MEN OF LAW
IN PRE-REFORMATION SCOTLAND

SCOTTISH HISTORICAL REVIEW

MONOGRAPH SERIES

No. 9

CURRENT AND FORTHCOMING VOLUMES

1 Helen M. Dingwall — Physicians, Surgeons and Apothecaries: Medicine in Seventeenth-Century Edinburgh

2 Ewen A. Cameron — Land for the People? The British Government and the Scottish Highlands, c.1880–1925

3 Richard Anthony — Herds and Hinds: Farm Labour in Lowland Scotland, 1900–1939

4 R. Andrew McDonald — The Kingdom of the Isles: Scotland's Western Seaboard, c.1100–c.1336

5 John R. McIntosh — Church and Theology in Enlightenment Scotland: The Evangelical Party, 1740–1800

6 Graeme Morton — Unionist-Nationalism: Governing Urban Scotland, 1830–1860

7 Catriona M. M. Macdonald — The Radical Thread: Political Change in Scotland. Paisley Politics, 1885–1924

8 James L. MacLeod — The Second Disruption: The Free Church in Victorian Scotland and the Origins of the Free Presbyterian Church

9 John Finlay — Men of Law in Pre-Reformation Scotland

10 William Kenefick — 'Rebellious and Contrary': The Glasgow Dockers, 1853–1932

11 James J. Smyth — Labour in Glasgow, 1896–1936: Socialism, Suffrage, Sectarianism

MEN OF LAW
in Pre-Reformation Scotland

JOHN FINLAY

TUCKWELL PRESS

First published in Great Britain in 2000 by
Tuckwell Press
The Mill House
Phantassie
East Linton
East Lothian EH40 3DG
Scotland

ISBN 1 86232 165 5

British Library Cataloguing-in-Publication Data

A Catalogue record for this book is available
on request from the British Library

Printed and bound by Cromwell Press, Trowbridge, Wiltshire

Contents

Acknowledgements   vi

Conventions and Abbreviations   vii

Glossary   viii

1 Legal Practitioners in Sixteenth-Century Scotland   1

2 Lawyer and Client   21

3 The 'advocatis and procuratouris' of the College of Justice   53

4 Compelling Counsel and the Procurators of the Court   72

5 The Life of the Law: Practice and Procedure   87

6 Comparing Counsel: Robert Leslie and Robert Galbraith   123

7 The Office of King's Advocate   170

8 The King's Men of Law, 1493–1561   206

9 Conclusion   225

Appendix 1: General Procurators of the College of Justice, 1532–1549   229

Appendix 2: Crown Advocates, 1493–1582   230

Bibliography   231

Index   243

ACKNOWLEDGEMENTS

This books stems from a doctoral thesis undertaken within the Centre for Legal History of the University of Edinburgh. I would like to thank my supervisors, David Sellar and Hector MacQueen, for their advice and encouragement, both when the research was being carried out and since. I would also like to record my gratitude to John Cairns and Margaret Sanderson for their criticism and encouragement. I am also grateful to my new colleagues in the School of Law at the University of Glasgow for their support and for providing the conditions in which the final text could be prepared.

Much of my time as a postgraduate was spent within the Department of Scottish History at Edinburgh and I would like to thank the staff and, in particular, my contemporaries as postgraduate students, who made the process of research much more enjoyable than it might have been.

I would also like to record my thanks to the staffs of the record repositories and libraries who have shown me such consideration, particularly at the National Archives (when it was still the Scottish Record Office) and the National Library of Scotland.

I am obliged to John Tuckwell for agreeing to publish the text and to the Scottish Historical Review Trust for rendering assistance toward that end. I am grateful to the anonymous copy-editor for suggesting presentational improvements and also to Greig McDonell for carrying out the task of proof reading at an earlier stage. I am, of course, responsible for any errors that remain. Finally, and above all, I should like to thank my parents for their support and it is to them that this volume is respectfully dedicated.

JF
Stair Building, Glasgow
28 August, 2000

CONVENTIONS AND ABBREVIATIONS

Dates are given in old style (Julian calendar), but with the year beginning on 1 January. Quotations from manuscripts are given in the original spelling but the letters *u* and *v* have been modernised where the sense required. Contractions have been expanded. Currency referred to is Scots currency unless otherwise indicated.

The following abbreviations are used:

ADA	*Acts of the Lords Auditors of Causes and Complaints*, 1466–1496 ed. T. Thomson, (Record Commission, Edinburgh, 1839)
ADC, i	*Acts of the Lords of Council in Civil Causes, 1478–1495* ed. T. Thomson (Record Commission, Edinburgh, 1839)
ADC, ii	*Acts of the Lords of Council in Civil Causes 1496-1501* eds. G. Neilson & H. Paton (Edinburgh, 1918)
ADC, iii	*Acts of the Lords of Council, 1501–1503*, eds. A.B. Calderwood (Edinburgh, 1993)
ADCP	*Acts of the Lords of Council in Public Affairs, 1501–1554*, ed. R.K. Hannay (Edinburgh, 1932)
Acta Concilii (Stair)	*Acta Dominorum Concilii, 1501–1503*, ed. J.A. Clyde, (Stair Society, 1943)
APS	*Acts of the Parliaments of Scotland,* eds. T. Thomson & C. Innes (Record Commission, Edinburgh, 1844–1875)
CC 8	Commissary Court of Edinburgh, Manuscript Register of Testaments
CS 1	Manuscript Books of Sederunt
CS 5	Manuscript Acts of the Lords of Council
CS 6	Manuscript Acts of the Lords of Council and Session
CS 7	Manuscript Register of Acts and Decreets
EUL	Edinburgh University Library
HMC	Historic Manuscripts Commission
JR	*Juridical Review*
NAS	National Archives of Scotland, Edinburgh
NLS	National Library of Scotland, Edinburgh
NRA(S)	National Register of Archives (Scotland)
PS	Manuscript Register of the Privy Seal
PSAS	Proceedings of the Society of Antiquaries in Scotland
RPC	*Register of the Privy Council*
SAUL	St Andrews University Library
SHR	*Scottish Historical Review*
SHS	Scottish History Society
TA	*Accounts of the Lord High Treasurer of Scotland*, eds. T. Dickson *et al.*, 13 vols., (Edinburgh, 1877–1978)
TDGNHAS	*Transactions of the Dumfries and Galloway Natural History and Antiquarian Society*

Other abbreviations follow the conventions laid down in (1963) *SHR* supplement.

Glossary of Terms

Annualrent: a right taken by a creditor to receive a yearly rent from land.

Bailie: the chief executive officer of a barony or regality; often responsible for convening the barony or regality court.

Barratry: trading in ecclesiastical preferments at Rome without royal authority.

Benefice: an ecclesiastical living, drawing revenues from the teinds and lands assigned to it.

Blenche ferme: holding land by nominal feu duty, such as a rose or a pair of spurs.

Brieve: a writ whereby one person demanded another do something. A *pleadable* brieve was addressed to a court-holder demanding that he resolve an issue between two parties, for example, which of them had right to lands disputed between them.

Caution ('cay-shun'):   a guarantee.

Cautioner ('cay-shun-er'):   a guarantor.

Commissary: the judicial deputy of the bishop's official.

Composition: an arrangement between a debtor and his creditor(s) whereby debts are discharged in return for partial payment.

Conjunct: rights taken by two or more persons jointly.

Cursing: excommunication; normally follows on from letters of cursing.

Decreet: final decision of the lords in the College of Justice in civil procedure.

Decreet arbitral: final decision of an arbiter or arbiters.

Deforcement: the forcible prevention of a court officer in executing the legal warrant of a competent court.

Dempster: court official who traditionally declared the sentence of the court and pronounced doom.

Diet: date [Latin *dies*] for court hearing.

Diligence: enforcement of a judgment debt.

Escheat: forfeit to the Crown.

Exception: a defence.

In solidum: for the whole; i.e. in a joint obligation, each party under the obligation is obliged to pay the whole debt with a right of relief against the other party.

Justice ayre: the name given to the practice of the justiciar going on circuit hearing criminal causes.

Justiciar: the chief criminal judge acting on behalf of the Crown.

Heritage: land or other immoveable property, as opposed to moveable property.

Letter of procuratory:	a mandate nominating a procurator to act on another's behalf and outlining his powers.
Letters of horning:	a method of diligence whereby debtor was charged to pay his debt on pain of horning. On default, a macer or other officer would go to the market cross and give three trumpet blasts signifying the outlawing of the debtor whose moveable goods were then escheat to the Crown.
Libel:	a statement of the grounds on which an action was brought; in modern practice this is a word restricted to describing only criminal indictments.
Macer:	mace bearer or usher in the College of Justice.
Maill:	rent.
Manrent and maintenance	in a bond of manrent a lesser man undertook to assist and serve a greater man in return for being maintained and supported under a bond of maintenance granted by the latter.
Oath *de calumnia*	an oath sworn by either party to an action declaring that the facts pleaded were believed to be true. Refusal by a party to take the oath meant that he or she lost the action.
Official:	the major ecclesiastical judicial officer of a diocese.
Poinding (pinding):	the impounding of a debtor's moveable goods in the execution of diligence to satisfy a debt lawfully due.
Practicks:	generally, collections of notes on decisions before the College of Justice which, in some cases, were digested under subject headings; distinguish the 'practick' of the College of Justice, which was the set of procedural rules particular to the College.
Pupil:	child up to the age of formal puberty which was 12 for girls and 14 for boys.
Quoniam Attachiamenta:	a fourteenth-century collection of brieves.
Reddendo	in feudal law, the return in consideration of which land was granted (e.g. money; services).
Regality:	a unit of local government in which the lord enjoyed certain exemptions from royal authority.
Regiam Majestatem:	an early fourteenth-century legal treatise.
Retourable brieve:	a non-pleadable brieve consisting of factual questions to be answered with the answers to be retoured (returned) to chancery for further action; the issues to be decided were fixed and did not arise though a process of pleading in court since no other party was summoned to contest the brieve.

Sasine:	putting into, or taking, lawful possession of land held by feudal tenure.
Spuilzie ('spooly'):	an action whereby a person in possession of property who is dispossessed without his consent or judicial warrant, may recover immediate possession.
Summons:	the initial document in a legal action whereby proceedings were raised and a person was called to appear in court to answer a claim against him. By the sixteenth century summonses were written in the vernacular on paper and issued under the royal signet.
Tailzie ('taily'):	an entail; this is a method of disponing heritage through a specified line of heirs rather than via general heirs-at-law, normally with the aim of keeping the heritage within a kin-group and avoiding inheritance by females.
Terce:	the right of a widow to a liferent interest in a one third part of the heritable estate in which her husband died infeft.
Tutor:	guardian (including the parents) of children in pupillarity.
Wadset	a contract that **was** an early form of right in security: the debtor ('the reverser') conveyed land in security to the creditor (the 'wadsetter') under a reversion whereby the creditor agreed to re-convey the land when the debt was paid.

CHAPTER ONE

Legal Practitioners in Sixteenth-Century Scotland

Was there a legal profession in Scotland during the reign of James V (1513–1542)? The answer to this question depends almost entirely on how the words 'profession' and 'professional' are defined and, in turn, any workable definition must take into account the nature and quality of the surviving historical sources. The major record for the activities of men of law in Scotland during the early sixteenth century is the *acta* of the lords of council.[1] The *acta* are unlike modern law reports, indeed their concern is with recording the procedural steps undertaken in the resolution of disputes coming before the king's judicial council and hardly at all with substantive points of law. But they do identify the most active men of law, who the clients were for whom they acted, and the kinds of legal action in which they were involved. From this single source, therefore, it is possible to reconstruct the activities of the generation of lawyers who came to be appointed to practise before the college of justice, the supreme civil court in Scotland, when it was founded in 1532.[2]

This reconstruction is greatly facilitated by the mention of lawyers in a wide variety of other contemporary records both ecclesiastical and civil, public and private. This provides personal information that allows greater insight into their professional activities. But the picture must always remain incomplete. It can never be known, for example, what proportion of their time Scottish men of law spent acting in court or preparing cases. Nor in most cases is it possible to assess what their income was, how high their fees were, or what proportion of their income they drew from their legal activity.

Historians of the early English legal profession, facing similar problems, have suggested useful base-line criteria. Paul Brand has argued that a person qualifies as a professional lawyer when he is recognised by others as having

---

[1] On which see W.M. Gordon, 'The acts of the Scottish lords of council in the late fifteenth and early-sixteenth centuries: records and reports' in *Law Reporting in Britain* ed. C. Stebbings (London, 1995), 59, and A.L. Murray, 'Sinclair's Practicks' in *Law, litigants and the legal profession* eds. E.W. Ives and A.H. Manchester (London, 1983), 102.

[2] On which, generally, see R.K. Hannay, *The College of Justice* (Edinburgh, Stair Society, 1990).

particular knowledge or expertise in relation to the law; he is willing to put that expertise at the disposal of others, receiving payment in return, and this activity takes up a major part of his time.[3] This elaborates broadly similar criteria earlier suggested by Robert Palmer, although the latter included the requirements that to qualify as a professional the greater part of a person's income must be derived from his legal activities and that these must be continued over a number of years.[4] Interestingly, neither set of guidelines referred to formal educational requirements nor did either consider it essential that the lawyer be willing to put his services at the disposal of all-comers.

By now, it will be evident that these guidelines can only go so far in helping us to define whether professional lawyers operated in early sixteenth-century Scotland. Even so, if Brand's criteria were applied to Scotland a significant number of men during the reigns of James IV and James V would potentially qualify as professional lawyers even though it is often impossible to find evidence that they were paid for their services. The original eight general procurators admitted to the college of justice in 1532, the men who form the core of this study, undoubtedly fulfil these criteria. But do they constitute a 'legal profession'?

The criteria offered by Brand in this regard are again interesting. In his view, a profession exists when professional lawyers are made subject to regulation, including a limit on their numbers in a particular court, or minimum standards of competence or behaviour.[5] Essentially, the defining characteristics of a legal profession in these terms are control over entry into its ranks and disciplinary control over recruits once entry has been gained. The lawyers themselves need not exercise the control; it can be imposed externally. In Scotland, as will be shown later, both criteria were met in 1532 with control over entry and discipline exercised by the lords of council.[6]

The danger in transplanting these criteria into Scotland lies in the fact that it invites the misconception that the legal profession was created along with the college of justice in 1532. In the past some scholars have even sought to retrace the existence of the Faculty of Advocates to that date.[7] The very title of Francis Grant's work *The Faculty of Advocates in Scotland,*

3   P. Brand, *The Origins of the English Legal Profession* (Oxford, 1992), preface, vi.
4   R.C. Palmer, *The County Courts of Medieval England, 1150–1350* (Princeton, 1982), 89.
5   Brand, *Legal Profession,* preface, vii.
6   Chapters three and four, below.
7   E.g. N. Wilson, 'The Scottish Bar: The evolution of the Faculty of Advocates in its historical social setting', *Louisiana Law Review,* xxviii (1968), 235.

1532–1943, suggests certainty as to the Faculty's origin.[8] Yet neither it nor the legal profession can be ascribed to legislative fiat in 1532. If, however, Brand's criteria are accepted as a basic litmus test for the existence of a legal profession, then it can be asserted with reasonable confidence that no such profession existed in Scotland prior to 1500. There were certainly professional men of law before that time but there is no evidence of control over entry to the profession or disciplinary control over a particular group. There are indications that these criteria were being fulfilled in the 1520s and the statutes of 1532 do provide evidence for the existence (as opposed to the creation) of a legal profession in terms of Brand's criteria.

As with contemporary England, the difficult question remains of precisely who should be included in its ranks. Professor J.H. Baker, in looking at English professional lawyers of the period 1450–1550, has questioned whether they comprised a single profession.[9] In looking at the diversity of English lawyers, and the lack of 'a comprehensive professional structure', he found a unifying factor in their association with the inns of court and chancery. Even so he acknowledged that membership of an inn was not exclusive to lawyers and so could not be accepted as defining the legal profession.

The very mention of 'inns of court', however, illustrates the divergence between Scots lawyers and their contemporaries in England in the fifteenth and sixteenth centuries. Professional lawyers were certainly diverse in Scotland, and from the outset advocates and Writers to the Signet performed different functions that were clearly reflected in the legislation of 1532.[10] As will be discussed further below, there were notaries, procurators, advocates and forespeakers. But these are not to be compared with the separate branches of the English legal profession. Indeed in Scotland the same individual might be a notary and be found in various records described as a procurator, forespeaker and advocate. Master John Williamson, a notary, was also one of the most active procurators before the lords of council during the reign of James IV.[11] Several of his contemporaries as procurators, including Adam Otterburn, James Henryson and John Lethame, were also notaries. This lack of a clear distinction creates some difficulty in deciding who should be included in the ranks of the Scottish legal profession in the 1530s. The king's advocate

---

8   F.J. Grant, ed., *The Faculty of Advocates in Scotland, 1532–1943* (Edinburgh, 1944). For criticism of Grant's work, see N.T. Phillipson, *The Scottish Whigs and the Reform of the Court of Session, 1785–1830* (Stair, Society, 1990), Appendix B.

9   J.H. Baker, 'The English legal profession, 1450–1550' in his collected essays, *The Legal Profession and the Common Law* (London, 1986), 75-78.

10 On writers to the signet see R.K. Hannay, *College of Justice* (Stair Society, 1990), 311-3.

11 E.g. National Archives of Scotland, NAS, Broughton and Cally Muniments, GD 10/623: 17 Oct. 1507.

is the most obvious candidate for inclusion and yet, eventually becoming a lord of session in his own right, he might be better classified as a member of the judiciary. It would be difficult to exclude those practising exclusively before the church courts. The same is true of those procurators who, while not named as general procurators to the college of justice, still appeared before it regularly in the 1530s (although at least some of these were probably men serving an apprenticeship and so cannot be considered fully-fledged professionals). Moreover it will be suggested later that the view that in 1532 a number of advocates were given the exclusive right to plead before the new college of justice is open to doubt. It may be enough simply to suggest, as Prest does in relation to English lawyers, that the general procurators admitted in 1532 represented a relatively small band of 'high-status practitioners', standing at the head of the profession.[12] To date, however, very little has been written about them, and even less about those who appeared in lower courts as procurators. Without knowing more about all those who might conceivably fulfil Brand's definition of 'professional lawyer' during the reign of James V, it is dangerous to attempt to define the membership of the legal profession at that date.

Nor is the emergence of a 'legal profession' in Scotland precisely dateable. The fact that prior to 1532 a small group of advocates was being regulated, to some extent, by the lords of council merely adds to the difficulty. The earliest evidence of an organisation akin to the Faculty of Advocates dates only from 1582. Significantly this refers to an individual, John Shairp, as 'dene of the advocattis of the session' rather than to the body itself.[13] No mention of a 'dean of faculty' has been found until 1619.[14] Although there are signs of corporate identity amongst the generation of lawyers examined in this study, it is true to say that the development of the Faculty of Advocates was vital to the development of a 'professional legal caste'.[15]

Unfortunately it is not until the 1550s that the books of sederunt survive which record the swearing of admission oaths by those admitted as advocates before the college of justice. The basis of the oath was an act of 1429 in which 'advocatis & forespekaris in temporalle courts pledande' were to swear that the cause that they put forward was just, and that they would not use false evidence nor seek to delay an action without cause.[16] In 1556 it was recorded on 12 November that:

[12]   *The Professions in Early Modern England*, ed. W. Prest (New York, 1987), 66.
[13]   *RPC*, iii, 530; M.H.B. Sanderson, *Mary Stewart's People* (Edinburgh, 1987), 23.
[14]   Hannay, *College of Justice*, 150.
[15]   Alexander Murdoch, 'The advocates, the law and the nation in Early Modern Scotland', in *Lawyers in Early Modern Europe and America*, ed. W. Prest (New York, 1981), 149.
[16]   *APS*, ii, 19.

> the haill advocattis & procuratouris maid feyth
> in presens of the haill lordis that thai sall lelelie &
> trewli procur for thir clientis & sall observe &
> keip the statutis of sessioun.[17]

The previous year, on 13 November, twelve advocates collectively swore the same oath and two others were then received and sworn for the first time.[18] This pattern, of annual oath-taking and new admissions of advocates on the first court day following Martinmas, was maintained throughout the 1560s. John Spens of Condie was sworn as an ordinary lord of session on 12 November 1561. This was followed by John Monypenny's admission as advocate, and then all the lords, procurators, scribes and macers 'maid fayth as use is conforme to the statutes'.[19] On the same day extraordinary lords and two new macers were also admitted. The significance of the period 'eftir martimes' (Martinmas), as the record put it, was underlined in 1562 when normal scribal practice was departed from and lords who were absent, instead of being simply ignored, were named and specifically 'excepted' from the sederunt.[20] Whether this particular court day had the same annual significance during the reign of James V is not particularly evident from the *acta*, although a new session can be dated to 12 November 1532.[21] Prior to this, a sederunt is not always recorded on that date, but thereafter, it appears to have been.[22] The first court day after Martinmas seems also to have had significance elsewhere. In France, for example, the earliest list of *avocats* before the *Parlement* of Paris dates from the first court day after Martinmas in the year 1340.[23]

In Scotland there were by 1590 some fifty advocates admitted to appear before the lords. There is evidence that in some cases they had been admitted on probation under the supervision of senior advocates. Even so, there was still no self-regulation. The number of advocates continued to increase dramatically throughout the seventeenth and eighteenth centuries

---

[17] CS 6/29 fo. 33v: 12 Nov. 1556.

[18] CS 6/29 fo. 4v: 13 Nov. 1555.

[19] CS 1/2/1 fos. 30r–31r: 12 Nov. 1561.

[20] CS 1/2/1 fo. 63r: 12 Nov. 1562. Normally the sederunt simply listed those lords who were present, either listing their names or comparing that day's sederunt to the previous day. Judges who were absent were therefore not named.

[21] CS 6/2 fo. 1r.: 12 Nov. 1532.

[22] On that day a sederunt was recorded in 1525 (CS 5/35 fo. 155v), but not in 1524 (CS 5/34) nor in 1526, although a parliament was called for 12 Nov. in this year (CS 5/36 fo. 95r). In 1533 (CS 6/3 fo. 74r) and 1534 (CS 6/5 fo. 131r) sederunts are recorded on 12 Nov.

[23] R. Delachenal, *Histoire des Avocats au Parlement de Paris, 1300–1600* (Paris, 1885), 24.

until, by around 1710, there were two hundred of them.[24] Similar increases were recorded during this period elsewhere in Europe and recent scholarship has stressed the international connections and experiences of Scottish advocates, in particular their tendency to be educated on the continent.[25]

This was also the time at which the legal dynasty came to prominence. Several notable examples, the Hope and Lockhart families and, perhaps the best known, the family and descendants of Thomas Craig of Riccarton, provide fascinating illustrations of the significance and increasing importance of family connections to anyone wishing to pursue a successful legal career.[26] Lawyers were capable of significant upward social mobility which, as the seventeenth century progressed, began to make the pursuit of a legal career a desirable prospect for younger sons of the nobility.[27] The social status of the advocate, and the social profile of the Faculty of Advocates, underwent a significant change that has been dated to the period of the Restoration. Between 1670 and 1730 men of higher social position began to seek and gain entry to the Faculty.[28] It has been argued that in the late seventeenth century, the advocates, led by Sir George Mackenzie, viewed themselves as a learned society almost equivalent to a university: a status underpinned by the foundation of the Advocates' Library in 1689.[29]

In conjunction with a continuing focus on the institutional development of the Faculty of Advocates, a great deal of work needs to be done on the status, professional careers, and family connections of individual advocates in the century-and-a-half following the foundation of the college of justice. But the general trends are clear. First, advocates were amongst the best-educated members of society. Late sixteenth-century figures such as Sir John Skene, Clement Litill and Thomas Craig (educated respectively at

---

[24]   N. Phillipson, 'Lawyers, landowners, and the civic leadership of Post-Union Scotland: an essay on the social role of the Faculty of Advocates 1661-1830 in 18th Century Scotland' (1976), *JR* 101.

[25]   F. Ranieri, 'From status to profession: the professionalisation of lawyers as a research field in modern European legal history', x (1989), *Journal of Legal History*, 184; J. Durkan, 'The French connection in the sixteenth and seventeenth centuries', in *Scotland and Europe 1200–1850*, ed. T.C. Smout (Edinburgh, 1986), 19; P. Neve, 'Disputations of Scots students attending universities in the Northern Netherlands', in *Legal History in the Making*, eds. W.M. Gordon & T. D. Fergus (London, 1991), 95; R Feenstra, 'Scottish-Dutch Legal Relations in the Seventeenth and Eighteenth Centuries', in *Scotland and Europe 1200–1850*, ed. T.C. Smout (Edinburgh, 1986), 128.

[26]   T.I. Rae, 'The origins of the Advocates' library', in *For the Encouragement of Learning: Scotland's National Library, 1689–1989*, eds. P. Cadell and A. Matheson (Edinburgh, 1989), 5.

[27]   Ibid., 6.

[28]   Phillipson, 'Civic leadership', 100.

[29]   J.W. Cairns, 'The formation of the Scottish legal mind in the eighteenth century: themes of humanism and enlightenment in the admission of advocates', in *The Legal Mind*, eds. N. MacCormick and P. Birks (Oxford, 1986), 259-60; ibid., 'Sir George Mackenzie, the Faculty of Advocates, and the Advocates Library', in G. Mackenzie, *Oratio Inauguralis* (Edinburgh, 1989), 23.

Wittenberg, Louvain and Paris) have been seen as representative of several generations of lawyer during the reign of James VI.[30] Hannay estimated that two-thirds of advocates admitted between 1575 and 1608 based their claim for admission on their academic qualifications.[31] Secondly, family connections were increasingly important. The profession of advocate was a useful vehicle to men ambitious for social and political advancement. Appointment as a judge was not based upon the criterion of legal knowledge, and the proportion of appointed judges who had been practising advocates fluctuated between 1532 and 1707. Even so, the prospects of advancement for an advocate either to the bench, or to a position within the Faculty or as a sheriff-depute or similar post, were good.[32] The third major characteristic of advocates was their wealth. As a result of their activities some advocates became very wealthy men, able to speculate in land and to lend out money.[33] As will be shown, all three of these characteristics of professional advocates may be found prior to 1550.

Having said that, it is doubtful whether those earlier professional lawyers could properly be described as forming a legal profession if criteria even slightly more demanding than Brand's minimal test were applied. But as Helen Dingwall, an historian of the Edinburgh medical profession, has acknowledged, it is questionable whether twentieth-century criteria defining what a profession is should be applied to the sixteenth or seventeenth centuries at all.[34] To apply the concept of a legal profession to the early sixteenth century is to apply an external, and anachronistic, standard to men who, although probably willing to accept the contemporary description 'men of law', would not necessarily have allowed it to define them. Some of them spent considerable time pursuing other avenues of employment while some held administrative positions.[35] The most that can be said is that the group of lawyers to be studied here does fulfil the base-line criteria for the existence of a legal profession suggested by Brand. Any more rigorous set of criteria, for instance entry requirements controlled by the group itself through entry examinations, or

---

[30] Cairns, *Stair Memorial Encyclopedia*, volume 13, para 1241. It has been suggested that as well as studying arts at Paris, Craig also studied law in France: J.W. Cairns, T.D. Fergus and H.L. MacQueen, 'Legal humanism in Renaissance Scotland' (1990) *Journal of Legal Studies*, 48.

[31] Hannay, *College of Justice*, 145.

[32] J.M. Simpson, 'The advocates as Scottish trade union pioneers', in *The Scottish Tradition*, ed. G.W.S. Barrow (Edinburgh, 1974), 166; Phillipson, 'Civic Leadership', 104; Rae, 'Advocates' Library', 7.

[33] Rae, 'Advocates' Library', 7.

[34] H. Dingwall, *Physicians, Surgeons and Apothecaries: Medical Practice in Seventeenth-Century Edinburgh* (East Linton, 1995), 11.

[35] Cf. Baker, 'The English legal profession', 76.

self-regulation, could not be fulfilled until much later when more is known of how the Faculty of Advocates operated.[36]

The advocates of 1532 have therefore been chosen for this study not because they represent the origins of the legal profession in Scotland. They have been selected because they are the first lawyers unambiguously connected with a particular court in Scotland whose names are known and whose careers may be studied in reasonable detail. It would have been possible to undertake a similar study in relation to an earlier generation of men of law although this would have involved identifying the most prominent practitioners according to more subjective criteria. It is doubtful if even this could be attempted for the period prior to the reign of James III, at which time the *acta* of the lords of council do not survive so comprehensively. Moreover, generally speaking, biographical information from the fifteenth century is less plentiful than it is in the early part of the sixteenth. If references in the *acta* were the only record of their activity, very little would ever be known of lawyers as individuals. Although a valuable source of information legal, political, economic, and biographical, the council record reveals surprisingly little about the personal lives of those men of law whose names appear in it most often. It is from supplementary information in other sources that meaningful study can be made of the lives and careers of these individuals.

The records used in this study cover primarily the period 1504 to 1537. Later material has also been used extensively but not as systematically, and use has been made of the published volumes of the *acta* between 1478 and 1504. But during the main period studied, the *acta* of the lords of council are unpublished. In 1932 R.K. Hannay produced a volume summarising some of the information contained in the *acta* from 1504 to 1554.[37] Although expertly transcribed and a work of great consequence containing much of interest to political and legal historians, it is unfortunately of limited value to anyone studying the men of law of this period not least because they are only very rarely named. Only by careful scrutiny of the manuscript volumes has it been possible to reconstruct and analyse their activities.

---

[36]   Slightly different criteria have also been suggested in general remarks by J.A. Brundage, 'The medieval advocate's profession' (1988), *Law and History Review*, 439–445.

[37]   *ADCP*, ed. R.K. Hannay (Edinburgh, 1932).

Terminology

> *In principio erat verbum et verbum erat deum et deus erat verbum etc.*[38]

In early sixteenth-century Scotland lawyers were variously described as advocates, forespeakers (or, in Latin, *prelocutors*), procurators and assessors. These terms were all of some antiquity but care should be taken in tracing their application since language changed over time and was used differently in different places. The Anglo-Saxon *forespeca*, for instance, probably developed into the English common-law 'narrator' (that is, someone empowered to make a statement of claim) although, as has recently been pointed out, the Scots 'forespeaker' could undertake the running of an entire litigation and was not restricted to uttering the statement of claim.[39]

Even sixteenth-century Scottish scribes were themselves not always consistent in their use of language. Some wrote 'forspeaker' rather than 'forespeaker', although whether this represented a substantive difference is doubtful.[40] Nonetheless this did mirror an inconsistency in the Latin equivalent of the term since both *prolocutor* and *prelocutor* are found. The sense is slightly different in that '*pro*' suggests a person speaking on another's behalf (whether or not he was present), whereas '*pre*' suggests someone specifically standing before another person and speaking on his behalf. This latter meaning was the basic meaning of *prelocutor* or 'forespeaker' in Scotland. Almost without exception, these words were used when the litigant was present and his man of law was speaking on his behalf.

It is unlikely however that there is any substantive difference in the meaning of the words 'forspeaker' and 'forespeaker', or *prelocutor* and *prolocutor,* as they were used by the clerks of the lords of council in the first half of the sixteenth century. This is in spite of the fact that in 1493 David Balfour of Caraldston was described as 'forespekkar, forspekkar and procurator for our soverane lord (i.e. the king)'.[41] There is no evidence that in practice a 'forespeaker' was in any way distinct from a 'forspeaker' and,

---

[38] CS 5/23 fo. 2r.: 27 June 1511. Portions of this phrase, evidently used as a writing exercise by the clerks of council, can be found in several places in the *acta*, although the quotation comes from the most complete example. On the significance of the text, see E. Duffy, *The Stripping of the Altars* (New Haven and London, 1992), 214-5.

[39] M.T. Clanchy, *From Memory to Written Record* (Oxford, 1993), 274; H.L. MacQueen, *Common Law,* 76.

[40] The word forspeaker was written in full; later it starts to be written with an obvious contraction, suggesting the spelling 'forespeaker'.

[41] *ADC*, i, 262: 21 Jan. 1493.

indeed, it is possible to find both words used in the *acta* on the same day ostensibly with identical meaning.[42]

The distinction between 'procurators' and 'forespeakers' in some ways mirrors the contemporary distinction between ambassadors and *nuncii*. The ambassador was empowered to negotiate and conclude specific business. By virtue of this authority he acted as the representative or agent of his sovereign. The *nuncius* was also the sovereign's representative but lacked the same authority. For this reason *nuncii* were described, by writers such as Azo, as 'speaking letters', that is, enjoying the role merely of communicating a message without having any power to influence its content.[43] The 'procurator' and the 'forespeaker' should similarly be distinguished in terms of authority although it would be misleading to characterise the forespeaker merely as a medium of communication between his client and the court. His role was to advise and to give counsel and, as the title suggests, to speak on his client's behalf and under his instructions. But it was the message that was important, the procedural steps taken, the argument adopted: those were the things that mattered. That is why in Scottish practice the presence of a forespeaker was not routinely recorded by the clerks of council. The presence of the principal was the important fact.

By standing at the bar of the court along with his man of law, the principal, in modern terminology, might be viewed as the 'controlling mind'. The responsibility for what was said on his behalf lay with him; if his forespeaker made a statement of which he disapproved then, presumably, he could disavow it and ensure that it was not recorded in the *acta* to his later disadvantage. Although the forespeaker had more influence over the content of the message he was delivering than was true of the *nuncius*, in both cases the message was unambiguously imputed to the principal.

By contrast the name of any procurator employed to represent another was almost without exception recorded. Therefore men of law are described in the record as 'procurator' three or four times as often as they are described as 'forespeaker'.[44] In practice the forespeaker may have had no less input into the argument put forward in court than a procurator

---

[42]   E.g. CS 5/40 fos. 21r-v: 10 May 1529. On this day there are references to Master Robert Leslie, 'forspekar', and Master James Foulis, 'forespekar'.

[43]   D. E. Queller, *The Office of Ambassador in the Middle Ages* (Princeton, 1967), 7; G. Mattingly, *Renaissance Diplomacy* (London, 1955), 28.

[44]   Robert Galbraith was described as 'procurator' on 340 occasions, as either 'forespeaker' (89) or 'prelocutor' (27) on 116; Robert Leslie was a procurator on 475 occasions and forespeaker or prelocutor on 110. These are only identifiable references; sometimes they acted 'in the name of' a client and this did not simply mean they were acting as a procurator since on occasion such clients were personally present.

might have had. But in court the procurator was the master of the message. His client was not present to contradict or disavow him. Provided the procurator was properly constituted, and was acting within his authority, he bound his client by what he said and did in his name. As an ambassador was employed to negotiate, within his terms of reference, the content of a treaty, so the procurator might, according to his mandate, have responsibility for reaching a settlement judicially or by arbitration. The similarity is one that would have been obvious to contemporaries, particularly since in the days before resident embassies ambassadors were also known as procurators.[45] In Scotland there is a lack of direct evidence concerning the precise extent of the powers of the forespeaker, and no details are known of when, or even whether, his client might disavow what he said. There is therefore much room for speculation, and to inform it a comparative approach is useful.

The word 'forespeaker' has its foreign equivalents, such as the *avant-parlier* found in France and in places such as Brabant. By the time of Vincent de Beaumanoir in the late thirteenth century, however, *avant-parlier* had fallen out of use in France in favour of the word *avocat*.[46] Interestingly, this followed a period when both words, *avocat* and *avant-parlier*, were used as synonyms by, for example, the compiler of the *Établissements de Saint Louis*.[47] According to Delachenal, the *avant parlier*, or *prolocutor*, was a true pleader; acting as the interpreter of his principal and treated as rigorously as if he himself were the principal. This meant that the *avant parlier* was unable to take back anything that he had said in court on behalf of the principal, even if prejudicial. Despite this formalism, means were soon found in practice to limit the mandate of an *avant parlier* and to introduce the possibility of the principal disavowing what had been said by him.[48] The French *avocat* clearly developed from the *avant parlier* (or *amparlier*) and, by 1274, the profession of *avocat* before the *Parlement* of Paris was being regulated.[49]

In Scotland there was certainly a progression in terminology from 'forespeaker' and 'procurator' to 'advocate'. There was also a clear distinction between those terms. But whichever term was applied to him, the central function of the man of law was to plead on behalf of his client in court. The functional division in Scotland, comparable to that between English serjeants-at-law and attorneys, was between advocates and writers.

[45] Mattingly, *Renaissance Diplomacy*, 28-9.
[46] Delachenal, *Histoire des Avocats*, introduction, xvii.
[47] Ibid., introduction, xvi.
[48] Ibid., introduction, viii.
[49] B. Auzary-Schmaltz and S. Dauchy, 'L'assistance dans la résolution des conflits au civil devant le Parlement de Paris au Moyen Age', 53; J.H. Shennan, *The Parlement of Paris* (London, 1968), 48.

These two groups had been distinct members of the college of justice from its inception but the distinction between them grew more pronounced as the sixteenth century progressed. However, this should not be pressed too far. At the end of the century the advocates and the writers to the signet, groups of similar size with many interests in common, even contemplated becoming a single incorporation.[50] The 1565 tax roll of Edinburgh (which for once included lawyers) reveals that there was no great social distinction between the writers and the advocates, nor was there necessarily a great difference in their respective incomes although the leading advocates were earning more than the busier writers.[51] This contrasts sharply with practice on the continent where the offices of *avocat* and *procureur* were kept quite distinct. At Malines, for example, legislation ensured that the same man could not perform both of these functions simultaneously.[52] By the early 1500s in Brabant *avocats* were distinguished from *procureurs* by the fact that they alone were graduates.[53] Such a clear distinction as that at Brabant was never made in Scotland. Even in the seventeenth century, the contrast between the educational standards of both branches of the profession should not be exaggerated, and many writers were graduates when, in fact, this was not a formal requirement.[54] The way in which the functional division arose in Scotland between advocates and writers, and the process by which it widened during the course of the seventeenth century and beyond, has not yet been properly investigated. Much later, Lord Cockburn was able to contrast sharply the individualism of the advocates with the 'pure corporation spirit' of the writers to the signet.[55]

But, as the following chapters will make clear, it would be a mistake to view advocates in the sixteenth century as, in any sense, isolated figures. Most directly, although they tended to appear alone in court, as the century progresses more becomes known of their servants and apprentices. For instance, a servant of Thomas McCalzeane was paid a small fee in 1564 by the town of Edinburgh for copying 'ane wryting...that was aganis the toun'.[56] To take a further example from the same period, the notary James

50 Hannay, *College of Justice*, 316; in 1586 there were about fifty advocates and forty writers to the signet: NAS, Professor Hannay's Papers, GD 214/14, quoting B.S. III, 354.
51 E.g. *Edinburgh Records: The Burgh Accounts*, ed. R. Adam (Edinburgh, 1899), 57-8 [*Edin. Accts.*], where the writers John Young and William Paterson were assessed at £40 and £20 respectively, whereas the advocates Alexander Sym and Clement Littil were assessed at £40 and £60.
52 C.H. van Rhee, 'Litigation and Leglislation Civil Procedure at First-Instance in the Great Council for the Netherlands in Malines (1522–1559)', (Ph.D Thesis, University of Leiden, 1997), 94-5.
53 Rousseaux, X., 'De l'assistance mutuelle à l'assitance professionelle. Le Brabant (XIVᵉ - XVIIIᵉ)', in *L'assistance dans la résolution des conflits* (Brussels, 1997), 155.
54 J.W. Cairns, 'Netherlands Influences on Scots Law and Lawyers', in *Scotland and the Low Countries*, ed. G.G. Simpson (East Linton, 1996), 141.
55 Henry Cockburn, *Memorials of his Time*, 419.
56 *Edin. Accts.*, 460. Cf. also, John Ochiltree and John Heriot, servants of Master David McGill, *Prot. Bk. King*, no. 123: 12 June 1556; Robert Cathcart, servant of Master David McGill, *Laing Chrs.*,

McCartney was described in 1563 as the servitor of the advocate, and clerk register, James McGill of Nether Rankeillor.[57] It is difficult to see much difference in the social status of master and servant in this case. As a notary, McCartney appears in his own right in the Edinburgh tax roll of 1565 assessed at £20, a relatively high figure.[58] Nor was he without social connections. His wife, Marion Hamilton, was the daughter of the macer (usher) Thomas Hamilton of Priestfield and the granddaughter of the advocate Robert Leslie. This made McCartney the uncle of Thomas Hamilton, lord advocate and earl of Haddington, better known as 'Tam o' the Cowgait'.[59] He was also, like McGill, a leading Protestant and indeed was appointed solicitor to the church of Scotland in 1564.[60] McGill remembered McCartney in his will in 1579, leaving him £54 6s.[61] It would be wrong to suggest that had McGill not been clerk register, then a man like McCartney would not have been his servant. The names of other advocates' servants are known and often these servants bore the same surname as other practising advocates, indicating that, at least in some cases, they may have been apprentices. For example, in 1561 James McGill, possibly the son of James McGill of Nether Rankeillor, was the servant of the advocate Alexander Sym.[62] John McCalzeane on at least two occasions was recorded as the servant of Master John Shairp.[63] McCalzeane, a notary, probably belonged to the same family as the leading advocate and lord of session Thomas McCalzeane.[64] The same could well be said of Henry McCalzeane, another advocate.[65] Although Thomas McCalzeane died without a male heir, in 1570 his daughter Euphemia married Patrick Moscrop, from another Edinburgh legal family, who took his wife's surname.[66] Patrick was the son of the advocate John Moscrop and may also

no. 927: 6 Nov. 1575; Thomas Horneuar and James Melville, servants of Master John Spens, *Laing Chrs.*, no. 662: 24 Nov. 1556. Writers also had servants, e.g. George Gibson, 'scryb[e] of consale', had a servant named Andrew Gray: *Laing Chrs.*, no. 757: 10 Apr. 1563.

57 *Prot. Bk. Grote, no. 242*: 8 Nov., 1563

58 Lynch, *Edinburgh and the Reformation*, (Edinburgh, 1981), 377.

59 G. Hamilton, *A History of the House of Hamilton* (Edinburgh, 1933), 413.

60 D. Shaw, *The General Assemblies of the Church of Scotland 1560–1600, Their Origins and Development* (Edinburgh, 1964), 154.

61 NAS, Register of Testaments, CC8/8/11 fo. 150v: 15 Oct. 1579.

62 *Prot. Bk. Grote, no. 202*: 24 Nov. 1561. James McGill did have a son called James; see, for example, the marriage contract of 1576 between McGill senior and Robert Stewart of Rossyth: NAS, Bruce of Kennet Papers, GD 11/65: 9 May 1576.

63 *RMS*, v, no. 846: 20 July 1585; and, along with James Donaldson as servant of Master Alexander Skene; Fraser, *Eglinton*, ii, 222-3: 10 Apr. 1582.

64 For his status as a notary public, see *RSS*, v, no. 611: 24 Oct. 1583.

65 For Henry, see, for example, *RMS*, v, no. 163: 11 Apr. 1581; *RSS*, viii, no. 212: 28 May 1584. He was also a justice depute: Pitcairn, *Criminal Trials*, I, ii, 98. They were also probably related to the mid-century notary James McCalzeane, for whom see, for example: NAS, Swinton Charters, GD 12/119: 5 Apr. 1544.

66 Lynch, *Edinburgh and the Reformation*, 340.

have been the nephew of the notary Adam Moscrop.[67] References such as these indicate that in terms of social status, it would be wrong to draw too sharp a distinction between advocates, on the one hand, and writers and notaries on the other. It is true that, as a group, the advocates were probably wealthier than writers and notaries and the Edinburgh tax roll of 1565 (which includes both groups) goes some way towards demonstrating this. But they often belonged to, or had married into, the same families and, as will be shown below in chapter three, the idea of the 'legal family' belongs as firmly in the sixteenth century, and even the fifteenth, as in the seventeenth.

By the 1580s the books of sederunt make specific reference to apprenticeship.[68] In December 1580 John and David McGill, sons of the late James McGill of Nether Rankeillor, returned from studying in France and were admitted as advocates, having given 'specimen doctrine'. But they were not to act 'without thai haif ane auld procuratour and advocat adjonit to thaim'.[69] The same happened, less than a month later, with John Moncreiff, a graduate of St Andrews and Poitiers.[70] Moncreiff was to appear with an experienced advocate until the lords were satisfied he was competent to act by himself. These cases are not unique nor do they constitute the earliest evidence of an effort by the judges to put entrants through a period of probation.[71] Probationary arrangements such as these represent the clearest indication of learning by practice and observation, although there is little doubt that such learning was even by then traditional. At least some of those recorded as 'servants' to advocates were aspiring advocates themselves, and although references to such servants are extremely rare prior to 1550, the basic method of learning their native law cannot have differed greatly.

'Advocates' in Scotland

In the past there has been a misreading of the original legislation by which the college of justice and its procedures were formally established. Lord Clyde determined judicially in 1924 that a particular chapter of the 1532

---

[67]   On John Moscrop see Lynch, *Edinburgh and the Reformation*, 344 and Finlayson, *Clement Litill and his Library*, 6-7; for Adam, see *Prot. Bk. King*, nos. 20, 55, 145: 27 July and 4 Nov. 1555; 4 Aug. 1556. Although these references indicate activity in Edinburgh, Adam, a notary by apostolic authority, was a priest of Glasgow diocese: NAS, Biel Muniments, GD 6/612: 11 Sep. 1554.

[68]   Cf. Brabant, where practical knowledge of procedure was, from 1501, a necessary requirement for admission as a *procureur* for those without a university degree; this involved a period of six or seven years functioning as a clerk to a *procureur*. Rousseaux, 'Brabant', 155-6.

[69]   NAS, Professor Hannay's Papers, GD 214/14, quoting B.S., iii, 137 (now CS 1/3/1 fo. 137r: 20 Dec. 1580). See also Hannay, *College of Justice*, 142.

[70]   CS 1/3/1 fos., 138r-v: 11 Jan. 1581.

[71]   See the case of John Moscrop described in chapter three.

legislation, which permitted only 'procurators' to enter the council chamber with their clients, was intended to refer to the 'advocates' whose office was instituted in 1532.[72] He assumed that procurators and advocates were the same thing. The general tenor of the legislation suggests this was the case, and it does use the phrase 'general procurators or advocates', although no effort was made to distinguish a general procurator from any other kind of procurator.[73] On the other hand, the historian Nan Wilson suggested that by the 1532 Act, the designation 'advocate' should be applied only to those procurators who had qualified to plead before the college of justice. On this view, 'advocates' were superior to 'procurators' (although not necessarily superior to 'general procurators').[74] Wilson's view is interesting, and may be correct, but it cannot be founded on the legislation as she suggests because no attempt was made in 1532 to restrict the meaning of the word 'advocate' in this way.[75] The difficulty with Lord Clyde's view is that his argument–which is still good law–must now be seen as poor history. The original advocates named to act before the college of justice did not have an exclusive right of audience. As will be shown in chapter four, they had no monopoly on business before the court. The weakness of Wilson's view lies in the fact that not only was the word 'advocate' used prior to 1532, but no evidence emerges until a considerable time after that date of men using the designation 'advocate' as a regular description of their status. That the word 'advocate' came to mean a man with the right to plead in the college of justice is quite true; but that it first had that meaning in 1532 is doubtful.

What appears to have happened is that the word 'advocate' attached particularly to the king's advocate from early in the reign of James IV.[76] A good example of this attachment can be found in 1505 when James Henryson, the king's advocate, acted on behalf of Mariota Calder and the earl of Angus. The clerk described him a 'thir ~~advocate~~-procuratour', and by bothering to correct himself, the scribe was surely indicating that the word 'advocate' should be reserved for when Henryson acted on the king's behalf.[77] Even so, other scribes were less fastidious and the term was never exclusively used to refer to the king's man of law. As early as June, 1478, the word 'advocate' was being used instead of the word 'procurator' in

72 *Gordon v Nokenski-Cumming* 1924 S.C. 939 at 941; 1924 S.L.T. 140 at 141. As well as editing Craig's *Jus Feudale* in 1934, Lord Clyde edited several other works and contributed several articles to Stair Society publications.

73 The legislation is quoted at the beginning of chapter three.

74 Wilson, 'Faculty of Advocates', 235.

75 On 12 Nov. 1556, there is a reference to 'the haill advocattis & procuratouris' who swore to uphold the statutes of session and to 'lelelie & trewlie procure for thir clientis'. This is consistent with Wilson's view, although it is still rather ambiguous: CS 6/29 fo. 33v.

76 See chapter seven.

77 CS 5/17 fo. 112v: 12 Dec. 1505.

reference to the representative of ordinary litigants.[78] References to advocates before the lords of council can also be found during the reign of James IV.[79] In an obligation that survives from 1509, Adam Otterburn promised to 'be advocat and procurator' for Robert, Lord Erskine.[80] Clearly 'procurator' and 'advocate' were synonyms which pre-supposed the provision of an identical service.

With the development of the role of the queen's advocate during the minority of James V, usage of the term widened although it was connected primarily with royal service. By the early 1520s James Beaton, archbishop of Glasgow, was also using his own advocate, Master James Simson. Simson, a churchman who was soon destined to hold the office of official of St Andrews, appeared on Beaton's behalf on five occasions between 18 December 1522 and 26 February 1524.[81] This follows a significant gap in the record, although at least once in 1518 Simson had acted as his advocate and it is likely that he continued to do so from then until 1524.[82] In the course of these six appearances in the record, Simson was described as advocate five times, and as the archbishop's procurator only four times (on some days he was described in more than one way). His appearances under the title of advocate cannot be put down to scribal error, and it seems likely that the unconventional usage was applied because of Beaton's position as chancellor and thus president of the court. There is no evidence of Beaton appearing by his advocate after he lost the chancellorship. The leading men of law Thomas Kincraigie, Thomas Marjoribankis and Abraham Crichton all acted for him when he was archbishop of St Andrews but they were always recorded as his procurators.[83] Simson's role may therefore represent a further, albeit modest, widening of the regular use of the term although Beaton's successors as chancellor did not use their own advocate.[84]

As time went on the term advocate was also used in relation to the representatives of litigants of lesser rank. There was no regularity about this usage, and it may be explicable simply on the basis of scribal laxity. For

[78]   NAS, Protocol Book of James Darow [*Prot. Bk. Darow*], B66/1/1/1, fo. 209: 16 June 1478.
[79]   E.g., *Acta Concilii* (Stair), nos. 426, 627.
[80]   NAS, Ailsa Muniments, GD 124/7/10: 7 July 1509.
[81]   CS 5/33 fos. 101v (18 Dec. 1522), 107v-109r (19 Dec. 1522, *bis*), 153v (5 Feb. 1523); CS 5/34 fo. 118v (26 Feb. 1524). Simson was official of St Andrews in 1525 and later was official of Lothian: *Fasti Ecclesiae Scoticanae Medii Aevi ad annum 1638*, Second draft, ed. D.E.R. Watt, (Edinburgh, 1969), 324, 326.
[82]   CS 5/32 fo. 6v: 19 Mar. 1518.
[83]   E.g. (Crichton): CS 5/43 fo. 28r (1 Aug. 1531), CS 6/1 fos. 117v (20 Sept. 1532), 119v (26 Sept. 1532); CS 6/2 fos. 1v (12 Nov. 1532), 4v (14 Nov. 1532); (Kincraigie): CS 5/40 fo. 162v (21 Jan. 1530); (Marjoribankis): CS 6/2 fo. 16v (27 Nov. 1532). Beaton was translated from Glasgow to St Andrews in 1522: J. Dowden, *The Bishops of Scotland* (Glasgow, 1912), 40.
[84]   Beaton vacated office in 1526, to be replaced briefly by the earl of Angus and then, for the remainder of the reign, by Gavin Dunbar: *Handbook of British Chronology*, 3rd edn., ed. E.B. Fryde (Royal Historical Society, 1986), 183.

example, in 1515 Adam Otterburn was described as advocate for Alexander and Robert Barton. The day before, he had appeared as Alexander's procurator, with Robert in attendance as Alexander's tutor.[85] In a deed drawn up and registered for execution before the lords of council in December 1526, Henry Spittall was described as advocate for Alexander, Lord Elphinstone.[86] In March 1530 James Foulis acted as the 'advocat' of William Anderson.[87] Prior to these may be found at least two references to advocates as a group. The first of these occurred in 1522, when there is reference to a meeting of 'certane advocatis & men of law' with the official of Lothian to advise him concerning an appealed case.[88] Then in March 1524, John Brown, in naming several procurators to act on his behalf before the lords, referred to 'the Remanent (remaining) advocates'.[89] References such as these indicate that the term advocate was beginning to enjoy wider currency even though at this stage the term was still not in general use as a standard designation.

As to the precise meaning of advocate in Scots usage, it is clear that the personal presence of the king, or the queen mother, had no effect on the title accorded to his or her legal representative. There are cases when Margaret Tudor was recorded as personally present before the lords when her advocate was acting on her behalf and the same is true of the king and the chancellor.[90] This suggests that the term 'advocate', as it was used in Scotland, was a hybrid term covering both a lawyer appearing in the absence of a client and one speaking on behalf of a client who also happened to be present. This wider meaning could distinguish the verb 'to advocate' from the verb 'to procure', assuming that there was a difference.[91] Alternatively, the verb 'to advocate' might simply mean 'to speak on behalf of' since there was no verb form of the noun 'forespeaker'. 'Advocation', as it was called, may conceivably have been more to do with putting forward a forensic argument rather than simply making appearance on another's behalf. For example, in 1513, the clerk described the experienced man of law Master Walter Laing as '~~procuratour~~ advocat' for the laird of Touch, having initially described him as his forespeaker.[92] Too much should not be read into this error however for some reason the clerk was unwilling to leave Laing, acting as forespeaker, designed as procurator.

---

[85]   CS 5/27 fo. 102v, 107v: 22 and 23 Nov. 1515.
[86]   CS 5/36 fo. 145r: 15 Dec. 1526.
[87]   CS 5/41 fo. 14r: 17 Mar. 1530. These examples are not exhaustive.
[88]   CS 5/33 fo. 93r: 15 Dec. 1522.
[89]   CS 5/34 fo. 154v: 19 Mar. 1524. For further comment, see chapter four.
[90]   E.g., CS 5/30 fo. 194v (23 Feb. 1518); CS 5/32 fo. 187v (27 Oct. 1519).
[91]   The verb 'to procure' is quite commonly found and meant simply 'to act as a procurator': e.g. C.S. 5/28 fos. 110r, 140v.
[92]   CS 5/25 fos. 124r-125r: 24 May, 1513.

Instead he settled for the word 'advocate' and it may be that he considered this a synonym or, as suggested above, a hybrid.

It is unfortunate that in 1597 Sir John Skene saw no need to include the terms 'advocate' or 'procurator' in his treatise *De Verborum Significatione*, since his purpose was only to define the difficult words which appeared in the treatise *Regiam Majestatem*. The clerks of the council who used these words knew what they meant and saw no need to define them. The precise significance of these terms, as they were used during the minority of James V, is therefore lost. However it seems unlikely that an advocate, in purely functional terms, was performing a task that differed substantially in kind from that carried out by either a procurator or a forespeaker: they made the same arguments and raised the same objections. There is little evidence to suggest that advocates were viewed as more important, or more permanent, office holders than procurators.

It seems to have been the case that during the reign of James IV, and more particularly that of James V, the word advocate was growing in popularity. Primarily used in connection with only a small number of very important litigants, especially the king, it came to be used even before 1532 to describe collectively the leading men of law in the kingdom. This development was replicated the following century in the Nordic countries and may perhaps be explained by reference to Romano-canonical procedure. Since in church courts in other jurisdictions advocates enjoyed higher status than procurators, it may have been the case that in Scotland, particularly in the years following 1532, men of law took that higher title for themselves. As the century progressed the word advocate enjoyed increasingly wide currency and began to be used as a regular designation in a way in which hitherto it had not. The clerks employed to make entries in the registers of the great seal or the privy seal, by the minority of Queen Mary, began to describe men such as David Borthwick or Thomas McCalzeane as *advocatus*.[93] The same is true of notaries such as Alexander King, Nicol Thounis and Gilbert Grote, whose protocol books in the 1550s and 1560s record the status of those advocates who bore witness to instruments they recorded.[94] Not until Mary's minority are significant numbers of lawyers regularly found designed by the term advocate. In the fifteenth century it was rarely used although, curiously enough, favoured by legislators and by poets such as Robert Henryson and William

---

[93]   E.g., *RSS*, iv, no. 758: 5 June 1550; *RMS*, iv, no. 725: 3 Dec. 1552.

[94]   E.g. 'Master John Moscrop advocate' in *Prot. Bk. King*, no. 211: 13 Feb. 1557; 'Master John Abircrummy advocate' in *Prot. Bk. Thounis*, no. 96: 17 Aug. 1562; 'Master Alexander Sym advocate' in *Prot. Bk. Grote*, no. 202: 24 Nov. 1561.

Dunbar.[95] Its widening popularity can be put down to the development of the college of justice, allied to the lawyers' own sense of corporate spirit and their own self-image as men of rank.

But the fundamental conclusion must be that the same man, in the same place and performing substantially the same task, might be called advocate, procurator or forespeaker depending merely upon the presence or status of his client. As already demonstrated, practice was not always consistent and the same person, in relation to the same client on the same day, might appear by more than one title. For example James Simson in 1523 appeared on one occasion described as 'procuratour & forspeker' for Sir Thomas Boswell and Henry Spittall did so in respect of Robert Scott six years later.[96]

The other main term used to describe men of law, albeit in specific circumstances, was 'assessor'. Normally the context was one in which a lawyer was called upon to advise laymen, operating in a judicial or administrative capacity, of the legal implications involved in the pursuit of their function. The most obvious example is that of the burgh council although so little is known of council assessors that even those of Edinburgh have been described as 'shadowy figures'.[97] More will be said about them in the next chapter, although it is interesting to note that, as with most of the terms in the present discussion, the designation assessor continued in use in connection with the burgh council for a very considerable period. In the 1490s *domini assessores* acted to assist the justiciar, who was usually a noblemen, by advising him on points of law and procedure.[98] Admirals, again laymen, also had lawyers acting as assessors. In 1544 the admiral, Patrick, earl Bothwell, was faced with an action by merchants of 'Sprewisland' (probably the Baltic port of Stralsund) concerning the spuilzie of a ship by Scotsmen.[99] He desired, and was given by parliament, an impressive array of leading judges and men of law, James Foulis, Thomas Bellenden, Henry Lauder, Hugh Rigg and Thomas Marjoribankis, as his assessors to help him decide the matter. At a lower level there is evidence that sheriff-deputes, at least on some occasions, also made use of men of law acting as their assessors although this would appear

95   Several fifteenth-century acts of parliament used the word 'advocate', such as the acts of James I anent advocates for the poor [*APS*, ii, 8 (c.24)] and the oath of calumny [*APS*, ii, 9 (c.9); 19 (c. 16)]. As for the poets, see J. Finlay, 'Professional Men of Law before the Lords of Council, *c.*1500–*c.*1550' (Edinburgh University Ph.D. thesis, 1997,) 30–40.

96   CS 5/33 fo. 179v: 12 Feb. 1523; CS 5/40 fo. 92r: 11 Aug. 1529. These should be distinguished from entries such as 'Robert Galbraith procuratour and forspekar for Robert Fogo and Patrick Barcar' since, clearly, Fogo may have been absent and Barcar present: CS 5/39 fo. 113v: 25 Feb. 1529.

97   M. Lynch, *Edinburgh and the Reformation* (Edinburgh, 1981), 15.

98   Hannay, *College of Justice*, 328.

99   *APS*, ii, 450: 12 Dec. 1544.

to have been the exception rather than the rule. The service of a brieve in 1505 in favour of George Rule by James Aldintraw, 'pretendit' sheriff-depute of Berwick, was annulled on the basis that James had not been properly sworn. Moreover, James had 'requirit the said george roullis advocate to sit as assessour with him and to geve him counsale in the said mater'.[100] In contrast Sir Alexander Lindsay petitioned the lords of council in 1512 to appoint assessors to advise the sheriff chosen to serve his 'brevis' (presumably brieves of succession or inquest) of the earldom of Crawford, in order to ensure that justice was 'equalie ministrat'.[101] Assessors could either improve the quality of justice or reduce it, depending upon the circumstances and, of course, the identity of the assessors in question.

[100] CS 5/17 fo. 155r: 19 Dec. 1505.
[101] CS 5/26 fo. 10v: 26 Oct. 1512.

CHAPTER TWO

Lawyer and Client

Secrecy surrounds most of the dealings between litigants and their men of law in the sixteenth century. Only later in the century does surviving correspondence between client and lawyer begin to cast light on the relationship. Prior to the Reformation virtually nothing of this kind survives. Instead it is necessary to fall back on a variety of less direct sources to understand the ways in which advocates were employed, the powers they had, and the relationships they had with their clients. These sources mainly reveal what went on in public; as to what happened behind the scenes much remains, as those privy to it always intended that it should, private and confidential.

Types of constitution

According to the fourteenth century treatise *Regiam Majestatem*, a litigant who wanted a man of law to act on his behalf before a judge had to appear personally in court and formally constitute one or more procurators to act for him.[1] This was apparently still the rule when Sir James Balfour of Pittendreich wrote his Practicks at the end of the 1570s. Sir John Skene, on the other hand, in his *Ane Short Form of Process* (1609), indicated that personal presence was unnecessary provided the procurator came to the bar of the court armed either with authentic letters of procuratory from his client or an extract from the books of council, subscribed by the clerk register, narrating his constitution.

The contemporary evidence consists in the main of formal constitutions of procurators written into the *acta* by the clerks of the council. As a source these constitutions are of limited value because as a matter of convenience for the scribes they became formulaic. Several examples will demonstrate the limitations that these entries in the record present for the historian. First, the most basic form of constitution:

---

[1]   Substantially the same text is found in *APS*, i, 94 and in the following manuscripts: NLS, Adv MS. 25.5.6 fo. 38r (1488); NLS, Adv. MS. 25.5.7 fo. 43r (c. 1475); Adv. MS. 25.5.9 fo. 35r (c. 1520).

Maister William bailze constitute maister thomas alane maister
matho ker procuratouris for him in all materis.[2]

This was a general constitution by which William named Thomas and
Matthew to represent him in all cases that might concern him before the lords
of council. Several clauses might have been included in this constitution but
were not. The ratification clause (*et promisit de Rato*) is the major absentee; it
appears so regularly at the end of each entry that where it does not, the reason
can usually be assigned to the forgetfulness of the scribe.[3] Another general
constitution, closely contemporary to that already cited, is closer to the norm:

> Schir alex[ander] brus constitute Edward brus david balfour of
> caraldstoun & Sir John elphinstoun proc[u]r[atou]ris for [him] in
> all actiounis *et promisit de Rato*.[4]

Here Sir Alexander is noted as specifically having promised to ratify
whatever his procurators might do on his behalf. This did not give them *carte
blanche*; they had to act within the scope of the powers granted to them. As
will be shown below, additional clauses were sometimes added to this basic
framework, further refining the scope of these powers.

The other basic type of constitution was the special constitution. By using
such a constitution the litigant nominated someone to represent him against a
party or parties named in the constitution or in a specific action. A good, if
unusually long-winded, example occurred six months after the battle of
Flodden:

> Comperit Johnne makane of Ardmurchane & constitut colyne
> erle of ergyle procuratour [for] him *cum potestate substitutendi*
> anent the clame of ane silver pece being in the hands of gilbert
> murray burges of Ed[inbu[r]gh and the sowme of viii[xx] merkis
> with certane uther jowell[is] being in ane box & tayne fra his
> servand in the feild of northumberland pertening to him as is
> allegit *et promisit de Rato*.[5]

Although this mentions what the action concerns, it does not clearly identify
the defender or defenders (although one of them, at least, was probably

---

[2]   CS 5/16 fo. 68v: 10 Feb. 1505.

[3]   On the *ratum* clause in church practice, see J.E. Sayers, *Papal Judges Delegate in the Provinces of Canterbury,
      1198–1254* (Oxford, 1971), 232. As she points out, the giving of a pledge comes from Roman law.

[4]   CS 5/16 fo. 122r: 20 Feb. 1505. Cf. '*in omnibus seu actionibus seu querelis motis aut movendis contra eosdem*':
      28 Mar. 1531: CS 5/42 fo. 148v.

[5]   CS 5/26 fo. 93r: 6 Mar. 1514.

Gilbert Murray). In rare cases there was no defender, or at least, none identifiable at the time the constitution was made. For example, the bailies of Haddington named procurators 'to heir and se[e] certane lettres be transumit befor the lordis of counsale'.[6] The normal procedure involved in the transumption, or copying, of deeds was for a notice to be posted on the tolbooth door advertising the date on which the transumpt was to be made and inviting anyone with an objection to attend and make his protest.[7]

Usually, however, there was no question as to the identity of the defender. A typical example was the constitution of procurators by John Shaw 'to persew & follow the actioun & caus movit be him apoun Johnne Crawford of Drongane'.[8] Conversely, special constitutions could be defensive, made in response to a summons already raised against the litigant in question. For example:

> Comperit Jhone Nudry william robesoun James prestoun alex[ande]r andersoun henry calendar thomas bad Jhone andersone robert gardner & constitut maister thomas marjorbankis procu[ratou]r for thame in the actioun movit at the instance of sir william lothiane aganis thame *Et promisit de Rato*.[9]

Similarly, John Cunningham named procurators 'to ansuer at the instance of the erle of Rothes quhatsoevir day or place eftir the tenour of the summondis' against him; and Alexander Stewart did so 'in defense' of an action moved against him by Elizabeth Stewart and her mother.[10] There were also special constitutions that were designed simultaneously to defend an action and to raise a counter-action. An example of this occurred in 1522 when Agnes, lady Bothwell, constituted procurators to act for her in actions which she brought against the provost of Guthrie and which he brought against her.[11]

There was a third type of constitution although it is questionable whether it should be classified separately. This was the special and general constitution. This typically provided for procurators against a named party and 'in all utheris actiounis quhatsumevir',[12] 'in all utheris materis',[13] or against all other parties. This differed from a special constitution in that the power was included to act

[6] CS 5/37 fo. 140r : 4 July 1527.
[7] E.g. CS 5/36 fo. 37v: 7 July 1526, where a deed containing a reversion was transumed because part of its seal was broken and the petitioner was afraid the rest might break by handling removing the deed's evidential value. Interested parties were summoned by open proclamation at the mercat cross in Dumfries.
[8] CS 5/26 fo. 31r: 10 Jan. 1514.
[9] CS 5/42 fo. 6r: 24 Jan. 1531.
[10] CS 5/28 fo. 49v: 6 Nov. 1516; CS 5/31 fo. 182r: 15 Nov. 1518.
[11] CS 5/33 fo. 67v: 5 Dec. 1522.
[12] E.g., CS 5/41 fo. 25r: 19 Mar. 1530.
[13] E.g., CS 5/22 fo. 106r: 29 Mar. 1511.

not only against a named party, but also 'in all other actions'. It was distinct from general constitutions, in that a specific party was named. The significance of this distinctiveness, if there was any, is more properly assessed in the discussion of procurators' powers which follows later.

The interaction between recorded constitutions and court appearances is far from straightforward. Litigants almost always constituted multiple procurators who acted jointly and severally.[14] Even if a particular procurator was constituted this was no guarantee that he would later act for the litigant in question. Men of law generally appeared only for a minority of those who actually constituted them. Conversely, they also appeared for clients by whom there is no record of their being constituted. For instance, recorded constitutions survive only in respect of 15 per cent of the clients for whom the advocate Robert Leslie appeared and this by no means unique.[15] Although modest gaps exist in the record, they are insufficient to explain these discrepancies and it is clear that if the recording of every constitution were essential then the clerks would have had to record very many more than they actually did.

The high number of constitutions may be accounted for by the fact that nominating procurators, like raising the action in the first place, may often simply have been a means of getting the other party's attention in the hope of out of court settlement. If it worked, then no subsequent proceedings would be recorded. But that does not explain why only a low proportion of clients actually recorded constitutions and the conclusion must be that the clerks did not record every constitution in the *acta*. There are several reasons why this might have been the case. Recording constitutions may not have been necessary. Litigants may not always have felt the need to pay the clerks of council to record in the *acta* the fact that they had constituted procurators, particularly if they could rely on other evidence, such as a letter of procuratory, that they had done so. Registration may have been a luxury that could be dispensed with, particularly if a well-known man of law was constituted. No advocate would risk his livelihood by acting without proper authority. Another possibility is that the constitutions once made might have been recorded elsewhere. Given the high degree of crossover in personnel between the civil and church courts, it is possible that constitutions recorded before a judge spiritual could retain their validity before judges temporal and vice-versa.[16]

---

[14] Constitutions naming multiple procurators invariably were made '*coniunctim et divisim*' or '*in solidum*'. The routine naming of multiple procurators also occurred in the English courts both ecclesiastical and common law: Sayers, *Papal Judges Delegate*, 230.

[15] Finlay, 'Professional Men of Law', 46.

[16] The interchange in personnel was also common elsewhere in Europe. See, for example, Martines, *Lawyers and Statecraft in Renaissance Florence* (Princeton, 1968), 91.

There is no mention of any separate book wherein constitutions might be registered until May 1534. The clerk register, James Foulis, was then ordered to make and maintain such a book and from 1535 only a very few constitutions were recorded in the *acta*.[17] If a book was made it has not survived. Registration therefore, although perhaps the best evidence that a valid constitution had been made, was merely one means of proving it. Any figures taken from those constitutions which were recorded—and which have survived—must be viewed with the *caveat* that there were other unrecorded constitutions. This will not invalidate the figures, of course, but it will perhaps only make them helpful as indications of general trends and most useful when supplemented by other evidence.

Letters of procuratory

Although letters of procuratory are less likely to survive than constitutions recorded in court books, they provide more evidence of the basis upon which such constitutions were made. Various types of letter might be issued corresponding to the different modes of constitution. They were witnessed and notarised, often subscribed by the granter, and sealed, sometimes with a burgh seal or a notary's seal.[18] In content, the letter could specify a particular court or indicate that the procurator might appear in any court to pursue a particular matter or matters relative to a particular party. Thus the earl of Errol in 1525 named procurators, including Robert Leslie, to appear before the king and council to pursue a summons at his instance.[19] In contrast, one of the tutors of Egidia Young named procurators to carry on processes on her behalf against Sir John Young before the lords of council or any other judge temporal or spiritual.[20] In a slight variation on this, the bishop of Brechin named procurators to act in his name '*coram dominis consiliariis seu dominis auditoribus*' ('in the presence of the lords of council or lords auditor') in an action moved against him by the burgh of Montrose.[21] As well as naming the court or courts where the procurators were to act, the place (however vaguely expressed) was also given. In unusual circumstances, such as plague, courts might move and often the procuratory might indicate that a procurator is to appear '*coram dominis consilii in pretorio de edynbrocht vel ubi contingit eos*'.[22] It was normal to include a date but again this was circumscribed by such phrases as

---

[17]   *ADCP*, 422.
[18]   *Prot. Bk. Alexander King*, no 118: 23 May 1556 (use of notary's seal).
[19]   *Errol Chrs.*, no. 341; NRA(S) no. 925.
[20]   *Prot. Bk. Foular*, iii, no. 421: 4 Sep. 1523.
[21]   *Registrum Episcopatus Brechinensis* (Bannatyne Club, 1856) [*Brechin Registrum*], ii, 161: 10 Nov. 1508. It is not clear whether '*auditoribus*' refers to the Lords auditor of Parliament or of the Exchequer. In the absence of the word '*scaccarii*' probably the former was meant.
[22]   NAS, Ailsa Muniments, GD 25/1/281.

'or any uther dais lauchfull', or 'with continuation of days' (that is, taking into account adjournments). In the case of the burgh of Montrose against the bishop of Brechin, the date expressed was *'quarto die cessionis vicecomitatus Angusiae seu quibuscunque aliis diebus'* referring to the geographical division of summonses heard before the lords of council.[23]

A letter of procuratory, as well as being special or general, might include not only reference to a particular action but also instruct the raising of a counter-action. The burgh of Cupar issued a procuratory in 1518 naming procurators to defend it against a summons brought by the king and the archbishop of St Andrews, and also to pursue a summons against the provost and bailies of St Andrews.[24] Other reasons, apart from the need to raise or defend an action, might be narrated as the basis for the procuratory. For instance, the letter might indicate that the granter was naming someone to act for him during an absence abroad.[25]

There are possible instances of letters of procuratory being issued without prior consultation with all of those named as procurators. Refusals to act by men of law will be discussed in greater depth in chapter four, however there are examples in the *acta* where the office of procuratory was specifically either accepted or declined.[26] The same is the case with arbiters who, having been chosen by a particular party, might decline the appointment.[27] A letter of procuratory from the English warden, Lord Dacre, was unsuccessful, even when presented by Margaret Tudor, since no one named in it was prepared to accept the office.[28] In this context, the extraordinary case of Marion Frog, an English-based litigant, is instructive. In 1517 Marion had paid £100 for royal letters licensing her to succeed to whomever she was 'nerest of kyn'.[29] She was to enjoy all lands and goods she obtained thereby even though she lived in England. On this basis, she inherited the lands of Janet Smith five years later and alienated them, as she had the right to do in terms of the licence, to the Edinburgh burgess James McCalzeane (the father of the advocate Thomas McCalzeane). It seems that Marion was then escheated for remaining in

---

[23] *Brechin Registrum*, ii, 161.
[24] NAS, B13/21/1/16: 20 July 1518.
[25] *Prot. Bk. Grote*, no. 83: 20 Jan. 1556. See also the abbot of Kilwinning, who named procurators during his absence in France: CS 6/4 fo. 112v: 29 Apr. 1534. It was normal for those going abroad on royal business to obtain letters of protection from the king safeguarding his property until his return. For example, Sir John Campbell of Lundie did so in 1530 during an absence in Flanders on business for the king (CS 5/41 fo. 2v: 11 Mar. 1530) as had John, Lord Hay of Yester in 1529 when he was on the king's service in the Borders: CS 5/39 fo. 133r: 2 Mar. 1529.
[26] E.g., CS 5/29 fo. 25v (acceptance of office by Patrick, abbot of Cambuskenneth, to act for William Lamb); CS 5/19 fo. 238r (renunciation of procuratory, by Master Walter Lang and Thomas Fleming, to act for George, earl of Rothes). The same practice was found in the church courts, Ollivant, *Court of the Official*, 58, fn. 179.
[27] E.g., CS 5/32 fo. 112r: 9 Mar. 1518.
[28] CS 5/32 fo. 90r: 28 Feb. 1518.
[29] CS 5/33 fo. 48r: 28 Nov. 1522; CS 5/34 fos. 129v–130r: 26 Feb. 1524.

England, despite having purchased the licence, and the Stirling burgess Alexander Forrester obtained the escheat.[30] He then raised an action against James, as the possessor of the lands, and James called on Marion as his warrantor to defend him. Marion sent a letter of procuratory to Edinburgh. Alexander's forespeaker, Master Henry Spittall, had it recorded that Masters Thomas Hamilton, Robert Galbraith and John Lethame 'acceptit the office upoun thaim as proc[uratou]ris for marioun frog remanand within Ingland'.[31] Over a year later the dispute was ongoing. Galbraith, for Marion, argued that the summons had not named his client but had named only James McCalzeane together with Marion Frog's procurators. He argued that 'the principall parti' should be called, and not her procurators. This was unsuccessful; Marion's 'pretendit procuratouris' were ordered to produce in evidence the letters of licence that she claimed to have. The significance of this case lies in the refusal of the procurators to be identified with their principal; this is a revealing attitude even though, in procedural terms, the argument was lost.

Types of procurator

Until now, the term 'procurator' has been used without further differentiation. But it is necessary, before discussing the powers granted to procurators, to consider in more detail how the term was used in the early sixteenth century. There is no explicit evidence of the distinction being used in Scotland between procurators *judicialis* (or *ad lites*) and procurators *de negotia* which was made by the Dutchman, Philip Wielant, in his *Practijke Civile* (1519).[32] Balfour makes no such distinction in this context.[33] Skene, in defining the word *actornatus* in his *De Verborum Significatione* (1597), does recognise the different functions that an attorney might perform. First, he mentions both the *responsalis* ('he quha makis answer for ane uther in judgement') and the *prolocutor* ('he quha speaks for the persewer'). Then he goes on:

> Alswa *actornatus* is he quha dois any thing in an uther mans name
> or behalfe, as he quha compeiris for an uther in courtes, or justice

---

[30] The precise legal basis of the escheat is unclear. The record indicated that Marion was escheated for remaining in England. It is possible that the goods were considered to be escheat because Janet was thought to have died without heirs.

[31] CS 5/33 fo. 48r: 28 Nov. 1522. On 17 July 1517, a constitution by Marion was recorded naming, in addition to those who later accepted office in 1522, James Simson and Abraham Crichton to represent her against the king and William and John Richardson in an action conerning land in the burgh of Edinburgh: CS 5/30 fo. 94r: 17 July 1517.

[32] A. Wijffels, 'Procureurs et avocats au Grand Conseil de Malines', *L'assistance dans la resolution des conflits* (Brussels, 1997), 170.

[33] But Balfour does distinguish curators *ad lites* and curators *ad negotia*: Balfour, *Practicks*, i, 122.

aire, to pass upon inqueistes, and serving of retoures to the kingis
chapel…

These alternative definitions are more akin to Wielant's distinction although
they fall some way short of actually making it.

Scottish practice in the early sixteenth century knew no great distinction, in
terms of personnel, between procurators who pled in court and those who
performed other tasks. These latter tasks might include the granting,
resignation and receiving of sasine in the civil context[34] or presenting
dispensations from the Roman penitentiary and making binding obligations
on oath under threat of excommunication in the ecclesiastical.[35] The same
people might perform both types of undertaking, although a larger number
and a greater variety of people undertook the latter. Skene does, however,
recognise a functional distinction between the two types of activity for which
procurators might be employed and it seems safe to apply, with due care,
Wielant's useful terminology in the context of Scotland.

In Scottish practice a judicial procurator was not simply a procurator who
appeared in court on behalf of another. There were two main reasons why a
procurator might appear before a court: either to plead the merits of the case
on behalf of his client, or to perform a formal act such as petitioning for a
curator, seeking to have a deed copied, or consenting to the registration of a
deed for preservation or execution. These two types of activity differ primarily
in the amount of discretion given to the procurator, and the degree to which
the client had to rely on the forensic skills of the particular man he had chosen
to represent him. Only those employed in court to use their own skill and
judgement as a procurator, independently of those who employed them,
should properly be considered judicial procurators. In practical terms such
procurators differed from every other kind of procurator in that it was not
possible to constitute them irrevocably.

In his *Practicks*, Balfour discusses the issue of revocation only in respect of the
procurator constituted 'in ony actioun or cause, the quhilk Procuratour
answeris in the samin cause, and dois that quhilk pertenis to the office of ane
Procuratour'.[36] This is somewhat enigmatic but clearly he had in mind
procurators who answered pleas on behalf of clients. By his time, the 'usual

---

[34]   In February 1510, John, earl of Crawford, resigned the office of sheriff of Aberdeen by using
    procurators: NAS, Errol Charters [NRA(S), no. 925].

[35]   An example of the latter indicates that the same procurators might appear in both contexts. In 1530 the
    advocates Masters Henry Lauder, James Carmuir, John Lethame and William Blackstock were among
    those named to present a dispensation on behalf of Robert Crawford of Beircriftis, before the
    archbishop of St Andrews: *Prot. Bk. Johnsoun*, 3 (no. 15): 2 Oct. 1530. For examples of procuratories
    naming procurators to enter obligations into church court act books see *Prot. Bk. Gaw*, nos 77, 159.
    161 and 162 and, for an earlier example, *Prot. Bk. Ros*, no. 541. For procurators producing a mandate
    '*lectum et admissum*' before a vicar general, see *Prot. Bk. Simon*, 88-9 (no. 116): 3 Apr. 1505.

[36]   Balfour, *Practicks*, ii, 301.

powers of a procurator' were so well known that he saw no need to define them closely.[37]

Surviving texts of letters of procuratory demonstrate that judicial procurators, as defined above, were not constituted irrevocably. Many examples could be given. In 1500 Lord Erskine, in perhaps the most comprehensive extant letter of procuratory, constituted six men his 'verray lauchfull and undowtit procuratouris, actouris, factouris and speciale erand beraris' to appear before the lords of council to answer a summons raised by the earl Bothwell.[38] Twenty years later, in identical terms, James Brown named five '*veros, legitimos et indubitatos, procuratores, actores, factores et negotiorum…gestores*' to raise a brieve of inquest.[39] In 1565 Matthew, earl of Lennox, named 'verray lauchfull and undoutit procuratouris' to raise a brieve of inquest to serve his wife as heir to her grandfather.[40] Nine years later, the principal of St Leonard's College in St Andrews, and others, named 'verry lauchfull & unduttit procuratouris' to defend them against an action of spuilzie raised by David Moneypenny of Pitmillie.[41] The two procuratories concerning brieves of inquest dealt with non-pleadable brieves (although it is not clear to what extent this distinction was properly observed at this period).[42] Even so, raising a brieve and ensuring that it was served correctly was a task which might easily lead to legal difficulties requiring independent thought by the procurator. One such procuratory instructs those named:

> to persew and follow [the brieves of inquest] be all proces and ordour of law that is requyrit, liticonstestatioun to mak, the aitht of suithfasnes to sweir, my absence to excuis, writtis, witnes, previs and documentis to produce and leid, and aganis me producit and led to except and impugne, actis, instrumentis, retouris, letteris of actornais, and preceptis of saising, and all utheris documentis and letteris necessar thairupoun to lift, ask and rais…[43]

This was clearly a potentially complex procedure. By contrast, those procurators who were constituted irrevocably tended to be those whose

---

[37] This phrase appears in a notarial instrument in November 1561: *Prot. Bk. Grote*, 45 (no. 202). Phrases such as '*in forma consueta*', 'in the largest form' or '*in uberiora forma*' are regularly found as part of the notation used when constitutions were recorded.

[38] *ADC*, ii , 473-4.

[39] Fraser, *Eglinton*, ii, 92: 7 Dec. 1520.

[40] Fraser, *Lennox*, ii, 262-3.

[41] *SAUL*, SL 110 L7.6: 29 Jan. 1574.

[42] The distinctions between different brieves appear to have become confused during the sixteenth century. Skene, *De Verborum Significatione*, wrongly identified the brieve of mortancestry with the brieve of succession, confusing a pleadable brieve with one that was retourable.

[43] Fraser, *Keir*, 364: 27 Oct. 1539.

activity involved following a set procedure in a mechanical way without the need for discretion on their part. In Dumfries in 1528 John Armstrong constituted Robert Leslie and others as his 'werray lachfull and irrevocable procuratouris' to resign the lands of Langholm to Robert, Lord Maxwell.[44] The previous month, in his lodging in Edinburgh, Hugh, Lord Somerville, gave his 'free, full and irrevocable power and mandate' to procurators named to resign a tenement of land in Edinburgh by delivery of earth and stone into the hands of one of the bailies of the burgh.[45] The same formulation, '*meam plenam liberam et irrevocabilem potestatem ac mandatum*' had been used by Master David Lauder in naming procurators in 1517 for resigning lands in favour of the Edinburgh burgess Gilbert Lauder and his wife.[46] Alexander Stewart of Grandtully, in resigning his lands in favour of his son, appointed '*veros, legitomos, indubitatos et irrevocabiles procuratores*' to do so.[47] In November 1560, the advocate Richard Strang ratified on behalf of Alexander Doles and his heirs, a decreet pronounced by the lords in favour of Lord Gordon, against him. Appearing in court, he renounced on Alexander's behalf any right to question the decreet, and to any action of warrandice which he or his heirs might have had against the earl of Huntly or his heirs. The procuratory by which Strang, and others, were constituted was preserved and it clearly shows that Alexander made them his 'verray lauchfull and undowtit and irrevocable procuratouris'.[48] This last example demonstrates that it was the task, not the procurator, which defined whether or not he might be constituted irrevocably. In short, the evidence suggests that although the terminology adopted by Wielant was not used in Scotland the concept that lay behind it was well known. More than that, the concept itself had a practical consequence in terms of the revocability of the relationship between procurator and the party he represented.

In the case of a procurator *de negotia*, the extent of the procurator's power was defined by the task assigned to him. The principal was able to pre-determine the extent to which the procurator might affect his position; in other words, he could control in advance his ultimate liability. The lands that were to be resigned or exchanged, or the rights to be given up or recorded, were carefully defined in the procuratory and the procurator need only comply. The very limits on the procurator's input explains why such procuratories tended to be irrevocable: the need to revoke them would not arise since the principal had already committed himself to act. In the case of a

---

44 Fraser, *Carlaverock*, ii, 465.
45 *Prot. Bk. Foular*, iii, 26 (no. 71).
46 NAS, Broughty and Cally Muniments, GD 10/47: 9 Feb. 1517. One of the procurators named was Master Henry Lauder, Gilbert's son and the future king's advocate.
47 Fraser, *Grandtully*, i, 75 (no. 44): 1 Mar. 1539.
48 NAS, Register of Deeds, RD 1/4 fo. 83b.

judicial procurator this was not the case. The procurator, by his own performance, might prejudice his principal's interests beyond his expectation; he might make concessions which the principal would not have made had he been present. The relationship between procurator and principal might break down as a result. After all, unlike other kinds of procurator, judicial procurators might spend years pursuing or defending an action; that is why on the continent such procurators, or *procureurs*, were sometimes called '*dominus litis*' or 'maître de la cause'.[49] If appointed irrevocably, the principal might find himself stuck with a procurator in whom he had lost confidence. Balfour makes this very point, when he says that a procurator may be replaced by his principal 'speciallie gif ony deidlie feid or inimitie has intervenit betwix thame'.[50]

The powers of a procurator

Two obvious issues present themselves when considering the scope of a procurator's authority: when was the procurator eligible to act for his client, and what could he do when he was? Clearly, a procurator constituted generally was eligible to act in all of his clients' future actions. If constituted specially then his ability to act was circumscribed and normally the clerks would give a brief indication of how it was limited (either to a particular action or to actions involving one or two particular opponents).[51] The third type of constitution, special and general, is more difficult to explain. It may be that these were simply general constitutions, entitling the procurator to act in all cases but mentioning one particular case for the avoidance of doubt because it was already depending before the lords and antecedent procedure had already been heard. Alternatively this type of constitution may essentially have been a special constitution but extending beyond a single action or a single

---

[49] Wijffels, 'Procureurs et avocats', 171. The Dutch phrase was '*meester vander sake*'.
[50] Balfour, *Practicks*, ii, 301.
[51] This differs from the interpretation of Dr Ollivant, who appears to consider general procurators to have more limited powers than special procurators: *Court of the Official*, 58, fn. 177. His argument, based on Balfour, would seem to be that a procurator, if he only held a general mandate, must find caution *de rato* as a guarantee of the client's subsequent ratification. The passage from Balfour, however, merely says that no one may be a procurator unless there is a *ratum* clause in his mandate; if there is no such clause, then even a procurator with a general mandate may be repelled unless he can find caution himself: Balfour, *Practicks*, ii, 299. This does not suggest that the general procurator has to find caution for each case in which he is involved, provided his client has promised to ratify his actions in the mandate. All sixteenth-century recorded constitutions, with very few exceptions, indicate that the mandate included the *ratum* clause regardless of whether the constitution was special, general or both. Balfour does also say that no one may be a procurator without a 'special' mandate, written and sealed and containing sufficient power to win or lose. This is straight from *Regiam Majestatem*. But Balfour does not here use the word 'special' in the sense in which I have used it; he simply means there must be a sufficient mandate. Otherwise, Balfour would be arguing the absurd proposition that only special procurators could appear in court when the evidence is clear that general procurators could do so and often did.

party to all actions resulting from a particular dispute and to all those who had an interest in that dispute. The evidence is ambivalent although there are reasons for preferring the second interpretation.[52]

Contrary to what might have been expected, there is no evidence that general constitutions were less subject to renewal or alteration than special, or special and general, constitutions. It is certainly true that some parties having made a general constitution are not thereafter recorded making any subsequent constitution.[53] In some cases, although a subsequent constitution (of whatever type) was made it was not made for several years.[54] There are a number of cases, however, in which a general constitution was repeated relatively quickly;[55] or was soon followed by an alternative type of constitution.[56] It cannot be concluded that special constitutions were short term whereas general constitutions, or special and general constitutions, were intended to be long-term. The evidence points to a more complex picture in which the nomination of procurators was driven by events rather than by the careful planning of litigants.

Presuming the procurator was entitled to act, the powers he enjoyed varied according to the terms of his constitution. He could be given the specific authority to pursue, to argue and finally to conclude the action ('*prosequi mediare et sine dubite terminare*')[57]. Phrases such as 'baith to persew follow and defend as law will' were not uncommon in recorded constitutions and would appear to represent the minimum in terms of the level of power granted.[58] To these might be added other powers. One litigant named procurators to defend

---

52   See Finlay, 'Professional Men of Law', 59-61.
53   For example, George, Lord Seton, whose general constitution was recorded on 31 Jan. 1509 (CS 5/20 fo. 78r); William, earl of Errol (13 Feb. 1509: CS 5/20 fo. 113v); John Brown, burgess of Ayr (31 July 1517: CS 5/30 fo. 131v); William, earl Marischall (23 July 1527: CS 5/37 fo. 174r, naming advocates as his curators); Henry Congilton of that ilk (25 Feb. 1531: CS 5/42 fo. 71r); Alexander Milne, abbot of Cambuskenneth (28 Mar. 1531: CS 5/42 fo. 148v).
54   For example, David Hoppringle made a general constitution that was recorded on 10 Feb. 1505 (CS 5/16 fo. 68v), and next appears making a special constitution on 4 Feb. 1510 (CS 5/21 fo. 118v). Robert Lauder of Bass made a general constitution that was recorded on 27 Jan. 1506 (CS 5/18/1 fo. 3v). He next appeared on 27 Feb. 1518 (CS 5/30 fo. 207r), making a special and general constitution.
55   For example, Alexander Hamilton, abbot of Kilwinning, made a general constitution on 13 Jan. 1533 (CS 6/2 fo. 43v), and made another one on 29 Apr. 1534 (CS 6/4 fo. 112v) naming different general procurators; William, Lord Carlyle did the same on 19 Jan. 1507 (CS 5/18/2 fo. 113r) which was followed by another on 10 Feb. 1508 (CS 5/19 fo. 153r).
56   For example, Robert Ayton made a general constitution on 26 Feb. 1529 (CS 5/39 fo. 116r) and then a special and general one a few months later (CS 5/40 fo. 132v: 23 Oct. 1529); John Murray of Fallahill made general procurators on 18 Jan. 1507 (CS 5/18/2 fo. 106r), and the same man may then have made special procurators on 5 Feb. 1508 (CS 5/19 fo. 137v); Robert Scott made special procurators on 4 Feb. 1506 and then, just ten days later, special and general procurators (CS 5/18/1/ fos. 37v, 83r).
57   For example, the constitution made by Neil Ferguson in 1527: NAS, Ailsa Muniments, GD 25/1/281. Cf. the constitution of James Brown in 1520 '*prosequi, mediare, terminare, finire et ad effectam producere*': Fraser, *Eglinton*, ii , 92.
58   CS 5/23 fo. 125v: 14 Aug. 1511.

and follow and 'to defer to the aith of george middilmas'.[59] More generally, the procurator might be given power to substitute another or others in his place (*cum potestate susbtituendi*), or to concord (*cum potestatione concordandi*), treat (*cum potestate tractandi*), or compromise (*cum potestate compromittendi*), that is, to submit the matter to arbitration.[60] It was possible for several procurators to be named but for a specific power to attach to only one of them.

The numerous references to a party being required to appear in court with a 'sufficient mandate' indicates that letters could be issued without the grant of sufficient authority to the procurator to allow him to bind the principal to a particular disposal of the case. Even when adequate power was granted, the procuratory might still be ineffective on a technical ground. Henry, Lord Sinclair, complained on one occasion that a procuratory produced on behalf of the burgh of Dysart was ineffectual because it contained the names neither of the bailies whom he had originally summoned, nor of those who then held office.[61] As a result, parties sometimes demanded that a cautioner guarantee the sufficiency of a procuratory. Adam Otterburn and James Logan, sheriff-depute of Edinburgh, were prepared to grant caution, to the value of £100, that James Edmonstone would appear before the lords the following week 'be [by] himself or his sufficient procur[atou]r[is]'.[62] In 1533, a notarial entry mentions that cautioners undertook to cause Mariota Fleming, widow of Alan Heriot, to appear in the tolbooth of Edinburgh '*per se vel sufficienis* (sic) *mandatum ad defendam in causa contra eam*'.[63] The action in question was raised by Master Robert Heriot, presumably a relative of her late husband, to be heard by the advocate, Henry Lauder, acting as bailie *in hac parte* of the regality of Glasgow. In another case, it was alleged that the sheriff of Elgin had refused to admit and maliciously repelled Thomas Guthrie, who had sought to put forward defences as Alexander Innes's procurator, even though he had 'sufficient mandate and power thirto'.[64] In long-running litigation between the prior of Whithorn and the burgh of Wigtown, the representatives of the latter promised 'to gett ane power of the toune...to compromitt and concord with quhithorne...or ellis to gett thair utir mynd and deliverance therein'.[65] Clearly they had not originally been given sufficient power to submit the dispute to arbitration.[66] Eventually the lords of session ordered both sides to produce and

---

[59] CS 5/18/2 fo. 206r: 18 Feb. 1507.
[60] It is doubtful whether there was any substantive difference in meaning between treating, compromising and componing. Cf. Sayers, *Papal Judges Delegate*, 235-6.
[61] CS 5/18/1 fo. 86v: 17 Feb. 1506.
[62] CS 5/24 fo. 121r: 18 Feb. 1513.
[63] NAS, N.P. 1/2A fo. 47r (*Prot. Bk. Thos. Keane*): 24 July 1533.
[64] CS 5/31 fo. 49r: 30 June 1518.
[65] CS 5/32 fo. 106r: 3 Mar. 1519; see SHS *Wigtownshire Charters*.
[66] Cf. the dispute between Malcolm, Lord Fleming, and John, Lord Hay of Yester, which was submitted to arbitration. John Lethame, Fleming's procurator, was specifically noted as being 'sufficientlie autorisit' to make the submission to arbitration on his client's behalf: CS 6/5 fo. 49v: 6 July 1534.

bring procuratories with them on a specified future date. The burgh's letters were to be sealed with the common seal of the burgh and to have sufficient authority 'to persew and defend the said actioun, to compromit in the samin gif neid be, and to be extendit in the best form with all clausis necessar'. The prior's procuratory was to be in similar terms although it was to be sealed 'under the chapel seile of the said place of quhithorne'.[67]

As well as guaranteeing adequate power, a procurator might be required to guarantee that in the event the action was lost any liability would be met by his principal. In one case, Master Robert Monorgund, kinsman to the earl of Huntly, sought to be admitted to procure in an action brought against the earl by the chancellor. He protested that he might do so provided he found 'caution de Ratihabitioune'. There is no indication of whether he contemplated obtaining this caution from Huntly or from some other party; provided he chose someone who was not a man of straw, presumably there was no objection to his finding a suitable local man to grant the guarantee.[68] Ultimately, however, the onus was on the principal to indemnify his procurator, and this will be discussed further below in relation to ratification.

In the areas of caution and sufficiency of mandate, foreign litigants were the most likely to present difficulties. It is from a case involving a foreigner that there is evidence that a procurator did not specifically need to be granted the power to take the oath of calumny on behalf of his client. A letter of procuratory sent to Scotland by the Englishman William Woodhouse was allowed by the lords even though it 'maid na mentioun *de iuramentum calumpnie*'.[69] Presumably a power so fundamental was implied in every letter of procuratory: if there was no one to swear the oath, no case could successfully be brought. In 1511, Bardo Altavite produced a procuratory, which was also described as an 'instrument of power', upon which he intended to act as procurator for some merchants in Flanders. Having produced it he promptly took it away again and refused to use it, whereupon the king's advocate, in the name of the entire realm and all the lords of session, offered to give him justice if he would show 'ane seyficient powere'. The implication is that the instrument he originally produced was in some way defective or inadequate, or that he was not sure of his instructions.[70] In May 1525, the Dane, Hans Sanderson, defending a charge that he had unjustly taken a ship and cargo

---

[67]　CS 6/2 fo. 20v: 2 Dec. 1532.

[68]　CS 5/33 fo. 110r: 19 Dec. 1522. Monorgund was parson of Culace. Huntly had used Monorgund's seal, not having his own with him, when he made a letter of procuratory naming Master John Garden to compone on his behalf with de la Bastie concerning the slaughter of Alexander Bannerman: CS 5/30 fo. 46r: 30 June 1517. If Monorgund was within the fourth degree of consanguinity or affinity to Huntly, he could speak on his behalf without a mandate, provided he found caution: Balfour, *Practicks*, ii, 298.

[69]　CS 6/6 fo. 65v: 3 Mar. 1535.

[70]　CS 5/22 fo. 105r: 29 Mar. 1511.

belonging to various men in St Andrews and Cupar, was required to find caution in case he was found liable. The men who were his cautioners indicate a high degree of inter-burgh co-operation since they include the Leith merchant and comptroller Robert Barton of Over Barnton, together with two burgesses from Aberdeen and two from Edinburgh. Hans had to promise to relieve them should he be unsuccessful; he then promptly named them his procurators together with the advocate James Foulis.[71] Although not a foreigner, Sir Alexander Fotheringham was a chaplain resident in Bruges.[72] His brother Charles, in producing a procuratory entitling him to act on his brother's behalf, required Lord Drummond to act as cautioner presumably because Alexander's assets were abroad.[73]

In 1531 another foreigner, James Eggart, a merchant in the Steelyard in London, made a constitution that indicates the variety of his needs and the demands which might be made upon his procurators. The Steelyard was the trading house of the Hansa and Eggart, a Baltic merchant, constituted three procurators and factors: his fellow countryman William Vicherling, Thomas Scott of Abbotshall and Gilbert Menzies provost of Aberdeen.[74] These were to act for him in all actions that might concern him in the realm of Scotland, and they were 'to ask craif and ressaif all soumes of money or uther geir pertening or that may pertene to him'. They were empowered jointly and severally, any two of them (provided Vicherling was one) being authorised to grant discharges and securities in his name. The circumstances explain the granting of these unusual powers.

Generally the powers granted in constitutions were expressed in a stereotypical way. The litigant committed to his procurators his 'full plane power, speciale mandement [*or* generale *and* speciale command], express bidding and charge' (the special form being expressed in Latin as '*veram, liberam, puram et expressum potestatem ac mandatum speciale*').[75] As was noted earlier, by Balfour's time the powers of a procurator had become a matter of generally understood custom. This was true for the whole of the sixteenth century. By 1500 procurators were being empowered to do all things that in law normally pertained to the 'office of procuratory'.[76] The letter of that date containing this phrase was made by Lord Erskine against Patrick, earl Bothwell, and since it provides the most explicit statement of the powers conferred it is worth quoting at length. 'Full plane power' having been committed to them, the procurators were

[71] CS 5/35 fo. 29v: 17 May 1525.
[72] CS 5/23 fo. 116r: 12 Aug. 1511.
[73] CS 5/23 fo. 64r: 23 July 1511.
[74] CS 5/41 fo. 159r: 14 Jan. 1531. Eggart is described as an 'Esterling' meaning that he was from the eastern Baltic.
[75] See *ADC*, ii, 473; Fraser, *Lennox*, ii, 262. For an example in Latin, see Fraser, *Eglinton*, ii, 92.
[76] *ADC*, ii, 474.

to ansuere to the said summondis and to al poynctis and articlis
contenit tharintill, myne absence til excuse, litiscontestatione to
mak, the aith of suthfastnes in my saule to swere, my parti
adversare til here be sworne, my ressons and richtis to schaw, my
pruffis, witnes, writtis and documentis to produce and leid, and
aganis thame producit and led be my parti adversare til object,
except agane and impung, actis, decretis and instrumentis to ask,
lift, raise and here be given, protestacions to mak, to tret,
compone, concord, compromyctand finalye to end, and
generalye al uthir and sundri thingis to do, exerce and use that to
the office of procuratory to sic thingis ordanis, pertenis or of law
is knawin to pertene, with full power to ane or maa procuratouris
or prelocutoris in thare stedis to make and substitut and at thair
willis for to revok and destitut, and like as my self micht do and I
war present in propir persone...[77]

So comprehensive is this that it is no surprise the clerks preferred to condense
such constitutions into standard three or four line notation. Even so, the
catch-all provision that the procurators were to enjoy all the other powers
generally pertaining to them in law was still included. This was probably
designed to give added security; there is no indication elsewhere that powers
additional to those specified actually existed although sometimes the phrase
'with full power to win and tyne (lose)' might be included.[78]

Although very unusual in being written into the *acta*, and extremely
detailed, it is unlikely that Lord Erskine's letter was different in its general
tenor from hundreds of others. There is certainly evidence, contrary to the
statement in *Regiam* that litigants must appear personally to name procurators,
that it was regularly done by letter.[79] Lord Erskine's procuratory is one
example. As has been seen, the brief entries made by the clerks normally begin
with the word 'comperit'. But sometimes the clerks go on to say that the

---

[77] *ADC*, ii, 473-4: 7 Dec. 1500. A near contemporary, although unpublished, letter of procuratory by Sir John Wemyss relating to litigation before the lords is very similar in its essentials; NAS, Leven and Melville Muniments, GD 26/4/661: 15 Feb. 1502. Cf. also CS 5/17 fo. 157v: 31 Dec. 1505. In the powers granted, these are heavily influenced by Romano-canonical practice: Sayers, *Papal Judges Delegate*, 234.

[78] The power 'finalye to end', in the constitution by Erskine, was probably regarded as the equivalent of this clause.

[79] *ADC*, iii, introduction, xxiv, where Dr Murray acknowledges that sometimes there was a written procuratory, sometimes the procurator was constituted in face of the court. The major difference in this context between the early thirteenth century, when *Regiam* was compiled, and the sixteenth century was in the proliferation of notaries whose appearance made it a great deal easier to have letters of procuratory drafted: G. G. Simpson, *Handwriting in Scotland 1150–1650* (Aberdeen, 1973), Introduction, 7*ff*.

litigant, having appeared, named procurators to represent 'me'; an indication that they were reading a letter of procuratory and summarising its contents.[80]

There is also evidence that litigants were sending letters of procuratory to men of law.[81] That is not to say that the litigant did not appear but personal appearances on such occasions seem unlikely or, at least, the litigant as well as appearing personally may also have produced a letter of procuratory. When John Carmichael personally appeared to name procurators in 1531, a memorandum was recorded intimating that his 'lettres' were with Robert Leslie, the first-named of his procurators.[82] It may well be that Scottish practice mirrored that before the *Grand Conseil de Malines* where the procurator, on his first appearance for his client, had to leave his 'power of attorney' with the clerk of registry.[83] There is certainly record of a letter of procuratory being delivered to the commissary of the official of St Andrews in 1517, although this nominated procurators to make a resignation of lands in favour of the sheriff-depute of Edinburgh.[84] The following year Master John Williamson produced before the lords a procuratory of the dean of Glasgow and 'acceptit the office of procur[ator]y apoun him'.[85] There are also references to cases where a 'power' was shown to the lords of session or the lords auditor of parliament.[86] In one case Master Edward Sinclair asked for an instrument on behalf of Elizabeth Sinclair only for her opponent to obtain an instrument of his own narrating that Edward had shown 'no power nor procuracioun of the said Elizabeth to ask the said instrument'.[87] In another, it was argued that a procuratory should be held invalid because it was interlined.[88]

As the constitution made by the Hanseatic merchant James Eggart, mentioned above, demonstrates, one procurator might be given more power than his colleagues. For example, in one constitution Robert Galbraith alone of those named was given the power to substitute. Presumably, the choice of any substitute was to be his.[89] On another occasion, only Nicol Crawford, of several procurators named, was to have power to agree with any opponent as if the client himself were present. Since the client was David Crawford, this is probably explained by a family connection.[90] In an ecclesiastical context,

[80] E.g. CS 5/34 fo. 70v: 13 July 25.
[81] E.g., James Ogilvy of Balfour sent a procuratory to Master Robert Galbraith in 1532 only to find that Galbraith was not in Edinburgh to receive it: CS 6/2 fo. 15v: 26 Nov. 1532.
[82] CS 5/43 fo. 59r: 19 Oct. 1531.
[83] Van Rhee, 'Grand Council of Malines', 1.4.
[84] NAS, RH 6/847: 29 Apr. 1517.
[85] CS 5/31 fo. 137v: 21 July 1518.
[86] E.g., CS 5/18/1 fo. 119r: 23 Feb. 1506. And, in parliament, *APS*, ii, 434: 11 Dec. 1543.
[87] CS 5/16 fo. 141r: 3 Mar. 1505. The opponent was Sir David Home of Wedderburn.
[88] CS 5/35 fo. 73r: 4 July 1525.
[89] CS 5/33 fo. 32r: 20 Nov. 1522.
[90] CS 6/1 fo. 114v: 12 Sep. 1532.

Edward Cockburn, parson of Ellon, named procurators to receive benefices, to conduct litigation concerning benefices or to resign them in favour of a richer benefice. Of the twelve procurators appointed, the laymen (except Sir John Home) had power to receive benefices only, while the clerics (together with Sir John) had power both to resign and receive them.[91] One of the clerics named as procurator was Master David Seton, parson of Fettercairn, who was one of the most active judicial procurators before the lords of council during James IV's reign.[92]

Payments to men of law

Unlike some other civil jurisdictions, such as that of the *Grand Conseil de Malines* or the *Conseil Provincial de Namur*, the lords of council in Scotland did not produce an official scale of remuneration for the advocates who appeared before them.[93] An Act of 1672 which did introduce the regulation of advocates' fees provoked a major conflict between the Faculty of Advocates and the judges who, acting on royal instructions, sought to impose an oath on advocates that they would accept no more than the prescribed fees.[94] This led to a withdrawal of co-operation by a number of advocates in 1670 and, although this short 'strike' was unsuccessful, so abhorrent was the concept of prescribed fees that the legislation was rescinded in 1681.[95] In the absence in the sixteenth century of a Scottish equivalent of the Burgundian *Ordonnance de Thionville* of 1470, it would only be possible to reconstruct the level of fees charged if contracts and receipts of payment survived in abundance. But such deeds had no permanent significance and very few have survived. Disputes concerning legal fees and pensions are also disappointingly rare.[96] Scots men of law appear to have taken to heart canonist advice to make sure of the fee before acting so as to minimise the need of going to law over it.[97] A more

91　　*Prot. Bk. Young*, no. 961: 26 Oct. 1497.

92　　On Seton, see chapter seven.

93　　A. Wijffels, '*Procureurs et avocats*', 181-2, 186; C. Vael, 'Avocats et procureurs au Conseil Provincial de Namur du XVᵉ au XVIIIᵉ', in *L'assistance dans la resolution des conflits* (Brussels, 1997), 215. The earliest known fee schedule was promulgated in the Sicilian chancery in the thirteenth century: J.A. Brundage, 'The profits of the law: legal fees of university-trained advocates', *American Journal of Legal History*, xxxii (1988), 12. In Scotland, at least during the reign of James IV, writers to the signet did operate according to a fixed rate of charges: Hannay, *College of Justice*, 312.

94　　Simpson, 'Advocates', 168-171.

95　　Simpson, Ibid., 171; Rae, 'Advocate's Library', 8.

96　　Cf. The early attorney in England, knowledge of payments to whom normally survives only where relevant to a dispute between lawyer and client: Brand, *English Legal Profession*, 91.

97　　Brundage, 'Profits of the Law', 10, quoting William of Drogheda (d. 1245): '[i]t is better to take pains about the fee than to go to law over it.' The same sentiment was expressed in thirteenth century practitioners' manuals. Cf. Sayers, *Papal Judges Delegate*, 222. Medieval legists however, did not recommend actual payment in advance as this was considered unethical: Brundage, ibid., 4-5. Moreover, agreeing fees in advance did not always prevent subsequent legal action as a last resort; numerous *causa salarii* were recorded in the English church courts: R.H. Helmholz, 'Ethical standards general survey of sources is therefore required even to lay the groundwork for inquiry into this issue.

Unfortunately the evidence in the records of ecclesiastical foundations of payments made to legal representatives is not extensive. It does appear that that abbeys such as Arbroath and Dryburgh retained leading men of law to represent them. The basic terms of appointment were simple. In return for an annual pension, the advocate was bound to give the abbey his best counsel and advice when it was required. This involved the obligation to act generally as procurator for the abbot and convent in all cases and against all persons, except any kinsman of the advocate or anyone to whom he had come under a prior obligation. These were the terms of a 1532 agreement whereby John Lethame was to act for the abbey of Coupar Angus receiving in return an annual pension of £10 for the rest of his life.[98] Good evidence of this type of obligation also comes from the abbey of Arbroath. In 1509 the abbot entered into an obligation with James Henryson, king's advocate and justice-clerk general, by which the latter was to give his '*optimum consilium*' to the abbey, and to advocate on its behalf, in return for a life pension.[99] Broadly similar terms were used in the agreement between Robert Leslie and David Beaton, abbot of Arbroath, in 1527; Leslie was to act generally except against those to whom he was previously engaged.[100] Henryson was to receive 40 merks and Leslie the lesser sum of £10, although in neither case are precise details given of what services this was intended to cover. Certainly Henryson did include the stipulation that if he was required to leave Edinburgh on abbey business he should receive extra expenses to cover this.[101] David McGill, who like Henryson went on to become king's advocate, was in receipt of a pension of £20 annually from Dryburgh abbey in the 1550s and 1560s although unfortunately nothing is known of the terms upon which it was held.[102] The same is true of a life pension granted to him in 1558 by the commendator of Holyrood, payment of which consisted of money and the teinds of the lands of Gorgie.[103] Leading men of law were retained elsewhere to act for abbeys, such as James Foulis for the abbey of Balmerino, and Thomas Hamilton and later

for advocates and Proctors in theory and practice', in ibid., *Canon Law and the Law of England* (London, 1987), 47.

[98]   *Rental Book of the Cistercian Abbey of Cupar Angus,* 2 vols (Grampian Club, 1979-80), i, 312: 18 July 1532.

[99]   *Liber S. Thome de Aberbrothoc* (Bannatyne Club, 1848), ii, 388.

[100]   Ibid., ii, 474.

[101]   Roman and canon law sources were explicit in acknowledging that lawyers were entitled to expenses: D. 3.3.46.4–6 (Gaius). According to Brundage, charging for additional expenses was an obvious means of circumventing strict fee schedules, as was establishing a separate schedule for *consilia*, or formal opinions: 'Profits of the Law', 13.

[102]   *Liber S. Marie de Drburgh* (Bannatyne Club, 1847), 51, 352, 401.

[103]   *Laing Chrs.*, No. 693.

John Lethame for the abbot and convent of Lindores.[104] Nothing is known of the terms on which they did so, or the pensions, if any, which they received.

The surviving accounts of the chamberlain of St Andrews indicate yearly payments made to procurators fiscal both in Edinburgh (appearing before the official of Lothian) and St Andrews (appearing before the official principal). Thomas Kincraigie, the procurator fiscal in Edinburgh, received £13 6s 8d yearly, at four terms in the year coinciding with the church festivals of the Invention, St Peter's Chains, All Saints and the Purification.[105] His colleague in St Andrews, Hugh Wishart, received £10 in two yearly instalments at Whitsunday and Martinmas.[106] This is more in line with other men of law; normally these were the two terms for payment of fees and pensions.

The retention of advocates by burgh councils is also well attested particularly in mid-century.[107] The three assessors of the burgh of Edinburgh, Thomas McCalzeane, Robert Heriot and John Spens, received £40 between them annually from 1554 onwards. It is clear from the burgh treasurer's accounts that additional payments might be made for specific actions performed by the assessors. Thus in 1555 McCalzeane received sixteen pence for making two protests before the privy council on the burgh's behalf.[108] But a few years later the assessor Richard Strang received no additional payment when ordered to ride to Stirling to 'ressoun with the Quenis maiestie' on the burgh's behalf. He did, however, receive eight pence on another occasion for making or obtaining 'instruments in the tailzears and broudstars matters'.[109] McCalzeane initially appears to have been the most active of the three assessors. Although formally replaced as an assessor by Robert Crichton in November 1556, after being suspended for using intemperate language towards Mary of Guise, his removal from office was short-lived. The regent may have relented, or McCalzeane's objection to the legality of his removal may have been upheld, but whatever the reason, the following year he received payment in respect of the Whitsunday term 1557, when he was supposedly suspended. Not only did the council pay him, they gave him twice what they had undertaken to pay Crichton.[110]

Perhaps as a means of spreading experience of handling the burgh's legal affairs amongst its leading burgesses, Edinburgh, although generally maintaining three assessors, varied the membership of the group. David

---

[104]   Finlay, 'Professional Men of Law', Appendix 2.
[105]   *St Andrews Rentale*, 95, 107, 121, 137, 176, 197, 209.
[106]   Ibid.; Ollivant, *Court of the Official*, 55.
[107]   The concept of the corporations, such as burghs and religious foundations, using accredited ('*attitres*') advocates is replicated on the continent: Wijffels, '*Procureurs et avocats*', 175; L. Martines, *Lawyers and Statecraft*, 103. It clearly derives from practice in the church courts, where corporate institutions such as monasteries used procurators to represent them: Sayers, *Papal Judges Delegate*, 224.
[108]   *Edin. Accts.*, 135.
[109]   *Edin. Burgh Recs.*, iii, 172; *Edin. Accts.*, 135.
[110]   *Edin. Burgh. Recs.*, ii, 255; *Edin. Accts.*, 205-6.

Borthwick and Richard Strang joined McCalzeane in 1562, each receiving £10 yearly to act as assessors for the burgh at the will of the council.[111] Two years later, Strang, Alexander Sym and John Shairp received a like amount for performing the same task.[112] In addition to the assessors John Moscrop was, prior to the Reformation, appointed the burgh's procurator fiscal, receiving in return the right to bring wine into the burgh for his own use free of customs charges.[113] He was charged with pursuing and defending actions relating to the burgh before all judges and he performed a similar function as procurator for the burgh of Ayr, receiving a fee and occasional gifts of herring.[114]

In 1548, by way of a bonus for good deeds done in the past on its behalf, Aberdeen burgh council ordered wine to be delivered to the advocates Robert Carnegie and Thomas Marjoribankis. The provost and bailies also determined to visit them and thank them personally by offering them such additional 'humanities' as they thought appropriate.[115] However the burgh does not appear to have retained permanent counsel. In 1562 it sent a man south with £6 to be paid to the advocate David Borthwick in return for defending the burgh in an action brought by William Forbes.[116] In 1527 the provost of Aberdeen was empowered to travel to Edinburgh to substitute advocates to act on the burgh's behalf and a similar expedition was made in 1557.[117] Danzig replicated Aberdeen's practice when its council in 1556 constituted a procurator, Hallibrand Lasar, to represent some of his fellow citizens in litigation in Scotland.[118] A Scot representing a foreign council might find himself faced with a conflict of interest especially if he himself belonged to a Scottish burgh. In 1526 James Foulis, acting as *prelocutor* for Cornelius Bertilson, procurator for the burgomeisters of Middleburg, protested that since he was sworn to the freedom of Edinburgh he would involve himself in nothing that might prejudice the common weal of merchants in the realm of Scotland.[119] Domestically, lawyers were even consulted on the legal aspects of burgh politics. In 1554 one of the bailies of Haddington was sent to Edinburgh to consult with men of law on what to do about James Oliphant, who was refusing to accept the office of provost.[120]

Burgh assessors of necessity were burgesses. But they were not the only lawyers who enjoyed that status. Many leading lawyers were involved in trading activity in some cases to supplement income and, in others, probably as

[111] *Edin. Burgh Recs.*, iii, 153.
[112] *Edin. Accts.*, 460.
[113] *Edin. Burgh Recs.*, iii, 28; C.P. Finlayson, *Clement Litill and His Library* (Edinburgh, 1980), 7.
[114] M.H.B. Sanderson, *Ayrshire and the Reformation* (East Lothian, 1997), 7.
[115] *Aberdeen Council Register [Abdn. Counc.]*, i, 263.
[116] Ibid., i, 346.
[117] CS 5/37 fo. 218r : 26 Aug. 1527; *Abdn. Counc.*, 294–5.
[118] NAS, Register of Deeds, RD 1/1 fo. 392a.
[119] CS 5/36 fo. 45r: 14 July 1526.
[120] NAS, Haddington Burgh Court Book, Transcript, GD 1/413/1: 9 Nov. 1554.

a major source of income. The assessor Thomas McCalzeane arranged to buy gunpowder for the council and also sold ammunition to it.[121] Lawyers who were also burgesses were well placed to make connections and they can often be found engaged in trading ventures and money-lending. Richard Lawson used his connections with the continent to import legal books and manuscripts.[122] In 1527 the earl of Cassillis acknowledged that he was 300 merks in debt to the advocate Adam Otterburn; a debt he could not repay.[123] Otterburn also appears to have acted as debt-collector on one occasion for George Shaw of Knockhill.[124] In 1555 Patrick Hamilton acknowledged an even larger debt, £1000, to the advocate Thomas Marjoribanks.[125] Leading lawyers who were also burgesses featured heavily at the foundation of the college of justice in 1532 and their importance will be discussed in the next chapter. A less significant man of law, the Edinburgh burgess and sometime judicial procurator Master Thomas Strachan, does however provide rare detail in his protocol book of the method by which he was paid to represent Alexander Jardine of Lauder in a legal action.[126] In a memorandum, Thomas noted that Alexander had:

> promittit me xl s[chillingis] for my labouris in the pley...of the
> quhilk I have gottin xvi s[chillingis] the condicioun was the tane
> half to be payit in hand & the tothir half at the end of the pley
> nayn p[rese]nt bot he & I Item payit thireftir iiii s[chillingis].[127]

This is a chance survival and there is no indication anywhere else of such terms of payment being used and therefore no way of telling how representative this is. Clearly the terms were agreed in advance between lawyer and client, part payment was made and an additional payment later added to meet the initial obligation of the litigant to pay half of the fee in advance.

Although many lawyers were undoubtedly wealthy, in the absence of testaments or tax records prior to 1550 it is impossible to know exactly how

---

[121] *Edin. Accts.*, 229-30, 253.

[122] Cosmo Innes ed., *The Ledger of Andrew Halyburton 1492–1503* (Edinburgh, 1867), 273. Not only lawyer-burgesses engaged in money lending. Master Thomas Couttis, canon of the chapel royal and official of Lothian, brought an action to recover £30 of 'lent money' from James Scrimgeour of Dudhope in 1526: CS 5/36 fo. 126r: 7 Dec. 1526.

[123] CS 5/37 fo. 73r: 1 Apr. 1527.

[124] CS 5/38 fo. 108v: 25 May 1528.

[125] NAS, Register of Deeds, RD 1/1 fo. 369.

[126] In the protocol book the name 'Thomas' has been scored out and replaced by the name 'Henry'. No 'Henry' is recorded as ever having been constituted as a judicial procurator, whereas Master Thomas Strathauchin was constituted on several occasions at around this time. It therefore seems sensible to suggest that the notary may have been Thomas, rather than Henry.

[127] NAS, B22/1/9/ fo. 6: 27 Sep. 1508.

wealthy they were or how they stood in comparison with others. The testaments of lawyers active before the Reformation which do exist tend not to appear until the 1570s and 1580s and are too late to be of value in assessing their earlier income.[128] Although the leading advocates in the college of justice were normally immune from burgh taxation, the Edinburgh tax roll of 1565 does include lawyers because it was the result of an extraordinary tax imposed to raise a loan to purchase the superiority of Leith.[129] The amount raised from 'men of law and scribes' was £1156 13s 4d, some £200 more than was raised from all of the crafts combined. The list is interesting for two main reasons. First, the lawyers were assessed individually as lawyers and not as merchants. Secondly, both advocates and scribes as individuals were assessed at high levels in comparison with most merchants; and the assessment of the leading advocates was considerably in excess of any demand made upon merchants.[130]

In the event of a client's refusal to pay, the advocate could rely on the obligation and recover whatever was due to him for his services.[131] This principle was certainly established early in the history of the college of justice. Balfour quoted two cases as authority for it but only one of these has been traced in the record.[132] This involved Henry Spittall's action against John Cummyng seeking payment of arrears of £12. The obligation entered into by John specified that he would pay Henry £4 in two annual instalments, in return for Henry's 'counsale and advocatioun in his materis before the lordis of counsale quhen he suld be requirit'. Presumably the obligation was made in 1528 because it specified that it was to last for three years 'nixt and immediatlie precedand' 19 March 1532. Without further surviving examples there is no way of knowing whether such a limited term agreement was unusual. Spittall does not appear to have wasted much time in resorting to legal action in pursuit of the debt although he did wait until the period specified in the agreement was complete.[133] Although an action such as this would not yet

---

[128] For example, John Spens died in 1574: NAS, Register of Testaments, CC 8/8/6 fos. 54v-55r; James McGill died in 1579: (NAS) CC 8/8/11 fos. 146v-152r; David Borthwick died in 1581: NAS, CC 8/8/10 fos. 239v-241v. The testmant of Henry Lauder (d. 1560) does not survive although an entry exists relating to debts which were left out of his confirmed testament: (NAS) CC 8/8/1 fos. 66v-67r. These shed no light on his legal activities.

[129] Lynch, *Edinburgh and the Reformation*, 373.

[130] David Borthwick, George Crichton, Thomas McCalzeane and John Moscrop were assessed at £100 each. The highest assessment for any individual merchant was £60.

[131] In contemporary England, it was the usual practice of serjeants in the sixteenth century to require payment in advance for legal advice and it was rare for them to sue over the matter: J. Baker, 'Counsellors and barristers', *Cambridge Law Journal* (1969), 210. In Scotland, the law regarding advocates' fees changed after Balfour and it became the rule that advocates could not sue for their fees. This was re-stated in *Batchelor v Pattison and Mackersy* (1876) 3 R. 914.

[132] Balfour, *Practicks*, ii, 300; CS 6/2 fo. 59v; *Selected Cases from Acta Dominorum Concilii et Sessionis 1532–33*, ed., I.H. Shearer (Stair Society, 1951) [*Acta Sessionis* (Stair)], case no. 108.

[133] Presumably he waited in order to sue for the whole debt. Personal obligations did not prescribe for 40 years and so negative prescription was not a factor in his decision to bring a relatively quick action.

have been privileged in 1533, and would have had to run its course like any other ordinary action, it is unusual in that of all the possible stages in the process, only the decreet is given. Conceivably that is all there was; the lords may have been persuaded by Spittall's evidence, as well as by his standing as one of the advocates of the council, to grant an immediate order in his favour. Even so, Spittall doubtless entered into correspondence with his reluctant client before bringing proceedings. Half a century later, the advocate John Russell sent a letter to his wayward client, Sir Patrick Waus, urgently reminding him of his obligation and subtly hinting at legal action.[134]

Arbitration afforded a less confrontational means of resolving a dispute with a client than raising an action.[135] A notarial instrument recorded in 1533 narrates a decreet arbitral by Alexander Milne, abbot of Cambuskenneth and first lord president of the college of justice, and Master George Scougal, in a dispute between the advocate Adam Otterburn and Andrew Murray of Blackbarony. At least part of the dispute seems to have involved payment for legal advice. Andrew was contractually bound to pay 200 merks to Adam, for food and drink for him and his servant for five years, '*ac pro consilio labore et industria dicte magistri adami*' in connection with Andrew's lands and leases.[136] It is possible that Robert Leslie was also involved in a dispute with his client Hector Bruce although the matter did not go the length either of legal action or arbitration.[137] Bruce had constituted him his procurator to represent him in an action against Lord Ruthven and William, master of Ruthven. Although Leslie did appear as instructed, at one stage Robert Bruce, a burgess of Edinburgh and presumably a kinsman of Hector, appeared and undertook to pay Leslie and to fulfil all conditions which he had made in return for the latter's 'labouris besyness and procuratiounis' in the dispute. Robert Bruce seems to have entered into a separate agreement to remunerate Leslie on Hector's behalf, probably acting as his cautioner. This might have occurred because Hector himself experienced difficulty in meeting his obligation.

An interesting point is that payment was to be made to Leslie or to his assignee. Such an arrangement is not found where annual pensions are paid.

---

[134]   Russell's letter was successful in obtaining payment of most of the debt. It is interesting that in relation to the sum outstanding, another advocate, David Reid, agreed to retain custody of a gold chain belonging to Waus as security for payment: *Correspondence of Sir Patrick Waus of Barnbarroch, knight*, ed. R.V. Agnew (Edinburgh, 1887), ii, 430–432. Cf. Brundage, 'Profits of Law', 12.

[135]   In the context of thirteenth-century England, many cases brought by sergeants for arrears of pensions did result in litigation but were often settled out of court: Brand, *Origins of the English Legal Profession*, 100.

[136]   NAS, Viscounts and Barons of Elibank, GD 32/6/9: 20 July 1533.

[137]   CS 5/37 fo. 88r: 4 Apr. 1527. A dispute in 1541 between the advocate Andrew Blackstock and William Cockburn of Scraling resulted in Andrew obtaining 20 merks by the judgement of the official of St Andrews. This may have been in respect of legal fees incurred in the church court where Andrew was most active (Ollivant, *Court of the Official*, 61). The dispute came before the lords of session after Andrew seized goods (including a Parisian-made velvet gown) belonging to William in satisfaction of the debt: CS 6/14 fo. 103v: 25 Jan. 1541.

Where a special constitution was involved, payment could be more flexible since the relationship would be relatively short term (or, at least, so it was hoped). Income from such arrangements might wholly or partly be used by the advocate as a convenient means to satisfy his own debts to others. Pensions, paid for life or for a fixed term of years, and intended to encompass general actions rather than only particular cases, were invariably paid only to the advocate involved and not his assignees. It is sometimes difficult to tell, however, whether an advocate who was suing over a debt was seeking payment of sums owed in respect of legal services.[138]

Master John Lethame, the only advocate for whom receipts survive, subscribed them sometime after the date the pension was due indicating he was prepared to wait at least a month or two for his money. Three of these receipts survive, all made out to servants acting for the earl of Cassillis, and all specifying different amounts. In the Whitsunday term 1518 he received five crowns.[139] In the Martinmas term 1522 he was given 50 shillings.[140] Earlier that year, in July, he also gave a receipt for either £4 or £5 (both figures are mentioned) in full payment 'of all tymes bipast before the dait of this my acquittance'.[141] Presumably this was in respect of the preceding year and, taken with the payment recorded for the Martinmas term, would indicate a pension of £5 *per annum*.

The type of obligation also varied. As well as the straightforward indenture, bonds of manrent and maintenance might be used to link the man of law with his client. The justice-clerk, Richard Lawson, also a judge, ambassador and man of law, bound himself in 1501 to the earl of Errol and his apparent heir by his bond of manrent. He promised to give them the 'best and trewast consall I can without disimulation in all caussis querellis and actionis mowit or to be mowit be thaim or at concernis to thaim or againnis (sic) thaim'.[142] In 1509 an indenture was made between Robert, Lord Erskine and Adam Otterburn, by which Adam agreed to be:

> advocat and procurator for the said lord In all & sindry his actiounis spiritual and temporall lefull & honeste agane qhatsumever persone exceptend the personis to quham he is

138 For example, in 1505 David Balfour of Careston sought payment of 11 merks 5s 4d from John Moutrie, brother of the late Thomas Moutrie of Markinch, which he alleged the latter was wrongfully withholding from him. There is no indication of how the debt was incurred: CS 5/16 fo. 127v: 21 Feb. 1505.
139 NAS, Ailsa Muniments, GD 25/1/242: 23 July 1518. Five crowns were worth 100s (i.e. £5).
140 Ibid., GD 25/1/261: 9 Dec. 1522.
141 Ibid., GD 25/1/254: 10 July 1522.
142 *Miscellany II*, ed. J. Stuart (Spalding Club, 1842), 278; NRA(S) no. 925, no. 167.

oblist of befor And sall gif to the said lord the best truth and afald consile he can in all his actiounis quhen he beis requirit thairto.[143]

As Henryson had done in his agreement with Arbroath abbey, Otterburn, another burgess of Edinburgh, specified that should he be required to leave the burgh to advocate, procure or even counsel Erskine, his expenses should be met. This was over and above the 8 merks to be paid to him yearly, in two equal instalments, so long as both parties lived.[144] A generation later George Crichton, bishop of Dunkeld, issued letters of maintenance to Thomas Bellenden, advocate and future justice-clerk, who in return bound himself in manrent to the bishop.[145]

The evidence is too fragmentary to permit a clear picture to emerge of precisely what the client was paying for. In return for his money he could certainly expect legal advice whenever he required it; but he could not always expect legal representation.[146] An advocate might, by prior obligation, find himself bound to represent a potential client's opponent and this was written into the agreement from the start. Pensions varied in value, probably according to the rank of the client and the likely amount of litigation in which he would be involved. Less regular payments made to advocates have left virtually no trace in the record. There is therefore no way of telling whether the rate of pay for their services varied according to the value of the sum sued for as it did in Florence, for example, where a tariff was set in 1415.[147]

On the limited evidence available, it seems that the legal basis of the advocate-client relationship did not greatly vary. In practice, however, it is likely that the expectations of clients differed according to their own knowledge and experience. Litigants with experience of making personal appearances before the lords may simply have been interested in getting the best advice at the appropriate time rather than being represented *in absentia*. The more litigious in society, and those who paid annual pensions to advocates, no doubt hoped to maintain someone in Edinburgh who was active in the council chamber and prepared to serve their interests in any litigation that might directly or indirectly affect them. It is not clear whether Scottish practice was similar to that in England where the payment of an annual retaining fee simply meant that the lawyer was prepared to offer occasional

---

[143] NAS, Mar and Kellie Muniments, GD 124/7/10: 6 July 1509.

[144] Robert, Lord Erskine named Otterburn as his procurator on two constitutions recorded in the *acta*, on 29 Mar. and 28 July 1511: CS 5/22 fo.101v, CS 5/23 fo. 72r. The first constitution was special and general (against Alexander Barclay and all others), the second was general. There is no recorded constitution of Henryson by Arbroath abbey, or of Bellenden by the bishop of Dunkeld.

[145] *HMC*, 14th Report (MSS. of the Duke of Roxburghe), part iii, 42; NRA(S), no. 1100, Appendix 4, 201: 27 Mar. 1530.

[146] In Scotland a certain vagueness always attached to the word *consilium*: J. Wormald, *Lords and Men in Scotland* (Edinburgh, 1985), 28-32.

[147] Martines, *Lawyers and Statecraft*, 100.

advice and that for pleading he would receive an additional fee.[148] It was certainly the case in both jurisdictions that if the lawyer were required to travel, the client would meet his expenses.

Ratification and revocation

The final clause in a procuratory was the ratification clause whereby the principal promised to hold 'firm and stable' whatever the procurator did as a result of his constitution. If the principal was a married woman then her husband's consent to the action was legally necessary and he was normally included in the procuratory for his interest.[149] Consent could be demonstrated by the spouse subscribing the procuratory and attaching his seal.[150] In one case it was objected that Helen Campbell was handfast and betrothed to Thomas Kennedy, and so she had no power to pursue a summons in which his name did not appear for his interest. Helen's procurator, Robert Galbraith, responded by arguing that Thomas was present for his interest and that, besides, 'thai war nocht spousit yit'. The objection was repelled.[151]

Ratification by the litigant was not merely for the benefit of the other party to the action. It also functioned as protection for the procurator. It was the equivalent of a warrandice clause, indemnifying the procurator from loss provided he lawfully followed the 'premises', or instructions, laid down in the letter of procuratory.[152] The principal promised to relieve the procurator 'under the pane and oblising [obliging] of al my gudis, movable and immoveable, present and tocum'.[153] In spite of the fact that the ratification clause was standard, there are entries in the *acta* narrating that caution had been found guaranteeing that the principal would adhere to the procurator's activities. Caution was often given in the context of husband and wife, with the husband promising 'under the pain of double' that his wife would 'hald ferme and stable' whatever he did on her behalf.[154] Presumably the penalty was double the value of the gain which the other party stood to make if successful

---

[148] Nigel Ramsay, 'Retained legal counsel, *c*.1275–*c*.1475' (1985) *T.R.H.S.*, 106–7. The word 'counsel' was defined much more tightly in England than in Scotland.
[149] Rosalind K. Marshall, *Virgins and Viragos: A History of Women in Scotland from 1080–1980* (London, 1983), 34–5.
[150] E.g. Fraser, *Stirlings*, 364.
[151] CS 5/34 fo. 110v: 22 Feb. 1524. In another case, the lords decided that an action against a widow might proceed even though her second husband had not been summoned, CS 5/32 fo. 15v: 23 Nov. 1518.
[152] E.g. *Prot. Bk. Foular*, iii, 26 (no. 71).
[153] E.g. *ADC*, ii, 373; Fraser, *Stirlings*, 364. Cf. '*sub ypotheca et obligatione omnium et singulorum bonorum suorum, mobilium et immobilium, presentium et futurum*': Fraser, *Eglinton*, ii, 92; Fraser, *Wemyss*, ii, 183; NAS, Crawford Priory Collection, GD 20/1/23: 4 Oct. 1497; and Ailsa Muniments, GD 25/1/281: 17 May 1527.
[154] Balfour, *Practicks*, 298. For examples, see CS 5/29 fos. 109r: 18 Mar. 1517; and 150v: 26 Mar. 1517; CS 5/30 fo. 72r: 8 July 1517.

in the action. A man, acting as procurator for his brother, might grant caution on identical terms.[155] It was also possible that a procurator could find another cautioner on his wife's behalf. For instance, William Crichton obtained surety from his brother John that William's wife would stand by what he did on her behalf.[156] Nor did the cautioner have to be related to the principal. Adam Otterburn agreed to act in this capacity, again under 'the payn of doubill', guaranteeing that the widow Margaret Hepburn would abide by the actions of her procurator Master James Johnstone.[157] Unusually for a professional advocate Robert Leslie agreed to become cautioner for his own client, Patrick Ogilvie of Inchmartin, again 'under the pain of double'.[158] On another occasion, when the chancellor in the name of all the lords promised to pay John Moutrie of Seafield the sum that he had recovered from the laird of Raith, the laird, and Leslie his procurator, jointly promised to relieve the lords 'be the extensioun of thir handis'.[159] According to Balfour, a procurator under a general mandate could be repelled unless he could find *caution de rato*.[160]

Considering the large number of constitutions made there are surprisingly few references in the *acta* to revocations. Yet nothing is so intriguing in the relationship between lawyer and client as the ending of it. In some cases the revocation clearly results from a litigant's decision to give up the action, perhaps because it became clear that he had no chance of winning. The case of John Nesbit of Newton is one example.[161] Having raised a summons of spuilzie against William Hay of Tallo, Nesbit renounced the summons, and his action, together with all procurators made in his name for pursuing it. He then admitted that the objects of the dispute, cows and oxen taken from his land by king's officers, were properly taken since William had lawfully apprised them. Alternatively, the litigant might change his mind and make a revocation because of a change of circumstances, as in the case of the Englishman John Brady, who 'was content to ansuer himself in the cause' and so revoked his procuratory.[162] The converse could also happen. James Henryson, 'allegeand him' procurator for Christine Muir, revoked all that her late husband had done on her behalf or that she herself had done.[163] It seems that Christine now wanted the experienced Henryson to represent her but from the wording used there must have been a doubt about the validity of his status. Despite these few

---

[155] E.g., CS 5/29 fo. 147r: 24 Mar. 1517; CS 5/32 fo. 8r: 19 Mar. 1518.
[156] CS 5/34 fo. 73r: 1 Feb. 1524.
[157] CS 5/30 fo. 91r: 16 July 1518. On the same day, along with others, Otterburn did the same for Sir William Sinclair of Roslin, guaranteeing that Sir William would hold firm whatever Otterburn himself, and the dean of Glasgow, did on his behalf.
[158] CS 5/29 fo. 30r: 20 Feb. 1517.
[159] CS 5/43 fo. 169r: 26 Feb. 1532.
[160] Balfour, *Practicks*, ii, 299.
[161] CS 5/42 fo. 30r: 1 Feb. 1531.
[162] CS 5/23 fo. 103r: 6 Aug. 1511.
[163] CS 5/18/1 fo. 119r: 23 Feb. 1506.

examples, it is generally the case that no reason was given when a revocation was made and usually there is insufficient information from which one might even be suggested.[164]

As well as having their authority revoked, it seems that lawyers themselves could renounce further participation in an action already begun. There appears to be a single example of this and it dates from 1506.[165] James Henryson, in an action concerning a poinding brought by William Keith of Inverugy against Lord Crichton, asked that it be recorded that 'he rennuncit to be procurator in this mater forsaid & wald nocht further defend it'. Once again, unfortunately, no reason was given. This unambiguous renunciation is unique in the *acta*, although it perhaps sheds light on a remark made by Robert Galbraith in 1529 that 'ane procuratory was bot ane office of will'.[166] This appears to mean that the office of procurator was the consequence of a voluntary agreement between litigant and representative, and remained valid only so long as both consented.

Although most of the evidence relates to litigants revoking procuratories, the Henryson example does indicate that procurators had a reciprocal right to bring the relationship to an end. This would be in line with the evidence raised earlier that procurators could accept or decline office.[167] The fact that a procuratory seems to have lapsed automatically in certain circumstances also adds strength to this view. Technically, it was said that the procurator was *functus officio*.[168] There is only one example of the use of this phrase but its circumstances are significant. James Foulis used it after he had acted for the abbot of Balmerino in a case eventually submitted to arbitration. The case came back to the lords of session, however, when the other party reclaimed from the decreet-arbitral for an alleged impropriety.[169] By the time the case returned to the lords, Foulis claimed that he was *functus officio*: conceivably either because of the passage of time, or because once the case was decided by arbitration his original authority lapsed. The latter explanation is more likely; reclamations from arbitration were rare and if the mere passing of time could cause a procuratory to lapse then there would have been many more examples of this phenomenon.

The clients least likely to revoke a procurator's authority were those closely related to him. Most of those who very rarely appeared as procurators did so because they were appearing for family members. When it comes to the

---

[164] E.g., CS 5/18/1 fo. 23v: 30 Jan. 1506; where the litigant 'revokit all that John Fery spake [sc. for] him' against his adversary. Nothing else is given.

[165] CS 5/18/1 fo. 187v: 10 Mar. 1506.

[166] CS 5/40 fo. 89r: 6 Aug. 1529.

[167] In some jurisdictions, such as Malines, this was possible in normal circumstances only up to the point of *litiscontestatio*. See, for example, Wijffels, 'Procureurs et avocats', 178.

[168] CS 5/39 fo. 52v: 19 Dec. 1528.

[169] For more on this case, see chapter seven.

leading professional lawyers however, only in a few cases is it known with certainty that the procurator was appearing for a member of his own family. The ubiquitous lawyer Abraham Crichton, who went on to become official of Lothian, appeared in separate actions on behalf of his father, his grandmother and his nephew.[170] Thomas Scott, later justice-clerk, appeared on behalf of his father Sir William Scott of Balwearie.[171] Henry Lauder also appeared on behalf of his father although Gilbert Lauder, sometime bailie of Edinburgh and dean of guild, had himself been no stranger to the courts in previous years.[172] In March 1536 Master Hugh Rigg appeared on behalf of John, Thomas and William, the sons of the late John Rigg, a burgess of Dumfries, Hugh's clients probably being his cousins.[173] Futher examples are Robert Leslie, who represented his sister Eufame; William Johnstone his father James, and Robert Galbraith appeared for his father, David Galbraith of Kimmergame in Berwickshire.[174] This latter court appearance is virtually the only surviving evidence that identifies Galbraith's origins.

Legal services

Mention has already been made of references to the counsel and advice which lawyers promised their clients. In the case of major magnates, such advice might be given within the context of the baronial council.[175] In comparison with England very little is known about such councils, or their place in wider magnatial affinities, in Scotland.[176] In 1527 John Moutrie of Seyfield offered to give himself in judgement to his overlord, the earl of Morton, and 'his weile

---

[170] CS 5/25 fo. 180r: CS 5/24 fo. 177v; CS 5/32 fo. 130v. He also appeared on behalf of Margaret Crichton, lady Sempill (CS 5/33 fo. 133r) and as tutor for John Crichton, son of the late Sir Adam Crichton of Rothiemains (CS 5/30 fo. 116v).

[171] CS 5/34 fo. 71v: 30 Jan. 1524.

[172] CS 6/7 fo. 124r: 23 Feb. 1536. Examples of Gilbert appearing personally in his own actions are numerous: e.g. CS 5/30 fo. 62r; CS 5/31 fo. 117r; CS 5/34 fos. 85r, 218r; CS 5/35 fo. 216r. As dean of guild, he is mentioned in 1532: CS 6/2 fo. 121v.

[173] CS 6/7 fo. 147r: 13 Mar. 1536. Rigg himself was clearly from Dumfries and became parish clerk of Buthill in Whithorn in 1532: *RMS*, ii, no. 1405. He was a burgess of Edinburgh by right of his wife, Janet Hoppar. Nonetheless he can still be found witnessing transactions as a notary public in Dumfries: e.g. *Prot. Bk. Carruthers*, no. 46: 16 Dec. 1535. His son, James, was also a notary public acting in Dumfries in the later sixteenth century: *Prot. Bk. Alexander King*, no. 70: 16 Jan. 1556; Fraser, *Carlaverock*, ii, 357: 28 Jan. 1590. Ultimately, Hugh settled in Carberry, Midlothian.

[174] Leslie: CS 6/1 fo. 76r; Johnstone: CS 5/43 fo. 80r: 17 Nov. 1531; Galbraith: CS 5/30 fo. 120v: 28 July 1517; CS 5/32 fo. 32r: 30 Nov. 1518. See also other references given in chapter five.

[175] C.A. Kelham, 'Bases of Magnatial Power in Later Fifteenth Century Scotland', (Ph.D. thesis, University of Edinburgh, 1986), 24.

[176] On the council learned in England, see C. Rawcliffe, 'Baronial councils in the later Middle Ages', in *Patronage, Pedigree and Power in Later Medieval England,* ed. C.D. Ross (Gloucester, 1979), 90. The high point of the notion of the council was probably Henry VII's famous 'council learned', extant from about 1500 to 1509. Of the twelve known members of this *consilium domini regis in lege eruditum*, ten were legally trained: S.B. Chrimes, *Henry VII* (London, 1977), 151.

avisit consale'.[177] Morton's regular advocate was John Lethame and it would require no leap of imagination to assign to him an important role in this council. Yet despite the odd tantalising reference, little trace survives of the activities which lawyers performed on behalf of their clients outwith the courts.

Certainly leading advocates do appear as procurators *de negotia*, carrying out important legal transactions. Those who were also notaries can be found drafting documents. John Lethame is only one significant example, while James Henryson and Adam Otterburn became successive town clerks of Edinburgh, using to advantage their burgess status.[178] But as well as drafting documents, advocates were often called upon to advise on the content of important deeds to ensure their legal efficacy. This required some skill. One bond that was registered in the *acta* confidently narrated that it had been made 'in the maist strate form & sicker (secure) stile of obligatioun that can be divisit but fraud or gile na remeid of law cannoun civile municipale or utheris quhatsumevir to be proponit in the contrar'.[179] This was not merely a matter of form: ensuring the security of an obligation would in many cases demand the involvement of men of law.

Loan agreements were particularly important in this regard. Juggling debts might require the expertise of an experienced lawyer. In negotiating a contract by which he hoped to relieve some of his debts, Lord Home promised the other party that he would cause his son Alexander 'to mak quhat securite that men of law will devise'.[180] In one case James Hering, who as the assignee of Robert Ferguson was owed money by the abbot of Dunfermline, promised to give the abbot a discharge for the debt provided the abbot caused three named individuals to bind themselves to make payment of the amount owed. This he did according to the advice and information of the man of law Richard Lawson.[181] Even more complex than debt negotiation were marriage contracts. This was especially the case since they were often made considerably in advance of the marriage and had to take into account numerous variables, such as the value of the tocher and terce, the consequences of non-fulfilment, or the possibility at any stage of impediments to the marriage being discovered.[182] One good example is the contract arranged in 1544 between William, earl Marischall and George, earl of Errol.[183] The Marischall's eldest son was to marry the eldest daughter of the late earl of Errol when he reached the age of fifteen. The new earl of Errol was to be infeft in certain lands within

[177] CS 5/27 fo. 91r: 5 Apr. 1527.
[178] See chapter eight.
[179] CS 5/33 fo. 200v: 18 June 1523.
[180] CS 6/8 fo. 162v: 12 Aug. 1536.
[181] *Prot. Bk. Jas. Young* no. 160: 3 Feb. 1489.
[182] On marriage contracts, see Marshall, *Virgins and Viragos*, 28-31, 74.
[183] NAS, Errol Charters, [NRA(S) no. 925]: 14 Jan. 1544.

forty days as security for the marriage going ahead and he was to give up those lands on completion of the marriage. Other financial details were arranged, including who was to pay in the event that a papal dispensation had to be obtained. Finally, it was agreed that if the contract proved not to be secure, it was to be 'reformed' with the advice of at least three men of law out of five who were named. Those named were Hugh Rigg, Thomas Marjoribankis, James McGill, Henry Lauder and Thomas Wemyss.

CHAPTER THREE

The 'advocatis and procuratouris' of the College of Justice

Item...that thir be ane certane nomer of advocatis and procuratouris to the nomer of tene personis that salbe callit general procuratouris of the counsall, of best name, knawlege and experience, admittit to procure in all actiounis...maister Robert Galbraith, maister Robert Leslie, maister Henry Spittall, maister Johne Lethame, maister Henry Lauder, maister Thomas Kincraigie, maister Thomas Marjoribankis, maister William Johnston...[1]

At the foundation of the college of justice in May 1532 the king expressly delegated power to the chancellor and the lords of session to 'avise, counsell and conclude upon sic rewlis, statutis and ordinancis as sall be thocht be thame expedient'. The 'statutes of session' produced in response to this were not particularly innovative. In the main, they merely consolidated in one place a body of rules that had been developed by the lords during the previous half-century at least. Where there does appear to have been considerable novelty is in the primary statute (quoted above) relating to the men of law who were to appear in the college. This provided for the creation of the office of general procurator of the council. Ten such general procurators were to be admitted although, in the first instance, only eight were named.[2] Those raised to the new office had to be sufficiently qualified to satisfy the lords that they were worthy of admission.

This foreshadowed later practice when the academic and practical qualification of advocates was scrutinised by the judges prior to their admission (although there is little evidence of such scrutiny actually taking place until the books of sederunt begin in 1553). Apart perhaps from the statutory duty placed in 1424 upon judges confronted by poor litigants who could not obtain representation to 'get a lele & wys advocate to folow sic pur creaturis causis', there is no evidence of procurators needing a particular qualification prior to

---

[1] *ADCP*, 377: 27 May 1532.
[2] The list is given in the Appendix.

1532.[3] The treatise *Regiam Majestatem* is silent on the question, other than to indicate that clerics below certain ranks could not act as procurators.[4] In practice, provided they were legally competent, it seems that most adult males could act as a procurator. There are also examples of women doing so.[5]

As a requirement for admission as a general procurator, the ability to demonstrate 'knawlege and experience' was extremely vague although no more so than some of the requirements demanded of procurators elsewhere.[6] The real comparison, however, is with foreign advocates. Scotland, unlike most continental jurisdictions, had no formal requirement that an advocate admitted to practise before the central civil court hold a university degree. French *avocats* in the *Parlement* of Paris had been, from as early as 1345, required to hold university degrees in civil or canon law.[7] Legislation in Malines (1522) and Brabant (1531) laid down that *avocats* had to be licentiates in both canon and civil law.[8] Similarly, in Castile, legislation in 1495 required every new advocate to have undergone a fixed term of study in both the laws at a recognised university.[9] As in most of the Italian city states, Florentine lawyers also had to be graduates in law and in fact the majority held doctorates.[10] Even in sixteenth-century England, the necessary preliminary to a professional career in law was a period of study in one of the inns of court and advocates before the ecclesiastical courts had to have studied civil and (prior to the Reformation) canon law, at university.[11]

Although in its formal requirements the college of justice in Scotland was out of step, it should not be concluded that the quality of those admitted as its advocates was in any way inferior to those in other jurisdictions. When, during the minority of Queen Mary, the lords began to increase the number of advocates admitted to practise before them they were much concerned with

[3]   *APS*, ii, 8.
[4]   Balfour is much more forthcoming (although still in a negative, exclusionary, sense). However he cannot always be relied on for the period prior to the Reformation.
[5]   E.g. Margaret Moncreiff, procurator for her husband: CS 5/39 fo. 169v; Margaret Cornwell, procurator for her son: CS CS 5/38 fos. 49r-v: 7 Dec. 1527. See J. Finlay, 'Women and legal representation in early Sixteenth-Century Scotland', in *Women in Scotland, c.1100–c.1750*, eds. E. Ewan & M. Meikle (East Linton, 1999).
[6]   For instance, it was laid in 1531 that *procureurs* in the provincial *Counseil soveraine de Brabant* had to be 'aptes, suffisants et convenables': X. Rousseaux, *'De l'assistance mutuelle à l'assitance professionelle le Brabant'*, 155.
[7]   B. Auzary-Schmaltz and S. Dauchy, 'L'assistance dans la résolution des conflits au civil devant le Parlement de Paris au Moyen Age', in *L'assistance dans la résolution des conflits* (Brussels, 1997), 53.
[8]   Wijffels, 'Procureurs et avocats', 173; Rousseaux, *'De l'assistance mutuelle à l'assitance professionelle le Brabant'*, 155. In the later sixteenth century requirements became even more stringent when political considerations required avocats to be graduates of pro-Spanish universities.
[9]   Kagan, *Lawsuits and Litigants*, 63. The requirements of the university of Salamanca in the fifteenth century are given by Juan Beneyto Perez, 'The Science of Law in the Spain of the Catholic Kings', in R. Highfield ed. *Spain in the Fifteenth Century*, 278.
[10] Martines, *Lawyers and Statecraft*, 80*ff.*
[11] E.W. Ives, *The Common Lawyers of Pre-Reformation England*, (Cambridge, 1983), 44; G.D. Squibb, *Doctors' Commons : A History of the College of Advocates and Doctors of Law*, (Oxford, 1977), 30.

the quality of the candidates. A university degree alone was not enough to satisfy them. In 1555 they wanted to receive Master John Moscrop on probation under the condition that 'gif thir beis ony falt or negligence fundin with him in tyme cuming' he should be punished and deprived of his office. Moscrop refused to accept office under such a condition. A week later the lords relented and admitted him unconditionally.[12] But their attitude was clear. All of those admitted in 1532 had studied at university, even if in some cases only the arts curriculum. Half of them had studied at Orléans, succinctly described by Durkan as 'the civil law faculty of the university of Paris', and a university which any aspiring continental *avocat* or *letrado* would have been proud to attend.[13]

The eight general procurators named in 1532 were men whose careers, to a significant extent, ran parallel. Three of them, Robert Leslie, Robert Galbraith and Henry Lauder, will be discussed in more detail in later chapters but, as a necessary preliminary, it is necessary to consider all of them in context.[14] Assessing each of this group solely as individual lawyers, without reference to each other or to other professional lawyers or, indeed, to the wider society in which they lived, runs the risk of presenting a misleading picture of them. The college of justice provides a unique common denominator for collective biography but it quickly becomes apparent that it is not the only common factor linking its earliest general procurators.

In terms of education, as many as six of them may have studied abroad, including the four who studied law at Orléans. They had all studied (or, at least, matriculated) at a university, with Johnstone, Leslie and Kincraigie recorded as students at St Andrews.[15] Their appearance there must be seen in the context of several others who studied arts at St Andrews during James V's reign and then went on to have significant legal careers later in the century. The most prominent of these were John Spens, James McGill, John Shairp, Thomas McCalzeane, David Borthwick, Alexander Sym and George Freir. The same is true of those studying at Orléans—Lethame, Spittall, Marjoribankis and Johnstone—who also found themselves in good company. David Beaton, the future cardinal, studied there around the time Johnstone and Marjoribankis did so, while Lethame was a near contemporary of James Foulis and Arthur Boece, a noted lawyer who became the university canonist at Aberdeen and a lord of session.[16]

---

[12]   CS 6/29 fos. 4v, 6v: 13 and 20 Nov. 1555.

[13]   J. Durkan, 'The cultural background in Sixteenth-Century Scotland', in *Essays on the Scottish Reformation,* ed. D. MacRoberts (Glasgow, 1962), 279.

[14]   For Robert Leslie and Robert Galbraith, see chapter six; for Henry Lauder, see chapter eight.

[15]   Anderson, *St Andrews Recs* (Leslie) 202-3; (Kincraigie) 208; (Johnston) 103, 105, 207.

[16]   Beaton was sworn and received as a novice by Johnstone on 16 Oct. 1519: 'Records of the Scottish nation at Orléans', ed. J. Kirkpatrick, in *Miscellany II* (Scottish History Society, 1903), 81; for Boece,

Slightly senior to Boece at Orléans, Henry Spittall also became university canonist at Aberdeen and, as the appointment demanded, rector of Snow Kirk.[17] Hector Boece describes Spittall as a relative of the bishop of Aberdeen, William Elphinstone.[18] Certainly there is record of him in the vicinity of the commissary court of Aberdeen in 1508 several months prior to his arrival at Orléans.[19] His subsequent career as reader of canon law at Aberdeen was cut short, probably by his decision to marry—an event that must have taken place before February 1517.[20] At that time he was admitted as a burgess of Edinburgh by right of his first wife, Margaret Bothwell and subsequently he was one of the bailies of the burgh.[21] His links with Aberdeen continued however, and in 1518 he was made clerk of the coquet of the burgh.[22] By this time he was also acting as a notary by apostolic authority, designing himself not only *apostolica autoritate notarius* but also *Caesarei juris utcunque licentiatus*.[23] Other contemporary advocates also began their careers as notaries. Perhaps the most prominent example was John Lethame who can be found working as a notary soon after leaving the University of Orléans.[24] But many others, including William Blackstock, a leading advocate of the 1520s, Adam Otterburn and James Henryson can be found drafting instruments as notaries.[25]

Spittall's rise to prominence was to a large extent based on his academic success which in turn probably owed much to his connection with Elphinstone. Thomas Kincraigie was another advocate with a family connection to Aberdeen. The natural son of James Kincraigie, dean of Aberdeen, and later provost of the church of the Virgin Mary de Rupe in St Andrews, Thomas was legitimated in 1531 by which time he was already a

see L.J. Macfarlane, *William Elphinstone and The Kingdom of Scotland 1531-1514*, (Aberdeen, 1985), 321.

[17]   Macfarlane, *Elphinstone*, 221, 339.

[18]   'Wilhelmi nostri cognatus': Boece, *Life of Elphinstone* (Spalding Club, 1844), 91.

[19]   NRA(S) no. 925 (Errol Charters), no. 226: 15 Jan. 1508. He became a novice in the Scottish nation at Orléans in Oct. 1508: Kirkpatrick, 'Scottish Nation at Orléans', 81.

[20]   Spittall was made Reader in Oct. 1512: *Fasti Aberdonensis*, 73; cf. Anderson, *Officers and Graduates*, 29, 50.

[21]   *Roll of Edinburgh Burgesses and Guild Brothers, 1406–1700*, ed. C.B.B. Watson (Scottish Record Society, 1929), 465 [*Edin. Burg.*]; as a bailie he appears in 1525: NAS, Register House Charters, RH 6/973a.

[22]   *RSS*, ii, no. 2973: 6 Mar. 1518. His links with the Elphinstones also continued. In 1526 he appeared as procurator for Mr Robert Elphinstone, parson of Kincardine, before the lords of the articles: *APS*, ii, 313. Three years later he held tenements in Edinburgh which had previously been owned by Andrew Elphinstone of Selmes: *Prot. Bk. Foular*, iii, no. 166.

[23]   Fraser, *Eglinton*, ii, 88: 24 Apr. 1518.

[24]   NAS, Register House Charters, RH 6/809: 8 Nov. 1513, at Melrose abbey. He was elected proctor of the Scots nation at Orléans on 3 Apr. 1511: Kirkpatrick, 'Scottish Nation at Orléans', 82. He was certainly back in Scotland by June 1512, when he is found in the diocese of Glasgow acting as an arbiter: *Prot. Bk. Simon*, no. 580.

[25]   For Blackstock as a notary, see an instrument of sasine involving Patrick, earl Bothwell, NAS, Lothian Muniments, GD 40/3/495(2): 28 May 1530. For Henryson and Otterburn, see chapter seven.

successful lawyer.[26] His early life is obscure although he seems to have attended the University of St Andrews.[27] More exotically, he may possibly be identified with a Scotsman of the same name from the diocese of Dunkeld who obtained a degree in medicine at Louvain in 1522.[28] This would certainly have been a novel approach to the bar, but study at Louvain was not unusual for aspiring Scots lawyers in the sixteenth century. John Abercrombie studied civil law there in the mid-1530s although it was not until the minority of Queen Mary that the better known lawyer Clement Litill became a student there.[29]

Unfortunately it has not proven possible to obtain a more complete record of university attendance from available sources. There are clues suggesting that other prominent men of law of the period studied abroad. Certainly it is clear from his poetry that James Foulis had studied under Robert Galbraith in the University of Paris and Galbraith himself studied in Paris before becoming a teacher there.[30] The first king's advocate, James Henryson, studied there during the last years of James III's reign. Henry Lauder was sufficiently skilled in spoken French to welcome James V's bride to the burgh of Edinburgh in 1538 which suggests that he had spent some time in France, possibly as a student.[31] Much the same might be said of David Borthwick who was sent to France as a servant of the king's secretary, Thomas Erskine of Brechin, in 1535.[32] The fact that Hugh Rigg was one of those called upon to translate letters of claim written in Dutch, which were produced in litigation by the Arnhem burgess Kerstan Martins in 1542, does not necessarily mean that he had studied in the Low Countries.[33] But it certainly indicates familiarity with the area obtained by trade if not by study.

The civic entry of Mary of Guise to Edinburgh in 1538 so heavily involved lawyers in the burgh that it demonstrates conclusively their contemporary social and cultural importance. Not only did Lauder make the speech of welcome, he was aided in its composition by Adam Otterburn and James Foulis, lawyers who were also noted poets, as well as the playwright and courtier David Lindsay. For the honour of the burgh, twelve men were

[26]   *RSS*, ii, no. 987; illegitimacy *per se* was no handicap to success as a lawyer and William Elphinstone himself is a good example. James Kincraigie was no stranger to appearing before the lords of council: e.g. he was constituted before them on 6 Feb. 1505: CS 5/16 fo. 58v. For him as provost of a church in St Andrews: NAS, Crawford Priory Collection, GD 20/70: 28 Aug. 1521.
[27]   Anderson, *St Andrews Recs.*, 208.
[28]   A. Schillings, *Matricule de L'Université de Louvain* (Brussels, 1958), iii, 673, no. 21.
[29]   Finlayson, *Clement Litill and his Library*, 3.
[30]   See chapter six.
[31]   *Edin. Burgh Recs.*, ii, 91. Lauder's father, Gilbert, had mercantile links with the continent. In 1525 these led to him being unable to leave Flanders until a debt which he had guaranteed on behalf of a fellow Edinburgh burgess was paid to a Flanders merchant: CS 5/35 fos. 216r, 218r: 3-5 Mar. 1525. It is likely that Gilbert had contacts in France and this might have facilitated Henry's education there.
[32]   CS 6/7 fo. 13r: 15 Nov. 1535.
[33]   CS 7/1/1 fo. 122r: 13 Nov. 1542.

dressed in velvet gowns of various colours. Of the twelve, two were lawyers, Thomas Marjoribankis and Hugh Rigg, one was the father of a lawyer, one the grandfather, and one was the son of a king's advocate.[34] If not necessarily a sign of learning, the privilege conferred was certainly a sign of respectability and it would be unlikely if any of the twelve was unable to speak French. Another lawyer who almost certainly would have participated in the festivities of 1538 was Robert Galbraith. As a philosopher and a poet, who enjoyed a considerable reputation in France prior to his legal career in Scotland, it is likely that he played a full part.[35]

Scottish advocates in general were men of good education in the sixteenth century, and those admitted in 1532 were certainly no exception to this. In terms of status there was a high degree of homogeneity within the group. Although they came from different areas of Scotland, Leslie from Fife, Spittall from Perthshire, Kincraigie from Aberdeen, Galbraith from Berwickshire, Johnstone and Lauder from Edinburgh, Lethame from somewhere within the diocese of Glasgow and Marjoribankis (possibly) from Dumfries, they necessarily had to spend a significant period of time in the capital pursuing their professions before the lords of session.[36] Of the eight, five were burgesses of Edinburgh in 1532 or later became so.[37] Evidence of any trading activity carried on by them is, however, relatively scarce except in the case of Thomas Marjoribankis who seems to have had considerable trading connections in France. He exchanged bills and exported goods, receiving in 1546 the privilege of exempting his merchandise from royal customs.[38] The law, traditionally regarded as a licence to print money, was almost literally true in Marjoribankis's case since in 1549, along with Robert Carnegie of Kinnaird, later treasurer-clerk, he even purchased a three-year lease of the mint.[39]

34   Gilbert Lauder, father of Henry; Alexander Mauchane, grandfather of Alexander; and George Henryson, son of James: *Edin. Burgh Recs.*, ii, 89; Edington, *Court and Culture in Renaissance Scotland: Sir David Lindsay of the Mount* (East Lothian, 1994), 36, 108-9. See also Van Heijnsebergen, 'The interaction between literature and history in Queen Mary's Edinburgh: The Bannatyne Manuscript and its prosopographical context', *The Renaissance in Scotland: Studies in Literature, Religion, History and Culture*, in eds. A.A. MacDonald, M. Lynch and I.B. Cowan (Leiden, 1994), 189.

35   None of Galbraith's poetry appears to have survived: A.A. Macdonald, 'William Stewart and court poetry' *Stewart Style 1513–1542: Essays on the Court of James V*, ed. J.H. Williams (East Linton, 1996), 180.

36   The evidence that Marjoribankis was originally from Dumfries is limited to place name evidence, the lands of Marjorybanks being in Dumfries, and also the fact that Thomas can be found associated in a witness list in the tolbooth of Ayr with Ninian Crichton of Bellibocht, sheriff-depute of Dumfries: *Prot. Bk. Ros*, no. 987: 23 Apr. 1529. William Johnstone's grandfather was from Marjorybanks: Durkan, 'Some local heretics', *TDGNHAS*, xxxvi (1957-8), 72. As to Lethame, it has not proven possible to locate his origins more precisely.

37   Henry Lauder, son of a burgess (1517); Henry Spittall, *iure uxoris* (1517); Robert Leslie (1517); Thomas Marjoribankis, *iure uxoris* (1538); and William Johnstone, son of a burgess (1538): see *Edinburgh Burgess Roll*, 298, 307, 337, 465; and, for Johnston, Ibid., 280, Lynch, *Edinburgh and the Reformation*, 83; and Durkan, 'Some Local Heretics', 72-3.

38   *RSS*, iii, no. 1693: 23 May 1546.

39   *RSS*, iv, no. 412: 2 Sep. 1549.

Since they worked, and, for the most part, lived, within the burgh of Edinburgh links easily developed between advocates. As early as August 1516 four of the eight general procurators of 1532—Galbraith, Lauder, Lethame and Spittall—together with James Foulis, can all be found witnessing proceedings in a commissary court held within St Giles.[40] In time, two of the eight, Lethame and Johnstone, themselves became commissaries in the church courts.[41] But records have not always survived that would clarify the family relationships of these men of law. For example, it is likely that the notary Edward Spittall, who became a burgess of Edinburgh during the 1490s, was related in some way to Henry Spittall. Edward, who acted for the earl of Montrose and others before the lords of council, was primarily a notary rather than a man of law. However his lack of direct contact with Henry makes any relationship between them tantalisingly difficult to determine. It is often equally difficult to trace parents. In Henry's case, it is likely that his father was James Spittall of Blairlogy in Perthshire although the evidence for this is not contemporary. In December 1516 James resigned his lands to the governor, Albany, so that they would be re-granted to Henry. This transaction is known only because its essentials were narrated in a charter of the lands of Blairlogy by the queen to Alexander Spittall, designed nephew and heir (*nepoti et heredi*) of James, in 1543 some seven years after Henry's death.[42] That Henry had held these lands is known through a charter of confirmation granted to him and his wife in 1530 and also through the designation 'de Blairlogy' applied to him in a precept legitimating his natural son, Master James Spittall, in 1558.[43] There appears to be no direct evidence naming Henry as the son of James although the circumstantial evidence is strong. This contrasts with the evidence concerning men such as Henry Lauder and Robert Galbraith who appeared in court for their fathers making their identity certain.

Of the eight general procurators, the fathers of all but two have been identified with a reasonable degree of certainty. The two exceptions are the fairly obscure figure of John Lethame and, more surprisingly, the ubiquitous Thomas Marjoribankis. Of the other six there is a neat symmetry to the position in society occupied by their fathers: two were clerics (Leslie and Kincraigie), two were lairds (Galbraith and Spittall) and two were Edinburgh burgesses (Lauder and Johnstone). This makes all the more remarkable the fact that five of the eight eventually became Edinburgh burgesses, either *iure uxorium* or through service to the burgh. The stigma of illegitimacy affecting

---

[40] *Charters of the Hospital of Trinity College, Edinburgh, and other Collegiate churches in Midlothian* (Bannatyne Club, 1861), 87*ff.*

[41] Watt, *Fasti*, 330-1. Both were commissary of Lothian, Lethame in 1521 and again in 1529, Johnstone in 1531.

[42] *RMS,* iii, no. 2975: 12 Dec. 1543.

[43] *RSS,* v, no. 482: 4 Sep. 1558.

the sons of the churchmen did not hold them. In Leslie's case this was due to a family relationship to the earl of Rothes, while Kincraigie's father, as already explained, was close to Bishop Elphinstone. Yet while family background might prove significant in terms of building up trade as a lawyer, there was nothing particularly special about the background of any of these men of law.

A clear indication of how close the day-to-day relations were between the leading advocates within Edinburgh society is given by looking briefly at the activities of James Foulis who, although not named as a general procurator in 1532, was one of the leading advocates of the 1520s.[44] Foulis had made his return to Scotland from his studies in France by early 1513 when he witnessed in Edinburgh a charter by John Crawford, prebendary of St Giles, in favour of the convent of Sciennes.[45] Following him on the witness list was William Johnstone (possibly the advocate), and the notaries John Foular and Henry Strachan. At this time, William Johnstone the advocate was studying at St Andrews, having matriculated there in 1512. He did not become a licentiate until May 1516.[46] This does not necessarily preclude his presence in St Giles in 1513, especially since he was from Edinburgh where his father was a leading burgess and one of the macers of the session. Of more immediate interest is the appearance of the notary Henry Strachan, since James's sister Isabel was married to Adam Strachan, probably Henry's brother.[47] Henry's son Vincent also became a notary and so Foulis, nephew of the king's advocate and perhaps a cousin of the notary Thomas Foulis, was also connected by marriage to men of considerable legal knowledge.[48] Henry Strachan was deputy common clerk of Edinburgh and, after his death, the earl of Arran, one of the regents of the kingdom and provost of the burgh, sought to put his own man in this position, going over the head of Adam Otterburn, principal common clerk. Foulis was on hand to witness Otterburn's successful defence of his position.[49]

In April 1514 Foulis began occupying a tenement on the north side of the High Street in Edinburgh, adjacent to one occupied by his cousin Robert

---

[44]   *Pace* D. Shaw, *General Assemblies, 1560–1600*, 143.

[45]   *Liber Conventus S. Katherine Senensis* (Abbotsford Club, 1841), 32: 15 Feb. 1513.

[46]   *St Andrews Recs.*, 207, 103, 105.

[47]   *Prot. Bk. Young*, no. 39: 31 Jan. 1508. For Isabel as the daughter of Henry Foulis, see *Prot. Bk. Foular*, i, no. vi: 20 Mar. 1502. Adam Strachan was dead by 16 Oct. 1503: *Prot. Bk. Foular*, i, no. viii.

[48]   His relationship with the king's advocate is discussed in chapter seven. In 1516 James can be found in a witness list to an instrument drawn up by Thomas Foulis, which included also Adam Otterburn and Master Gilbert Strachan, dean of Dunblane: *Prot. Bk. Strathauchin*, no. 232: 25 Sep. 1516. James was certainly linked to Robert Foulis, burgess of Linlithgow, described as his 'eme' in 1530: CS 5/41 fo. 102v: 4 Aug. 1530. Robert's nephew, Henry Foulis, who is mentioned here might be the same Henry Foulis who was in 1560 a notary public: NAS, Crown Writs, A.D. 1/119: 3 Apr. 1560. This Henry was dead by December 1561: CS 7/22 fo. 269v. The Foulises of Linlithgow produced a better known notary, another James Foulis, whose mid-sixteenth century protocol book survives: *The Protocol Book of James Foulis, 1546–1553*, eds. J. Beveridge and J. Russell (Scottish Record Society, 1927).

[49]   *Prot. Bk. Strathauchin*, no. 292: 3 Feb. 1518; Inglis, *Otterburn*, 6–7.

Henryson.[50] That winter, he witnessed a transumpt (an official copy of a deed) made in the consistory court of the official of St Andrews, William Wawane, again in St Giles. Others present included John Lethame, James Carmuir and Thomas Hamilton, all fellow advocates.[51] Eight years later, Foulis received further land in Edinburgh, this time in the Cowgate. Sasine was given to him by one of the bailies, Francis Bothwell, under reversion to John Halkerston.[52] Bothwell was married to Katherine Bellenden, sister of Foulis's fellow-student at Paris, Thomas Bellenden, who was by now director of the king's chancery and in future was to become the justice-clerk.[53] Bothwell, himself later provost of Edinburgh and a lord of session, owned a merchant booth in the High Street that was occupied in 1520 by James Marjoribankis, probably a relative of the advocate Thomas Marjoribankis.[54] Foulis, Bothwell and Adam Otterburn were all assessors of the town council at the Michaelmas head court of the burgh in 1528.[55]

Contact between Foulis and a number of men of law can therefore be documented prior to 1532. Of the eight general procurators named in that year, there are two—Robert Leslie and Thomas Kincraigie—with whom his only surviving connection before then is that he was named in letters of procuratory, or in a constitution of procurators, along with them. In relation to Kincraigie, Foulis does appear in a witness list of July 1531, along with Thomas's father, James Kincraigie, and the justice-clerk, Nicol Crawford.[56] But a connection between Thomas Kincraigie and Foulis can only be inferred from the fact that both were named general procurators of Robert Aiton in February 1529.[57] Foulis's name appeared with that of Leslie in an instrument of procuratory dating from 1520 made by James Brown; the other procurators named were Galbraith, Lethame and James Haliburton.[58]

Foulis can therefore be connected early in his career with most of the men who were to emerge as the leading advocates of James V's reign. His contact with them normally occurred in a legal context but this is due to the fact that most of the evidence comes from notarial protocol books which primarily record legal processes. What have not been recorded are the social and less formal relations between Foulis and his fellow leading advocates. Nor did Foulis cease contact with his erstwhile fellow advocates in 1532 when he

50 *Prot. Bk. Strathauchin*, no. 184: 28 Apr. 1514.
51 NAS, Register House Charters, RH6/827: 13 Nov. 1514.
52 *Prot. Bk. Foular*, ii, no. 299: 30 July 1522.
53 Bellenden was director of the chancery as early as 1514: CS 5/26 fo.174r: 23 Oct. 1514. His wife supplied velvet to the queen dowager in 1536: *TA*, vi, 327.
54 CS 5/34 fo. 167r: 16 May 1524.
55 *Prot. Bk. Foular*, ii, no. 75: 21 May 1520; *Edin. Burgh Recs.*, ii, 3: 6 Oct. 1528.
56 *Illustrations of the Topography and Antiquities of the Shires of Aberdeen and Banff* (Spalding Club, 1869), iv, 97: 8 July 1531.
57 CS 5/39 fo. 116r: 26 Feb. 1529.
58 Fraser, *Eglinton*, ii, 91 (no. 106): 15 May 1520.

became the first in a significant line of secular men of law appointed to the post of lord clerk register (an office in which he was succeeded by Thomas Marjoribankis in 1549).[59] Although this automatically led to his appointment as a judge in the new college of justice, and therefore curtailed his activities as an advocate, it in no way diminished his interest in law. The only surviving legal books which he is known to have owned were volumes of Bartolus's commentary on the *Old* and *New Digest* in a Lyons edition which was not published until 1538.[60] Like Marjoribankis, Foulis's status as a burgess of Edinburgh probably made it easier for him to import books of this kind and the fact that he and others did so merely underlines the point that Scottish advocates in general were men of good education in the sixteenth century.

There was also a good distribution of clients amongst the leading advocates at this time.[61] For example, Henry Lauder can be found acting for noblemen such as the earl Bothwell, and the earls of Crawford, Argyll and Glencairn, while John Lethame represented the earls of Morton and Cassillis as well as the master of Glencairn. Lethame also acted for a number of lesser magnates such as Lord Cathcart and Sir William Sinclair of Roslin. Both Lethame and Lauder acted for Lords Elphinstone and Fleming, while Lauder can also be found representing Lords Ogilvie, Ruthven and Sinclair. Lethame, himself a churchman (he became by 1527 subdean of Trinity collegiate church in Edinburgh, and later parson of Kirkchrist), had several clerical clients including the abbot of Lindores and the bishops of Brechin and Galloway.[62] Lauder's clients included the prioress of Eccles and the abbot of Dunfermline. A particularly active advocate was Thomas Hamilton. Even though he was dead by 1525, his major clients during this period included the earls of Moray and Glencairn, Lords Glamis, Herries and Maxwell, and the abbots of Holyrood, Lindores and Paisley.[63]

The crown was not slow to take advantage of the experience and ability of the leading advocates in the realm. This reflected a tradition of secular men of law who find a niche in royal service which can be traced back at least as far as David Guthrie of Kincaldrum in the 1460s and 1470s.[64] As well as holding the

59 A.L. Murray, 'The Lord Clerk Register', (1974) *SHR* 134; *RSS*, iv, no. 91: 5 Feb. 1549; *ADCP*, 580: 8 Feb. 1549; *DNB*, vii, 510. The existing DNB entry for Foulis indicates that he was knighted in 1539; however this seems doubtful since he was referred to in a variety of documents only as Master James Foulis until his death. The new DNB entry will contain this amendment.

60 Durkan and Ross, *Early Scottish Libraries* (Glasgow, 1961), 100. Foulis appears to have owned a manuscript copy of *Regiam Majestatem*, since his name appears frequently inscribed on the Cuyk MS. which bears the date 28 July 1528: *APS*, i, 203.

61 See Finlay, 'Professional Men of Law', Appendix 2.

62 *RMS*, iii, no. 447: 15 Apr. 1527; G. Brunton & D. Haig, *An Historical Account of the Senators of the College of Justice from its Institution in MDXXXII* (Edinburgh, 1832), 62.

63 *Prot. Bk. Foular*, no. 554: 1 Feb. 1525.

64 Guthrie's career has received notable scholarly attention in recent years. He was a graduate laird (having attended university of Cologne), who was active as a forespeaker certainly in the 1460s and in royal government prior to his death in 1474. See, for example, A.R. Borthwick and H.L. MacQueen, 'Three

offices of treasurer and comptroller in the royal household, Guthrie also acted as justiciar-depute south of the Forth and was sheriff-depute of his native Forfar.[65] The tradition was continued in the reigns of James III and IV by figures such as Richard Lawson, justice-clerk general and a royal councillor, and James Henryson. Of the eight general procurators named in 1532, four (Galbraith, Marjoribankis, Lauder and Lethame) became lords of session. This is impressive considering that Hannay recorded the fact that of the first seventy-four senators of the college of justice, less than a third had been practising advocates.[66] It has already been noted that Marjoribankis followed in the footsteps of James Foulis in the office of clerk register while, as a later chapter will demonstrate, use was made of the talents of Henry Lauder by appointing him king's advocate in 1538. Ten years after this, Kincraigie was appointed advocate for the poor, a post that had previously been held (at least jointly) by Marjoribankis.

From the ranks of this same group of lawyers came several sheriff-deputes, normally constituted as sheriffs *in hac parte* under commissions to carry out specific tasks, normally serving brieves of inquest. For example, Henry Spittall, and two fellow Edinburgh burgesses, were appointed sheriffs of Selkirk *in hac parte* for this purpose in 1527.[67] For the same reason William Johnstone, Henry Lauder and James Lawson had sworn in 1524 that two of them would 'minister in the schirrefship of Linlithgow'.[68] Thomas Kincraigie in 1528 acted as *commissaris in hac parte* of the archbishop of St Andrews in repledging to the church courts Andrew Kincraigie, who had been implicated in an unlawful killing.[69] In 1552 Kincraigie was sheriff of Dumfries *in hac parte*, and the following year he can be found, again acting with other advocates, as a sheriff of Roxburgh and Peebles *in hac parte*.[70] Others, such as Francis Bothwell, and later advocates like David McGill and Alexander Mauchane, can also be found in a similar capacity.[71] Men of law might also be found constituted by sheriffs to serve as their deputes; an example being the appointment by the sheriff of

---

fifteenth-century cases' (1986) *JR* 123; ibid., "'Rare creatures for their age': Alexander and David Guthrie, graduate lairds and royal servants", *Church, Chronicle and Learning in Medieval and Early Renaissance Scotland*, ed. B.E. Crawford (Edinburgh, 1999) 227–239.

[65]   Crawfurd, *Lives and Characters*, 360–1; *HMC*, 14th Report (MSS of the duke of Roxburghe), part iii, 27; *HMC*, 5th Report, Appendix (Lord Wharncliffe), 622.

[66]   NAS, Professor Hannay's Papers, GD 214/14. Hannay mentioned that 24 of the 74 lords created between 1532 and 1608 were advocates, but did not distinguish between ordinary and extra-ordinary lords of session.

[67]   CS 5/37 fo. 15v: 13 Mar. 1527.

[68]   CS 5/34 fo. 183r: 21 July 1524.

[69]   NAS, JC. 1/3: 21 Aug. 1528. Andrew Kincraigie had not been further identified.

[70]   *RMS*, iv, no. 1621: 28 May 1552; NAS, A.D.1/110: 21 Apr. 1553. Kincraigie took the oath *de fideli administratione* in respect of the latter office on 2 May 1553.

[71]   CS 5/34 fo. 162r: 11 May 1524. Bothwell was sheriff-depute of Edinburgh, perhaps indicating a family link with earl Bothwell, the sheriff. For McGill and Mauchane as sheriffs of Haddington *in hac parte*, see NAS, Biel Muniments, GD 6/84: 14 July 1554.

Stirling, John, Lord Erskine, of Adam Otterburn and Sir William Scott of Balwearie as joint sheriff-deputes.[72] In 1529 the advocate James Carmuir was appointed one of the clerks *closete domini regis*, indicating a yet closer degree of royal service. Marjoribankis, as well as having been treasurer's clerk, was appointed custumar of the burgh of Inverness in 1545.[73] He also served in parliament.[74] Royal service was often instrumental in enabling men of law to amass sufficient landed interests to found significant dynasties like the Lawsons of Cairnmuir, the Henrysons of Fordell and the Foulises of Colinton. The descendants of Thomas Marjoribankis can be traced all the way down to Lord Tweedmouth in the nineteenth century.[75]

Unorthodoxy in religion, on the other hand, was a factor that could retard or even destroy promising legal careers. William Johnstone's ambitions as an advocate were ended abruptly in 1534 by a crisis of faith that was to be replicated in the following years amongst other lawyers. Since they were well read, often educated abroad, and came into contact with large numbers of people both native and foreign, men of law were exposed more than most to new ideas particularly in matters of religion. In 1532 there was no hint that Johnstone had been unduly influenced by heretical teaching. His education at St Andrews and Orléans was not unusual and he had risen to the rank of commissary of Lothian. In 1534 he was part of an embassy to England and it has been argued that his heresy was due to this contact.[76] Adam Abell, in his chronicle *Rota Temporum*, recorded that in 1534, at the feast of the Eucharist in the kirk of Holyrood, the king being present, two heretics were examined and burned for denying that man had free will.[77] Two others, the sheriff of Linlithgow (James Hamilton of Kincavil) and Master William Johnstone fled and were abjured. Johnstone's goods were escheated and granted to the bishop of Aberdeen in September.[78] The subsequent history of Johnstone is difficult to follow, although he seems to have recanted more than once and certainly survived beyond the Reformation.[79]

Johnstone was the first of several prominent advocates who espoused Protestantism leading up to the Reformation crisis and beyond. It has been suggested that the most notorious heretic of the period, George Wishart, was a

---

[72]   CS 5/34 fo. 163v: 11 May 1524.

[73]   *RSS*, iii, no. 1245: 20 Aug. 1545.

[74]   E.g., *APS*, ii, 479: 16 Aug. 1546.

[75]   *Book of the Old Edinburgh Club*, iii, 295.

[76]   CS 6/4 fo. 18r: 25 Feb. 1534; Durkan, 'Some local heretics', 72.

[77]   NLS, Adv. MS. 1746, fo. 122r. Part of this manuscript, including the portion referred to, has recently been published by A.M. Stewart, "The final folios of Adam Abell's 'Roit or Quheill of Tyme': An Observantine Friar's reflections on the 1520s and 30s", in ed. J. Hadley Williams, *Stewart Style, 1513–1542* (East Linton, 1996), 246.

[78]   *RSS*, ii, 1583: 16 Sep. 1534.

[79]   Durkan, 'Some local heretics', 72-3.

younger brother of James Wishart, the king's advocate.[80] The future king's advocate, David Borthwick, part of Arran's circle in the 1540s, was suspected, and the justice-clerk of the time, Thomas Bellenden, may also have had Protestant sympathies.[81] Amongst the eight procurators of 1532, however, Johnstone's case was unique. Even a man like Robert Leslie, who was probably within a fairly close degree of kinship to Norman Leslie, the murderer of Cardinal Beaton in 1546, was conservative in religious matters.[82] But his was the last generation in Scotland relatively untouched by religious controversy, and even amongst his clients were several who were suspected of heresy. The most obvious of these was Johnstone's fellow refugee, James Hamilton of Kincavil. But he was merely one of half a dozen men for whom Leslie acted who at one time or another during their lives came under suspicion of heresy.[83]

One of Leslie's clients, John Melville of Raith, was closely connected to the young advocate Henry Balnavis, another native of Fife. Balnavis may have been converted to Protestantism on the continent prior to his studies at St Salvator's College in St Andrews in 1526.[84] His career as a man of law belongs primarily to the 1530s. Like James Foulis and Thomas Marjoribankis, Balnavis had his career in private practice truncated by the acceptance of administrative office which eventually led to a seat in the college of justice to which he was sworn on 29 July 1538.[85] He was one of the justices on the Jedburgh ayre in 1541, but prior to this was a clerk to the treasurer, James Kirkcaldy of Grange, a close Protestant ally, and he also acted as substitute for the king's advocate.[86] Indeed Balnavis quickly rose to the rank of ambassador when he was one of those sent to discuss the proposed marriage of the infant Mary with Henry VIII's son in 1543.[87] A tenant of Beaton as the archbishop of St Andrews, he was not directly implicated in his murder in 1546 although he certainly supported it and entered the castle of St Andrews to join the besieged, a political act which interrupted severely his career as a lord of session.[88] As a prisoner at Rouen he wrote the *Treatise on the Justification* for which he is best

---

[80]   Knox, *History of the Reformation in Scotland*, ed. D. Laing (Wodrow Society; Edinburgh, 1855-6), vi, 669.

[81]   Lynch, *Edinburgh and the Reformation*, 277; Sanderson, *Cardinal of Scotland*, 271.

[82]   This is discussed in chapter six.

[83]   Those with suspected Protestant sympathies include John Erskine of Dun, Patrick, Lord Gray, James Hamilton of Kincavil, James Kirkcaldy of Grange, and Robert, Lord Maxwell: see Finlay, 'Professional men of law', Appendix 8, and Sanderson, *Cardinal of Scotland*, Appendix 3.

[84]   Knox, *History*, iii, 405-6; H. Watt, 'Henry Balnavis and the Scottish Reformation' in (1935) *Records of the Scottish Church History Society*, 25.

[85]   CS 6/10 fo. 164v.

[86]   *Hamilton Papers*, i, 99-100; NAS, Ailsa Muniments, GD 25/1/426: 13 July 1542. See also chapter seven.

[87]   *Hamilton Papers*, i, 472, 492: 20 and 27 Mar. 1543

[88]   Lease to Balnavis by Beaton: Fraser, *Melvilles*, iii, 81: 7 Mar. 1541; Knox, *History*, 408-10.

remembered.[89] Nonetheless it is his legal career which is most significant here because he provides a bridge between the generation of lawyers prominent in 1532 and those who became increasingly important in the 1540s and beyond not only as men of law, but also as office holders and political figures. When Queen Mary resigned the crown in favour of her son in 1568, she had plenty of invective for Protestant lawyers such as Balnavis, James Balfour, James McGill, 'and the rest of that pestiferous factioun'.[90] The study of the role of advocates in the Reformation requires to be done, but there is plenty of evidence that some of them were in the ranks of the most committed Protestants, whilst others, such as Thomas McCalzeane, saw the religious upheaval as an opportunity to make money.[91]

In 1532, when the eight general procurators were named and the college of justice set up with funding from the church, there can have been little hint of future religious difficulties. Indeed, the choice of the procurators appears to have been amongst the least innovative aspects of the foundation. As the discussion so far has indicated, they were experienced men who knew each other well. Moreover they were following in an established tradition. During the reign of James IV the same names appear repeatedly acting as procurators before the lords of council. In using the printed record from 1496 to 1501, Lord Cooper found that James Henryson appeared in private practice on ninety-three occasions, Thomas Allan on forty-three and David Beaton of Caraldston on thirty-three.[92] These were certainly some of the leading practitioners, but their activities only tell part of the story. In looking at those who were constituted to act as procurators in roughly the last decade of James IV's reign, from 25 March 1504 to 24 March 1514, these three men account for almost 13 per cent of all constitutions. If the leading nine procurators from that period are taken, they account as a group for some 41 per cent of all named procurators.[93] Clearly they fell short of enjoying a dominant position. But this figure does illustrate a natural tendency amongst those litigants who named others to represent them to select people who already had some experience of the courts. This tendency increased sharply during the reign of James V. During the decade from 25 March 1524 to 24 March 1534 almost 70

---

[89] Knox, *History*, 411.

[90] Fraser, *Lennox*, ii, 437.

[91] Although Protestant, McCalzeane become custodian of Edinburgh's most treasured Catholic relics, and, after the Protestant Lords of the Congregation had left Edinburgh in July 1559, he even rented out his house to the returning Catholic lord provost, George, Lord Seton: Lynch, *Edinburgh and the Reformation*, 74, 81.

[92] Donaldson, 'The Legal Profession', 7; Cooper, *Selected Papers*, 330.

[93] Finlay, 'Professional Men of Law', Appendix 4. The leading nine were: Mr John Williamson (7.38%), Mr Walter Lang (6.95%), Mr Matthew Kerr (5.65%), Mr Thomas Allan (4.94%), Mr Adam Otterburn (5.37%), Mr James Henryson (4.13%), Mr David Balfour (3.8%), Mr John Murray (2.71%), Mr Hugh Gifford (1.63%).

per cent of all nominations made by litigants went to just nine procurators.[94] Four of these account for 42 per cent of nominations.[95]

By the time of the foundation of the college of justice, there was therefore a strong line of social and professional continuity within the original group of those licensed 'to procure in all actions'. Although recorded constitutions afford the best measure available of procurators' activity, they must be used with caution. As was shown in the previous chapter, not all constitutions were recorded and, of those that were, only a minority of those named jointly and severally in any particular procuratory actually appeared as procurators. At best, therefore, recorded constitutions can only indicate the trend. However, in the years leading to 1532 the trend, using this measure, was for a small group of procurators increasingly to dominate court business. Simultaneously, fewer procurators were being named in each constitution. Thus the nine procurators named most often in the year to 24 March 1517 represented some 60 per cent of all nominations. In the year prior to the foundation of the college this had risen to 73 per cent and, in the subsequent year, to 95 per cent. In the year to 24 March 1532, for example, of the 149 nominations, Henry Lauder alone had 24 of them (16 per cent). The following year John Lethame on his own had almost 23 per cent. That means that almost one in four litigants whose constitution of procurators was recorded, named him as one of their procurators. Increasingly, only two or three procurators were being nominated in each constitution, and it is likely that this led to a significant growth in the proportion of the court's business that went to the leading advocates. As the statistics demonstrate, those individuals admitted in 1532 were increasingly at the forefront of activity.

The reliability of this trend can be tested by looking at court appearances. In chapter six the careers of Robert Leslie and Robert Galbraith will be investigated in more detail. In regard to these individuals, further statistical evidence can be drawn by discovering which advocates opposed them most often in cases brought before the lords of session.[96]

The trend is confirmed by looking at the procurators whose presence before the lords was actually recorded by the clerks. On its own this is not a particularly reliable measure but it does demonstrate the trend. The problem is that in many cases in the record the presence of men of law is not indicated. The clerks were understandably selective in the facts that they recorded. Wherever a party was personally present then this was stated because it was the

---

[94] The leading nine were: Mr Robert Galbraith (12.5%), Mr Robert Leslie (11.2%), Mr Henry Spittall (9.25%), Mr John Lethame (9.25%), Mr Henry Lauder (9%), Mr Thomas Marjoribankis (7.2%), Mr James Foulis (6.6%), Mr William Blackstock (2.9%) and Mr William Johnstone (1.87%).

[95] Galbraith, Leslie, Spittall and Lethame. See previous footnote.

[96] This has been done, but ther eis no room to include the statistics here: J. Finlay, 'Professional Men of Law', Appendix 7.

legally relevant fact. Sometimes, a man of law was recorded as that party's forespeaker if he did something that the clerks were required to record. Otherwise his presence was insignificant and was ignored. It is therefore impossible to tell in many cases whether a party who appeared personally did so alone or together with a legal adviser. What can be done, however, is to take note of the definite appearances made by men of law. Although this represents only a guaranteed minimum there is no reason to suspect that the statistical outcome would be significantly different if the clerks had routinely recorded all appearances by legal representatives. The evidence shows that a few advocates were increasingly dominant in practice as well as being increasingly popular amongst litigants.[97]

Procurators of the court

From 1527 onwards the phrase *cum ceteris procuratoribus curie* or its vernacular equivalents such as 'with the rest of the advocates of the court' or 'with the remaining advocates', is increasingly found in recorded constitutions before the lords of council immediately following the names of those nominated. Out of 1138 recorded constitutions between 1504 and 1535, the phrase appears in 107 of them.[98] There are two isolated examples of its use from 1507 and 1524, but generally it was most used in the years immediately preceding and following 1532. A similar phrase can be found in the act book of the official of Lothian in the 1540s.[99] Nothing definite is known about who these 'procurators of the court' were, or what their status was in each court, although the fact that they were 'of the court' clearly implies that some kind of judicial control was being exercised over them.

In seeking to identify the 'procurators of the court' the most likely candidates are obviously those already mentioned as being the most active advocates. Most of the constitutions containing the *cum ceteris curie* clause named at least one of the general procurators of 1532. The only exceptions to this were constitutions that named only one procurator and this occurred in three cases where Master William Blackstock, Master Hugh Rigg and Master John Gledstanes were named alone together with the phrase *cum ceteris curie*. Perhaps the best guide to identifying the procurators of the court is to isolate all those constitutions where only one man was named together with 'the rest of the procurators of the court'. In addition to the three mentioned, this occurred only in the cases of the following advocates: Robert Galbraith, Henry Lauder, John Lethame, Robert Leslie, Henry Spittall and Thomas Marjoribankis. Rigg and Gledstanes only came onto the scene after the

[97]   Finlay, 'Professional men of law', Appendix 7.
[98]   Ibid., Appendix 1.
[99]   Ollivant, *Court of the Official*, 58, fn. 178.

foundation of the college in 1532 while Blackstock died shortly before it. There can be little doubt that the other six, together with Blackstock, were 'of the court' prior to 1532. It is difficult to say whether any others enjoyed this status. William Johnstone and Thomas Kincraigie, the remainder of those licensed in 1532, are the most obvious candidates.

A possible hypothesis is that the group of 'procurators of the court' numbered ten. This would also explain why provision was made at the setting up of the college of justice for ten general procurators when only eight were admitted. The lords were not creating a new system from scratch; they were simply regulating an existing framework that until then is not directly revealed by the record. They were prevented from naming ten procurators straight away in May 1532, because of the untimely death of Blackstock towards the end of 1531 and the promotion of James Foulis to their own ranks as lord clerk register in March. Besides, it seems likely that the number admitted was quickly increased to nine with the addition of Hugh Rigg. The other possible candidate as a procurator of the court in 1532 was James Carmuir. Although his level of activity was relatively low, he seems to have been active as a procurator from about 1513 until the early 1540s. His appointment as *clericus closete regis* in 1529, mentioned earlier, may however have excluded him from being admitted as a general procurator.

A central civil court with only a small number of licensed advocates was not unusual. The concept of a *numerus clausus* can be found in secular courts in other jurisdictions. In England quotas can be found as early as the late thirteenth century.[100] Limits on the number of *avocats* were imposed in the *Grand Conseil de Malines* and the *Conseil Provincial de Namur*.[101] By legislation introduced in 1500, only six *avocats* and eight *procureurs* were permitted to appear before the *Counseil Soveraine de Brabant,* although the number of lawyers increased to one hundred in the second half of the sixteenth century.[102] In Dijon there was a clear growth of legal professionals at the expense of notaries during the sixteenth century and as a phenomenon this may have been replicated elsewhere.[103] Castile also saw a dramatic rise in numbers during the sixteenth century with eight advocates registered in the chancillería of Valladolid in 1497 and fifty-six registered there in 1589.[104] This mirrors the increase in Scotland although the reasons why such an increase should have occurred across Western Europe at this time must involve economic, social, political and even religious factors requiring broader study.

---

[100] Brand, *English Legal Profession*, 149.
[101] Wijffels, 'Procureurs et avocats', 173-4; Vael, 'Conseil Provincial de Namur', 225.
[102] Rousseaux, '*De l'assistance mutuelle à l'assistance professionelle le Brabant*', 157.
[103] J.R. Farr, 'Dijon's Social Structure 1450-1750', in *Cities and Social Change in Early Modern France*, ed. P. Benedict (London, 1992), 141.
[104] Kagan, *Lawyers and Litigation*, 63. The Spanish kingdoms, of course, did have a much greater number of lawyers in absolute terms than Scotland.

It has been suggested that numbers of advocates in the major English church courts remained small because the advocates who enjoyed a monopoly sought to maintain their practice, and so their high fees, by excluding others.[105] This meant that no new advocate might be appointed until the death or removal of an existing advocate. The latter rule was not explicitly stated in Scotland until 1590 by which time the upper limit on the number of advocates was to be fifty.[106] For the first two decades of the college of justice, however, the number of licensed advocates did not rise above the original limit of ten. It does appear to have been the case in practice that a new advocate was admitted only after another had died or been created a senator of the college. Since there is no record of advocates' admission oaths until the 1550s this is impossible to prove. However a list of those admitted to practise as general procurators was recorded in 1549 and contains only nine names.[107] An anonymous seventeenth-century writer, commenting on the *acta* as he read them, made a list of those he regarded as the major advocates in the year 1537. This consisted of eight names, none of which can be argued with although the list is not contemporary nor does it purport to indicate that those eight were admitted on any particular day.[108] Indeed the '1537 list' is demonstrably incomplete because it does not include Thomas Kincraigie who was certainly still active before the lords and who, in the 1549 list, was the only original general procurator still practising.[109] His caseload was never large and the seventeenth-century compiler, whose purpose was to record the 'cheiff advocattis in Sessioun', may therefore have excluded him.[110]

Kincraigie's long survival underlines the fact that the advocates who were thrust into the limelight by the foundation of the college of justice in 1532 represent in some ways the end of a generation. Although Marjoribankis, Lethame, Lauder and Johnstone were all also still alive in 1549, with the exception of the disgraced Johnstone they were all lords of session. As practising lawyers they had largely been replaced by a new generation which had begun to make its appearance within the first few years of the new court's existence. Men such as Hugh Rigg, George Strang, William Wightman, James

---

[105] Helmholz, 'Ethical Standards', 47.
[106] EUL, Lord Fountainhall's Collection, La. III. 399, fo. 116: 18 July 1590.
[107] See Appendix 1.
[108] EUL, Lord Fountainhall's Collection, La. III. 399, fo. 2. This MS is entitled 'Notices and Observations out of the buikis of sederunt of the Lordis of Sessioun: Statutes of Session'. It seems that Francis Grant, *Advocates*, has accepted the date of the entry in this list of excerpts from the *acta* as the date of admission of the lawyers that it names. This was clearly not what the compiler meant to convey. There is no evidence that any of these lawyers was admitted on the day in question.
[109] *ADCP*, 584.
[110] EUL, La. III. 399, fo. 2.

McGill and Thomas McCalzeane had taken over.[111] Although the earliest appearance of Thomas McCalzeane as a procurator before the lords of council was on 1 February 1535, he can be found in another source in connection with a legal dispute as early as 1527.[112] These were men who went on to have significant careers as advocates, government officials and, in the cases of McGill and McCalzeane, lords of session.

---

[111] Rigg appeared as a procurator from 1532; Strang was regularly appearing as a procurator by 1540 (e.g. CS 6/13 fo. 47v: 30 June 1540); Wightman was appearing by late 1538 (e.g. CS 6/11 fo. 53r: 19 Dec. 1538); McGill was also a regular by 1540 (e.g. CS 6/13 fo. 83v: 15 July 1540).

[112] CS 6/6 fo. 30r; NAS, Protocal Book of John Feyrn, NP1/168, no pagination: 18 Oct. 1527. This underlines the inaccuracy of Grant's assertion that McCalzeane was one of a group admitted as an advocate on 16 Nov. 1537.

CHAPTER FOUR

Compelling Counsel and

the Procurators of the Court

> ...and that thir forsaidis procuratouris procure for every man for
> thair waigis bot giff thai have ressonable excus.[1]

The lords in 1532 gave no reason as to why so few advocates were admitted
by them into the college of justice. There may have been a lack of suitable
candidates, with most educated men preferring careers in the church or in
royal service; or the lords, desiring to maintain a tight control over the quality
of advocates, may have selected only the most experienced. Pressure may have
come from the advocates themselves, as happened in other jurisdictions, to
limit numbers and so to protect their client-base and their income. But there is
no real evidence to support any of these theories.[2] What the lords patently did
not do was to create a monopoly. They created the office of 'general
procurator'. Those who held it clearly had a special status, one consequence of
which was the dominant position that between them they enjoyed in terms of
their share of court business. But other procurators continued to appear before
the lords although probably in a smaller proportion of cases. In the year from
November 1535 there were at least thirty-seven different procurators who
appeared before the court and who did not enjoy the special status of general
procurator.[3] The precise content of that status is unknown. Cases involving
general procurators were not privileged, unlike cases involving the lords, so
initially they were subject to the same delays and accorded the same

---

[1] *ADCP.*, 377: 27 May 1532.

[2] Ollivant was impressed by the large number of procurators who appeared before the official of Lothian
in the 1540s. This runs somewhat against the trend described in the college of justice but, even on his
own figures, it seems that a small proportion of the procurators dominated the business of the court:
Ollivant, *Court of the Official*, 175.

[3] If judges, scribes, and macers of the court who sometimes acted as procurators (and who come broadly
under the umbrella of 'members of the court') are excluded from this list, along with those appearing in
1536 who only later became general procurators (men who were regular professional advocates but
who were younger, less experienced and so inferior in status), that still leaves 28 special procurators
who had no obvious connection with the court.

precedence as any other ordinary action. In 1537 Thomas Marjoribankis, on behalf of himself and his colleagues, secured a concession permitting summonses concerning general procurators to be placed in the privileged table. This, the earliest example in the record of advocates as a group working together to achieve a common goal, does not necessarily indicate that they had a corporate identity. But it does underline the fact that real power lay with the lords rather than the advocates notwithstanding their special status.

The obvious inference is that in 1532 eight advocates were given the sole right to act generally on behalf of clients, representing them in all matters which might concern them arising before the court. To ensure the smooth running of business, these advocates may have enjoyed other privileges that were understood but not written down at the time. Since the law was to a great extent their livelihood, and the right of audience was vital to them, it was probably a reasonable assumption that they would not willingly jeopardise that right by engaging in sharp practice. On that basis there may have been a certain leniency permitted to general procurators, in terms of proving that they had a mandate and so on, which the lords would not have allowed to other procurators with whom they were less familiar. This, however, is necessarily speculative. Those formally admitted to practice before the college predictably dominate the constitutions of general procurators recorded after May 1532.

Whatever advantages these eight general procurators enjoyed, it is clear from the case law of the court that the right to act as a general procurator also carried with it the obligation to do so in certain circumstances. The significance of the group referred to in the late 1520s as 'procurators of the court' is directly related to the rule, laid down by the lords in 1532, that a procurator must act unless he had a reasonable excuse for not doing so. By implication, what was 'reasonable' was a question for the lords to determine. But the issue of judicial control over advocates was not one which arose suddenly in 1532: to understand the intricacies of this rule it is necessary to investigate how the lords dealt with the issue of refusals by advocates to represent clients.

The rules concerning representation

During the 1520s there had been several cases in which advocates had refused to act on behalf of litigants. Sometimes the reasons behind such refusals are obscure. Money does not appear to have been the motive. Advocates declined to act even where potential clients offered considerable sums to secure their services. James Pantoun even offered 'large expensis' to 'divers' advocates to defend him against an action of spuilzie but he was still unsuccessful.[4] For some reason none was prepared to appear for him in court, although it is possible that an advocate helped him draft his defences. In 1530, John Tweedie of Drummelzier protested that no advocate would represent him 'nowthir for command nor reward howbeit he wald have gevin quhat thai wald have askit'.[5] Such claims should be viewed in context; they were made by litigants seeking to delay actions against them on the basis that they could not obtain the services of an advocate. In order to get such a delay, they had to persuade the court that their claim was not frivolous and that they had been diligent in trying to hire an advocate. The clearest way to demonstrate diligence was to indicate that money had been offered and declined. But that does not mean there is any reason to doubt that such offers had been made.

Refusals to act, and a general difficulty encountered by litigants in securing advocates' services, led the courts to develop procedural rules in regard to representation. So far as is known these rules were not written down in any contemporary treatise; they were part of the practick of the courts in the 1520s and their existence can only be inferred from the case law of the period. The first rule is evident from the defences put forward against a summons of treason in 1528 on behalf of the earl of Angus by his secretary, John Ballantyne.[6] These defences stated that, since Angus and his fellow accused could not secure the services of a man of law, they should not be compelled to answer the summons unless one was provided to them. It was specifically asserted that it was the legal duty of a judge to provide an advocate to any person called before him at that person's expense. There is irony in the fact that Ballantyne appeared before the lords to speak on behalf of Angus in order to argue that Angus could not find anyone to speak on his behalf. This might merely indicate prevarication. But the fact that this argument seems to have been accepted indicates the degree of specialisation that had by now attached to the profession of advocate; Ballantyne could state the grounds of defence but he was not sufficiently skilled forensically to argue the merits of the case. The idea that it was a judge's duty to provide an advocate appears to have been generally applicable at this time. As early as 1516 the chancellor, in a letter subscribed on 16 May, implied that he was prepared to order a man of law to act on behalf of Dean Alexander Cunningham.[7] In 1523 Robert Barton and other men of Leith, in a dispute with Edinburgh concerning profits from prize ships, protested that they desired an advocate but could not get one and

---

[4] CS 5/37 fo. 40v: 21 Mar. 1527.
[5] CS 5/41 fo. 7v: 14 Mar. 1530. See below.
[6] *APS*, ii, 322-4.
[7] CS 5/27 fo. 230v: 16 May 1516. Cunningham, a monk at Glenluce, was accused of barratry. For barratry, see chapter seven.

so should not be compelled to answer until they had one.[8] Eventually Robert Leslie agreed to act on their behalf having been instructed to do so by the lords.[9]

Six years later it was argued before the bailies of the regality court of Dunfermline that they could not proceed in an action because of the defenders' claim that they should not be required to answer the summons without an expert man of law.[10] This argument was initially rejected but on appeal to the lords of council the bailies' decision was effectively reversed. The lords found that the judges in the regality court had shown themselves to be partial by failing to appoint an advocate to the defenders as the law had required them to do. The case concerned the validity of the assignation of a lease made to the defenders by a deceased relative of theirs. In so important a matter, alleged the defenders, they should have an advocate to put forward their case and they were prepared to prove before the bailies that 'thai had maid exact deligence in all the partiis of this realm quhare expert men in the law was'.[11]

The final case illustrating the rule involved Andrew Baron and the other heirs of the late Sir William Brown.[12] Balfour cited this case as authority for the rule, as he expressed it, that:

> Gif ony partie beand persewit dois diligence befoir ane Judge to
> get a Procuratour for himself, and cannot obtene the samin, he
> sould not be compellit to answer to the summondis, quhill (until)
> the Judge provide him an Advocat upon his expensis.[13]

Brown had been summoned for treason although Baron argued that he had done nothing that could competently give rise to such a charge.[14] In stating his argument Baron was careful not to make himself an accomplice to Brown's alleged crimes by appearing to defend them. Responding to the allegation that he had shown himself to be art and part in Brown's crimes by making his plea, Baron made it clear that it was not his intention to defend Brown but rather to

---

8   CS 5/33 fo. 117r. On this litigation see J.C. Irons, *Leith and Its Antiquities* (Edinburgh, 1897), chapter thirteen, 149, and Appendices 29-31; W.S. Reid, 'Robert Barton of Ovir Barnton' in *Medievalia et Humanistica*, v, (1948), 55-6; ibid., *Skipper from Leith: A History of Robert Barton of Over Barnton* (Philadelphia, 1965), 54-5, 164-8.
9   CS 5/33 fo. 119r.
10   CS 5/39 fos. 141r-142v.
11   No reason is given for their lack of success: CS fo. 141v. Several men of law were natives of Fife. Even non-native men of law can be found practising before courts in Fife and it is clear that distance was no object for them. For example, Henry Spittall appeared in the court of John, Lord Lindsay of the Byres, sheriff principal of Fife, on 28 Mar. 1528: CS 5/39 fo. 67v.
12   Baron's name is clearly written as 'Baron' and not as 'Brown' although, in the circumstances, scribal error cannot be ruled out.
13   Balfour, *Practicks*, ii, 299.
14   CS 5/41 fos. 158v-160r: 19 Jan. 1531.

defend his own right to Brown's goods which would be lost if they were forfeited to the crown.[15] Baron and his co-defenders, all with interests in these goods, were unable to employ procurators to represent them having tried diligently to do so. Indeed they had gone so far as to instruct a macer to charge Robert Galbraith, Robert Leslie, Henry Spittall and James Carmuir to act for them but they had all refused.[16] On the basis of this refusal, the defender successfully argued that they should not be compelled to answer the summons against them until the lords provided them with advocates upon their expenses. It seems that Balfour was unaware that the rule he was describing pre-dated the case he cited.

The second rule created by the lords prior to the foundation of the college of justice was that no advocate could see a party's summons, or the evidence which he intended to use in a case, unless he first agreed to accept the case and to act for that party.[17] The lords explicitly enacted this rule in 1528 probably in response to an action that was heard in 1527. There is no need to go into the political background of the case in detail but it is clear that the principal defender, Isabel Stewart, countess of Lennox, was politically isolated. Her husband had been killed the previous year in a failed attempt to liberate the king, who was still a minor, from the custody of the earl of Angus. Angus had been in illegal possession of the king since 1525 and it was on the basis of this control over the person of the king that he controlled the government. It was an accepted fact of late medieval Scottish government that during periods of minority, control of the king was vital to effective government. The action that Angus brought against Isabel, and two local lairds, in 1527 was brought in conjunction with the earl of Arran and others who formed the governing faction. Angus's government was very narrowly based and depended mainly on his control of patronage and government offices, many of which were given to his relatives and allies. In order to obtain control of Lennox lands Angus had made numerous grants of ward on lands in that area all going to a fairly small number of people. Wardship of the lands of the earldom of Lennox was granted jointly to Angus and his ally, the earl of Arran. The aim of the grants, to divert the revenue of the earldom during the minority of the new earl, was not successful because the tenants, rather unsurprisingly, refused to pay up.[18]

---

[15] This allegation was made by Thomas Scott on behalf of the king. Adam Otterburn, the king's advocate, was present and on the sederunt. For the division of responsibility between treasury officials such as Scott, and the king's advocate, see chapter seven.

[16] This appears to be the only recorded case in which a defender named specific men of law who were not willing to represent him.

[17] CS 5/38 fo. 127r : 8 July 1528.

[18] W.K. Emond, 'Minority of James V' (Ph.D. thesis, University of St Andrews, 1988), 529-31.

The particular dispute in 1527 appears to have given rise to an action and a counter-action. First Angus and his associates sought payment of rents and, secondly, Isabel counter-claimed arguing that she had been jointly infeft in the lands with her husband, and therefore had the right to continue in possession of them, and that the rents belonged to her. Although the legal issue was straightforward, it must have been obvious in political terms that Isabel had no realistic chance of success. Her co-defenders, two local landowners who were affected by the action, protested that they should not be prejudiced by it because 'thai couth nocht have a procuratour to procure for thame'. Sir James Hamilton then asked that it be noted that the lords had appointed Master Henry Spittall to be procurator for the defenders. In response, the defenders pointed out that Spittall had admitted to having already given counsel against them in the matter and that therefore he could not act in the case. It was an unwritten rule of legal practice that an advocate could not appear for both sides at once and it was clearly accepted in this case that Spittall, having advised one side, could not then act for the other. It is clear from the record of the case that Isabel, as she put it, 'can get na advocate to gif hir counsale nor yit that dare spek for hir'.[19] This is not surprising since any advocate representing her would have been faced with the motley crew of Angus, Arran and James Hamilton of Finnart—the man rumoured to have murdered her husband Lennox, after he had already surrendered.

In the circumstances, Spittall was no doubt rather relieved that he could not act for the defence enjoying, as he did, an excuse which in 1527 the lords undoubtedly accepted as 'reasonable'. As a result of the rule made in 1528 his excuse would not have been admitted (since he should not have looked at the summons without agreeing to take the case); and it is likely that the lords after 1532 would have considered such an excuse to be unreasonable. Indeed the rules under discussion were not specifically mentioned in the acts of sederunt of 1532 and it seems likely that they were subsumed in the general principle laid down in that year that advocates must accept a case unless they had a reasonable excuse for not doing so.

These rules could not have been enforced without sanctions and the sanctions applied were twofold: an advocate who refused to act could either be fined or have his right of audience before the court suspended. The latter penalty was particularly meaningful to those 'procurators of the court' who appeared regularly before the lords. There is only one example of this ultimate sanction being applied and it occurred in the context of one of the most acrimonious disputes to come before the lords in the years preceding the foundation of the college of justice. This was the feud that raged between the Tweedies of Drummelzier, supporters of Angus and aligned with the pro-

---

[19]   CS 5/37 fos. 74v, 131r: 2 Apr. and 29 May 1527.

English faction in Scotland, and the Flemings, strong supporters of the Albany governorship and pro-French in outlook. The dispute between the families centred on Katherine Fraser, heiress of Fruid in Peebleshire.[20] Both sides disputed the ward and marriage of Fruid. The feud was sparked in 1524 by the murder in Edinburgh of John, Lord Fleming, an act for which John Tweedie was outlawed.[21] Fleming's son Malcolm was imprisoned until he agreed to a marriage between Katherine and one of John Tweedie's sons. He later alleged that his 'consent' had been given only under duress whilst in captivity. In spite of an apparent accommodation, leading to the payment of assythment and the issuing of a respite to the Tweedies, the dispute concerning Katherine continued into the 1530s. Malcolm, Lord Fleming, demanded either her delivery in an unmarried state (rather impractical in the circumstances) or the avail of her marriage.

By March 1530 Tweedie was clearly finding it difficult to obtain the services of an advocate. He pointed out that although the lords 'had commandit all the advocatis or ane part of thame to procure for him in the actioun movit be him aganis the lord [F]lemyng', none would do so no matter how much money he offered.[22] This obviously suggests that the advocates of the court were regarded as a group. His difficulties were unresolved by December, at which time the lords appointed Henry Spittall and Thomas Marjoribankis to represent him. When they refused, the lords responded by withdrawing permission for both of them to procure before them.[23] This draconian ban seems to have had the desired result. The following month both advocates, together with John Lethame who may have taken on the role of mediator, appear in the record acting for Tweedie. But in doing so, they took the precaution of extracting a promise from Tweedie that he would not look upon their efforts with displeasure.[24] This suggests fear of their client but they may have been as much afraid of his opponent, Lord Fleming.[25]

Two other instances of judicial compulsion in the 1520s illustrate not only the need for intervention by the lords to provide unpopular litigants with advocates, but also their willingness to do so. These cases dealt with common enough topics; only the element of compulsion makes them unusual. The

[20] M.F. Tweedie, *The History of the Tweedie or Tweedy Family* (1902), 26-30; J.W. Buchan and H. Paton, *History of Peeblesshire* (Glasgow, 1927), iii, 403-4, 425*ff.*

[21] Fleming, the great chamberlain, appears to have been murdered shortly after sitting in judgment in the Tolbooth: *Edin. Burgh Recs.*, ii, 224-6; CS 5/42 fo. 5r.

[22] CS 5/41 fo. 7v: 14 Mar. 1530.

[23] CS 5/41 fo. 140v. Spittall was representing Tweedie on 19 Jun. 1525:CS 5/35 fo. 44r but this was two months before he was put to the horn.

[24] CS 5/42 fo. 2v.

[25] Fleming appears to have been as unsavoury a character as Tweedie. Others were certainly afraid of him: when, in August 1527, Walter Scott of Branxholm complained that he could not have sure passage to appear in court in Edinburgh, Fleming stated that he was ready to give him assurance that he might appear 'unhurt unharmit or trublit' by him: CS 5/37 fo. 191r.

first, in December 1522, involved an action raised in the king's name against Andrew Ballon. Ballon was a canon of St Andrews and it was alleged that he had committed barratry—the offence of trafficking in ecclesiastical appointments without royal licence.[26] He was alleged to have purchased the priory of Inchmahome at Rome without the king's permission. Inchmahome had been annexed to the chapel royal at Stirling by Pope Julius II in 1508 and so this transgression was perhaps particularly blatant.[27] Robert Leslie was compelled to procure for the alleged prior and protested that 'na actioune nor cryme suld be impute to him' for so doing. Barratry was a civil matter although the major penalty was banishment. Quite often it is described as being treasonable and inasmuch as it was an attack on the privileges of the crown it was a serious matter.

The second case, that of the bishop of Brechin against Euphemia Ramsay, was also of a kind fairly typical in the sixteenth century. It involved the wrongful occupation of lands. Euphemia alleged that she had received a lease of the lands of Balrony in Forfar from the prior of St Andrews. She claimed that the prior had been given power by the bishop to grant the lease. The bishop denied this and he also denied that he had promised on oath that he would never remove Euphemia from the lands. John Lethame, acting for the bishop, claimed that he had been discharged by the vicar general in Brechin and so wanted to withdraw from the case. Despite this, the lords compelled him to continue with the case. This is a difficult case to interpret. Clearly there was compulsion but Lethame was not being forced to act for someone for whom he was unwilling to act. The issue may have involved the competence of the discharge made by the vicar general as the representative of the bishop. In substance this was a revocation of Lethame's mandate, but it had not been made by the bishop and the lords might have taken the view that it was technically invalid and that Lethame should therefore continue. The case seems out of step with the others mentioned above in that the lords were interfering in an established advocate-client relationship rather than seeking to form such a relationship.

It is evident that when the lords came to frame the general concept concerning representation in 1532 they simply restated rules that had already been developed and applied to the small group of procurators of the court which increasingly dominated business and which alone was subject to compulsion. These were conflated into the principle that an advocate could not, without good reason, refuse to act for a client who offered to pay his fee. The principle enunciated in 1532 was not entirely satisfactory however. It did not remove the concerns of advocates that they might suffer from being too

---

[26] On barratry, see also chapter seven.
[27] Cowan and Easson, *Medieval Religious Houses*, 92.

closely identified with the interest, and sins, of their clients. Nor did it address the needs of a significant part of the population who could simply not afford to offer payment to secure the services of an advocate.

In the remaining years of James V's reign, advocates can still be found refusing to act for clients or protesting about the fact that the court was compelling them to act. In November 1537 Master Hugh Rigg had to be compelled by the lords to procure on behalf of John Leslie, an alleged barrator. Rigg ensured that his protest was entered in the record so that in the future no crime could be 'impute' to him, explaining that he acted by 'compulsion & obedience that he aucht (owed) to the command of the saidis lordis & na uther wyse.'[28] Two years later Rigg, this time with unnamed colleagues, was ordered to represent James Colville of East Wemyss, the former comptroller, who had been charged by the king with treason.[29] Rigg agreed to act but again wanted it made clear that he did so under protest and that his agreement in these circumstances should not make him criminally liable in future.[30] The tendency of men of law to look after their own interests by distancing themselves from those who were accused of criminal or quasi-criminal activity cannot have inspired much confidence in their clients.

In 1540 Alexander Forrester of Corstorphine brought an action against David Forrester of Garden.[31] Alexander had given David the barony of Corstorphine under a reversion. David, having been warned to come to the altar of St James in the church of St Giles on a specific day to receive payment of the sum under the reversion, failed to do so. Alexander, having appeared and offered the money then consigned it to the safekeeping of Thomas Marjoribankis. The lords decided that the barony had been lawfully redeemed and ordered David to resign and quitclaim the land in terms of the reversion. This was all rather straightforward apart from the fact that for some reason David could not persuade an advocate to represent him. Even though the lords ordered certain advocates to procure for him, 'nane of thaim wald except [accept] the samin bot refusit aluterlie to procure for him'.[32] Unfortunately no reason was given for their refusal.

It is clear that the lords' attempt in 1532 to solve the problem of litigants who could not obtain the services of an advocate was unsuccessful. Two acts of sederunt in the mid-1550s indicate that the problem still existed. In 1554

[28]   CS 6/9 fo. 29v.
[29]   Colville was charged on the basis that he had communicated with Angus. Rigg's reluctance to represent him was understandable given that at this period, following the execution of Janet Douglas, lady Glamis, in 1537, James V was on the lookout for signs of conspiracy against him and suspicious of anyone with links to Angus. Robert Leslie, albeit posthumously, was also accused of treason in the wake of James's anxieties; see pp. 129-30.
[30]   APS, ii, 353. Compare the case involving Andrew Baron, above, pp. 75-6.
[31]   CS 6/14 fos. 15r-v: 27 Nov. 1540; CS 6/14 fo. 46v: 17 Dec. 1540.
[32]   CS 6/14 fo. 15v.

the lords declared that litigants, both pursuers and defenders, were 'daily and continualie' coming before them and making the excuse that they could not get a procurator, with the result that the lords were greatly hindered and justice much delayed. Such excuses, as a result, were no longer to be heard or admitted.[33] This merely indicates that the defence was no longer acceptable; it does not mean that the defence was genuine. The following year, it was decided that no party could choose more than two advocates (including his pensioners), without then giving his adversary the opportunity to choose any other two he pleased, provided he did not seek a delay 'throw pretence of wanting of thame'.[34] They also took the opportunity to reiterate the rule of 1532, slightly recasting it in even stronger terms by stating that:

> no advocattis, without verrie gret cause, [may] refuise to procure
> for ony partie upoune thair ressonable expensis under the pane of
> deprivatioun of thame of thair offices of advocatioune.

Power clearly still lay with the judges rather than the advocates. It is questionable whether this in itself worked to the disadvantage of the advocates as a group. The small number of advocates who were admitted to the college in its first twenty years were not self selecting, nor did they exercise a monopoly, but they did dominate the market place for legal services. There is no indication that they were dissatisfied with their lot. When numbers of advocates began to increase, from the 1550s onwards, this may have changed. The earliest known evidence of the existence of some kind of official body representing the advocates does not come until 1582 when John Shairp was described as 'dene of the advocatiis of the session'.[35] Arguably it was when they grew in number that the collective power of advocates, vis-à-vis the judges, increased. But this very growth in numbers, overseen as it was by the judges, may have been the catalyst to closer co-operation amongst existing advocates: the admission of too many young 'expectants' would have threatened the position and income of those already established in practice.

This leaves one other aspect of 1532, and the rule concerning representation, to be discussed: the poor. It can be no accident that the lords did not impose on advocates an obligation to represent any person, irrespective of ability to pay, who might require their services. Given the high number of poor litigants, this would have created an intolerable burden. Nonetheless, this discrimination did give the poor a genuine ground for complaint. The king was required to give justice to all his people, not merely those who could afford advocates to represent them, and it appeared to be

---

[33]   CS 1/1 fo. 1r.
[34]   *Acts of Sederunt*, ed. I. Campbell (Edinburgh, 1811), 60.
[35]   Sanderson, *Mary Stewart's People*, 23.

only the latter group whom the lords were willing to help by the use of compulsion. It may have been pressure from the poor that led, in March 1535, to a very public resurrection of the office of advocate for the poor, a move that occurred in tandem with a drive to regulate and limit begging.[36]

The advocate for the poor

To the medieval mind knowledge was seen as a gift from God. There was therefore considerable questioning in the later medieval period as to whether or not it might be sold.[37] The debate centred on university teachers, who often held regular salaries or had income from benefices, and many were of the view that they should transmit knowledge to their students without a fee. To some, heavily influenced by Roman law, this view equally applied to professors of law and other jurists.[38] According to Ulpian, the teacher of law should neither demand money nor seek gifts, although he could honourably accept them.[39]

When this view encountered Christian teaching concerning the alleviation of the suffering of the poor the result, from the council of Chalcedon in 451 onwards, was a positive duty on clerics to give legal counsel to widows, orphans and the poor.[40] Bishops in particular came under a duty to protect what the canonists called *miserabiles personae*, a term not always easily defined but generally including those disadvantaged because of their status, such as widows and orphans, always provided they were also poor in fact.[41] A decretal of Honorius III authorised judges to appoint advocates for poor people. Little is known about how court-appointees in such circumstances were remunerated although the number of poor litigants indicates some relief was given, either from public funds or by the advocates themselves in the form of remission of fees. The provision of legal advice to the poor has been viewed as 'an integral characteristic of professional status'.[42]

In Scotland, legislation dating from the reign of James I instructed judges to provide an advocate for those 'pur creaturis' who were unable to secure the

---

[36]   J.M. Goodare, 'Parliament and Society in Scotland 1560–1603', (Ph.D. thesis, University of Edinburgh, 1989), 416. As Dr Goodare has shown, municipal initiatives for the relief of poverty were not introduced in Scotland until the 1550s, although they did build on the network of poor hospitals already in existence. It is interesting that pre 1535 legislation concerning the poor drew its inspiration from legislation dating from 1424, the time when the general concept of advocate for the poor is first mentioned (*infra*): Goodare, ibid., 417.

[37]   G. Post *et al.*, "The medieval heritage of a humanistic ideal: '*Scientia Donum Dei Est, Unde Vendi Non Potest*'", 11 *Traditio* (1955), 197*ff*.

[38]   Ibid., 204.

[39]   D.50.13.1.4–5.

[40]   J.A. Brundage, 'Legal aid for the poor and the professionalization of law in the Middle Ages' (1988), *Journal of Legal History*, 170.

[41]   On the various definitions of this term, see R.H. Helmholz, *The Spirit of Classical Canon Law* (Georgia, 1996), 128–132.

[42]   Brundage, 'Legal Aid', 175.

services of one.[43] This was done, ostensibly 'for the love of God', at a time of significant innovation in the administration of justice. No provision was made to pay any advocate who might be instructed to act for a poor litigant, except that if the litigant were successful the losing party was to pay for the advocate's 'costis and travale'. This was a potentially attractive incentive but it is not known how successful this legislation was. Scotland was not unique in providing poor litigants with advocates in the civil sphere, nor was it the first kingdom in Europe to maintain an advocate for the poor from crown revenues. From the late thirteenth century kings of Castile paid for an *abogado de pobres* to represent the poor, while from 1473 provision was made for an *avocat* and a *procureur* to act for poor people, *pro Deo*, at the *Grand Conseil de Malines*.[44] Nor indeed is there much in the way of evidence that the rule was being observed in practice in Scotland during the fifteenth century. Not until 1502 is there a reference to a case in which there appeared an 'advocat til the pure folkis'; and the man who fulfilled this role was the king's advocate, James Henryson.[45]

As was common elsewhere in Europe, a large number of cases involving the poor, normally described as 'poor tenants', can be found in the record. Normally they used procurators and most of the leading procurators of the day appeared for such clients on occasion. For example, Master William Blackstock appeared in January, 1530, for the poor tenant, John Bruce, who acted against Patrick, master of Hailes, sheriff-depute of Edinburgh, and Helen Shaw who had been served to the lands of which John was a tenant.[46] Since inordinate process was alleged, John's summons also ran in the king's name but it is noticeable that he was represented separately, not by the king's advocate. Nothing is known about the basis upon which these procurators were employed or whether they remitted all or part of their fee. Nor is it easy to know how poor the poor actually were. Since most of them were described as 'poor tenants' the courts were obviously dealing with the settled poor, those who had little and yet something to lose, rather than vagrants and beggars.[47] It is clear that for his summons to be placed in the 'pure folkis table', and therefore to benefit from the services of the advocate for the poor, a litigant had to show that his income fell below a certain monetary threshold. At the end of James V's reign, William Mowbray was disqualified from asserting the

[43]   *APS*, ii, 8 (c.24).

[44]   Kagan, *Lawsuits and Litigants*, 13; Wijffels, 'Procureurs et avocats', 175 (*Ordonnance of Thionville*, 1473, art. 22). An *Ordonnance* of 1364 made similar provision before the *Parlement de Paris*, imposing upon judges the duty to provide a *procureur* to impoverished litigants: B. Auzary-Schmaltz and S. Dauchy, 'L'assistance dans la résolution des conflits au civil devant le Parlement de Paris au Moyen Age', 55.

[45]   *ADC*, iii, 323.

[46]   CS 5/40 fo. 156r: 12 Jan. 1530.

[47]   The settled poor were the great majority, and tended to be viewed as more deserving than vagrants: Goodare, 'Parliament and Society', 414. In principle, however, there seems to be no reason why the advocate for the poor might not represent a vagrant, provided he had just cause to litigate.

privilege of the poor's table because he had sufficient land in liferent as to afford him the modest sum of seven shillings worth of food annually.[48] In 1536, by contrast, Janet Newton was allowed to benefit from the privilege even though her opponent alleged that she was a landowner and also that she was to receive five £500 from him.[49] According to canon law, poverty was to be defined according to current means, not future expectations, and this might be an example of that principle being applied in the college of justice.[50]

As mentioned above, it was in March 1535 that steps were taken to put the office of advocate for the poor on a firmer footing. Narrating that numerous poor lieges daily complained that there were no advocates to procure for them, and that they lacked the money to pay for one, the king directed the lords to choose a man of good conscience as *advocatus pauperum*.[51] He was to swear to represent all those who came to him for help and who themselves were prepared to take an oath that they lacked the means to pursue justice themselves. In return he was to receive £10 *per annum*. This was a small amount in return for a potentially extremely burdensome task but it seems clear that the role of advocate for the poor was not envisaged as being a full-time one. In the event of the advocate being found false, the lords were instructed to remove him from office and also to prevent him appearing as an advocate in any other cases until he was reconciled to the king. This is reminiscent of the sanction at the *Conseil Provincial de Namur* where apparently any *avocat* who refused to work for a poor person might be suspended from appearing before the court.[52] The motive behind the 1535 appointment was partly to respond to demand and partly, once again, for the honour of God. To supplement this new office, provision was soon made to speed up procedure for 'pur miserable persounis' because they lacked the substance to remain in Edinburgh to await the ordinary course of litigation.[53] Cases concerning the poor were thenceforward to be heard on a Friday, which was normally one of the days set aside for the king's matters. It is significant that in his brief discussion of the role of the advocate for the poor, Balfour only mentioned the steps taken in 1535; he ignored, or was ignorant of, the legislation of James I.[54]

In response to the king's instruction, the lords nominated not one but two advocates to act jointly and severally for the poor: Thomas Marjoribankis and John Gledstanes. With Marjoribankis's consent, Gledstanes alone was to

48   CS 6/19 fo. 38r: 8 May 1542.
49   CS 6/7 fo. 164r: 23 Mar. 1536.
50   Helmholz, *Classical Canon Law*, 131.
51   *ADCP*, 434-5: 2 Mar. 1535.
52   Vael, 'Conseil Provincial de Namur', 217.
53   CS 6/6 fo. 111v: 27 Apr. 1535.
54   Balfour, *Practicks*, ii, 299.

receive the annual salary. It has been plausibly suggested that this meant Gledstanes was working under the supervision of Marjoribankis.[55]

Gledstanes probably began his career as a chancery scribe, having received £3 from the fees of the privy seal in 1532.[56] Shortly thereafter he may have gone to study in France although by this time he was already a licentiate in both the laws. Gledstanes and his cousin, Robert Fraser, with their voyage in mind, petitioned the lords of council to certify that they were of noble status.[57] His tenure as *advocatus pauperum* was brief. In 1537 his appointment as commissary of Glasgow made it impossible to continue as advocate for the poor in Edinburgh.[58]

There is no record of any payment actually being made from the treasury to an advocate for the poor until 1537 when Master John Williamson received the £10 fee.[59] He is further recorded as receiving this pension in the two subsequent years.[60] Like Gledstanes, Williamson was a churchman. Governor of the hospital of the Virgin Mary in Edinburgh in 1525, and provost of Seton, by 1534 he was also commissary of Lothian although this did not affect his ability to appear for the poor before the lords of council.[61] In the years leading to his appointment as advocate for the poor he was also responsible for collecting ecclesiastical taxes from various deaneries within the diocese of St Andrews. By 1540 Williamson was sharing the role of advocate for the poor with Andrew Blackstock, the pension having been raised to £20 annually shared equally between them and payable in two instalments.[62] Thereafter only Blackstock is recorded as *advocatus pauperum* in the treasurer's accounts, with payments of £20 to him recorded in 1542 and £40 in 1546 (made in arrears in respect of the previous three years).[63] This indicates that the pension had reverted to £10 when he held office on his own. There is no indication of why Blackstock replaced Williamson. Blackstock himself was replaced by Thomas Kincraigie, probably in 1546. This time the pension was increased, although Kincraigie was not paid until 1550 then receiving £80 (at the rate of £20 per year probably in respect of the previous four years).[64] Further payments indicate that Kincraigie was connected to the office of advocate to the poor until 1563, although he was not always sole office holder.[65] From

---

55 Hannay, *College of Justice*, 69.
56 *RSS*, ii, 770.
57 *RMS*, iii, no. 1263. Gledstanes' subsequent appearances before the lords suggest that he did not go to France for very long, if at all.
58 Watt, *Fasti*, 191.
59 *TA*, vi, 357.
60 *TA*, vi, 447; vii, 200.
61 NAS, Register House Charters, RH 6/973a: 11 Oct. 1525; *RMS*, iii, no. 2172; Watt, *Fasti*, 331, 373.
62 *RSS*, ii, no. 3261: 7 Jan. 1540.
63 *TA*, viii, 106, 487.
64 *TA*, ix, 447.
65 *TA*, x, 132, 214, 294, 296, 444; xi, 36, 256.

1558 Master Edward Henryson was also being paid £10 yearly for representing the poor.[66] His fee was paid at the special command of the queen whereas Kincraigie was paid out of ordinary revenue from the treasury.

Henryson was a renowned scholar and former lecturer at Bourges. He was employed as a translator of Greek in the household of Henry Sinclair, dean of Glasgow and lord of session and he had numerous other links with educated Scots churchmen.[67] His post as advocate for the poor may have been provided to augment his income; Marie of Guise had already employed him to read one lecture in the laws and one in Greek thrice weekly in Edinburgh. After February 1563 there is no further record of payments made to Kincraigie or Henryson. In May 1564, Master John Logie was appointed advocate to the poor.[68] Although he was to receive the same fee as his predecessors, to be paid out of 'the reddiest of hir graces casualiteis', there is no record of any payments made to advocates for the poor in the treasurer's accounts until the 1570s, when the fee of £60 annually was disbursed to unidentified procurators for the poor.[69] Unless the customary pension had by then been raised once again, this would indicate an innovation in that there were by now three office-holders.

In sum, the evidence indicates that the office of advocate for the poor was held consistently from 1535 onwards until a short gap in the mid-1560s. The office holders were without exception skilled lawyers although in the main they were men whose backgrounds tended towards practice in the church courts. Despite the fairly rapid turnover of staff, the attention given to the office of king's advocate during the latter part of James V's reign does indicate a serious attempt to address a perceived imbalance in the provision of legal services.

---

[66] *TA*, x, 354, 402; xi, 220.
[67] Durkan, 'The beginnings of humanism', 16; ibid., 'The royal lectureships under Mary of Lorraine' (1983) *SHR* 74.
[68] *RSS*, v, no. 1701: 24 May 1564.
[69] *TA*, xiii, 104 (1575), 233 (1578-3 years in arrears), 312 (1579).

CHAPTER FIVE

The Life of the Law: Practice and Procedure

In 1532, having been explicitly granted the power to make such rules, statutes and ordinances as were required to regulate procedure before the college of justice, the lords of session set out in broad terms the content of that procedure.[1] Judging from what can be gleaned from the *acta* in the 1520s there was little novelty in the procedural rules that the lords enunciated: they largely confirmed the 'stile and consuetude' of the court as it had been developing in previous decades. This 'stile', the body of rules particular to a specific court, is the factor that distinguishes the procedural rules of the major courts of western Europe at this period. Procedure developed through legal practice and, to the legal practitioner, the obvious reservoir of procedural knowledge was the authoritative texts relating to Romano-canonical procedure which was the most influential and successful system then devised. There are signs that it would be unwise to draw too sharp a distinction in the early sixteenth century between the procedures adopted in the spiritual jurisdiction and those used before the lords of session.[2] Experienced canonists, such as William Elphinstone, William Wawane and Abraham Crichton, were key personnel not only in the consistory but also in the session. Many of the thirty or so men of law practising before the court of the official of Lothian in the middle of the sixteenth century also appeared before the lords of session.[3] Such a free interchange of personnel would certainly have affected the development of procedural rules.[4]

Numerous texts of canon and civilian writers circulated in Scotland in the fifteenth and sixteenth centuries and amongst these were works on procedure including the extremely influential *Speculum Judiciale* of Guillaume Durand.[5]

---

[1]   For the various interpretations of this event see H.L. MacQueen 'Jurisdiction in heritage and the lords of council and session after 1532' in *Miscellany II,* ed. W.D.H. Sellar, (Stair Society, 1984), 61.

[2]   On the similarities between canonist practice and modern civil court practice see T.M. Cooper, *Select Scottish Cases of the Thirteenth Century* (Edinburgh and London, 1944), Introduction, xxxv-xxxvii.

[3]   Ollivant, *Court of the Official,* 60-1.

[4]   J.J. Robertson has drawn attention to the similarity of the interlocutors of the Roman Rota and the acts of the lords of council in civil causes. The significance of this relates to the fact that in the majority of cases the pleadings before the Rota were made in Rome by Scottish procurators: Robertson, 'The development of the law', *Scottish Society in the Fifteenth Century,* ed. J.M. Brown (London, 1977), 151-2.

[5]   J. Durkan and A. Ross, 'Early Scottish Libraries' (1958) *Innes Review* 5-167.

Such texts were often purchased by those studying abroad, some of whom then returned and practised law in the Scottish courts. But it should not be overlooked that, once in Scotland, these texts were widely borrowed and consulted. For example, in his testament written in 1555 Master David Whitelaw mentioned several civilian and canonist works some of which were in the hands of others including the man of law Master Thomas McCalzeane.[6] An inscription on a breviary owned by Clement Litill indicates that the book, originally owned by Master John Moscrop, was taken by Master John Monypenny from whom Litill obtained it.[7] This was apparently done covertly although the amount of overt borrowing between men of law of other—in particular legal and procedural—texts would have been significant not only in the 1550s but earlier. Such works were not only loaned but were passed on from generation to generation. Thus Abraham Crichton, official of Lothian and an extremely active man of law in the secular courts, almost certainly passed on canonist texts to his legitimated son George, who was admitted as an advocate in November 1557.[8] Such behaviour would have been widespread and important in disseminating legal knowledge.[9]

The libraries built up in the second half of the sixteenth century by men such as Clement Litill and Thomas Hamilton, James VI's advocate, had counterparts earlier in the century in the libraries of printed books owned by such men as William Elphinstone, Robert Reid and Henry Sinclair.[10] In addition to these printed works numerous manuscripts were in circulation. The most important of these were manuscripts of *Regiam Majestatem* which were still being produced in the sixteenth century.[11] There is clear evidence of the use of *Regiam* before the lords of council although few citations of it were recorded during the 1520s.[12] Men of law certainly owned manuscript copies of it, often compiled with other material such as collections of old statutes and

---

6   *Prot. Bk. Grote* no. 107. McCalzeane was a graduate of St Andrews; there is no evidence that he himself studied abroad although he clearly had access to a reasonably good library.

7   Finlayson, *Clement Litill*, 6. Litill, Moscrop and Monypenny were all advocates.

8   Master George Crichton was legitimated in March 1554: *RSS*, iv, no. 2584. He was admitted advocate on 12 Nov. 1557: CS 6/29 fo. 55r.

9   The importance of the possession of books on professional advancement was demonstrated by the eminent Spanish lawyer, Doctor Alonso Diaz de Montalvo, who divided his books into works on canon law and civil law and then left them to his two grandsons instructing them to cast lots to determine which subject each should study and so which kind of lawyer each would become: Juan Beneyto Perez, 'The science of law in the Spain of the Catholic Kings', in R. Highfield ed. *Spain in the Fifteenth Century*, 279.

10   On Littil's library see Finlayson, *Clement Litill*; on Hamilton, see B. Hillyard '"Durkan and Ross' and beyond", in eds. A.A. MacDonald, M. Lynch and I.B. Cowan, *The Renaissance in Scotland* (Leiden, 1994), 367; as for Elphinstone, Reid and Sinclair see Durkan and Ross, 'Early Scottish Libraries', 5-167.

11   On the extant manuscripts, see Buchanan 'The MSS. of Regiam Majestatem: an experiment' (1937) *JR* 217. The treatise was not printed until Skene's editions of 1609.

12   It is cited by James Henryson in 1503: *ADC*, iii, 193; on the evidence for its use in practice, see MacQueen *Common Law* 89-98.

assises and *Quoniam Attachiamenta*. These collections formed core materials, designed for practical use, and were probably often bundled together for the aid those wishing to learn the practick.[13]

Nonetheless it is the case that direct evidence of authority being taken from the learned law does not often reach the record.[14] The reason is simply scribal practice: the focus was on noting procedural points and only rarely was the substance of arguments given or the authorities used cited.[15] These rare examples, such as the citation of Nicolas de Tudeschis, John de Ferrarriis and Johannes Andreae by the earl of Buchan's forespeaker George Stirling in 1503, or John Moscrop quoting Cicero to the the provost and bailies of Edinburgh in 1562, confirm that there is no reason to doubt that many of the texts in circulation were actually used in argument before the courts.[16] An impressive array of sources is quoted in Sinclair's *Practicks*.[17] But from the *acta* it is impossible to measure the influence which such writings had on the development of practick before the lords of session.[18] What is clear is that this practick was unique to the session. A similar range of authorities might have stood at the basis of procedure in contemporary courts abroad such as the *Reichskammergericht*, the *Parlement de Paris* and the *Grand Counseil de Malines*.[19] But what distinguish these courts are the particular rules developed by the courts themselves. There was a clear differentiation between the 'stile' or practick of the lords of session and the 'theorik of the legistes and canonistes'.[20] While the content of this practick certainly owed much to Romano-canonical sources and to those familiar with church procedure, it increasingly came to represent an independent body of rules in much the same way as has been argued in relation to the courts of the Low Countries that distinctive features emerged making the manner of litigation more or less unique.[21]

---

[13] It is clear that scribes involved in copying the manuscripts of *Quoniam* were producing texts for the practitioner's library: T.D. Fergus, *Quoniam Attachiamenta* (Stair Society, 1996), 95. Robert Galbraith compiled one of the surviving manuscripts containing this kind of material (see chapter six) and, as was mentioned in chapter three, James Foulis almost certainly owned another: *APS*, 192-3, 203.

[14] Murray, 'Sinclair's Practicks', 102.

[15] W.M. Gordon, 'The acts of the Scottish lords of council in the late fifteenth and early-sixteenth centuries: records and reports' in *Law Reporting in Britain* ed. C. Stebbings (London, 1995) 59.

[16] *ADC*, iii, 309-310 (cited by Murray, 'Sinclair's Practicks', 102); *Edin. Burgh Recs.*, iii, 149.

[17] See the sources cited by Murray, 'Sinclair's Practicks', 103. Dr Murray correctly points out that the impression gained from Balfour, of solid concentration on native sources, is misleading as an indication of the absence of more sophisticated legal knowledge.

[18] An example of the more typical reference to the learned law found in the *acta* occurred in 1517 when Thomas Hamilton, in relation to a summons of error, 'offerit to produce lawis baith civile & canoun makand the said summondis inept in the self becaus thir wes no mencioun of the day zeit nor place of the serving of the brief & retour': CS 5/29 fo. 83v: 19 Mar. 1517.

[19] R.C. Van Caenegem, 'The developed procedure of the second Middle Ages XI-XV Century' *Encyclopaedia of Comparative Law*, XVI, iii; C.H. van Rhee, 'Grand Council of Malines', 12-14.

[20] Sinclair, *Practicks*, c. 132: cited by Murray, 'Sinclair's Practicks', 102.

[21] Van Rhee, *Grand Council of Malines*, 1.6.

The technicality of the practick of the session during James V's reign was not yet sufficient to discourage litigants appearing personally, without a man of law, at least in relatively routine matters. In assessing this legal process from the viewpoint of the advocates most intimately involved with it, it is necessary to include discussion of the physical environment in which it operated and the practical difficulties faced by them in preparing cases for litigation.

The physical environment

Originally courts were often held in the open air in the vicinity of local strongholds. Churchyards were also a popular meeting place.[22] With the castle being the original *caput* of the sheriffdom, open air courts continued to be held, even into the sixteenth century, on 'motte-hills', the original sites of castles that had fallen into decay and been rebuilt nearby, as well as within the castles themselves.[23] As late as 1539, for instance, there is reference to the sheriff court of Perth being held 'at the Court hill of Skone'.[24] But by the end of the fifteenth century outdoor courts were rare and the castle had begun to give way to the burgh tolbooth or *praetorium* as the place where secular courts were customarily held.[25] For example, the head courts of the burgh of Glasgow met in the tolbooth by the fifteenth century[26]; in 1529 the sheriff of Ayr is recorded as sitting in the tolbooth of that burgh while a justice court was held in the tolbooth of Peebles and, in 1530, the regality court of Dunfermline sat 'in *pretorio* de kirkcaldy'.[27] In 1540 Master David Borthwick, a future king's advocate, is recorded as presenting letters from the king to the bailies, council and community of Haddington convened 'within the pretor' of the burgh.[28] A similar assembly of bailies, councillors and masters of the crafts was meeting within the tolbooth of Edinburgh in February 1518 when Adam Otterburn, common clerk of the burgh, rose from his seat to protest at

---

[22]   Elizabeth Ewan, *Townlife in Fourteenth Century Scotland* (Edinburgh 1990), 11; *Fife Court Bk.*, xix. It is even possible to find an example of procurators being constituted in the cemetery of Abernethy parish church in 1556: *Prot. Bk. Gaw,* no. 159.

[23]   *Fife Court Bk.,* introduction, xii–xiii .

[24]   Fraser, *Keir*, 364.

[25]   *Fife Court Bk.,* introduction, xix and Appendix I. Consistory courts were held in cathedral churches within each diocese; Glasgow consistory court, built on three storeys, projected from the southwest of Glasgow Cathedral: Macfarlane, *Elphinstone,* 61. The court of the official of Lothian sat in St Giles: Ollivant, *The Official,* 45. Men of law more associated with secular courts might still be present there on occasion e.g. Foulis and Marjoribankis were at a consistory court in St Giles in April 1521: NAS, Register House Charters, RH6/909.

[26]   Norman F. Shead, 'Glasgow: an ecclesiastical burgh', *The Scottish Medieval Town*, eds. M. Lynch, M. Spearman, G. Stell, (Edinburgh, 1988), 126.

[27]   *Prot. Bk. Ros,* no. 987 (Ayr); CS 5/39 fo. 64v (Peebles); CS 15/1 (Dunfermline) notarial instrument drawn up by George Gude. A year earlier, in March 1529, the bailies of the regality of Dunfermline met in the tolbooth of that burgh: CS 5/39 fo. 141r: 5 Mar. 1529.

[28]   NAS, Haddington Burgh Court Book (transcript), GD 1/413/1.

an attempt to usurp his right of appointing a deputy clerk; a stand for burghal independence that ended with triumphant shouts of 'Otterburn, Otterburn'.[29]

Given that tolbooths also functioned as prisons justiciary courts also came to be held within them. Thus, in Lauder in 1506 a charter was transumed in the court of Andrew, Lord Gray, the justiciar, meeting in the burgh tolbooth in the presence also of the justice-clerk and the king's advocate.[30] In the tolbooth of Dundee, in March 1531, Sir John Campbell of Lundie, sitting as justiciar-depute for the earl of Argyll, heard a case presented against John Ramsay accusing him of robberies and other crimes.[31] The man of law Master Thomas Marjoribankis was fined in a justiciary court held in the tolbooth of Edinburgh in July 1536 for failing to produce certain letters summoning his clients to appear before the justiciar charged with mutilation. Marjoribankis, having become surety to the justice-clerk that he would bring the letters to court, incurred the same penalty prescribed for the offence of his clients and was therefore forced to pay a large fine although he had a right of recourse against the accused.[32]

Although most burghs had a tolbooth by the early sixteenth century very few of these buildings survive in their original form. Many have been demolished, in whole or in part, and much re-building was done in the century following the reformation.[33] Nonetheless the pre-Reformation tolbooth, because of its importance within the burgh as council house, courthouse and prison, was normally placed in a central location. In Edinburgh the tolbooth had added significance. Built next to St Giles it was the site at which parliament assembled and where the lords of session met, as well as the building used for sittings of the burgh court.[34] It was also used for sheriff court business and not only by the sheriff of Edinburgh: the sheriffs of other areas, such as Stirling or Perth, also occasionally fenced their courts in the tolbooth of Edinburgh.[35] This explains why the lords of session, when

---

[29] *Prot. Bk. Strathauchin*, no. 292. Interestingly Francis Bothwell, Otterburn's neighbour, was one of those specifically named as having supported him. Another large meeting of prominent men of the burgh was called to assemble in the tolbooth in April 1516: *Edin. Burgh Recs.*, i., 160.

[30] NAS, GD150/269 (Morton Papers).

[31] NAS, Register House Charters , RH6/1066.

[32] *RSS* no. 2125. References appear to persons called before the justiciar in the tolbooth in the *acta* of the lords of council; for example, John Allerdes was called in 1526 'to underlie the law' for hurting David Balfour and drawing blood: CS 5/36 fo. 86r: 16 Aug. 1526.

[33] Stell, 'Urban buildings', in *The Medieval Scottish Town*, 63, states that the only surviving tolbooth' type structures date from the second half of the sixteenth century with the possible exception of the tolbooth tower in Crail. See also *Tolbooths and Town-Houses: Civic Architecture in Scotland to 1833* (Royal Commission on the Ancient and Historical Monuments of Scotland, 1996), 1–23.

[34] It was whilst on their way to the tolbooth one morning for judicial business that the two regents James, Archbishop of Glasgow, and James, earl of Arran, were attacked in the street in the 'cleanse the causeway' affair on 30 Apr. 1520: 'Discours Particulier d'Ecosse', *Miscellany II* (Stair Society, 1984), 127; Emond, 'Minority of James V', chapter six.

[35] For example, John Stewart, sheriff of Banff, held his court there in August 1488 (*Prot. Bk. Young* no. 111) and Thomas Stewart, sheriff of Perth, did the same in 1492 (*Prot. Bk. Young* no. 523). For a later

sitting in Edinburgh, mainly used the tolbooth but did not do so exclusively. It was perhaps a consequence of the diverse purposes to which that building was put that other venues for the lords within the vicinity of the High Street were occasionally used, such as the chancellor's house, Holyroodhouse or the chapter-house of the Friar's Preachers.[36]

Stell points out that in architectural terms the tolbooth was designed to be functional and to accommodate, as it had to, the town guard house and the weigh house as well as the council chamber and common prison.[37] This functionality tended to diminish the aesthetic value of tolbooths compared to churches which, as symbols of civic pride, were much more ornate; although it has been suggested that post-Reformation re-building, notably in Edinburgh, altered this trend.[38] Just after Christmas 1554 there was a short period of building activity repairing and enlarging Edinburgh's tolbooth and building a dwelling house for the jailer.[39] There was specific reference to the 'over hous' at this time and, two years later the burgh council convened in the 'Inner counsalhous of the ovir tolbuith'.[40]

Most legal business was performed below this level, on the first floor reached by a stairway from which general proclamations might be issued and where notices or tables might be attached to the tolbooth door.[41] Little is known about the chamber in which the court sat at this time. There was clearly a bar in the court and there are numerous references to persons standing at it and addressing the lords.[42] The macers (i.e. ushers) of the session controlled entry to the council chamber. Preserved in a manuscript in Edinburgh University

---

example, a court of the sheriffdom of Dumfries was held in Edinburgh's tolbooth in May 1552: *RMS*, iv, no., 1621.

[36] Holyroodhouse was used on one occasion at the king's command: CS 5/43 fo. 197v: 13 May 1532. But this use was not unique; see, for example, CS 5/35 fo. 131v: 30 Aug. 1525.

[37] G.Stell, 'The earliest tolbooths: a preliminary account' (1981) *PSAS* 446.

[38] R. Fawcett, *Architectural History of Scotland: Scottish Architecture from the Accession of the Stewarts to the Reformation 1371–1560* (Edinburgh, 1994) 278.

[39] *Old Edinburgh Club*, iv, (1911) 86.

[40] *Protocol Book of Alexander King* (transcript in Edinburgh City Archive), no. 109.

[41] *Fife Court Bk.*, introduction, xx. A good example of the way this was done occurs in 1542. A transumpt of a charter dating from the reign of William the Lion narrating a gift made to the abbey of Arbroath was to be registered in the books of the lords of session. A public edict was fixed to the tolbooth door instructing all persons with an interest in the matter to appear and make their objections between 1 March (presumably when the edict was presented) and 24 March. No one appeared and so the transumpt was registered on 25 March: *Yester Writs*, no. 593. In ecclesiastical courts, it appears that notices, for instance of cursings (excommunications) might be 'tikkat ... apoun kirk durris': CS 5/27 fo. 141v: 14 Jan. 1516. This is in line with Romano-canonical procedure: A. Engelmann, 'System of the Romano-canonical procedure', *Continental Legal History Series* vol. VII (London, 1928), 23.

[42] There also appears to have been a bar in the tolbooth of the Canongate where the regality court of Broughton sat. In 1490 William Blakfurd, Thomas Bell's prelocutor, moved from the bar to where the judge was seated, a thing which *'Willelmus non tenetur facere neque removere suos articulos pedum ubi sui tali seu talones steterunt'* (he was bound not to do nor to remove his toes where his heels stood), in order to examine a witness. On moving he 'came to the feet of the judge' indicating that the judge was sitting in an area that was elevated, looking down on those behind the bar of the court. This may also have been the position within Edinburgh's tolbooth: *Prot Bk. Young* nos. 342, 343.

Library are 'Directions frome the Lordis of Sessioun to the bailies of Edinburgh' in January 1604. These state that the bailies are to appoint one or two officers to stand at the outer door of the tolbooth when the lords were sitting to 'debarr all rascallis vagaboundis beggaris' and other undesirables from entering.[43] By that time they had been performing the same function for at least a century with apparent success.[44] The rule was that men of law were permitted to enter with their clients but had to leave with them while the lords considered their case in privacy.[45] When a member of the court was successfully objected to he had to pass from his colleagues towards the bar and was not permitted to vote with them.[46]

The judges were seated behind a large table which, around September 1557, was re-covered with four ells of green cloth.[47] Nearby perhaps sitting on 'a lang bynk' were, at the discretion of the chancellor, men able 'to leir practick'.[48] These would be the students and apprentices hoping to learn by observation. The scene that faced them would have been colourful even apart from the green coverings on the lords' chairs and table and the bright livery worn by the macers.[49] The lords, both spiritual and temporal, may have worn gowns relative to their social standing and the men of law may also have worn clothes appropriate to their position.[50] According to one sixteenth-century source, which may record an act of sederunt, advocates who were not appropriately dressed would not be heard before the lords.[51] The judges appear

---

[43] EUL, Laing MS III-388a fo. 105.

[44] I have only come across one instance of a person gaining access to the chamber without licence. This was 'the inopertune entering of robert betoun of creich within the counsalehous at his awn hand this being quiet ... all partyis being removit': CS 6/29 fo. 53v: 30 July 1557. Betoun was ordered to ward himself in Edinburgh castle for ten days and to pay £10 to be delivered to the grey friars. The lords also delayed the action which he had sought to pursue 'for the space of xxx sitting dayis'.

[45] The role of macers will be considered in the next section.

[46] CS 6/28 fo. 69v: 4 Feb. 1547.

[47] *Edin. Accts.*, 206. This table may have been that ordered to be made in 1532 'ane burd quadrangulare or rownd about the quhilk that may sit xviii personis eselie' *ADCP*, 375. But there is reference to 'the burd' used by the lords in 1527: CS 5/38 fo. 35v: 28 Nov. 1527.

[48] Hannay, *College of Justice*, 36.

[49] The receipt of livery by macers is regularly recorded in the Accounts of the Lord High Treasurer. For the dress of officers of arms see Charles J. Burnett, 'The Officers of Arms and Heraldic Art under King James the Sixth and First 1567-1625' (Unpublished M.Litt. dissertation, University of Edinburgh, 1992), i, 11. The names of twelve virtuous and honest men chosen by the Lyon King of Arms to act as messengers on 12 July 1527 are recorded in the *acta*: CS 5/37 fos. 157v-158r.

[50] In a well known statute of 1455 it was laid down that 'all men of lawe that ar forspekaris for the cost haif habitis of grene of the sassane of any tunykill and the slevis to be opyn as a tabart' (*APS*, ii, 43, c. 12). Despite the detailed description of this outfit, there is unfortunately no evidence that this act was ever enforced.

[51] This source, a manuscript in Edinburgh University Library (Laing MS. III-388a), is dated by Atholl Murray to about 1581: Murray, 'Sinclair's Practicks', 91. It contains, in addition to a version of Sinclair's Practicks, a copy of various Acts of Sederunt from June 1532. One undated entry 'Anent the habitis of the lordis and advocattis' is as follows: '*Item*, that the lordis bayth spirituale and temporall at all tyme quhen thai cum to the counsalhous have syk gownis everie man efferand to his estait and

to have sat in an elevated position and it is likely that dress was used, as in the case of heralds and messengers, in order to reinforce the social hierarchy and impress upon litigants the lords' position as representatives of the king. It is known that on the eve of the Reformation the lords were kept warm during the long winter days by coal supplied to them by Thomas Hall.[52] But, beyond this, there seem to be few near contemporary references to conditions inside the chamber. It is clear that those who had business before the lords waited outside the hall to be called to their presence. When the lords, in August 1526, assigned two days in the week 'to compeire in the tolbuith and sitt apoun privelegit actiounis', they instructed that 'all persounis that has sic actiounis a do [sic] awayte apoun the said dayis that justice may be ministerit as efferis.'[53] A diagram of the layout inside the tolbooth dating from 1629 indicates that there was an ante-room as large as the court room itself set aside as a waiting area for those with business before the court.[54]

In Edinburgh a row of booths, the luckenbooths, ran east from the tolbooth along the north side of St Giles and down the High Street. In the early sixteenth century these booths, along with the booths rented within the tolbooth itself, were described as 'offices' rather than shops; places where notaries and men of law might do business.[55] It is clear that from at least the mid-fifteenth century Edinburgh's tolbooth contained various booths which were let to burgesses. In 1482, at around the same time as a booth is first recorded as being used as a prison, the 'eistmaist' booth *ex boreali parte pretorii* was let to Master Richard Lawson who was later to become justice-clerk general.[56] Other men of law appear to have held booths within close proximity to the tolbooth and the luckenbooths and much business was recorded there. In 1532 there is reference to a booth on the north side of the tolbooth that was the dwelling place of Thomas Marjoribankis.[57]

The luckenbooths, from 1508, tended to have wooden fronts in common with other buildings along the High Street facing north and forming what

---

utherwayes to have na voic and the advocattis inlykwess or ellis to haiv na audience' (fo. 6r). This act may conceivably belong to the 1530s but it does not seem to be recorded elsewhere.

52 *Edin. Accts.*, 305.

53 CS 5/36 fo. 91r: 26 Aug. 1526.

54 Lowther, *Our Journall into Scotland anno Domini 1629* (Edinburgh, 1894). There was also a small conference room in which private business was transacted.

55 P. Miller, 'The origins and early history of the old tolbuith of Edinburgh, the heart of Midlothian and the luckenbooths', (1886) *PSAS* 372.

56 *Edin. Burgh Recs.* 41-2.; for reference to the prison, see (1886) *PSAS* 370.

57 *Prot. Bk. Foular*, iii, no. 412. In 1557 agreement was reached concerning assythment between Robert Weir and Thomas Hammil for the mutilation of Robert's thumb and forefinger in 1550. The agreement was made in the 'tavern' of Marjoribankis on the north side of the High Street; obviously not the same as the building mentioned in 1532, but Thomas Kincragy was among the witnesses: *Prot. Bk. Grote*, no. 93.

have been described as piazzas, cutting the width of the street slightly.[58] The booths themselves, half the width of the tolbooth, appear like the tolbooth itself to have been built on more than one level.[59] Thus in 1521 Adam Otterburn resigned in the hands of Gilbert Lauder, bailie, his booth 'under the stair of the land in Buthraw' together with another booth above the stair.[60] The typical town house of the period was built of wattle or timber and, although stone building among the more prosperous was growing more common by the sixteenth century the luckenbooths appear to have been at this time quite flimsy structures.[61] Mention was even made before the lords in December 1525 of the wind having blown down the 'luckin buthis' the previous Epiphany.[62]

In January 1531 there was a resignation of land in the 'Buithraw' on the south side of the High Street by a certain Andrew Borthwick with the consent of his curator, John Pardouin. Pardouin was himself one of the macers of the session but more notable is the fact that this land was next to areas belonging to Adam Otterburn, the king's advocate, and James McCalzeane, father of the advocate, Thomas.[63] James McCalzeane, himself a writer, had held his booth for at least a decade and seems to have been in receipt of rent from another booth nearby which interest he sold in February 1523 to the hospital of the Virgin in St Mary's Wynd.[64] Ultimately James resigned his interests in his two booths in the 'buthraw' on his death-bed to his second son, Master Thomas, much to the annoyance of Thomas's elder brother.[65] Among these merchant

---

[58] Miller, 'Tolbooth', *PSAS* (1886) 362. It has been plausibly suggested that the road prior to 1508 was 30 feet in breadth being narrowed by 7 feet thereafter. This was still wider than the present day High Street at this point.

[59] There is reference in a charter of sale by James McCalzeane in February 1523 to a low booth in the 'Buithraw': NAS, Register House Charters, RH6/934. This presupposes that some booths were built on more than one level as does the reference in 1556 to a 'lower' booth on the north side of the High Street next to the foreland of Master Thomas McCalzeane, James's son: *Prot. Bk. Alexander King*, no. 118.

[60] *Prot. Bk. Strauthauchin*, no. 330. Sasine of these booths was given to James McCalzeane and the booth beneath the stairs may have been that mentioned in the previous footnote. It is interesting to note that this booth stood between areas occupied by Alexander Mauchane, whose sister was married to Gilbert Lauder and whose son, also Alexander, had become a prominent advocate by the 1550s; and John Young, a notary public: *Prot. Bk. Alexander King*, no. 191. Lauder's son was Henry Lauder, another prominent advocate (for whom, see chapter eight). This illustrates well the already developing links between 'legal families' in Edinburgh at the time.

[61] Fawcett, *Architecture*, 282. For the significance of stone building as an indication of social standing see G. Stell, 'Architecture: the changing needs of society', *Scottish Society in the Fifteenth Century*, ed. J.M. Brown (London, 1977), 163-4, 181.

[62] CS 5/35 fo. 169v: 1 Dec. 1525. Mentioned again at CS 5/37 fo. 174r: 23 July 1527.

[63] *Prot. Bk. Foular*, iii, no. 284.

[64] NAS, Register House Charters, RH6/934.

[65] CS 6/10 fo. 88r: 1 June 1538. The elder son, Sir James McCalzeane, designed as a chaplain, failed in a bid to have the resignation annulled in June 1538.

booths on the north side of the tolbooth included in 1520 one held by Francis Bothwell, one of the original senators in 1532.[66]

Although the leading men of law were no strangers to the tolbooths of other burghs, the tolbooth of Edinburgh in the sixteenth century was without doubt the centre of their activity in Scotland. Edinburgh's economic and political predominance dates at least from the reign of James III, a king who spent much of his time in Edinburgh and who oversaw the establishment there of the royal administration.[67] By 1567 it was acknowledged that 'of procuratouris and advocattis the gretast plentie ar at Edinburgh.'[68] What this meant in practical terms was illustrated in 1556 when the burgh of Aberdeen found itself in dispute with the Crown over the right to control fishing in the Dee. The burgh council sent six commissioners to Edinburgh 'to consult with men of law, experience, and knawledge, the best way for defence of the said actioune, and to constitut procuratouris, ane or ma, to that effect'.[69] It is significant that they did not send men of law; they sent burgesses to hire men of law. But the concentration of legal talent swarming around the central court had by then been evident for generations.

Procedure before the Lords of Council

The first thing required by any procedure is the articulation of a dispute. In Scottish terms some 'richt' had to be infringed or some 'wrang' had to be done. By far the most typical type of action involved debt, spuilzie or wrongful occupation of land. The client became a client typically when someone else came on to his land and carried off something of value to him: a few bolls of wheat, barley or oats, or, if the client was a man of substance, perhaps some horses[70] or jewellery or even one of his daughters.

The client, feeling aggrieved, now made contact with a man of law.[71] This might have been done directly by the client going to one of the booths in the vicinity of the tolbooth mentioned earlier or by letter or intermediary. Once contact was made the situation would have been explained and the appropriate course of action agreed or, at least, the desire of a particular outcome expressed. Normally the achievement of this outcome involved the

---

[66]　*Prot. Bk. Foular*, ii, no. 75. For business being conducted in the chamber of James McCalzeane see *Prot. Bk. Foular*, iii, no. 734.

[67]　Normal Macdougall, *James III: A Political Study* (Edinburgh, 1982), 304, points out that Edinburgh, with its financiers, became the obvious choice as the permanent home for the royal administration.

[68]　Hannay, *The College of Justice*, 138.

[69]　*Abdn. Counc.*, 294-5.

[70]　For example, CS 5/26 fo. 5v: 30 Sept. 1513: wrongful intromission with 'tua gray horsis worth xx libratas & ane quhyte hors worth ane hundreth merkis'; CS 5/34 fo. 4v: 11 Sept. 1523: spuilzie of 'ane blak horss price xl libratas ane gray hors price xl libratas and of utheris horsis...'.

[71]　The word client was a contemporary term. For example, there is a protest by Master Robert Galbraith 'for him self and his clientis': CS 5/34 fo. 129v: 28 Feb. 1524.

purchase of 'kingis lettres' from the chancery. A summons was issued and the action was tabled. This means that a note of the action was written in summary form in a table along with a list of other actions to be heard. The names of the parties would certainly be noted, perhaps a note of the pursuer's procurator may have been included with a brief description of the nature of the summons. At this time, or on a later occasion, the procurator would be constituted in line with the procedure described in chapter two.

Normally parties appeared by a single procurator, or appeared in person in conjunction with only one forespeaker. But it was not uncommon to find two procurators in attendance, although sometimes only one would be a man of law. For example, Thomas Hunter appeared by his procurators Master Adam Hunter and Adam Otterburn.[72] James Dunbar's procurators were Sir Alexander Dunbar, vicar of Crail, and the man of law Master James Simson.[73] Sir William Murray of Tullibardine appeared by his son, Patrick, and Robert Leslie, his procurators in an action of spuilzie brought against him by the abbot of Culross.[74] Two days previously Leslie had asked the lords for time to produce an annualrent by which William claimed that lands had been held of the abbey for a century. Leslie admitted that goods had been removed from these lands, but when pressed he refused to swear that he would produce William's alleged deed. At this point there was no mention of William's son being present although he may have been. It is clear, and to be expected, that Leslie was the more active of the two. Slightly more unusual was litigation involving Peter Carmichael who appeared by his wife, Eufame Wemyss, and Thomas Hamilton.[75] Hamilton had earlier acted as Eufame's forespeaker and, again, there is little doubt that he was in charge of presenting her case. The tendency to name family members in letters of procuratory was followed through in practice as these examples demonstrate, although their attendance in conjunction with an advocate indicates that their position was probably supervisory, and that the lead would be taken by the man of law. Some litigants preferred to use two men of law as their procurators. In May, 1517, Patrick Home was 'lawfully' warned to answer a summons brought against him by Elizabeth Martin, lady Fastcastle, by his procurators, Master Thomas Hamilton and Master Robert Galbraith, 'personaly apprehendit'.[76] Clearly the macer who issued the warning could not personally apprehend Patrick. This does not mean that both Hamilton and Galbraith would have appeared on Patrick's behalf; if named jointly and severally, only one would have sufficed and, as it happened, neither did so. By contrast, Walter Tyry was represented

[72] CS 5/30 fo. 23r: 15 June 1517.
[73] CS 5/29 fo. 98v: 17 Mar. 1517.
[74] CS 5/30 fo. 239r: 18 Mar. 1518.
[75] CS 5/30 fo. 148v: 25 Aug. 1517; Cf. CS 5/33 fo. 129v: 27 Jan. 1523.
[76] CS 5/30 fo. 5r: 22 May 1530.

by both William Scott of Balwearie and Robert Leslie in a case which he brought against James Fenton of Ogill although the procurators appeared merely to acknowledge that a summons raised by Walter should be held *pro deleto*.[77] There are several other references to procurators in the plural acting before the lords of council. Lord Seton had it recorded that William Cranston's procurators had produced royal letters suspending a process of recognition.[78] Less ambiguously, Robert Galbraith and Thomas Kincraigie both appeared as procurators for John McGillies in a case in 1527.[79] There are also indications that men of law might take turns to act in cases. For example, John Lethame acted as prelocutor for Janet Rutherford in an action brought against her by Helen Rutherford.[80] During the course of the argument, reference was made to a concession granted by James Foulis, Janet's prelocutor in an earlier diet of the same case. The same litigant could also use different men of law in respect of separate cases, even when those cases were concurrent. For example, Richard Maitland of Lethington used Robert Leslie as his forespeaker in an action, alleging the spuilzie of two horses, which he brought against William Duntreath of Edmonstone in September 1523.[81] The following January, Thomas Hamilton was Maitland's forespeaker against John, Lord Hay of Yester.[82]

But however many procurators appeared, or were constituted, the litigant was required to ratify prospectively whatever his procurator might do in conformity with the authority granted under the procuratory. Most clients, trusting to God and the justness of their cause, and relying on their man of law, now disappeared from the record. A minority, however, re-appeared later when their case was called.

The summons tables

In the meantime the summons was served, calling the defender to appear on a certain day to hear and answer the allegations against him. The defender could then constitute his own procurators. Sometime before the appointed day the table, having been drafted, was fixed to the door of the tolbooth for public display.[83] If the summons was not tabled on the tolbooth door but was

---

[77] CS 5/33 fo. 27v: 19 Nov. 1522. Walter had been served to the lands of Drumkilbo, a retour that James disputed. James had evidently obtained a decreet suspending the retour. Walter than issued a summons appealing against the decreet. It was admitted that this summons was for some reason invalid (*pro deleto*) and no answer should be made until a new summons was made.

[78] CS 5/24 fo. 47r: 3 Dec. 1512.

[79] CS 5/37 fo. 62v: 29 Mar. 1527. *McGillies v Richard Lekky of Wester Lekky and Malcolm, Lord Fleming.*

[80] CS 5/36 fo. 126v: 7 Dec. 1526.

[81] CS 5/34 fos. 4r–4v, 6v: 7, 9 and 11 Sep. 1523.

[82] CS 5/34 fo. 60v: 27 Jan. 1524.

[83] According to John Lethame in one case a summons had been, on command of the king, 'tabulit on the tolbuith dur be ane tikkat and had remanit apoun the samin be the space of xvj dais with the mair': CS

subsequently called then the whole process was null.[84] If the summons was tabled but the table was not fixed to the tolbooth door or, presumably, otherwise displayed ('tikkatit'), then the defender might have a delay to answer the summons.[85] The lords of council, however, were on occasion not above proceeding with a summons that had not first been tabled,[86] or giving precedence to a summons which should have been heard later according to its position in the table.[87]

It was probably the wisest course to enter a protest just in case an opponent sought to advance the hearing of his summons. Robert Leslie, forespeaker for Gilbert McDowall, adopted this tactic when he protested that a summons raised by Patrick Sinclair against Gilbert had only been libelled within the previous two months and did not appear on the table and so his client should not have to answer it. Gilbert, although he had come to Edinburgh, had done so not to defend Patrick's summons but to defend other actions against him.[88]

The word 'libell' was used in both verb and noun form. The libel was a statement of the grounds on which the action was brought.[89] Its use may be illustrated by reference to one particular action in which the compromise was reached following arbitration.[90] Once the decreet arbitral had been issued, however, one of the parties reclaimed from it back to the lords of session. The written reclamation functioned as a libel. However the reclaimer argued that, although he could not produce another libel apart from the reclamation, under

5/37 fo. 49v: 26 Mar. 1527. The abuse of using 'tikkets' - notices posted on the tolbooth door - to promote the calling of a summons which did not appear in the table is adverted to by Hannay, *College of Justice*, 36. The pressure on the lords to keep to the order of the table rendered any process following upon a summons called by 'tikket' invalid according to a decreet in February 1529 (CS 5/39 fo. 111v). Before this it would appear that the use of 'tikkets' *per se* was not an abuse and they seem to have been countenanced notwithstanding this decreet. Sixteen days' notice is excessive; the norm, for actions involving the king, was set down in 1532 as being three days: *ADCP*, 378. The three day notice period appears to have been used generally: for example, the earl of Cassillis was charged by the macer Oliver Maxton on Wednesday 13 Aug. 1527 to defend himself against an action raised by Hugh Campbell on Friday 16 August. Campbell did not appear on 16 August and, a week later, Cassillis, having still not been called, entered the familiar protest that he should not be required to answer until freshly summoned: CS 5/37 fos. 205r, 213v: 17 and 23 Aug. 1527.

84 CS 5/34 fo. 82v: 5 Feb. 1524. The summons, once tabled, may have been marked by the scribe in some way to indicate its appearance on the table; on one occasion Robert Leslie alleged that a certain summons was 'nethir tablit nor tikat': CS 5/34 fo. 110v: 22 Feb. 1524.

85 CS 5/37 fo. 56v: 27 Mar. 1527: Robert Leslie 'askit instrument that the table was nocht on the dur & at he desirit viij dais'. Summonses could be 'tikkatit or tabilit' according to the rules laid down in 1532 although the 'tikketing' would presumably require to have been authorised: *ADCP*, 378.

86 E.g. CS 5/34 fo. 129v: 28 Feb. 1524: 'Maister Robert galbraith for him self and his clientis protestit that gif the lordis wald proceid apoun the summondis raisit be alexander forestar aganis James m^ccalzeane and thame the samin nocht beand tabulit for remeid.'

87 CS 5/41 fo. 20r: 18 Mar. 1530.

88 CS 5/36 fo. 133r: 11 Dec. 1526. Leslie next unsuccessfully sought to argue, three months later, that he need not answer the summons until his client's expenses were paid: CS 5/37 fo. 60v: 28 Mar. 1527.

89 For the libel in the church courts see Ollivant, *The Court of the Official*, 100; Brundage, *The Medieval Canon Law* 130.

90 CS 5/37 fos. 161r, 164r: 15 and 16 July 1527.

the common law he could 'supple his reclamatioune and support and eike the samin as he plesit'.[91] In other words, he argued that he had the right to modify the grounds on which he claimed the decreet arbitral was not valid. Whether he would have had a similar right to modify the libel of the summons is not clear; and it is also unclear whether a case once presented might be substantially modified.

Once all the summonses on a table had been called and dealt with, often simply by being continued to another day, the next table would be called. Sometimes things did not run smoothly. A summons might be called in a table before all the summonses in the old table had been called. This would invite the argument that the new summons should not be heard the old table being 'unendit becaus ther is divers summondis theron as yit dependand nother under continewatioun nor desert'.[92] In one exchange, it was argued by Robert Leslie that a summons against his client was identical to a summons which had been 'lang syne lyk taiblit' by the same pursuer and which had later been renounced by that pursuer's advocate. This he offered to prove 'be the taibler & certane lordis thir sittand'.[93] Despite this argument, and Leslie's attempt to have the question of whether or not the two summonses were identical referred to the pursuer's oath, the lords ordered him to answer the summons.

Despite frequent statements by the lords of session of their aspiration to keep to the order of the table, and reminders from men of law that summonses should only be called according to the table, actions tabled to be heard on a particular day might nonetheless be heard on some other day.[94] For example, an action raised by the king was continued to a Monday when it was to be called and have process notwithstanding the fact, as the lords pointed out, that Monday 'is nocht the kingis day'.[95] But it appears that this was done with the consent of the defender's procurator. In another action a summons raised by the king and Robert Orrock, and tabled to be called on the king's day, was called on another day. James Foulis protested on the defender's behalf. Henry Spittall, procurator for Orrock, admitted that the summons was in the 'kingis table' but alleged it had been called on the king's day and continued (i.e. adjourned) to the instant day and so should have process. Foulis responded that even though the summons had been continued his client had not been

---

[91]   CS 5/37 fo. 194r: 9 Aug. 1527; CS 5/38 fo. 83v: 20 Dec. 1527.
[92]   *Morton Registrum,* ii, 287: 16 Apr. 1543.
[93]   CS 5/37 fo. 32v: 19 Mar. 1537. This entry is difficult to decipher; the writing is slightly compressed and side notes have been added in a confusing way. The central issue, although not stated in the record, appears to be personal bar: Leslie seems to be arguing that the renunciation by Galbraith bound the pursuer and so an identical summons was not competent. As to the 'taibler' his identity is unknown although it appears here that he may have been one of the lords. It was presumably the tabler who recorded on each tabled summons the word 'tabulit' on the reverse side of the signet. There is another reference to him in 1532: *ADCP,* 378 and there are also references in Nov. 1528: CS 5/39 fos. 2v, 5v.
[94]   For such reminders, see CS 5/36 fo. 112r: 1 Dec. 1526; and CS 5/37 fo. 74r: 1 Apr. 1527.
[95]   CS 5/37 fo. 55r: 27 Mar. 1527.

present and had not consented to the continuation and therefore under the law it should not be heard. In the end the lords decided that the process should be heard the following day.[96]

No copies of the table survive, but something is known of how it would have been set out. Firstly there appeared a list of those causes that were privileged. This might be a sizeable list: in 1525 Janet Rutherford wrote to the lords concerning a summons brought against her stating that the summons had been[97]

> tablit on the tolbuithe dur in the latter end of the privlegiate table and thir is to be callit befoir it in the said table fourty summondis or thirby... And I dissasentit expreslie to the calling of it quhill the remanent of the saidis tablit summondis befour it be callit.[98]

Actions involving the king, strangers, recent spuilzie or rescinding of decrees or of letters for inordinate process and entry to superiorities were privileged.[99] In February 1538 Thomas Marjoribankis produced a royal letter before the lords granting to 'advocattis' the same 'privilege and ordour of table' as enjoyed by the lords of session and prelates thus widening still further the range of privileged causes.[100] The table then listed the remainder of the actions and this may have run to dozens of cases, covering the period during which the court was expected to sit.[101] On Wednesdays the king's business was attended to[102]; on Saturdays bills of complaint were dealt with so as not to

---

[96]   CS 5/37 fo. 41v: 21 Mar. 1527.
[97]   The summons related to the 'retreting of ane decreet' which Janet had earlier obtained. That explains why it was a privileged summons.
[98]   CS 5/35 fo. 79r: 7 July 1525.
[99]   Hannay, *College of Justice,* 203, 213. In 1527 Robert Galbraith distinguished between the 'previleget table' and the 'unprevileget table' (CS 5/37 fo. 82r); taken together with the reference to the 'kingis table' already mentioned and, in the 1540s, the 'puir folkis table' (Sinclair, *Practicks* no. 249, fo. 88; also no. 315 fo. 115) this may indicate either one table which was subdivided or, more likely, a number of tables all in use simultaneously and, presumably, all fixed to the tolbooth door at the same time. There are instances of the 'tabillar' being instructed to place all summonses raised by and against a particular party in a separate table by themselves. An example of this occurred in November 1528 when Malcolm, Lord Fleming, was unable to remain and 'vaik' upon the session because of unrest in his own lands and actions concerning him were all put in a separate table to be called at a later date so that he might depart the king's service temporarily to restore order at home: CS 5/39 fo. 5v: 14 Nov. 1528.
[100]   *ADCP,* 465. Saturday was the day on which summonses in 'the prelatis tabill' were called early in Mary's reign: CS 7/1/1/ fo. 173r: 15 Jan. 1543.
[101]   In one case Robert Leslie that a summons should not be called because it was 'ferr doune in the table' and there were 'mony aboune uncallit': CS 5/36 fo. 152v: 18 Dec. 1526.
[102]   CS 5/35 fo. 50r: 21 June 1525. Any decree given on a summons called on a Wednesday that did not involve the king was to be null. There seems to have been some doubt about this before the lords clarified the matter. On 19 June Henry Spittal argued that a summons issued against his clients was principally at the king's instance and had been called on a day that was 'nocht the kingis day in the sessioune' and so should be called again when that day arose. He specifically alleged that calling the summons on the wrong day 'was contrar the tenour of the act of parliament maid apoun tabuling of summondis'. Gilding the lily, Henry 'presentlie requirit the clerk of registre and his deputis to deliver to

interfere with the hearing of the tabled summonses during the rest of the week.[103]

The initial trial procedure

When the day scheduled for the hearing of the case arrived, and after having been summoned himself by the ringing of the bell in St Giles early in the morning, the chancellor would have begun by dealing with cases adjourned from the last diet. Then he would have read out the new summonses in the order in which they appeared in the table.[104] If neither party nor their representatives appeared when the case was called the chancellor would simply call the next summons.[105] The macer positioned on the floor of the chamber would then be ordered to call each case several times at the outer door of the council house.[106] In the *acta* the absence of a litigant is always indicated by the formula that he or she was 'lauchfullie warnit to this actioun oftymes callit be ane maissar and nocht comperit'.[107] When the case was called, it perhaps would have been this macer who conducted the parties and/or their men of law to stand before the bar of the court.[108] As they entered they passed through the outer door, guarded by two macers, and then an inner door, again guarded by two macers. No one else could enter without leave of the court on pain of being summarily warded.[109] So, for example, in July 1540 the king's advocate

---

him the autentik copy of the act of parliament maid laidie anent tabuling of summondis' only to meet the response that, in fact, 'thir was nocht sic ane act': CS 5/35 fo. 44v: 19 June 1525. In August 1526 the lords assigned Wednesday and Friday weekly to privileged actions: CS 5/36 fo. 91r, but in May 1532 Fridays were set aside for the king's matters: *ADCP*, 375.

[103] CS 5/35 fo. 53r: 23 June 1525. In the 1540s there appears to have been a 'puir folkis table': Sinclair, *Practicks* no. 249 fo. 88; see also no. 315 fo. 115.

[104] This appears to have been the customary practice. The treasurer of Edinburgh paid 10 shillings to 'Hanislie' (Ainslie?) the bell-ringer for ringing the bell at nine in the morning for convening the lords in the tolbooth in 1556/7: *Edin. Accts.*, 206. It appears as though the lords convened at eight in the morning from 1 March to 1 August, except on 'dayes of preiching' when they convened at nine (until eleven); and in the winter, from 4 Nov. until 1 March, they convened at nine (until twelve). The seventeenth-century source of this information, Lord Fountainhall's Collection – 'Notes and Observations gatherit out of the buikis of sederunt of the Lordis of Session', gives an act of sederunt but sadly is not specific as to its date: EUL, Laing MS III-388a fo. 2v. It should be added that the lords regularly also sat in the afternoons, often with the sederunt *post meridiem* differing slightly from that *ante meridiem*.

[105] This might result in a case lower in the table being reached earlier than expected. The chancellor on one occasion asked that it be recorded that he had read all the summonses in the table down to the case of the Heirs of Blacater v Master Patrik Blacater and that no parties had appeared to pursue or defend in any of those cases: CS 5/35 fo. 83v: 13 July 1525.

[106] CS 6/1 fo. 98r (31 July 1532) which refers to a party 'beand lauchfullie callit at the counsalehouss dure diverss tymes'. Provision was made for a bell to be used to call the macers: *ADCP*, 375.

[107] This phrase, or variants of it, is found throughout the *acta*.

[108] CS 6/2 fo. 203r: 25 June 1533.

[109] CS 5/42 fo. 53r: 14 Feb. 1531.

and another procurator had to be admitted by permission of the lords to plead defences in an action in which their clients had an interest.[110]

At this stage, there were several possibilities. The client was not present but the procurator was; the procurator was present but so was the client; the procurator was not present but the client was; the client had not constituted a procurator but was present to represent himself; or the client was simply not present at all and there was no procurator to represent him. If the pursuer or his man of law failed to appear or, for some reason—such as excommunication—could not appear, then the defender would protest that his client should not be required to answer the summons until newly summonsed and that the other party shuold meet his expenses.[111] In one case Master Thomas Marjoribankis complained that he 'had remanyt lang upoun the calling' of a summons of recent spuilzie and the lords admitted his protest that his client's expenses should be paid and a new summons issued.[112] But this was relatively unusual: for obvious reasons, it was far more common for the defender or his procurator to make no appearance at all than it was for them to be kept waiting. Another possibility that might arise was that both parties, having appeared ready for their case to proceed, were not heard because the lords refused or failed to call the summons. Robert Galbraith, procurator for the poor tenants of the abbey of Glenluce, protested that any detriment suffered by his clients because of the failure of the archbishop of Glasgow (i.e. the chancellor), and the rest of the lords, to call their case should be ascribed to the fault of the lords. The case, a long-standing dispute with the bishop of Galloway, had already been adjourned on several occasions and the day on which Galbraith made his protest was the day that had been assigned for final judgement. Galbraith stated that although he had remained until six o'clock in the evening he had been unable to obtain process in the matter. Consequently, as he alleged, the lords had thereby incurred excommunication in terms of papal letters that had been granted to his clients and previously produced in court. This was an unusual protest and, if Galbraith is to be believed, the lords' failure to call the action was wilful rather than due to the pressure imposed by a high case-load.[113]

Little is known about the contemporary seating arrangement in the tolbooth or the Chancellor's residence or wherever else the lords happened to be

[110] CS 6/13 fo. 107r: 20 July 1540.
[111] An example of a pursuer repelled *ab agendo* due to cursing is found at CS 6/1 fo. 76r: 17 July 1532.
[112] CS 5/42 fo. 122r: 16 Mar. 1531. Such protests were extremely common and almost always admitted by the lords. They provide an example of men of law seeking *not* to prolong litigation by demanding that the party which has kept the defender waiting be required to go to the expense of starting his action again by obtaining a new summons. Attempts by lawyers to accelerate proceedings were not uncommon in the church courts: see Helmholz, 'Ethical standards for advocates and proctors', in ibid., *The Canon Law and the Law of England* (London, 1987), 49–50.
[113] CS 5/37 fo. 78r: 2 Apr. 1527.

sitting. The pleaders—amateur or professional—stood at the bar and presumably this was an area facing the seated lords who generally numbered at least six in the 1520s. Lords, clerks, macers and pleaders would all, however, have required space, although the number of lords of session actually in attendance varied: for example, in one case involving an act of parliament controlling the importation of books into Scotland, the lords present held that 'thai war our [i.e. over] few at that tyme to deliver thirapoun the said act'.[114]

Audience in the council chamber

The parties and their procurators would have waited outside the council chamber before being called to transact their business. In 1511 it was complained that justice was being hindered by the 'multitud of peple that cumis in the consale hous makand gret noys and misreule'; although many of these people would have been engaged in commerce rather than law, with the tolbooth the centre of Edinburgh's bustling market place.[115] There were occasional supplications to the king by those in his service who could not spare the time to 'waik (wait) apoun the table & diettis' of the session and so requested their cases to be heard immediately.[116] Some waited longer than others. In December 1516, Robert Leslie protested that his clients had been summoned to 'ane schort day' in October at the instance of John, Lord Hay of Yester, and had since then remained waiting for the summons to be called but lord Hay would not pursue it.[117] The parties awaiting the pleasure of the lords of council were as diverse as the business that they sought to bring to the lords' attention. They ranged from Marion Andrew, waiting with her mother Janet Lethame to petition for curators *ad litem* to be appointed for the duration of her minority;[118] to leading figures in the realm such as the Marischall,[119] and experienced men of law receiving last minute instructions from anxious clients

---

[114] CS 5/26 fo. 180v: 26 Jan. 1514. This was not an isolated example of a deficiency in the numbers of the lords of council in the sederunt: see, for instance, CS 6/28 fo. 80v (14 Mar. 1547), where Mr James McGill 'becaus thai war nocht now of nomer desirit the lordis to byd quhill that war sufficient nomer', and CS 5/43 fo. 118v (13 Dec. 1541) where in answer to the claim that no decision should be made until all those ordained to the session were present it was alleged that the most part of the lords temporal ordained for the session were present. In November 1532 three extraordinary lords were named to be 'ekit' to the lords 'becaus thar is divers deid sum seik & sum away': CS 6/2 fo. 5v: 16 Nov. 1532.

[115] Hannay, *College of Justice*, 21. H.L. MacQueen, 'The temples of Themis', unpublished address to the Old Edinburgh Club, 1996.

[116] CS 5/37 fo. 12r: 5 Feb. 1527, an example in which Archibald Douglas of Kilspindie, the king's treasurer, was granted the privilege of having his summons called 'without ony delay of table or diettis' in a letter from the king to the lords because 'of oure speciall service daily & hourlie to be done to ws'.

[117] CS 5/28 fo. 68r. Walter Scott of Branxholm was also called to underly the law 'at ane schort day' (CS 5/37 fo. 191r: 8 Aug. 1527) i.e. he was summoned to enter appearance at short notice.

[118] CS 5/34 fo. 160v: 28 Apr. 1524.

[119] CS 5/40 fo. 28v: 13 May 1529.

until called to appear. Men of law may have waited outside the lords' chamber hoping to be admitted into actions in which their clients potentially had an interest in order to plead defences or to make protests.[120]

The man of law had no greater right to be present than his client had. Once the arguments had been made, and the client had to withdraw while the lords debated the merits of the case and decided upon their interlocutor, the man of law had to withdraw as well. They were only permitted to return once the lords were agreed and then only to hear the interlocutor being pronounced. The length of time that it took to present an argument cannot readily be deduced from the records.[121] The clerks recorded major procedural steps but most of their entries record occasions upon which one or other side 'askit instrumentis', or made protests. Asking instruments was simply a technique to ensure that the clerk would record the procedural step then being taken, or the particular objection being raised, and so preserve it for future reference. It was commonly done even outwith the context of a legal dispute. Registering a deed for preservation, in which the maker of the deed or his procurator appeared and asked the lords to register the deed, was very common and the text of numerous deeds are copied into the *acta* for this purpose. They would have been copied either by the clerk register himself or, more likely, by his depute Sir Alexander Scott.[122] Whether parties entered with their own notaries is doubtful although an act of parliament in 1540, regulating the practice in sheriff courts, suggests that parties did bring their own notaries with them and that this caused confusion with conflicting instruments being recorded.[123]

Initial objections

The first thing a procurator might do was to raise an objection against the lords hearing the case. This could involve one of two things: attacking the jurisdiction of the lords or objecting to one or more lords as being partial judges. There are several examples of objection being raised to the lords' jurisdiction. Most obviously this might be done on behalf of a cleric. Thomas Marjoribankis, procurator for the abbot of Holyrood, called to warrant an

---

[120] For example, CS 6/13 fo. 107r: 20 July 1540; Henry Lauder, king's advocate and Hugh Rigg, procurator for William Cunningham of Glengarnock 'desirit to be admittit for thir enteres' to an action for spuilzie involving parties who were not their clients. They then put forward defences in the matter. At this date Lauder, as king's advocate, had been granted the right to be present in the chamber but Rigg had not.

[121] In one case, presumably to save time, a charter which was produced was 'held as redd': CS 5/26 fo. 118r: 29 Mar. 1514.

[122] Scott appears by name in March 1526 along with Mr James Douglas another notary: CS 5/36 fo. 8v: 13 Mar. 1526; he appears designed as 'deput to the clerk of Reg[ist]re' a year later: CS 5/27 fo. 55r: 17 Aug. 1515. For a deed registered by the clerk register himself see CS 5/37 fo. 53r: 27 Mar. 1527.

[123] *APS*, ii, 360.

assignation to John Carmichael of the vicarage of Crawford-Lindsay, alleged that 'becaus the said abbot was ane spiritual man he suld nocht be haldin to ansuer in the said mater befor the lordis but befor his jugis competent'.[124] The argument was unsuccessful as most such arguments appear to have been.

Failure to object to the court when initially raising exceptions against the summons meant that the exception could not be raised at all. Dilatory exceptions, that is, objections against the form of action, had to be raised first and in a particular order with exceptions against the judge to be made first.[125] So when Robert Leslie objected to a summons on the basis that it had been called without first appearing in the table, his opponent James Foulis protested that he should not then be allowed to raise an exception against the judges.[126] That explains why Thomas McCalzeane in one case protested that should the principal matter come to disputation he should still be allowed to speak against the lords in regard to their 'parciale consale'.[127] He specifically wanted no other matters discussed until he had the court's interlocutor on the issue of partiality; thus, in the formulation used at the time, he would avoid passing from that exception by default through raising another. If an exception once raised was repelled by the lords, however, then the rule was that any further exceptions which the procurator wished to raise all had to be made together at one time.[128]

As for allegations that particular lords were biased these are comparatively rare. In an action between Hugh Campbell, sheriff of Ayr, and William Cunningham, master of Glencairn, objections were raised to three of the lords. William showed that the prior of St Andrews had confessed to having 'advertisit & informit the shireff of airis procuratour how he mycht have ansuerit better to the resounis contenit in the libell na (than) he did'.[129] This made him 'parciale & suspect' in William's submission. The lords agreed and removed the prior from voting. Two days later the prior himself appeared on the sheriff's behalf questioning whether the abbots of Kelso and Dryburgh had given 'parcial counsale' in the matter.[130] The abbot of Dryburgh admitted that he was kin to the sheriff's children and according to William's procurator, the abbot said 'I will nocht purge me of parciale counsale'. However he appears to have sworn on oath that he was not partial and the lords do not seem to have removed either abbot from the sederunt at that time. It is interesting to note, however, that three months later the sheriff protested that no lords should vote

---

[124]   CS 6/1 fo. 37v: 22 June 1532.
[125]   See H.L. MacQueen, *Common Law and Feudal Society in Medieval Scotland* (Edinburgh, 1993), 77; ibid., 'Pleadable brieves, pleading and the development of Scots Law', *Law and History Review*, iv (1986) 403.
[126]   CS 5/36 fo. 112r: 1 Dec. 1526.
[127]   *Morton Registrum*, ii, 283.
[128]   CS 5/38 fo. 118r: 28 May 1528.
[129]   CS 5/43 fo. 152v: 15 Feb. 1532.
[130]   CS 5/43 fo. 157v: 17 Feb. 1532.

in the matter 'except thaim alanerly quhilk was chosin of befor to the session that arguint the mater & had the samin ripe in thir hedis'.[131]

The most vulnerable member of the sederunt to the charge of exhibiting partiality was the king's advocate. In February and March 1547 the then advocate, Henry Lauder, was twice successfully challenged as a judge.[132] On the first occasion the ground of challenge was that the action in question was brought by him at the king's instance; for that reason the lords instructed him to rise and pass to the bar of the court and not vote in the matter. The second challenge was different: it involved a case in which Lauder had represented one of the parties at a previous diet. The lords held that he should not vote in what was now the second instance of the cause. Lauder protested against this decision and 'purgit himself be his aith that he haid nocht gevin parciale consale in this mater'. Clearly he had been acting as procurator in a private capacity; his response seems to indicate that he had given counsel but that this did not necessarily make him biased. Lauder's reaction suggests that his initial involvement had been viewed by him—and might reasonably be viewed by his colleagues on the bench—as purely a business transaction. The fact that Lauder left the bench and immediately began again to represent the client in question does not disturb this view. Since he had to pass to the bar of the court and was debarred from voting, there was no reason why his services as a forespeaker should not have been secured.[133]

In fact the first thing Lauder did when he passed to the bar was to object to his opponent, alleging a lack of title or interest to sue. This was a familiar tactic and in the case in question Lauder asked that his opponent, Sir John Campbell of Lundie, produce his title for verifying his interest in the matter. When Campbell produced an apprising, containing an assignation in his favour of the lands that were subject to dispute, this was accepted by the lords even though Lauder's client, John, Lord Ogilvy, continued to object. Matters appear to have become rather heated since Campbell alleged that Ogilvy had threatened that should 'sir jhone come in the northland he suld nocht cum sa wele hame agane' although, despite calling several witnesses, he failed to prove that this statement had been made.[134] The practice of questioning an opponent's title and interest to sue was common. So much so, that Master Archibald Crichton, procurator for James Beaton, archbishop of St Andrews, alleged that James's nephew, the abbot of Arbroath, had no interest to reduce letters issued in

---

[131] CS 5/43 fo. 194r: 10 May 1532.
[132] CS 6/28 fos. 69v, 79v (4 Feb. and 10 Mar. 1547).
[133] CS 6/28 fo. 80r: 13 Mar. 1547. The client in question was John, Lord Ogilvy. It made sense for Ogilvy, as it had made sense for the sheriff of Ayr, to employ a disqualified lord of council to represent him.
[134] CS 6/28 fo. 82r: 21 Mar. 1547.

favour of the archbishop seeking half the fruits of his abbey.[135] Failure to mention by what right or interest a summons was being pursued might result in the lords ordering a new summons to be libelled.[136]

Litigation strategies and the use of evidence

In one case the lords, notwithstanding an exception that the pursuer had no title to sue, ordered the defender to answer 'the haile summondis' (i.e. the substantive allegations) *affirmatione vel negative aut excipiendo.*[137] As this phrase suggests, the procurator had several strategies available to him. He might admit the truth of an allegation, in which case his opponent would ask for an instrument to be made recording this concession; or deny something entirely, in which case he would himself ask for an instrument to be made.[138] Alternatively, the procurator might choose not to deny something but to challenge its relevance.[139] Occasionally the lords would assign a particular day on which to hear argument concerning the relevance of allegations contained in a summons. In February 1525 the lords assigned the next Thursday to the laird of Balbirny 'to produce sic lawis and resounis as he will verify that the punctes of the summondis raisit be him aganis helene stewart is relevant'. In the meantime, Helen and her forespeaker were to produce authority showing that the summons was not relevant so that the 'lordis may be avisit with baith thair lawis and resounis'.[140]

Objections to the relevance of a summons might be of a technical or complex nature. Hugh Rigg objected to a summons because it was 'coniunctlie libellat' by both the king and William Gourlaw. Gourlaw, having renounced his interest to proceed and given it over to the king, had thereby rendered the summons inaccurate, a technicality that in Rigg's submission made it invalid.[141] In another case, Henry Spittall objected to a summons addressed against his client and another person *in solidum* as cautioners. The ground of objection was that since the other cautioner was dead, Spittall's client, as the only surviving cautioner, should have been libelled 'in speciall' with the summons specifying precisely what he was required to pay.[142] Neither of these objections achieved its purpose nor, surprisingly, did Robert

---

[135]   CS 6/1 fo. 119v: 26 Sept. 1532. For a short discussion of this dispute see Sanderson, *Cardinal of Scotland*, 22-3.

[136]   As happened to William, master of Glencairn: CS 5/43 fo. 106v: 4 Dec. 1531.

[137]   CS 5/39 fo. 26v: 10 Dec. 1528. This clearly illustrates the preliminary (or dilatory) nature of an exception as to title.

[138]   An example of a concession is given at CS 5/40 fo. 16r: 5 May 1529.

[139]   Robert Leslie, for example, in relation to a retour given for lord Lovat 'allegit always that he denyit nocht the secund punct bot said the samin was nocht relevant': CS 5/40 fo. 19v: 8 May 1529.

[140]   CS 5/34 fo. 127v: 26 Feb. 1524.

[141]   CS 6/13 fo. 166v: 31 July 1540. A similar example occurs at CS 6/38 fos. 25v-26r.

[142]   CS 5/37 fo. 26v: 18 Mar. 1527.

Galbraith's much more straightforward objection in another case to a summons raised by the earl of Rothes that it 'was generall & buir nothir the moneth nor day'.[143] A slightly more sophisticated objection was made by Master John Lethame that a summons by Dutchmen against his French clients lacked specification (i.e. that the libel was general). The French had taken the Dutchmen's ship claiming it as a lawful prize; the Dutch responded by asserting that they had been sailing under a safe conduct of the great admiral of France and Brittany. Lethame responded by arguing that the summons was flawed because it failed to mention that the admiral had received authority from his king to grant such a safe conduct.[144]

In order to make such objections in the first place it was, of course, essential to have a copy of the summons.[145] In the event that the party who raised a summons failed to deliver a copy of it to the defender, the latter had the right to ask the lords to order delivery to be made.[146] The possibility of making technical objections to summonses made the drafting of the summons an important part of the legal process. Summonses were often referred to in the *acta* as 'kingis lettres' reflecting the fact that they were purchased under the signet.[147] The infinite variety of the summons, which made it the most popular means of initiating a legal action at this period, contrasted with the stereotyped nature of the brieve. This may have given the man of law a significant role in giving initial advice on points of drafting to his client who would then seek to obtain a summons drafted by Writers to the Signet in conformity with this advice.[148] But summonses, although formulaic, were essentially flexible. They could certainly be amended during the hearing of the action and there are numerous references to parts of the summons being regarded as *pro deleto* by the pursuer. Defenders often asked that it be noted that the pursuer no longer intended to pursue his claim against them but only against others named in the summons.[149] Any input which men of law may have had into the content of

---

[143] CS 5/38 fo. 63r: 13 Dec. 1527. Straightforward objections such as this were more common than the complex examples noted above. For instance John Lethame protested that a summons of spuilzie of lands raised by the countess of Cassillis failed to mentioned that she was in possession of those lands; Lethame did not fail to make the obvious point that she could not be spuilzied of that which she did not possess: CS 5/35 fo. 104v: 24 July 1525.

[144] CS 6/9 fos. 76r-v; 171r-v (28 Feb. 1538).

[145] CS 5/39 fo. 3r: 18 Nov. 1528: Robert Leslie, on his client's behalf, required the pursuer to deliver a copy of the summons so that thereby his client might use his defences.

[146] CS 5/37 fo. 56r: 27 Mar. 1527.

[147] H. McKechnie, *Judicial process upon Brieves, 1219–1532* (Glasgow, 1956), 23, 28-9.

[148] On writers to the signet during this period see Hannay, *College of Justice,* 301-2. The signet summonses in CS 15/1 are drafted by notaries such as Maben, Gude and Wallace. The statement that men of law gave initial advice is speculative. In Sinclair's *Practicks* there is reference to the procurator James McGill who is said to have 'faillit in the libelling of his summondis and in the conclusione thirof' (c. 123) although this does not necessarily mean that he helped draft the summons. Also, see the advice note (c. 1476) given in Fraser, *Lennox,* ii, 106-9.

[149] For example CS 5/39 fo. 125v: 1 Mar. 1529.

the summons was less direct than in the case of written defences in the drafting of which men of law had a more active role.[150] Moreover it was certainly the practice later in the century for the defences once drafted to be delivered by one man of law to another so that he might then draft his answers.[151]

As well as legal argument the procurator could produce physical evidence backing his claims. This may have consisted of documentary evidence such as a sheriff court roll, protocol book or notarial instruments or even a decreet in a similar case heard previously by the lords.[152] Written evidence and pleadings were very important. In one case a foreign litigant arrived with certain 'wrytingis' and protested, through his man of law, that he would not 'enter to pley the said mater' but desired only to have an answer to the writ he produced.[153] It appears to have been standard practice for the lords to receive 'exceptionis and informationis gevin in write befor thaim'.[154] Indeed in matters concerning heritage written evidence was essential or, at least, Robert Galbraith objected to witnesses being examined in relation to heritage because this was something that he alleged should 'be evidentlie previt and nocht be witnessis'.[155] It is equally clear, however, that there was also a great deal of oral debate before the lords. One late source indicates, in reference to exceptions, that they might be proponed by tongue, or given in by writ at the bar and so left 'in the lordis handis to be discussit.'[156] There are examples of actions in which written exceptions and other written evidence, as well as entire witness depositions, were read over in court by men of law at the command of the

---

[150] CS 15/1 *Bonar of Rossy v Patrick, Lord Crichton, sheriff principal of Perth and his deputes* (1544). The defences in this case were subscribed by the man of law Master David McGill. An extract *ex libro actorum* subscribed by Master James Scott in this process, bearing the marginal note 'for production of defensis', narrates that the lords continued the matter in dispute to allow the defender 'to geif in all his defenses quhilkis he hes or will uss relevantlie qualifiit in writt aganis the summondis'. This is a rare example of surviving defences from this period written, as with other documents in the process, on paper. As for the flexibility in framing the summons, see Murray, 'Sinclair's Practicks', 98, quoting the Practicks as indicating that the order of the parts of the summons was not vital, allowing the conclusion to be placed before the beginning without invalidating the summons.

[151] For example, CS 7/31 fo. 87v: *Perth v. Dundee* (11 July 1564). In this case Master David Borthwick, having produced written defences, delivered them to Master Thomas McCalzeane, the procurator for the burgh of Perth, who was then assigned a term by the lords on which to give in his answers. Whether such a procedure occurred in the 1520s is certainly possible although there are no cognate examples of it in the *acta* during that period. Instead there are references to parties handing in their 'lawis' for example CS 5/36 fo. 35v: 7 July 1526. On the *Perth v Dundee* case, see also CS 1/2/1 fo. 85v: 11 Dec. 1563.

[152] For a decreet in a similar case being used see CS 5/43 fo. 157v. For a rolment of court being produced see, for example, CS 6/1 fo. 9r: 28 May 1532.

[153] CS 5/36 fo. 45r: 14 July 1526.

[154] *Morton Registrum*, ii, 286.

[155] CS 5/37 fo. 79v: 3 Apr. 1527; 'evidentlie' i.e. by 'evidentis'. This was by no means a new rule; see, for example, *ADC*, i, 177.

[156] EUL, Laing MS III-388a, fo. 5r, 'Anent the proponing of exceptions quhilk concerne the procuratouris'.

lords and in the presence of the opposing counsel.[157] In one case James Foulis acting as prelocutor for the defender protested that he should not be required to answer the second point of the summons until the first point had been discussed and held relevant.[158]

The best evidence was undoubtedly written and this caused its own difficulties. Cases were adjourned while searches were made for old letters, instruments and other documents that might provide more clarity to the dispute, especially when land was involved. In one case, Master Henry Lauder offered on behalf of the earl of Glencairn and his son William to prove that the land in question belonged to the barony of Kilmaurs and 'sa has bene reput and haldin past memorie of man'.[159] His opponent, Master John Lethame forespeaker for William Hamilton, responded that Henry had produced no evidence other than an assignation of those lands made by the late lord Kilmaurs. The action was continued to allow both parties to seek out documentary evidence with which to back their respective claims. As a corollary of this, it was competent to petition the lords in the hope of recovering evidence that was in the possession of another party.[160]

But once written evidence was obtained and produced its authenticity might be called into question, particularly when some years had passed since it was made. In another case involving William, master of Glencairn, he managed to establish that a charter which had been produced allegedly bearing his seal and his signature along with those of his father had not in fact been subscribed by him because he was not present when the charter was sealed.[161] Forgery was almost routinely alleged. Robert Leslie offered to prove that a charter of tailzie was 'fals & feynzeit & scrapit away eftir it was first written & writtin agane of the new' and so should have no faith in prejudice to his client.[162] If necessary the lords could issue letters to a party by which he might require the clerk register to extract the authoritative copy of a deed so that it might be used to verify the authenticity of the copy in that party's possession.[163]

---

[157] For example, in a maritime case in March 1554 James McGill and David Borthwick repeated in court 'the haill deposiciounis of the witnesis producit be thair said clientis ... with the clerkis bukis and charter parteis producit be thame ... with ane missive writtin in franche': CS 1/1 fo. 13r; in a later case Borthwick read out all his exceptions which he offered to prove on his client's behalf which he then left in the lords' possession: CS 6/29 fo. 23r:18 May 1556.

[158] CS 5/39 fo. 74r: 5 Feb. 1529.

[159] CS 6/1 fo. 63v-64r: 12 July 1532.

[160] For example, Walter Drummond sought to recover a summons of error belonging to him which he claimed was in the keeping of John Stirling of Keir. The matter was referred to Stirling's oath and, following his admission that he possesed the document the lords ordered him to produce it: CS 5/37 fo. 116r: 4 May 1527.

[161] CS 6/2 fo. 11v: 23 Nov. 1532.

[162] CS 5/37 fo. 50v: 26 Mar. 1527; also CS 5/38 fo. 74r: 18 Dec. 1527.

[163] CS 5/37 fo. 72v: 1 Apr. 1527 The exchequer rolls might also be used; in a case involving the nonentry of the lands of Carlton Thomas Marjoribankis produced a 'draucht of the chekkir billis berand quhair the airis of carltoun was interit': CS 6/1 fo. 21r: 15 June 1532.

Sometimes actions were raised in order to obtain possession of documentary evidence such as a charter or instrument of sasine that was known to exist. Thus Janet Balfour sought the delivery of an instrument of sasine of an annualrent in the lands of Caraldston in Forfar which had been given by her father to David Pitcairn, archdean of Brechin. The action is described as an *actio depositi*. Pitcairn, through his procurator Hugh Rigg, argued that he ought not to be ordered to return the instrument because there was no question of *dolus* or *culpa lata*. He claimed he had placed it, along with documents of his own, in 'the place of Ferchir' from where those 'writingis and evidentis war negligentlie tint efter the ressait thirof and befor the moving of the pley'. In other words, as depositee he had not been negligent and so should not be required to hand back possession of the now missing instrument to the representative of the depositor.[164] Shortly afterward this in the record another example occurs, this time relating to a charter narrating a gift of nonentry made by James Beaton when archbishop of St Andrews to James Strang, the pursuer. The charter had been in the possession of Strang's man of law, Robert Leslie, until his recent death and was now in the possession of his heir Andrew who had allegedly refused to return it and had been intromitting with the lands to which it related. Strang required the document in order to prove, in a dispute with another party, that the lands in question belonged to him.[165]

In actions of proving the tenor of a document that had been produced, custody of the document in question might be given to Sir Alexander Scott, depute clerk register.[166] Scott was clearly in the habit of acting as custodian of written documents: in 1528 he declared that documents relating to the lordship of Dirleton had been in his care for nine years.[167]

Witnesses were summoned by letters issued by the lords. If the witnesses failed to appear in answer to the summons then the lords would issue new letters under which they might be summoned 'undir greter painys'[168] unless there was a reasonable excuse, such as absence on the king's service, in which circumstance the action would be adjourned without prejudice.[169] Once a

---

164   CS 6/13 fo. 172v: 31 July 1540.
165   CS 6/13 fo. 219v: 17 Nov. 1540.
166   CS 5/37 fo. 54v: 27 Mar. 1527. Scott (d. 14 May 1544) was appointed one of the deputies of the clerk register in 1516 and enjoyed a long career in the king's service: A.L. Murray, 'The Exchequer and Crown Revenue of Scotland, 1437–1542' (Ph.D. thesis, University of Edinburgh, 1962), 25–6.
167   CS 5/38 fo. 132r: 17 July 1528. The documents were to be delivered to the husbands of the three heiresses to the lands of Dirleton although one of those husbands, the master of Ruthven, would not compear to receive them.
168   For example, CS 5/34 fos. 4v–6v: 7 Sept. 1523. The procedure in some ways is similar to that before the court of the official, see Ollivant, *The Court of the Official*, 105–6.
169   For example, Sir John Scott procurator for the earl of Morton stated that although he was ready to pursue his action his witness was in the Borders on the king's service with the earl of Angus and therefore the lords continued the action: CS 5/35 fo. 152v: 5 Aug. 1525.

party produced his witnesses a time would be assigned for their examination. A small committee of the lords would make this examination, the witnesses being under oath, and neither the parties nor their procurators were allowed to be present.[170] Those lords, once they had examined the witnesses, sealed a document containing their depositions that could then only be opened on the command of a quorum of the lords.[171] In the event that the case was adjourned to a later session, as it often was, the depositions of the witnesses might not be opened for a considerable time.[172] Either party might renounce further production of witnesses and, once the depositions were published, no new witness could validly be deponed. In the event that further witnesses were to be called, or witnesses were to be summoned again, existing depositions had to remain closed.[173] The parties might each submit an interrogatory (a list of questions) based upon the points raised in the summons and this would form part of the lords' examination.[174] In one case the lords apparently proceeded to examine witnesses while the defender was absent on the king's service. On hearing of this the defender, John Hay, Lord of Yester, asked the lords to recall the witnesses that he might put forward exceptions against them and also that they might be examined upon his interrogatory because he had been informed that they had been suborned by the pursuer.[175]

In order to 'found his defensis' a party was entitled to obtain a copy of the summons against him and it would have been on the basis of the points raised in that summons that the interrogatory would have been framed.[176] In the case

---

[170] Three lords were chosen in September 1523 for this purpose: the abbot of Dundrennan, the justice-clerk and Adam Otterburn: CS 5/34 fo. 4v. Only two were assigned to examine witnesses in a case heard in November 1527: the official of Lothian and Master James Lawson: CS 5/38 fo. 34v. In 1532 the procedure seems to have been regularised when it was laid down that a committee of three was to be chosen weekly to hear witnesses. They were to convene in the afternoons as required. Of the three one was to be temporal and two spiritual and then the following week two were to be spiritual and one temporal and so on: *ADCP*, 375–6. However it is questionable whether this was rigidly adhered to. The evidence from CS 15/1 (see below) indicates that only one or two lords might be present to examine witnesses e.g. *Angus v Seton* (1539) begins 'Examinators dominus Ruthven M John Letham'; and in *Scott v Seton* (1539) two diets of examination were held, on 3 and 23 July 1539, each held by one examiner.

[171] CS 5/35 fo. 128r: 5 Aug. 1525.

[172] CS 5/35 fo. 170v: 1 Dec. 1525.

[173] For an example of a renunciation of further witnesses see CS 5/38 fo. 109r: 25 May 1528. In one case (CS 5/38 fo. 83v: 20 Dec. 1527) Galbraith protested that the bishop of Galloway should not be received as a witness against Lady Lochleven because prior to his examination the depositions of the other witnesses had been published rendering his deposition invalid 'sen be the lawis and pretick *post publicacionem productionis non licet testes de novo producere*'. However, exceptions against witnesses might be proponed following their examination but prior to publication of their depositions: CS 5/36 fo. 58v: 23 July 1526. An example of depositions ordered to remain closed while witnesses were summoned 'undir gretar panys' occurred in 1526: CS 5/36 fos. 92r-v: 29 Aug. 1526.

[174] CS 5/38 fo. 150v: 5 Aug. 1528.

[175] CS 5/39 fo. 133r: 2 Mar. 1529.

[176] CS 5/35 fo. 139r: 5 July 1525: protest that the defender 'mycht haif the copy of the said Williamis summondis that thirby he may found his defensis aganis the samin failzeing thirof that he suld nocht be haldin to ansuer to the samin'.

of *William Scott v Andrew Seton* (1539) the interrogatory given in on Seton's behalf survives.[177] The case involved an allegation that Scott had been wrongfully ejected from his lands. Seton requested that the lords ask witnesses whether they 'gif thai war present hard & saw ony sic eiectioun as is libellit And quhat zere moneth & oulk the said pretendit eiectioun was done'. Secondly, in relation to an allegation that Seton had laid waste to the lands in question, the lords were to examine the witnesses diligently to discover 'be quhat force & maner the said andro laid the saidis landis waist & quhat baisting & manising (menacing) he maid to the said william & his servandis'.[178] The interrogatory ends with the phrase '*reliqua interrogatoria referuntur prudencio domini examinatoris*'.

The earliest extant process in which the depositions have been preserved dates from January 1539, a case of spuilzie brought by Thomas Angus against Ninian Seton.[179] The alleged spuilzie had occurred over a decade earlier but the witnesses, once sworn, deponed as to their whereabouts at that time and as to what they remembered of the events in dispute.[180] Thus Adam Broun gave a description of the goods taken and an estimate of their value; the summary of his deposition ends with the phrase 'And this he kennis becaus he saw the gudis ga by he beand present in the toun'.[181] John Bas, although not himself present, spoke to the fact that 'the commoun voce was that sic gudis was spulzeit be sir niniane setoun fra the libellar'. Other witnesses produced what nowadays would be described as hearsay evidence deponing as to the state of common knowledge (*ex commune voce et fama* or 'the vo[i]ce of the cuntre') and indicating what they had heard from others. The witnesses varied as to their recollections and the details that they could give. Robert Anderson indicated that sixteen milk cows, three 'tydy' (pregnant) cows and fourteen young 'nolts' had been spuilzied but Thomas Donaldson deponed that 'he saw certane ky ga by the nomer he kennis nocht'. In contrast, William Bennet stated that about eleven years ago he 'saw ane poynd gang by castell campbell tane be the lard of cowtis servandis' placing an altogether different gloss on events. All the witnesses appear to have been asked how much the goods

---

[177] This interrogatory omits mention of the first point that appears in some other extant interrogatories, namely a reminder to the judges to show to 'everilk ane of the saidis witnesis the payne of ony persoun berand fals witnessing in ony caus...'. This is found, for example, in CS 15/1 *Scott of Buccleuch v Scott of Howpasley*, n.d.

[178] CS 15/1 *Scott v Seytoun* (1539).

[179] CS 15/1. This source consists of a box of extracted and unextracted processes dating from 1527 to 1549. These documents can only be identified according to the name of the case from which they emanate.

[180] One witness, Rob Rowend, deponed that he was 'in his awn hous' when he saw 'certan gudis cum by quhilk tha said wes tane fra thomas angus'. Some witnesses stated that ten years had passed since these events, others that ten or eleven years had elapsed.

[181] CS 15/1 *Thomas Angus v. Ninian Seytoun*. At the end of another deposition, by the witness Robert Anderson, it is stated: 'And this he kennis becaus he was present hard & saw'.

taken were worth. Answers varied from those who gave precise figures per head of cattle taken to those who stated that they did not know. The question of value was clearly important and it is likely that the lords carrying out the examination were following an interrogatory framed by one of the parties in which witnesses were asked to estimate the value of the goods they saw. In the circumstances it would not seem unreasonable to ask for a valuation of the value of livestock from those who worked the land. But not everyone was qualified to comment. In the case of *Scott v Seton* mentioned earlier one witness, asked to speak to the yearly profit one might expect to draw from a ewe and some lambs which had been driven off Scott's land, responded that 'he kennis nathing becaus he is bot ane millar & kennis nocht the proffit of na gudis & can nocht estym the samyn'.[182]

No more than three diets of examination of witnesses were permitted and any witness thereafter produced could not be admitted.[183] When witnesses were called there were rules concerning the precise matters on which they might be questioned. An example of this occurred in a case between William, master of Glencairn and Hector Bruce.[184] Hector raised a summons against William to rescind a charter made by the deceased Henry Bruce to William's father. William protested that he had only been called to appear to hear an action involving the rescission of a charter granted by his father to the late Henry. Therefore his *prelocutor* argued that any witnesses produced by Hector should only be examined concerning the points of the summons relating to this matter and not relating to anything else in the summons. No regard should be given, he argued, to any depositions made relating to other points in the summons. Witnesses gave their evidence on oath and generally they were asked to speak to things within their own experience. For example, Master Thomas Bellenden, director of the chancery, appeared and deponed that Isobel Hopper had renounced her conjunct-infeftment in relation to the lands of Blackbarony and that, 'as he rememberis' the renunciation reserved to her the liferent of the lands.[185] Memory played an important part not only in questions of land-holding but also in relation to matters such as proving a person's age which was an issue of importance in relation to questions of wardship or tutory.[186] Moreover, witnesses might be summoned to 'impreuve'

---

[182] CS 15/1 *William Scott v Andro Seytoun* (1539). In contrast the concept of the expert witness apears to have been known, at least in one case, in the chuch courts shortly after this date: Ollivant, *Official*, 105. There is no evidence of the use of expert witnesses in the secular courts but only very few depositions have survived.

[183] E.g. CS 5/38 fo. 109r: 25 May 1528.

[184] CS 5/34 fo. 93r: 18 Feb. 1524.

[185] CS 5/40 fo. 22r: 11 May 1529.

[186] This was an action between David, abbot of Arbroath and Margaret Forbes in relation to the wardship and marriage of Alexander Bannerman, Margaret's son. Robert Leslie, for the abbot, offered to prove that Alexander was over the age of seven (and should therefore be in the abbot's custody) whereas Thomas Marjoribankis for Margaret offered to prove he was under seven: CS 6/1 fo. 72v: 16 July

(disprove) a deed, typically an instrument of sasine. In one case a number of witnesses called to disprove the authenticity of such an instrument were objected to because their names did not appear in the instrument. This objection was repelled by the lords because the witnesses in question

> war for the maist notaris and know the notar that maid the instrument And thai wald examine thaim gif the instrument was the notaris hand writ or nocht.[187]

When witnesses were called they could claim their reasonable expenses for appearing in Edinburgh from the party who had summoned them. The Aberdeen burgess John Rattray, summoned by Robert Lumsden to give evidence against Gilbert Menzies, complained that although his expenses of two shillings per day had been 'taxt' by the lords, John was dilatory in paying him. He therefore sought an order that he should continue to receive this sum daily for as long as John defaulted.[188]

A fairly common procedure was the reference by one party to the oath of the other. When James Kennedy of Blairquhan asserted that he had in fact paid maills for the non-payment of which he had been poinded by Lady Janet Stewart, Robert Leslie for Janet referred the matter to his oath. James was assigned a day to depone and give his oath that he had paid the sums owed; he was instructed in the meantime to 'aviss apoun his deposicioun' presumably with his own man of law and eventually he appears to have submitted a written deposition.[189]

Witnesses could be objected to not only on the basis that the accuracy of their testimony might be suspect but also where there was a suspicion of partiality based on, for instance, affinity or consanguinity.[190] A good example of this occurred in 1543 when Thomas McCalzeane, for Robert Douglas of Lochleven, protested against two witnesses introduced by his opponent the earl of Morton. The first, John Tenent, he objected to on ground of affinity

---

1532. Similarly age was important in determining whether or not a tutory was still effective; thus it was established 'upoun the deposicounis of famous witnesis' that Alexander, Lord Elphinstone, was 'past xiiii zeris of age and out of tutorie': CS 5/35 fo. 190r: 18 Dec. 1525.

[187] CS 6/1 fo. 51v: 6 July 1532. There was precedent for a notary being cited as a witness because the lords considered that points made in an instrument he had drawn up were obscure: *ADC*, i, 189: 22 Mar. 1491.

[188] CS 5/41 fo. 158r: 19 Jan. 1530.

[189] CS 5/38 fo. 51v, 87v (Dec. 1527–Jan. 1528). James appeared personally. This action took the form of an action of spuilzie in relation to oxen and cows belonging to James which Janet and her accomplices had seized. Janet responded by producing royal letters and a decreet of the lords giving her authority to exercise diligence by poinding. Once James gave his oath, Robert Leslie as Janet's forespeaker immediately and without question confessed the spuilzie.

[190] For instance in February 1524 the Master of Ruthven protested against Mr. Lawrence Oliphant and his brother 'becaus the saidis persounis war within greis of consanguinitie and affinite to his wif and suld nocht be admittit be the law to beir witnes': CS 5/34 fo. 107v: 22 Feb. 1524.

averring that he was married to a woman within the fourth degree to the earl and the second witness, the laird of Sheriffhall, was 'thrid and ferd in consanguinite' to the earl. The earl denied the first averment on oath and then asserted that Sheriffhall was of the fifth degree in consanguinity to him, and had been purged of partial counsel, therefore making him a competent witness.[191] In one spuilzie action, in which a box containing 19,000 merks was allegedly taken from the Perth lodging of George, earl of Rothes, witnesses appearing for the earl were objected to because they had not been summoned by a macer but had been 'solistit' to come to the Edinburgh by Patrick Charters at the earl's request.[192] Patrick, it was said, had bribed the witnesses who were described as 'pure simple vile persounis that suld nocht be admittit previs in sa grete a mater & actioun'. To underline this point specific allegations including adultery, murder, fire-raising and theft were made against some of these witnesses.

Although normally witnesses had to go the lords, in rare cases of particular difficulty, the lords might go to the witnesses. Thus in one case the king's advocate, the dean of Restalrig and the parson of Spott were sent to the tolbooth of the burgh of Dundee as assessors to summon an inquest of those in the best position to know the truth of the facts in issue.[193] This procedure, reminiscent of the *enquête* procedure in contemporary France, arose because 'the witnesis producit be aither of the saidis partyis hes provit direct contrar utheris'. Particular difficulty seems to have been caused where witnesses or men of law were in direct contradiction to each other; so much so that according to Sinclair's *Practicks* one party could not produce an exception, article or reply directly contrary to the summons or an exception of the other party.[194] On other occasions notaries might be sent to receive depositions from witnesses unable to attend. In one case Robert Galbraith alleged that three men, summoned to give evidence, were 'waik aigit & febill persounis at mycht nocht travale'. The lords granted his request that 'ane notar of the court or uther famous notar' visit them and take their evidence, closing the depositions and returning them to the lords.[195] In such a case it was competent for the other party to appear before the notary and raise lawful exceptions against the witnesses.[196] In cases involving a foreign element, depositions could

[191] *Morton Registrum*, ii, 286. The lands of Sheriffhall were held by the Gifford family. Balfour states that anyone within the fourth degree of consanguinity or affinity may be repelled as a witness, quoting a case from 1541 as authority for this: Balfour, *Practicks*, ii, 377.
[192] CS 5/38 fos. 63r, 75r, 75v (15 and 18 Dec. 1527). Patrick Charters had allegedly usurped the office of provost on an annual basis without allowing free elections: CS 5/38 fo. 189v: 10 Nov. 1528.
[193] CS 6/13 fo. 163v: 30 July 1540.
[194] Sinclair, *Practicks*, nos. 113 and 126: EUL Laing MS III-388a fos. 49r., 50v.
[195] CS 5/31 fos. 37r-v: 22 June 1518.
[196] E.g., CS 5/30 fo. 114v: 27 July 1517: reference to a commission to the notary Robert Josse, to hear on a specified certain infirm witnesses in Brechin, allowing the opposing party or his procurator to attend and raise exceptions.

be obtained from abroad. In one case John Moffat, Scots conservator in Flanders, alleged that he had already paid a debt owing to Thomas Niddry, abbot of Culross, which the abbot's executor was seeking to recover. A commission was sent to the bailies of Veere who returned depositions of witnesses, together with copies of a letter from the abbot in which he appointed procurators to receive the money and their receipt indicating that they had done so.[197]

Procurators often had custody of their client's evidence during the dependence of the action.[198] It was normally up to the client to provide the evidence that would form the basis of the legal argument in the case. Thus when Gilbert McDowall came to Edinburgh in the winter of 1526 to defend himself in actions raised against him, he brought with him the relevant instruments, precepts and writs with which he planned to do so.[199] This evidence would then have been handed over to the man of law who would use it to prepare his case.[200] In one action the lords, announcing an adjournment, instructed Walter Lundie, the defender, to appear personally on a specific day to answer the matter or else to 'send his procuratour with his informacioun'.[201] Not everyone kept their legally significant documents and contracts with them. For more security the more prominent members of society might place their documents in a stronghold or ecclesiastical centre for safe keeping.[202] For example, in his minority Alexander, Lord Elphinstone, sought recovery from his erstwhile tutor, Robert Elphinstone, parson of Kincardine, of writs and contracts pertaining to him which were in Robert's control. Most of these were kept in the priory of the Black Friars in Stirling and Robert was ordered by the lords of session to hand control of them over to Alexander and his curators together with any relevant deeds not in Stirling which Robert also had in his possession. Once these were handed over, and Robert was given a receipt, the documents were placed in a chest and returned to the priory for safekeeping. For extra security three locks were apparently placed on the chest and Alexander, the prior and Henry Spittall 'advocat for the said lord', each received a key. This was an arrangement

---

[197]   CS 6/2 fo.125r: 19 Mar. 1533.

[198]   One woman even called Master Adam Otterburn before the lords to deliver to her 'certane evidentis' which she alleged belonged to her; presumably she was a former client or Otterburn had acted against her on behalf of someone else: CS 5/43 fo. 92v: 23 Nov. 1531.

[199]   CS 5/36 fo. 133r: 11 Dec. 1526. This case was mentioned supra. McDowall clearly did not bring all his writs with him, merely those relevant to the actions he was involved in. The case re-appears in the record at CS 5/37 fo. 72r: 1 Apr. 1527.

[200]   In 1527 James McGill's spouse, in his name, placed on the lord's 'burd' (i.e. table) a box with documents belonging to the laird of Galston who had the key to the box in his possession. Sir Alexander Scott, depute clerk register, immediately delivered the box to the laird and may personally have recorded this fact at the end of this entry in the *acta*: CS 5/38 fo. 35v: 28 Nov. 1527.

[201]   CS 5/37 fo. 50r: 26 Mar. 1527.

[202]   As will be seen shortly, the earl of Huntly kept his significant charters and documents in his main strength, the castle of Strathbogie.

which was to last four years until Alexander reached his majority and was designed to allow Alexander and his man of law access to the deeds 'for the defence of his pleyis at altyme quhen neid beis.'[203] Not everyone was so security conscious.[204] In a case brought by George, Lord Home against Helen Shaw, lady Dirleton, Helen's man of law produced a charter of her lands of Haliburton together with a precept of sasine but the vital instrument of sasine was missing. It was said that it must have been destroyed or lost by reckless keeping and this loss undoubtedly weakened her case.[205]

Procedural delays

The failure of a man of law to arrive, and to bring with him this evidence, was a serious matter for his client. Normally, the lords would grant a delay. In one case the allegation that the defenders had no procurator caused an action to be adjourned with the result that, according to the *acta*, it 'hes slept this lang tyme bipast'.[206] But this was open to abuse and the delay could not go on indefinitely. Thus the sheriff of Fife complained that no process should be given against him because he had given his defences to Thomas Scott his procurator who had gone to Berwick as one of the king's commissioners.[207] Similarly George Gray argued that because Thomas Marjoribankis his procurator 'was now lyand seik & had his evidentis and writtingis' an action against him should be delayed 'quhill he mycht be avisit with his procuratour'.[208] The lords did not allow him a delay because he had used the same argument before and the onus was on him in the interim to instruct another procurator. However, it was possible to avoid such a result by

---

[203] CS 5/36 fo. 145r: 15 Dec. 1525. This information comes from a deed registered before the lords and preserved in the *acta*. The reference is to 'thre lokis put apoun the kist' which does suggest that three separate keys would be required to unlock it, rather than three keys each capable of opening the same lock.

[204] Although the charter chest of the earl of Lennox was also kept with the Black Friars, this time in Glasgow. It was broken into after his death in 1526 by his mother and his son's tutor, Allan Stewart, in the absence of his widow who held the key. A new lock was placed on the chest and Lennox's widow was denied entry: CS 5/38 fo. 144r: 31 July 1528. It is also interesting that one of the advocate John Shairp's clients, rather than giving his last testament to Shairp to keep for him, put it in a writing desk, locked the desk, and then gave Shairp the key: *Correspondence of Sir Patrick Waus of Barnbarroch, knight*, ed. R.V. Agnew (Edinburgh, 1887), ii, 385.

[205] CS 5/38 fo. 64r: 13 Dec. 1527. That her case was weakened can be seen from the fact that her procurator sought to rely also on positive prescription whilst her adversary's man of law sought an instrument narrating that her instrument of sasine 'coud nocht be gottin'.

[206] CS 6/13 fo. 127r: 26 July 1540. The notion of actions going to sleep, only to be awakened some years later, was not unusual in an era when actions could outlive lawyers. In one case Robert Galbraith alleged that six or seven years had passed since the lords had set a date for the disproving of an assignation and that, nothing having happened in that time, his client should be freshly summoned to answer in the matter: CS 5/37 fo. 68r: 30 Mar. 1527.

[207] CS 5/39 fo. 31r: 12 Dec. 1528. Presumably Scott was given the note containing the defences in order to advise upon and amend them if necessary.

[208] CS 6/6 fo. 159v: 3 July 1536.

obtaining a letter from the king instructing the lords to continue the calling of a summons thus giving a client the opportunity 'in the meyntyme [to] pas hame & feche his evidentis & just defensis'.[209]

Similarly, delay might be granted so that a procurator might seek instructions from his client. In July 1525, for example, James Gordon of Westpark was placed in possession of the castle of Strathbogie by the third earl of Huntly on his deathbed. Gordon was to hold the castle, which contained Huntly's deeds and charters, for the benefit of his nephew, the new earl, during his minority. The countess of Huntly, however, obtained letters demanding that the castle be handed over to her within twenty-four hours unless reasonable cause was shown why they should not be. As a result Gordon was put to the horn. A petition was later presented on his behalf against the countess. The lords suspended the horning against Gordon for a period of twenty days in the hope of an amicable settlement. The countess's procurator, Robert Galbraith, asked for a copy of the supplication that he 'mycht send the samyn to the countes to haif hir aviss in the samyn'.[210]

It was difficult for a procurator to argue that an action should be delayed or adjourned because his client had to be somewhere else. Such an argument did not find favour when Robert Leslie tried it on behalf of David Beaton, abbot of Arbroath, who was said to be 'at the erding (burial) of his fader'. The abbot's tenants in Arbroath, acting against him, were allowed to proceed.[211] The opposite situation also raised difficulties. When James Ogilvy of Balfour sent instructions to Master Robert Galbraith to make a plea for him, Galbraith 'than happynit to be furth of the toun' and in his absence James's opponent managed to secure decree *simpliciter* against him.[212]

Litigation could thus take considerable time and in the end could be very costly. Of course delay could be tactically desirable where it led to the prospect of financial gain. Walter Gourlay, in a letter to the lords, complained that whereas his summons of error had been called every Wednesday since the beginning of the session it had been adjourned from day to day by the activities of the treasurer and the king's advocate 'for the kingis proffit'.[213] This suggests that the king was drawing the fruits of lands that Walter believed were his and that tactical legal delays were being used to maintain this situation. The rather sad example of Robert Arnot is equally illustrative. In the furtherance of

---

[209]   CS 5/36 fo. 148r: 17 Dec. 1526.
[210]   CS 5/35 fo. 115r: 28 July 1525. The horning was suspended for twenty days 'that gud wais may be had in the said mater'. On 30 August Elizabeth's letters were suspended by the lords because they were 'inordourlie procedit': CS 5/35 fo. 131v: 30 Aug. 1525.
[211]   CS 6/2 fo. 9r: 20 Nov. 1532; see also fo. 7v where the lords refused to accept 'the excusation maid be robert lesly procuratour for the said abbot that he was at the funerale supulcur of his fader & mycht nocht compeir & thirfor the lords mycht not proceid be the law in the said mater'.
[212]   CS 6/2 fo. 15v: 26 Nov. 1532.
[213]   CS 5/35 fo. 135r: 30 Sep. 1525.

a dispute with the earl of Crawford, Arnot came with his servant 'foure sessioun tymes in the zeir to the burgh of Edinburgh and awaittand therein every time upoun the calling of the said mater xij dayis he his man and thir horsis expensis every day estimat to viij s & for maisaris feis iiij s'.[214] These were the least of his expenses in an action that had he had been pursuing for thirteen years.

On the other hand, speed could also be tactically desirable especially for the pursuer. The dean of Glasgow, having had two of his horses poinded by John Moutrie of Markinche and his son for non-payment of a debt, sought to have the horses restored by purchasing letters on a Thursday charging John to appear before noon the following day in the Edinburgh's tolbooth. John appeared before noon having crossed to Edinburgh as soon as he could get passage on the ferry, only to find that that he had already been put to the horn because the dean had that morning purchased yet more letters.[215] Immediately warded, John sought his release complaining that the procedure used by the dean was not only against the 'commone stile and practick of the court' but had never been 'practickit nor usit' before. Similarly when Master John Spens of Mareston obtained letters discharging unlaws (fines) of the sheriff court of Fife the sheriff summoned him at his home on Monday to appear before the lords the following day. Spens, in St Andrews when he heard of the summons, immediately rushed to Edinburgh to be heard but was too late: the sheriff had already had Spens's letters suspended and his goods poinded to the value of the debt.[216] Deliberately failing to give a copy of the summons to the defender, however, was not an acceptable tactic for a pursuer. The defender might simply ask the lords to order the party who raised the summons to deliver a copy of it to him. This in turn would engender a delay with the lords granting a period for the defender to seek advice on what, if any, exceptions might be raised against the summons.[217]

The ultimate means of delay was to keep an action alive until there was a general continuation of actions to a later date. The practice of adjourning actions to a fresh diet was frequent but was not all-encompassing. Actions involving the king or strangers were always excepted in proclamations authorising adjournments and sometimes specific actions involving named parties were also excepted. However, when an action was not specifically

[214]   CS 6/13 fo. 130r: 26 July 1540.
[215]   CS 5/33 fos. 138v, 140r-v, 146r, 181v, 182r, 188v. (Jan./Feb. 1523). The dean had alleged that John had sworn before the lords 'be goddis boddy that the said dene suld nevir gett thai horsis restorit' and that they should take his home 'doun about his luggis' before he would give them up.
[216]   CS 5/36 fo. 114v: 3 Dec. 1526.
[217]   CS 5/37 fo. 56r: 27 Mar. 1527. In this particular case, *Thomas Kerr v John Cranston*, Kerr was granted a period of 21 days 'to be avisit'.

excepted in this way, any attempt to hear it prior to the date to which it had been continued was subject to protests for nullity of process.[218]

In conclusion, from beginning to end of the legal process it was increasingly important, especially for those unfamiliar with the courts, to obtain the services of a man of law. The vast majority of procedural points raised before the lords were made by a small number of men of law and it is clear that opportunities existed for them to delay the final resolution of cases significantly if it was in the interests of their clients to do so. Often this led to cases being ended by arbitrated settlement rather than by final decreet of the lords. There can be little doubt that formal legal proceedings were sometimes raised by a party in order to encourage his adversary to negotiate. Indeed in some circumstances negotiation might be the more socially acceptable solution. According to his prelocutor Henry Lauder, Alexander Dunbar of Cumnock was willing to submit himself to any three of the lords of session 'amicably' because he was loathe to stand against his superior if he could do otherwise.[219]

The influence of Romano-canonical procedure in the session is clear. The number of written documents in use; the citation and secret examination before only one or two judges of witnesses who were speaking to facts rather than acting as compurgators; the use of documentary evidence and the terminology of the libel, exception, probation and litiscontestation are major features, as is the frequent use of arbitration. Equally, however, the lords created rules particular to the procedure used before them and in this way the practick of the session was constantly evolving.[220]

---

[218] CS 5/37 fo. 198r: 14 Aug. 1527.

[219] CS 6/11 fo. 156r: 25 Feb. 1539.

[220] Although Balfour cited cases from the reign of James V which still stood as authority for contemporary practice in the 1570s, it was only to be expected that there were also areas of procedure in which significant change had occurred. An example is the general rule stated by Balfour that neither priests nor women could act as procurators (Balfour, *Practicks*, ii, 298-9), a rule which clearly did not apply in James V's reign.

CHAPTER SIX

Comparing Counsel:
Robert Leslie and Robert Galbraith

In this chapter particular attention is given to the careers of two advocates, Robert Leslie and Robert Galbraith. Several considerations have influenced this choice. First, they represent a contrast: Leslie was a secular man of law who never became a lord of session, Galbraith was a churchman who did. Secondly, the careers of both were virtually contemporary. Thirdly, neither man, unlike for example Thomas Marjoribankis or Henry Lauder, enjoyed a legal or administrative career lasting significantly beyond the reign of James V; most of what is known about them is known only because of their legal activities. Finally, it must be remembered that there was no strict *cursus honorum* and, although several men of law shared similar backgrounds during this period, no single career can be considered paradigmatic. By looking at two careers in parallel a slightly more representative picture may emerge.

(1) The career of Master Robert Leslie

Of the personal history of Robert Leslie only a few facts are known. If it is correct to identify him with a student from Angus of the same name who matriculated at St Andrews in 1508 or 1509, then this would place his date of birth some time in the mid-1490s.[1] According to Grant, he was the son of Master Walter Leslie, parson of Menmuir.[2] As Walter was commissary of Dunkeld from about 1517 he must have been a skilled canonist because the diocese contained a considerable number of trained canon lawyers at that time.[3] Described by Alexander Milne, in his *Vitae Episcoporum Dunkeldensium*,

---

[1]   Anderson, *St Andrews Recs.*, 202. Of all the general procurators named in 1532 Leslie's graduate status is the least certain. He was not consistently described as 'Master', even by the clerks of the council. This might indicate that it was, in his case, merely a courtesy title. There is no evidence that he was a determinant at St Andrews, let alone that he graduated. However if he did indeed matriculate in 1508/9, he would have been a contemporary of David Beaton.

[2]   Grant, *Faculty of Advocates*, 123.

[3]   Watt, *Fasti*, 125; I.B. Cowan and M.J. Yellowlees, 'The cathedral clergy of Dunkeld', *The Renaissance in Scotland*, eds. A.A. MacDonald, M. Lynch & I.B.Cowan (Leiden, 1994), 141-2.

as a person of noble birth on both sides, Walter was probably the illegitimate son of one of the Leslies of Rothes.[4] Who Robert's mother was is not known nor is much known about his siblings. He certainly had a sister named Euphemia and, although he appeared together with a chaplain named James Leslie in a document dated 1525 there was no indication that they were related.[5] In the following year, in the sheriff court of Fife, Robert acted for Margaret Leslie, described as a tenant of Glasmont, who was probably a relative since she still lived there in 1530 when Robert purchased the barony.[6]

By 1527, and probably much earlier, he had married Christine Wardlaw by whom he was to have six children.[7] Christine may have been one of the Wardlaws of Torrie in Fife. Leslie certainly had links with this family in his professional career; he acted for William Wardlaw, brother of the laird of Torrie, and for Hector Bruce of Coultmalindie who was married to Gelis Wardlaw, probably another member of the family.[8] Identifying Christine with this family is not helpful in explaining how Leslie became a burgess of Edinburgh. Had he married another Christine Wardlaw, one of the sisters of the Edinburgh burgess Thomas Wardlaw, his burgess status would have been more easily explained. But this Christine, and her sister Elizabeth, were minors in 1522 being represented by Robert Galbraith, their curator *ad litem*.[9] Considering the age of his own children (two of his sons were graduates by December, 1540), it is likely that Leslie was already long married by this date.[10] Nor does the Edinburgh burgess roll specify that Leslie became a burgess by right of his wife.[11] But the fact that he was a burgess is beyond doubt since it is mentioned in several contemporary instruments as well as in the roll of burgesses.[12]

That does not mean that Leslie engaged in trade; indeed there is no evidence that he did so. His only recorded activity within the burgh was directed towards legal matters, witnessing and receiving sasine and acting before the lords in the tolbooth. Yet this does not serve to explain why he agreed to defend the port of Leith in 1522 against Edinburgh at the climax of what Knox later called the 'auld hatrent'. The particular argument in that year

4   *Dunkeld Rentale*, 326.
5   NRA(S), no. 925, Erroll Charters, no. 341: 24 Apr. 1525.
6   *Fife Ct. Bk.*, 46; *RMS*,, iii, no. 968: 7 Oct. 1530.
7   Leslie's family tree is given in Finlay, 'Professional Men of Law', Appendix 13.
8   Leslie also acted for William Scott of Montrose against John Wardlaw, laird of Torrie, in 1527: CS 5/38 fo. 54v: 10 Dec. 1527. Wardlaw was personally present and no forespeaker for him was named although he later used William Johnstone as his procurator: CS 6/2 fo. 112v. For Gelis as wife of Hector: CS 5/32 fo. 2r.
9   CS 5/33 fo. 14v: 15 Nov. 1522.
10   *APS*, ii, 366. His eldest son, Andrew, was a graduate by May 1537: NAS, NP1/5A fo. 6v: 11 May 1537.
11   *Edin. Burg.*, 307: 26 Mar. 1518.
12   *Prot. Bk. Foular*, ii, no. 522: 29 Nov. 1524; *Prot. Bk. Foular*, iii, no. 310: 27 Apr. 1531.

concerned the profits of prize ships and who should receive them, but it was part of an older and wider dispute concerning the burgh privileges of Edinburgh and what was viewed as increasing encroachment upon them by the men of Leith.[13] The men of the port were led by Robert Barton of Over Barnton, Leith's leading sea captain who had risen to the rank of royal comptroller. Given the unpopularity of the cause of Leith in Edinburgh, Barton's claim to have experienced difficulty in obtaining an advocate to act for him must be accepted.[14] But it is more difficult to accept that in January 1523, Leslie voluntarily agreed to resolve Barton's difficulty by acting on Leith's behalf merely because the lords directed him to do so. As a burgess, sworn to defend the freedoms of Edinburgh, he could surely have ignored the direction with impunity especially since he would run the risk of alienating opinion in Edinburgh. It is hard to believe, even with Leslie's Perthshire background, that as a burgess of Edinburgh he would have been considered neutral by the men of Leith. Nor did he have many clients in the port. The only other examples of him acting for Leith litigants occurred in 1530 and 1531.[15] On the other hand, his practice amongst Edinburgh burgesses was not large, including only two burgesses and the widow of another. However one of the burgesses was Adam Hopper, who was the dean of guild, and it is probably the case that little long term damage was done. The Leith episode is unusual, and should perhaps be explained on the basis that Leslie was put under more pressure to act than the scarce detail of the record reveals.

As well as being a burgess of Edinburgh, Leslie had close links with the Cistercian convent at Elcho, in the parish of Rhynd on the south bank of the Tay, where his sister, Eufame, was one of a community of about twelve nuns.[16] This led to another curious episode. In the mid-1520s Elizabeth Swinton, prioress of Elcho, resigned the convent in favour of Eufame Leslie in contentious circumstances. Elizabeth later alleged that the earl of Atholl and the bishop of Caithness, together with eighty armed men, violently broke down the doors of the monastery, seized her person and compelled her to make letters of procuratory resigning her rights as prioress in Eufame's favour. According to Elizabeth, using these letters Eufame:

> be menys and ways of Robert lesly hir broder causit
> resignacioune to be maid of the said abbay of elcho And

---

[13]   J.C. Irons, *Leith and Its Antiquities* (Edinburgh, 1897), chapter thirteen, 149*ff*, and appendices 29-31.

[14]   *Pace* Reid, who accused him merely of time wasting: W.S. Reid, 'Robert Barton of Ovir Barnton' *Medievalia et Humanistica*, v, (1948), 55-6.

[15]   *John Brown of Anstruther v Master George Forrester in Leith*, a case concerning alleged intromission with goods belonging to the former and delivered by the latter to English merchants: CS 5/41 fo. 9r: 15 Mar. 1530; and *Kirkmasters of Leith v Adam Dais*, skipper of a ship from Flanders, concerning unpaid primegilt: 5/43 fo. 72v: 13 Nov. 1531.

[16]   Fraser, *Wemyss*, i, 134; *Essays on the Scottish Reformation,* ed. D. McRoberts (Glasgow, 1962), 236.

thirthrow optenit pretendit bullis of the courte of Rome And be circumventioune of oure soverane lord he nocht knawing the ground of the mater...optenit his admissioune admittand the said dame eufame to the temporalite of the said benefice.[17]

Elizabeth appealed to Rome to have these bulls annulled and petitioned the lords of session to have the king's letters in Eufame's favour which followed on from them reduced. This litigation was expensive and lasted until Elizabeth's death, which occurred probably towards the end of 1529. It was vigorously defended by Robert Leslie on his sister's behalf.[18] According to a charter made early in 1530 by Eufame, in favour of her brother, Elizabeth had been removed from the administration of her office because of unspecified "excesses".[19] Since then she had molested the monastery, forcibly removing its fruits and possessions, and raising legal pleas against it. In turn, this had obliged the nuns to put valuables in pledge and to contract other debts. According to the charter, Robert Leslie provided the funds to redeem the monastery's goods from pledge and to pay its debts; he also provided money for necessaries and paid for the prioress's bulls of provision at Rome.

Given Leslie's status as man of law to both the second and third earls of Atholl, it is likely that he was also involved in the initial seizure of Elizabeth Swinton.[20] This event must have occurred around 1526 and so the earl complained of would have been John Stewart, the third earl, who was at this time in his late teens.[21] In July 1526 pursuivants had been sent to Dunkeld to summon the earl of Atholl and the master of Ruthven for despoiling king's officers.[22] Evidently Atholl was later fined at the justice ayre of Perth and it was Leslie who delivered his composition of £100 to the treasurer, Master John Campbell of Lundie.[23] This was not the last time he would find himself responsible for making a payment to a royal official on behalf of the earl of Atholl.[24]

---

[17]   CS 5/38 fo. 82v: 20 Dec. 1527.
[18]   CS 5/36 fols 83r: 13 Aug. 1526, 98r; CS 5/37 fols 2v, 123v, 136r; CS 5/38 fols 4r, 18r, 19v, 82v: 20 Dec. 1527.
[19]   Fraser, *Wemyss*, ii, no. 190.
[20]   See Appendices 2 and 8. Leslie was a witness to an indenture between the earl of Atholl and the bishop of Dunkeld made on 8 Feb. 1527, further indication of his closeness to the young earl: *Chron. Atholl*, i, 32.
[21]   This is dated to 1526 because Elizabeth Swinton was alleged early in 1530 to have been bringing pleas against the monastery for three years; Jamie Cameron, *James V* (East Linton, 1998), Appendix iii, 356, estimated the third earl of Atholl to have been about 21 in 1528.
[22]   *TA*, v, 278.
[23]   Ibid., v, 331, 464.
[24]   CS 6/7 fo. 97v: 4 Feb. 1536. On this date the lords issued a decreet by which Atholl and Leslie were to pay before Easter to the comptroller, Sir James Colville of East Wemyss, £117 6s 8d. The payment was in respect of the *grassum* of certain lands to which the earl sought entry; evidently it was a composition since it represented the complete payment of 'of ane mair sowm'.

Grateful for his help, the prioress and convent acknowledged a debt to Leslie of some £290 5s 4d (although he remitted a hundred merks of this). It was arranged that compensation should be paid with a grant in feu-farm to Leslie and his heirs of the lands of Kinnaird in Fife, and an assignation of the rents of Binning near Linlithgow.[25] This grant in itself led to further litigation in 1536 when Archibald Swinton, a tenant of the priory in part of the lands of Kinnaird, refused to hand over the maills of those lands when Leslie demanded that he do so. Swinton's nineteen-year lease with the convent still had a considerable period to run, but the lords upheld Leslie's claim and directed that the rents should be paid to him on the basis of the grant made in 1530. Two years after Leslie's death, his eldest son Andrew, designed 'of Kinnaird', brought an action against his aunt the prioress, and several others, alleging that they had broken down the doors of his chamber in his house in Kinnaird and spuilzied his goods.[26] This episode was probably symptomatic of a deeper dispute but it appears to have been settled amicably.

It is difficult to characterise Leslie's involvement in the Elcho affair. It would be churlish to cast doubt on whether he spent so large a sum of money in aid of the priory. In view of the fact that he remitted part of his expenditure, and received only modest grants in compensation for the remainder of it, he clearly had no motive of personal profit and the figure suggested can be taken as reasonably accurate. Nor was such expenditure of time, money and effort likely to have been undertaken simply to satisfy his sister's ambition. This appears to have been a genuine act of personal piety, albeit influenced by family involvement; not only was his sister the prioress but his daughter, Janet, took the name Euphemia and by 1542 had also become one of the dwindling band of nuns at Elcho.[27] By the time of the Reformation there were only about seven nuns left when they were attacked by reformers and driven out.[28] This had followed an attack in December 1547 when the priory was burned by the English at which time the nuns and 'many gentleman's daughters at school with them' were removed.[29] Despite the aid of Sir John Wemyss, the priory, in decline since at least the 1520s, ceased to be inhabited prior to the death in 1570 of its last prioress, Eufame Leslie.[30]

Of Leslie's six children, there were four sons (Andrew, John, George and Gilbert) and two daughters (Elizabeth and Janet or Euphemia). Presumably

---

[25] The priory's possession of these lands was confirmed by Benedict XIII in 1418: Cowan and Easson, *Medieval Religious Houses*, 146.

[26] CS 6/11 fo. 10v: 20 Nov. 1538.

[27] That Janet was a nun is clear from *APS,* ii, 423; that she was at Elcho appears from an obligation subscribed in September 1554: Fraser, *Wemyss,* ii, no. 209. The latter document was also subscribed by Euphemia Swinton who may have been related to Elizabeth, the earlier prioress.

[28] Cowan and Easson, *Medieval Religious Houses,* 146.

[29] *Cal. Scot. Papers,* i, 56. It is possible that Leslie's own two daughters were educated at the priory in the 1520s, giving him another reason to intervene there.

[30] Fraser, *Wemyss,* i, 135; Cowan and Easson, *Medieval Religious Houses,* 146.

Andrew and John, who both went on to become graduates—the first becoming a lawyer, although his death in 1543 prevented his career from developing, and the latter becoming parson of Kinnoul—were involved in a transaction before the lords in 1528.[31] With the authority and consent of their father, they constituted Sir John Dingwall, Master William Meldrum, Sir Ninian Douglas, Thomas Lawson and Alexander Young, their procurators for raising brieves, taking sasine, resigning or alienating land or moveable goods.[32] The procurators were to act with Robert Leslie's advice, but they were empowered to accept benefices or offices and to resign the same *per mutationis causa vel simpliciter.* Andrew was certainly the eldest son and John was probably next eldest (or perhaps he was merely the next most suited to university training). The wording of the constitution suggests that a church career was already being contemplated for him. Sir John Dingwall was provost of Trinity collegiate church in Edinburgh. In 1524, when he was rector of Strabrok in Linlithgow, Leslie had witnessed a charter by which he donated land to the local church and, a decade later, Dingwall named Leslie in his will as one of his executors.[33] Meldrum was archdean of Dunkeld, and was probably a connection of Robert's father.[34] The others have not been traced. This decision to make procurators may represent the moment that Andrew and John were to leave the country to begin studying; no reason was given as to why their father was not named although it was laid down that the procurators could not act without his advice.

The same procurators were named at the same time by Thomas Hamilton, the son of the late advocate of that name. Leslie's daughter Elizabeth later married Thomas and became the grandmother of Thomas Hamilton of Priestfield who became king's advocate during James VI's reign.[35] This constitution, and the subsequent marriage, suggests that Leslie was close to Thomas's late father who had an extensive practice and was probably the leading advocate in the period following Flodden until his death in 1526. Leslie inherited several clients from him as did Robert Galbraith.[36] Master Andrew Leslie, Robert's eldest son, may also have married into a legal family since by 1538 he was married to Katherine Henryson, possibly the granddaughter of James Henryson, king's advocate. In that year Andrew resigned the lands of Glasmonth, which he had inherited from his father, and

---

[31]   Andrew was undoubtedly a man of law; Master George Leslie also appeared as a procurator before the lords. For instance, he appeared for William Stewart in 1546: CS 6/23 fo. 78r: 9 May 1546.

[32]   CS 5/38 fo. 169r: 18 Sep. 1528.

[33]   *RMS,*, iii, no. 281: 10 Nov. 1524; CS 6/4 fo. 95v: 19 Mar. 1534. The other executors were Master William Gibson, dean of Lestalrig and Master Gilbert Strathauchin, parson of Fettercairn.

[34]   *Fife Ct. Bk.,* 92.

[35]   *A History of the House of Hamilton,* ed. G. Hamilton, (Edinburgh, 1933), 412-4.

[36]   E.g. Patrick Sinclair (represented by Hamilton at CS 5/27 fo. 172r); James Kennedy of Blairquhan (CS 5/34 fo. 46r); Sir Ninian Seton of Tullibody (CS 5/32 fo. 12v); Robert, Lord Maxwell (CS 5/32 fo. 109r) and John, Lord Glamis (CS 5/32 fo. 47v; 5/34 fo. 133v).

received sasine jointly with Katherine.[37] After Andrew's early death Katherine, as her husband had been in 1538, was involved in another dispute concerning the lands of Kinnaird when she accused Norman Leslie, the master of Rothes, of spuilzie of the crop cultivated there in 1544, the year after Andrew's death.[38]

As well as Kinnaird, Leslie held the estate of Inverpeffer in the parish of Arbroath and sheriffdom of Forfar. There is no indication of how or when he came by these lands, although he certainly had them by 1525.[39] In 1527 Leslie and his wife received from the abbot of Arbroath a nineteen-year lease of the teinds of Inverpeffer in return for a yearly payment of wheat, barley and oatmeal to the abbey.[40] His relationship with David Beaton appears to have been fairly close, and it was due to Beaton's influence that Leslie was custodian of the privy seal in 1529.[41] Three years earlier he was described in the council record as keeper of the signet. On this occasion, the lords instructed him that whenever a deliverance, which might have the effect of discharging any process following on from a decreet given by the lords, came to be signeted, he was not to proceed without bringing the deliverance before them and taking their advice.[42] It is not clear how long Leslie held the office of keeper of the signet nor whether his custody of the privy seal was restricted to only a couple of occasions; nonetheless possession of either the signet or the privy seal meant potentially lucrative additional income even if it was only short term.

Leslie's last appearance before the lords was on 31 July 1536. He was dead by 1 December that year.[43] After his death, Leslie's estate was subject to the opportunism of James V when his corpse was exhumed in 1540 so that it could be tried for *lèse majesté*.[44] The allegation made against him was that in February 1529 he had conspired with James Hamilton of Finnart, Archibald Douglas of Kilspindie and James Douglas of Parkhead to assassinate the king.[45] During the last five years of his reign James V had become increasingly obsessed by the fear of plots against his life particularly when connected with

---

[37] *RMS*,, iii, no. 1828: 25 Aug. 1528.
[38] CS 6/21 fo. 114r: 28 July 1546. Katherine asserted that the lands of Kinnaird pertained to her because of a lease from the abbey of Lindores. No details of her terce survive and presumably she had come to some arrangement with the abbot concerning these lands.
[39] NRA(S), no. 925 (Erroll Charters), no. 341: 24 Apr. 1525.
[40] *Liber S. Thome de Aberbrothoc* (Spalding Club, 1848–56) [*Arbroath Liber*], ii, 474: 5 Dec. 1527.
[41] *RSS*, ii, Appendix, 765: 11 July 1529, 766: 14 Dec. 1529. Leslie also received a gift of nonentry from James Beaton, Archbishop of St Andrews. Knowledge of this survives only because it became the subject of litigation by Master Andrew Leslie early in 1540: CS 6/14 fo. 161r: 11 Feb. 1540.
[42] CS 5/36 fo. 46r: 16 July 1526.
[43] CS 15/1, box containing document marked 'Renunciation of Christian Wardlaw or Leslie'.
[44] Kelley, 'Douglas Earls of Angus', 437, 751–2.
[45] *APS*, ii, 355, 366–7, 423.

the exiled earl of Angus.[46] Nonetheless there is nothing in Leslie's career that would indicate complicity with Hamilton of Finnart in a plot to kill the king. It is true that in 1530 Hamilton had sold the lands of Glasmont in Fife to Leslie, *pro consilio et servitio*.[47] But the only other evidence of direct contact between them revealed in the record is one appearance before the lords by Leslie as Hamilton's forespeaker in 1527, and Leslie's presence the following year as witness to a charter in Hamilton's favour.[48] Cameron has examined the evidence against Hamilton and found it wanting. The same conclusion must apply even more strongly to his alleged co-conspirator, Leslie, who was probably only on the periphery of Hamilton's circle.[49]

Leslie and his clients

Given the necessity of a lawyer, once established, residing part of the year in Edinburgh, and thus coming into contact with potential clients from throughout Scotland, the clients who tell us most about the lawyer tend to be those from his earliest years in practice. In Leslie's case, the first 25 of his clients who can be identified with a particular geographical area came mainly from Fife, Perth and the north-east.[50] This covers the period 7 February 1514 to 19 March 1517. The sheriffdoms from which he gained most of his initial clients were Fife and Forfar with 6 clients coming from each; but Perth (3), Aberdeen (2), Kinross (1) and the burgh of Dundee (1) also feature and all of these together account for 19 of the 25 (76 per cent). His other clients in this sample came from Dumfries (2), Edinburgh (1), Berwick (1), Ayr (1) and Dumbarton (1). Apart from an appearance for Gilbert MacDowall of Spott in the sheriffdom of Dumfries in December 1514, his first client from south of the Forth was not until February 1517, when he acted for Janet Smalame, widow of the Edinburgh burgess Alexander Napier. This demonstrates that clients from the north-east were vital to Leslie at the beginning of his career.

In terms of social composition, his first 25 clients included 4 earls (and also some of their adherents), the son of the countess of Montrose, two burgesses and the widow of a burgess. He also acted for Richard Stewart, Lord

---

[46]   Kelley, 'Douglas Earls of Angus', Appendix III. Kelley (at 527-9) connects James's almost pathological fear to the death of his first wife in 1536 and the trials of Lady Glamis and Master of Forbes for treason in 1537. Angus was found guilty of treason in September 1528. For the political circumstances surrounding this, see Emond, 'Minority of James V', chapter 13. Angus left for England in December 1528 although, perhaps significantly, there was mention of his return in March 1529: Emond, 'Minority of James V', 559.

[47]   *RMS*,, iii, no. 968: 7 Oct. 1530.

[48]   NAS, GD 1/1155/1: 14 Apr. 1528.

[49]   Cameron, *James V*, chapter nine.

[50]   Unfortunately, space does not permit replication of lists of clients. Readers are referred to Finlay, 'Professional Men of Law', Appendices 8 & 9.

Innermeath, a man who had close family connections to the north-east.[51] His employment by the earls of Atholl, Crawford, Lennox and, in particular, Rothes, are significant in terms of patronage. These were all major landholders in the environs of Fife and Perth and, as will be shown below, they formed the centre of networks based on land tenure and service that represented one of the means by which Leslie increased his legal practice.

Looking at his entire body of clients more widely, not all of them were given a designation in the record. Of those whose full name and designation were given, not all of them can be identified. Nonetheless, of the 284 clients for whom he appeared, the geographical origin of 262 can be stated with some degree of confidence.[52] By far the highest number, 47, came from the sheriffdom of Fife. Next in importance were the sheriffdoms of Perth (39) and Forfar (25). If Aberdeen (15) is added, and the burgh of Dundee (3) is considered part of Forfar with the regality of Dunfermline (3) included as part of Fife, then 132 of these identifiable clients, that is, just over half, came from just five contiguous sheriffdoms in the east of Scotland north of the Forth. South of the Forth, Edinburgh (20) including the port of Leith (3) and the constabulary of Haddington (7) constituted a significant recruiting ground for clients. Lanark (13), Dumfries (12) and Ayr (9) including Cunningham (3), came some way behind.

An analysis of Leslie's client-base is more usefully conducted by subdividing his clients into smaller groups according to three criteria: geographical proximity, family relationship, or consensual relationship. In some cases there is a considerable overlap between these criteria and a combination of reasons might serve to explain why a particular client employed Leslie rather than any of the other advocates available. Conversely, in selecting these criteria it must be remembered that any of Leslie's clients might be linked to others in ways that have left no trace in the record or which would require more research to uncover. In what follows, Leslie's client list has been investigated only with a view to trying to discover how he built up business.

(i) Geographical proximity

This is the most obvious of the three criteria. Leslie's clients came from as far afield as the sheriffdoms of Inverness, Aberdeen, Wigtown and Roxburgh. Their designations do show that a preponderance (around 58 per cent) came

---

51 *Scots Peerage*, v, 4.
52 There are doubts about some given that the same place name can appear in different sheriffdoms. Certain individuals, particularly the nobility, also held land in more than one place. Generally, the land at the centre of the litigation has been used to categorise the client unless, in the case of the nobility in particular, he was a sheriff or sheriff depute in which case that sheriffdom has been taken. Even if minor errors have been made in identification, this cannot seriously affect the conclusions.

from the area described in the medieval period as Scotia (the area north of the Forth) but, taking his career and list of clients as a whole, such bias as there was is by no means overwhelming.

The area closest to Leslie's roots in Fife provided a large number of his clients, from the earl of Rothes down to the Dishingtons of Ardross and the laird of Raith. From Fife alone he drew almost 50 clients, with Perth and Forfar not too far behind. In Aberdeenshire, although he had only about 15 clients, they were of no less importance, including as they did George, fourth earl of Huntly, and men such as Andrew Tulidaff of that ilk, Sir James Crichton of Frendraught and Alexander Seton of Meldrum. Presumably recommendations concerning men of law passed by word of mouth amongst people of broadly equal rank in society. This would explain why all the burgesses Leslie represented, other than burgesses of Edinburgh, came from a group of burghs in the north: Aberdeen, Dundee, Montrose, Kinghorn, Crail and Dysart. More exotically, he also acted for the burgh of Whithorn but this was not a geographically isolated case since several of his clients came from Dumfries and Wigtown. If anything, it might seem surprising that burgesses did not represent a higher proportion of Leslie's client list. In July 1517, when acting for Walter Bunche, Leslie was prepared to prove a point of custom pertaining to the burghs of Perth and Dundee. He contended that the heirs of burgesses might alienate their lands at the age of fourteen since that was the age at which they were taken to the tolbooth to count out money and to measure cloth in order to qualify as a burgess.[53] Presumably, he had gone through some similar procedure in Edinburgh and, even if he had not, most leading men of law would have had knowledge of the laws of the burghs as part of their stock-in-trade. But to a large extent most cases involving burgesses before the lords of council could have been dealt with by the burgesses representing themselves, provided they lived close enough to Edinburgh. This probably explains why Leslie, and indeed other men of law, appear to have drawn only a modest number of clients from the burghs.

Outwith the north-east, and Edinburgh, the major source of Leslie's clients was Ayrshire, centred on the bailiary of Cunningham and the bailie, Hugh, first earl of Eglinton, for whom he made more appearances than any other client. As well as the Montgomeries, Leslie appeared for locals such as Alexander Kennedy of Bargany, James Kennedy of Blairquhan, James Dunbar of Cumnock and Margaret Boyd, countess of Cassillis. The other major area of his client-base was Lanark, a sheriffdom in which he represented at least 14 people including the hereditary sheriffs, the first 2 earls of Arran.

Indeed sheriff courts, as an administrative focal point in local communities, probably formed a major recruiting opportunity for men of law such as Leslie.

---

[53]   CS 5/30 fo. 97r: 17 July 1517.

It is only through chance survivals that documents exist demonstrating that leading advocates in Edinburgh did appear in local courts. Even in the surviving sheriff court book of Fife, Leslie makes only one appearance. Nonetheless a significant number of those local lairds who owed suit to the sheriff court in Fife were clients of his: John Moutrie of Seafield, William Lumsden of Airdrie, Walter Heriot of Burnturk, David Wemyss of that ilk, Andrew Seton of Parbroath, David Ramsay of Cullothie, and Sir Peter Crichton of Naughton.[54] Both Ramsay and Crichton also held their own baron courts, as did another of Leslie's Fife clients, John Seton of Lathrisk, and no doubt he was available to assist them in doing so even if only by giving advice from Edinburgh in difficult cases.[55] As well as representing the sheriffs of Fife, initially John, Lord Lindsay of the Byres and then George, earl of Rothes, Leslie also acted as one of the procurators of David Beaton, abbot of Arbroath, who presided in the regality court. Unfortunately, the court book is lost.[56] But it is known who Beaton's leading friends, tenants and servants were and amongst them are included some of Leslie's clients such as Robert Maule of Panmure and William Wardlaw of Torrie, the brother-in-law of Elizabeth, one of the abbot's sisters.[57] No doubt they owed suit to the regality court. Similarly, some of Leslie's clients who owed suit in Fife sheriff court also did so to the regality court of Dunfermline. Amongst these included Robert Orrock, Melville of Raith and Crichton of Naughton in Kirkcaldy. Clients who owed suit only in the regality court included Sir William Scott of Balwearie, Janet Inglis, William Dishington of Ardross, Master William Lundie and Master Thomas Wemyss.[58] As in the sheriff court, there is only one instance of Leslie being named in the surviving record of the regality court of Dunfermline although it was as an arbiter rather than a procurator.[59] On the other side of the country, it is likely that Leslie met clients old and new at the bailie courts of Cunningham held in the council house of Irvine by his patron, the earl of Eglinton.[60] Much the same could be said about the sheriff courts of Lanark and Linlithgow, where his clients, the first two earls of Arran and James Hamilton of Kingscavil respectively, were sheriffs; and also in Dumfries, where another client, Ninian Crichton of Bellibocht, carried out

---

[54]   These are taken from the index of names in the *Sheriff Court Book of Fife* [*Fife Sheriff Ct. Bk.*], ed. W.C. Dickinson (Edinburgh, 1928).
[55]   For these baron courts, see *Fife Sheriff Ct. Bk.*, 41, 43, 63, 273-4. Leslie also acted for William Lumsden's wife, Janet Inglis.
[56]   Sanderson, *Cardinal of Scotland*, 23-4.
[57]   Ibid., 58.
[58]   *Dunfermline Regality Court Bk.*, 41, 59.
[59]   Ibid., 121. See below.
[60]   For an instrument taken at such a meeting, but not mentioning the presence of Leslie, see NAS, Glancairn Muniments, GD 39/1/30: 13 Mar. 1520.

the *SHR*ieval duties during the nonage of Robert Crichton, fourth lord Sanquhar.[61]

It would be wrong however to give the impression that Leslie had a complete monopoly on local business in any particular area. After all, most legal disputes involved near neighbours and he could hardly act for both sides. Henry Spittall, in particular, being from the north-east, had a number of clients in that area, including the Forbeses and the Grahams of Montrose. In Fife, the range of Spittall's clients is impressive: it included the burgh of Dysart, William Lindsay of Pyeston, William Lindsay of Airdrie, John Beaton of Balfour, David Spens of Wormistone, Sir John Melville of Raith and Robert Orrock of that ilk. The Melvilles and Orrocks were themselves brought together in a bond of manrent in 1520.[62]

Robert Orrock married Spittall's widow, Elizabeth Forbes, probably in 1536.[63] Orrock also appears as one of Leslie's clients and he was not the only client Leslie shared with Spittall. For example, Richard Stewart, Lord Innermeath, William Lindsay of Airdrie, William Dishington of Ardross and Roger Herries, were all represented in different cases by both Leslie and Spittall. In the case of Innermeath and William Lindsay, Spittall acted for them in actions where Leslie appeared as opposing counsel. In the other two cases Spittall acted for occasional clients of Leslie in actions where Robert Galbraith was the opposing counsel. This underlines the fact that there was no necessary exclusivity in the relationship between client and man of law. In general, particularly for clients with larger estates, it made sense to rely primarily on one advocate who might then become familiar with all the necessary details of the client's business. But it was shown in chapter two that many clients did call upon the services of more than one advocate and it would be as wrong to imagine that a litigant had a particular bond of loyalty to an advocate as it would be to think that advocates would refrain from appearing against former clients. Not every relationship between a litigant and his advocate lasted a lifetime; normally, it survived only the duration of a single lawsuit.

This is exemplified in Leslie's career. Some of his clients were of long standing, whereas for others he made only a few appearances within a short space of time. Relationships in which he was involved for over a decade included those with the earl of Rothes (21 years), the earl of Eglinton (18 years), James Kennedy of Blairqhuan (14 years), John Carmichael of Meadowflat (12 years) and Margaret Boyd, countess of Cassillis (10 years). His relationship with the following clients spanned 9 years: William, Lord Borthwick; Gilbert McDowall of Spott; Patrick Ogilvy of Inchmartin and

---

[61] On Crichton, see T.I. Rae, *The Administration of the Scottish Frontier 1513–1603* (Edinburgh, 1966), 234.

[62] Wormald, *Lords and Men*, 341.

[63] *Edin. Burgh Recs.*, ii, 81: 27 Jan. 1537.

John Lindsay of Covington. In the absence of a large number of documents bearing Leslie's name it is impossible to tell, in most cases, whether these long-standing relationships produced closer personal ties than is the case with short-term clients. Ogilvy of Inchmartin can be linked with Leslie's widow and eldest son shortly after his death but, generally speaking, such links are elusive.[64] Of course, durability of relationship is not the same as intensity of activity especially in the context of a legal system where a single action might drag on for years. For example, Leslie acted on behalf of Hector Bruce of Coultmalindie for some nine years but only against one opponent, William, Lord Ruthven. In total, during this period he appeared on thirteen separate occasions arguing on Bruce's behalf in the same action.

In terms of religious houses, Leslie's most direct contact was with the priory of Elcho in Perthshire and this has already been described. Churchmen of high rank do not particularly feature in his client list. In particular there are no bishops or archbishops (although he did act for David Beaton, but only when he was abbot of Arbroath). This in part reflects the fact that senior churchmen often had considerable legal knowledge themselves and so had no need to hire a man of law; indeed several leading bishops and abbots were lords of session. But even experienced lawyers, and law graduates such as Alexander Milne or David Beaton, did on occasion use procurators. Another reason for this clerical deficiency may lie in Leslie's status as a lay lawyer; other men of law who were also secular priests might have had an advantage in recruiting such clients. Nonetheless, Leslie did represent the abbots of Arbroath, Glenluce, Holyrood, Lindores, Jedburgh and Paisley; the priors of Inchmahome, St Andrews and Whithorn, and the prioresses of Elcho and Haddington, as well as less significant figures in the secular clergy such as the dean, and chanter of Moray, and the vicars of Perth and Inverness. There is no pattern to the monastic houses represented by Leslie: there was no discrimination on his part between Cistercian, Cluniac, Augustinian and Tironensian foundations.[65] Nor is there any particular geographical link between the foundations he represented, although in no case are they entirely isolated from other clients which he had in that area. This might suggest that representing a major abbey was a means of gaining other clients locally. Take for example Robert Shaw, abbot of Paisley. Leslie first appeared on his behalf in 1526. Thereafter he began to appear for other clients in the Renfrew area, such as James Crawford of Auchinhame (in 1527) and Henry Maxwell of Bishopton (in 1528). This may have drawn him to the attention of Ninian, Lord Ross, for whom he appeared in 1531. There is no way to be certain that recruitment of clients occurred in this way but it seems plausible. The abbot was not Leslie's first

---

[64] CS 15/1: 1 Dec. 1536.
[65] See Finlay, 'Professional Men of Law', Appendix 2.

client in Renfrew since he was already representing John Muir of Caldwell. But this was probably the result of Muir's relationship with the Montgomeries of Eglinton which will be discussed below. Equally, appearances for lay clients in the vicinity of a priory might have led to Leslie's employment by the latter. This may have happened with the priory of Whithorn, where in the years before his appearances for the prior Leslie acted for locals such as Dame Janet Stewart, lady Mochrum and Gilbert Graham of Knockdoliane. The importance of local knowledge in building a client-base should not be underestimated.

A strictly geographical analysis of Leslie's clients does therefore provide useful insight into the importance of his own locality in their recruitment as well as the localities of figures whom he represented who were in a position of local influence and patronage. The number of clients drawn from the burgh of Edinburgh and its environs is equally significant since that is where Leslie spent much of his time in practice before the lords of council. From Edinburgh itself came eighteen clients, including two of his fellow burgesses with the widow of one and the son of another, and to this should be added a further eleven from the constabulary of Haddington and two from Linlithgow.

(ii) Kin relationships

The 284 clients whom Leslie represented shared only 141 surnames. As well as fathers and sons, such the first two successive earls of Arran or the seventh and eighth earls of Crawford; there were included siblings such as Bartholomew and Gilbert McDowall in Dumfries.[66] From Fife came lairds such as Paul, Patrick, William and George Dishington whilst from the north-east came Janet Gordon, lady Lindsay, and her nephew, George, earl of Huntly.

Perhaps the most significant kin group represented by Leslie were the Montgomeries of Eglinton in Ayrshire. Hugh, first earl of Eglinton, has already been mentioned as one of his major clients but the family provided him with several other clients one of whom was probably Adam Montgomerie for whom he acted in 1532.[67] The context suggests that Adam was related to the earl and tentatively he can be identified with Adam Montgomerie of Giffen, in Ayrshire, who was certainly related to the main Montgomerie line.[68] More easily identified is Sir Neil Montgomerie of Langshaw, a grandson of the first earl of Eglinton. In 1535 Leslie acted for him against John Boyd who sought payment of £40 allegedly owing to him in assythment from Sir Neil and his elder brother, Master William Montgomerie

[66]   CS 5/37 fo. 49r: 26 Mar. 1527.
[67]   CS 5/43 fo. 150v: 10 Feb. 1532.
[68]   Douglas, *Baronage*, 525.

of Greenfield, as cautioner.[69] Seven years earlier Leslie had acted for Sir Neil's wife, Margaret Muir, heiress of Quentin Muir of Ard, in an action against William Muir of Skeldon and Hugh Campbell of Loudoun. The case concerned the lands of Ard, of which Campbell was the superior. He had entered William into these lands on the basis that he was entitled to them as heir of entail. Margaret objected to this on the basis that the entail was made by Campbell, or his predecessor, in defraud of the rightful heir. She sought to have William's sasine annulled on the basis that the charter of tailzie (or entail) from which it proceeded was false. There was some dispute as to how many charters of entail were made; Leslie alleged that Campbell made one on 20 October 1507 but William Muir also had one dated April 1440. Leslie therefore summoned notaries to produce their protocol books so that the authenticity of the charter might be verified. Despite various procedural objections by Robert Galbraith, acting for William and Hugh Campbell, in which he seems to have argued that the action had prescribed, and then that they should not be allowed more time to summon witnesses when none appeared, the case was resolved in favour of the pursuers. The lords found that the charter of entail relied on by the defenders was invalid because the original writing had been scraped away and it had been rewritten. This case is significant because some years prior to it Leslie had acted for a John Campbell of Skeldon, very probably an adherent of the Campbells of Loudoun. If he had faced a conflict of interest it must have been easily resolved in favour of his allegiance to the Montgomeries of Eglinton.

The major player on the Eglinton side in the Montgomerie-Cunningham feud, which raged during the reign of James V, was John, master of Montgomerie, the earl's eldest son. Leslie also acted for him, in an action of spuilzie in 1518 brought by Master John Forman, chanter of Glasgow.[70] In the context of the Ayrshire feud, it is worth noting that there is not a single Cunningham for whom Leslie appeared as procurator.[71]

Of more direct concern to him was Leslie's own kin. His most significant client in Fife, and probably his most important patron, was George Leslie, fourth earl of Rothes, for whom he made twenty-nine appearances in the course of dealing with fifteen separate actions involving the earl between 1514 and 1535. It would seem likely that the agreement to represent the earl, as his chief kinsman, would have been his primary obligation and would have excepted no one apart from the king (and perhaps his own closest relatives). When Lord Lindsay of the Byres was dismissed as sheriff principal of Fife in 1529 because he had acted partially, it is significant that Leslie did not act on

---

[69] CS 6/6 fos. 24v, 47r.

[70] CS 5/31 fo. 100v: 13 July 1518.

[71] William Cunningham, parson of Hawick, did however constitute him as a procurator: CS 5/28 fo. 130r: 24 Jan. 1517.

his behalf even though he had acted for him on previous occasions. The case involved direct conflict between Lindsay and Robert Orrock, another man for whom Leslie had acted in the past, and this might explain his non-involvement. But the man to benefit from Lindsay's loss of office was his replacement as sheriff, the earl of Rothes, and there is a temptation to conclude that Leslie did not represent Lindsay because it was not in Rothes's interest to advance Lindsay's cause.

Leslie's closeness to Rothes can be demonstrated in numerous ways, some of which will be mentioned later. At the moment only two pieces of evidence need be mentioned. On 1 December 1528 an agreement between the earl of Rothes and John Crichton of Strathord was made and registered in the books of council. Under its terms, Crichton and his wife were to appear on 11 December and declare on oath how much money, jewellery and other goods they had obtained, without the earl's permission, from his late wife, Elizabeth, countess of Huntly, from the day she married him until the hour the agreement was made. They then bound themselves to deliver to him all of these items except 'small thingis' worth less than £100. Added at the bottom of the folio on which this agreement appears, is a short entry as follows: 'And gif the said erle keipis nocht that day the said John is contentit that his procuratour robert lesley reassaif thir ayth for him'.[72] In November 1530 Rothes and Leslie, as the curators of Robert Mercer of Balleif in Perthshire, brought an action on Robert's behalf against the Perth burgess John Pyper, to remove John from lands in the burgh of Perth belonging to Robert.[73] Only Leslie was actually required to appear. But as curators they had replaced Master Alexander McBrek, who had been Robert Mercer's tutor when the previous year Leslie had acted for his mother, Margaret Moncreiff, against him in an action concerning her terce.[74]

Leslie did not draw clients from the Aberdeenshire branch of the Leslie family, the Leslies of Balquhain. It was alleged before the lords in 1525, however, that he was a 'couiunct persoun' to the laird of Meldrum, Alexander Seton.[75] This was in the context of an action between William Forbes and Seton which was raised by Forbes, and his procurator Henry Spittall, despite an obligation dating from 3 March 1484 which was described as an 'assourance'. Leslie alleged that this assurance, which included the kin on either side, had been broken by the raising of the action and that a penalty

---

[72]   CS 5/39 fos. 15v–16r: 28 Nov. 1528.
[73]   CS 5/41 fo. 127r: 18 Nov. 1530.
[74]   CS 5/39 fo. 169v: 13 Mar. 1529. McBrek was another burgess of–and sometime bailie and dean of guild in–Perth: *Perth Guildry Book 1542–1601*, ed. Marion L. Stewart (Scottish Record Society, 1993), 120. He claimed to be standard clerk of Perth in 1523, a claim refuted by the sheriff principal, William Ruthven: CS 5/33 fo. 124v.
[75]   Leslie first acted for Seton of Meldrum in 1518: CS 5/32 fo. 6v: 19 Nov. 1518. He may have done so again prior to 1525, but a large portion of the record is missing during that period.

mentioned therein should now be paid.[76] The legal action formed one episode in a feud between the Forbeses and the Leslies. In 1526 both John Leslie of Kinawty and Alexander Seton of Meldrum were murdered by Lord Forbes and his kin.[77] When the feud was resolved in 1530, at Aberdeen, with a mutual agreement to keep the peace, only one of the witnesses, George, earl of Huntly, was connected to Leslie although the first evidence of their relationship does not appear until some time later. Indeed, two of the witnesses—Sir Alexander Irvine of Drum and Gilbert Keith of Troup—were at the time clients of Robert Galbraith.[78] Apart from Leslie's connection with Seton, and despite sharing their surname, there is no evidence of a link with the Leslies of Balquhain. This is surprising given his extensive number of clients in the sheriffdom of Aberdeen, and the fact that lands in the burgh were gifted to him by the king in 1531 for gratuitous, albeit undefined, service.[79]

Equally significant, but more difficult to trace, are relationships by affinity. According to Dr Wormald, marriage contracts were the weakest form of alliance in a Scotland dominated by agnatic kin groups. They were weaker than the personal bond, which directly cemented a relationship between men of different kindreds, in that marriage did not directly join the husband to his wife's kindred; nor was the wife assimilated into her husband's kin group.[80] A marriage alliance cannot therefore be taken as an automatic indication of closeness between the families of the husband and wife and, indeed, the client lists examined in this chapter reflect this. It would be absurd to imagine that a man of law used by the husband's family should also thereafter be used by his wife's kin. The process is more subtle and needs to be viewed from the advocate's perspective. If he is known and trusted by one kindred, then there is no reason why he should not meet and interact with their supporters and allies. Obviously, advocates were to be found in Edinburgh and some clients might be guided independently to a particular man because of his reputation alone; but the recommendation of a friend or kinsman would no doubt help.

Nonetheless, the limits of taking a prosopographical approach to client lists should be stressed. The following example demonstrates the potential pitfalls. It would not be difficult to imagine that when Patrick, earl Bothwell, was released from ward during 1533 he decided to instruct Leslie to act for him (which he did the following year) on the basis that Leslie was Lord Maxwell's man of law.[81] Bothwell was linked to Maxwell through his mother, Agnes,

[76] CS 5/35 fo. 58v: 1 July 1525.
[77] *The House of Forbe*, eds. A.N. Tayler & H.A.H. Tayler (Spalding Club, 1937), 73.
[78] Ibid., 62.
[79] *RSS*, ii, no. 892: 28 Apr. 1531. This was probably in recognition of his roles of custodian of the privy seal, and keeper of the signet.
[80] Wormald, *Lords and Men*, 79.
[81] Patrick was warded in 1531 for entering into treasonable correspondence with Henry VIII of England: *Scots Peerage*, iii, 157.

whose second husband was Maxwell's father. Yet this involves reasoning backwards on the assumption that Bothwell's choice was inevitable. It was not. If anything, it is easier to construct a link between Bothwell and Robert Galbraith than between him and Leslie. Since Agnes was the half-sister of the earl of Buchan, who used Galbraith as his regular procurator, then had Bothwell chosen Galbraith his decision might easily have been ascribed to his maternal link with the Stewart earls of Buchan. After all, Agnes had a blood relationship with Buchan, but only a relationship by marriage with Maxwell and Galbraith's relationship with Buchan was of much longer standing than Leslie's with Maxwell. But Bothwell did not choose Galbraith, and his decision to use Leslie might have been influenced by a myriad of personal considerations about which nothing can be known. This emphasises the potential danger in making assumptions about marriage links. In the absence of extraneous information—and in most cases court appearances are the only surviving link between lawyer and client—there is necessarily an element of speculation in building a picture of how the lawyer went about building his client-base. But that does not invalidate the approach, it merely counsels caution.

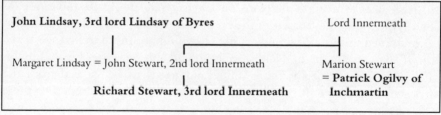

Figure 6.1 (Leslie's clients are in bold type.)

Another example of how relationships by affinity might be responsible for augmenting Leslie's clientele, is that of one of his Fife clients John, third lord Lindsay of Byres (see **Figure 6.1**). John's daughter Margaret had married John Stewart, Lord Innermeath.[82] Their son, Richard became one of Leslie's clients. Richard's aunt, Marion Stewart, was in turn married to a third client of Leslie, Patrick Ogilvy of Inchmartin.[83] This could be simple coincidence although the conclusion that Richard was influenced in his choice of advocate by his grandfather John, or his uncle Patrick, cannot be discounted. To complete the picture, Margaret Lindsay's brother, Patrick, was succeeded in 1526 by his grandson, John, fifth lord Lindsay of Byres. John, himself a client of Leslie, married the daughter of another client, John, second earl of Atholl.[84] In

82   *Scots Peerage*, v, 4.
83   Ibid..
84   Ibid., v, 398.

Forfarshire, two of Leslie's clients—some fourteen years apart—were also linked by marriage: John Erskine of Dun and Alexander Durham of Grange.[85] The latter was married before 1525 to Erskine's daughter, Janet.[86]

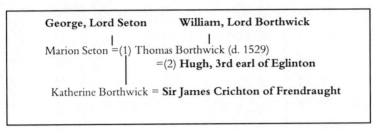

Figure 6.2 (Leslie's clients are in bold type)

More geographically removed from the north-east of Scotland, Marion Seton provides a further example. Both her father, George, Lord Seton, and William, Lord Borthwick, who was the father of her first husband Thomas, were clients of Leslie. Marion and Thomas had a daughter, Katherine, who in turn married Sir James Crichton of Frendraught, one of Leslie's Aberdeenshire clients. After Thomas died in 1529, Marion herself married Hugh, earl of Eglinton, Leslie's major client in the south-west. Again, it could be a coincidence that Leslie acted for all of these people who, at first sight, have little in common. But the very fact they have so little in common is significant because without this relationship by affinity it is difficult to explain how Leslie could have become involved with such diverse clients. The same is true in the example of Patrick, Lord Gray and his brother Gilbert, given in Figure 6.3, which illustrate the importance of marriage and its ramifications to building up a clientele.

Finally, widows as a group formed a significant class of clients in the sixteenth century. Often they were left to live out a significant portion of their life sometimes in quite comfortable circumstances and yet their sex and, in some cases, their age, made them peculiarly vulnerable. This was especially the case should disputes arise, as they often did, between the widow and her late husband's kin (even with her own children) concerning her terce. When the threat was external, in the sense of coming from a party who was a member of neither kin, then the widow might become involved in a legal action with the blessing and advice of her sons. This occurred in the case of David Beaton, abbot of Arbroath, and his mother Isobel Monypenny. David arranged for Leslie, as one of his own legal advisers, to act on Isobel's behalf in an action she had against James Lundie of Balgonie concerning her terce of the lands of

---

[85] CS 5/32 107r-v: 3-4 Mar. 1519; CS 6/2 fo. 168r: 5 May 1533.
[86] Douglas, *Baronage*, 472.

Figure 6.3

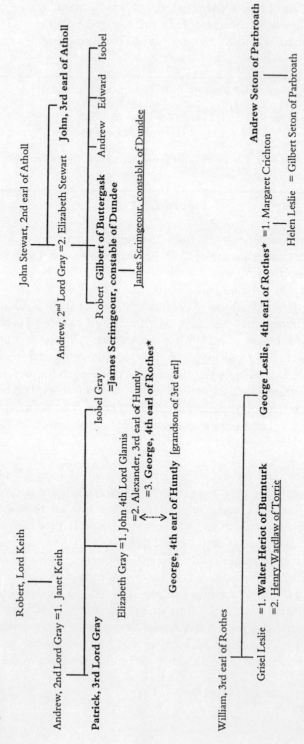

Bold: a party for whom Leslie appeared before the lords of session.
Underlined: a party who constituted Leslie as one of his procurators.

Balfour.[87] This was the fourth time Leslie had acted for an opponent of Lundie of Balgonie, and he may have been involved as an adviser when a fifth client of his, William Wardlaw, made an arbitrated settlement with Lundie in 1527.[88] Isobel was one of over a dozen widows whom Leslie represented and in the main they were women who had been married to lesser lairds and burgesses.

(iii) Consensual relationships

This category primarily relates to magnatial affinities and relationships between men of whatever rank created and underpinned by bonds given consensually (even if through the necessity of acting for financial or other reasons). According to Kelham, the raison d'être of the affinity was service: from man to lord and vice-versa.[89] As he points out, identifying the members of a magnatial affinity is necessarily a process of inference and mere kinship and geographical proximity cannot always be relied on as automatic indicators of bonds between lords and men. An instructive example of this is the fifth earl of Angus. In 1483 only half of his council were his vassals while most of the bailies on his estates had no tenurial ties to him.[90] Given the fact that in the reign of James V there were twenty-one earldoms and only eight general procurators of the college of justice, some advocates inevitably came to be identified with more than one magnatial affinity. The service that they provided was primarily in the form of counsel and legal representation and it is questionable whether the inference can safely be drawn from such activities that they belonged to a particular affinity. In the present context the approach taken has been not to look at the advocate's impact on, or importance within, any given affinity, but to assess the importance of the affinity in advancing the advocate's career.

Robert Leslie provides an excellent case study in this respect. The evidence strongly suggests that he was part of the earl of Rothes's affinity. Apart from the probable family relationship between them, at least one charter, made by the earl in 1529, was witnessed by Leslie although only its confirmation seems to survive.[91] The following year he was also a witness to the marriage contract, signed in Haddington, between Rothes and John Wardlaw, laird of Torrie, for the marriage of the earl's sister Isobel and John's son and heir, Henry.[92] On the basis that appearances in charter witness lists provide evidence of a role in the

---

[87] CS 6/7 fo. 150r: 15 Mar. 1536.
[88] *Prot. Bk. Foular*, ii, no. 830: 25 May 1527. The other cases against Lundie were on behalf of David Learmonth (twice: CS 5/33 fos. 28v, 94v), and William Murray of Tullibardine (CS 5/39 fo. 79r).
[89] Kelham, 'Magnatial Power', 20.
[90] Kelley, 'Douglas Earls of Angus', 175.
[91] *RMS*,, iii, no. 717.
[92] CS 5/40 fo. 54r: 8 June 1529. The other witness to the contract was Bernard Bailie, another man close to the abbot of Arbroath: Sanderson, *Cardinal of Scotland*, 58.

magnatial affinity, Leslie must also be considered as a candidate for membership of the affinities of the earls of Errol, Atholl and, perhaps, Crawford. In the narrower context of representation in court, he certainly appeared on behalf of all of these as well as the earls of Arran, Bothwell, Lennox, Huntly, Eglinton and, of course, Rothes, although in the case of most of these earls no additional information concerning their links to Leslie survives.

In terms of the importance of a magnatial affinity on Leslie's burgeoning career, probably the best example, after the earl of Rothes (already mentioned in the previous section), are Alexander and David Lindsay, the seventh and eighth earls of Crawford. Charles Kelham's work on the affinity of the fifth earl has been of value in identifying which of Leslie's clients he may have met through his connection to the seventh earl and his successor. Leslie's relationship to the earls can be traced back at least to 1517 when he witnessed a charter by David, master of Crawford, granting lands in Perthshire, and appeared before the lords of council on behalf of his father.[93] The definite Lindsay adherents represented by Leslie are as follows: Thomas Fotheringham of Powrie, Thomas Ogilvy of Clova, John Lindsay of Covington, Robert Carnegie of Kinnaird, Richard, Lord Innermeath, Robert Maule of Panmure, Andrew Guthrie of that ilk and John Carmichael of Meadowflat, captain of Crawford castle.[94] Of these eight clients three were from Forfar, three from Perth and two from Lanarkshire and apart from the common denominator of adherence to Crawford there is no obvious link between them.[95] Ogilvy of Clova, however, was one of the tenants of the kirk of Alyth in Menmuir, which pertained to the bishopric of Dunkeld. A connection through his father might explain why Leslie acted for these tenants in 1524 against Lord Glamis and George Hepburn, vicar general of Dunkeld, in a dispute concerning payment of teinds.[96] Leslie's relationship with Lindsay of Covington was well known, even to the extent that he complained on one occasion that John Campbell, the treasurer, had known well that Leslie was Covington's procurator and had chosen to call a summons against him when Leslie was absent.[97]

Clearly his early start with the earls of Crawford was of considerable value to Leslie because it allowed him to recruit numerous clients from the ranks of their adherents. The effect that success like this had on his reputation probably

93 *RMS,*, iii, no. 180.
94 The Fotheringhams of Powrie were also important vassals of the earls of Angus in the regality of Kirriemuir, however as Kelley points out, their primary allegiance was to the earls of Crawford: Kelley, 'Douglas Earls of Angus', 139–141.
95 To this list can probably be added master Charles Fotheringham, parson of Edzell, who constituted Leslie in 1524 but for whom Leslie is not recording as appearing.
96 CS 5/34 fo. 133v: 1 Mar. 1524.
97 CS 5/33 fo. 83r: 11 Dec. 1522.

had a knock-on effect and may have brought him significantly more than those eight clients named above. For example, Robert, fifth lord Maxwell, was served heir to his father in lands in Lanarkshire which he then held of Lindsay of Covington.[98] Maxwell was an important figure and a significant client for Leslie on the West March of which he was warden, as well as holding the offices of steward of Annandale, steward of Kirkcudbright, sheriff of Dumfries and keeper of Lochmaben castle. The tenurial link with Lindsay of Covington aside, Maxwell was linked by service to other Leslie clients. John Carmichael of Meadowflat, like Covington part of the Crawford affinity, entered into a bond of manrent with Maxwell in 1528.[99] Carmichael had been a client of Leslie's since 1524 and Leslie did not appear for Maxwell until the 1530s. But it is not possible to infer whether he did so through the influence of Carmichael, or Lindsay, or even his wife, Lady Bothwell. Leslie can be directly linked with two other men close to Maxwell, his brother-in-law Alexander Jardine of Applegirth and John Armstrong who entered a bond of manrent with him in 1525. Three years after this, Leslie and Jardine were named by Armstrong as procurators for resigning his lands in Langholm.[100] Another Leslie client, Thomas Kirkpatrick of Closeburn, was also to make a bond of manrent with Maxwell but not until 1543. This is the opposite situation from that described in relation to the earldom of Crawford. Instead of a geographically diverse earldom providing the means to obtain clients in sheriffdoms far removed from one another, Leslie also made use of local networks to meet the same objective. Rather than kin relationship or mere proximity, the key element here was service to a local figure. Of course, other men of law might tap into the same network although moving from a different point of origin. Thus James Douglas of Drumlanrig and James Gordon of Lochinver, both clients of Robert Galbraith, also made bonds of manrent with Lord Maxwell in 1518 and 1525 respectively.[101]

In Ayrshire, another local network operated to Leslie's potential benefit. It was centred on the Montgomeries of Eglinton and included the Muirs of Caldwell who were their close neighbours. John Muir, laird of Caldwell, entered into a bond of manrent with Earl Hugh in 1527. This was prompted by Caldwell's financial difficulties stemming from a lawsuit which followed an attack he had unwisely made on chancellor James Beaton's residence in

[98] CS 5/26 fo. 150v: 20 July 1514: *Robert, Lord Maxwell v John Lindsay of Covington*, concerning his service to the lands of Waranhill in the sheriffdom of Lanark. Lindsay was absent from the realm and the lords decided that Robert should be served as heir to his late father on Lindsay's return.
[99] William Carmichael of Meadowflat was captain of Crawford castle at least from early in James IV's reign and may have succeeded John Lindsay of Covington who was bailie of the barony of Crawford Lindsay in the 1470s: Kelley, 'Douglas Earls of Angus', 171.
[100] Fraser, *Caerlaverock*, ii, 465, no. 84.
[101] Wormald, *Lords and Men*, 334-5.

Glasgow in 1515 prior to the arrival of the regent, Albany.[102] Although John Lethame was his procurator in 1517, defending Beaton's action of spuilzie, Leslie had become his man of law by 1524.[103] The bond of manrent cemented a marriage link between the two families with Caldwell's eldest son having married Eglinton's daughter and it would be reasonable to assume that Leslie became involved with the Muirs of Caldwell because of his Eglinton connection. The link with both families was maintained when in 1527 Leslie represented Margaret Muir, who was the wife of Neil Montgomerie. In 1534 David Caldwell produced in court a bond stating that he, and his heirs, had become man and servant to Eglinton for all the days of his life.[104]

(2) The career of Master Robert Galbraith

Robert Galbraith had his origins in Berwickshire, the son of David Galbraith of Kimmergame, a lesser laird and a tenant of the Homes of Wedderburn. There is nothing particularly notable about this minor branch of the Galbraith family: it did not even merit a mention in Home of Godscroft's history of the Homes of Wedderburn published in 1611. According to a recent study, the Galbraiths of East Windshiel, as they had become known by the mid-sixteenth century, were at that time still lesser Berwickshire lairds with no evidence of upward social mobility.[105]

Very little is known of Robert's early life until he came to prominence in Paris in the early 1500s as a lecturer in logic at the *College de Coqueret*. He is known, hoever, to have obtained a degree at the university of Paris in 1503.[106] Recent study has demonstrated the significance of Galbraith's academic work on philosophy and he is regarded as an important figure in the circle of John Major.[107] In 1510 Galbraith dedicated his major work on logic, *Quadrupertitum*, to James IV's advocate James Henryson. Given the obscurity of Galbraith's early life it is impossible to know whether he personally knew or corresponded with Henryson. The latter was a graduate of Paris and his nephew James Foulis, later clerk register, was one of Galbraith's students and it is certainly possible that they had corresponded. Another of his Scots students was Thomas Bellenden, who was director of chancery by 1514 and later justice-clerk general.[108]

---

[102] *Caldwell Papers*, i, 10: 19 Oct. 1527.

[103] This dispute was still going on in 1518 with Lethame again acting as the laird of Caldwell's forespeaker: CS 5/30 fo. 210r: 1 Mar. 1518.

[104] CS 6/5 fo. 82r: 23 July 1534. Unfortunately, there is no indication of why Caldwell was required to produce this document.

[105] M. Meikle, 'Lairds and Gentlemen', 489.

[106] Galbraith took his B.A. in 1502 and his licence and inception as M.A. in 1503. There is no record of him in the university's register of law students. I am grateful to Dr John Durkan for this information.

[107] A. Broadie, *The Circle of John Major: Logic and Logicians in Pre-Reformation Scotland* (Oxford, 1985), 4-5.

[108] For Bellenden as director of chancery, see CS 5/26 fo. 174r: 23 Oct. 1514.

With his successful track record in law and philosophy, and perhaps known also as a poet, Galbraith no doubt returned to Scotland with considerable aspirations. His return should probably be dated to 1515, since his first appearance before the lords of council was in August of that year although his first constitution as a procurator before them was not recorded until 11 January, 1516.[109] There is no evidence of a link between Galbraith and the duke of Albany and his return to Scotland was probably independent of the new governor's arrival on 16 May, 1515.

It seems likely that Galbraith returned in order to pursue a legal career. That this was his long term aim may be inferred from the dedication to Henryson, although in the event Galbraith arrived too late to profit from the latter's undoubted influence in royal and legal circles. His main family connection was with the Homes, staunch allies of the earl of Angus and, after his marriage to her in the summer of 1514, of Margaret Tudor. Lord Home's involvement in the confused politics of the period were to have fatal consequences. Within months of arriving in Scotland, Albany sought to secure possession of the young king and his brother. Lord Home was one of those to whom Margaret was prepared to surrender possession of her sons, although Albany rejected him as untrustworthy given his support for Angus. It was at this point that Lord Home became embroiled in a plot by Lord Dacre to kidnap the king from Stirling castle where Margaret was being beseiged by forces loyal to the Governor. Emond suggests Home broke with Albany, whose return he had hitherto welcomed, because of disappointed ambition. Whatever the reason, it had disastrous consequences, with Home, his four brothers, and David Heriot of Trabroun all charged with treason.[110] Albany raised significant forces in pursuit of Home, and the pressure he exerted led David Home of Wedderburn to compear before the lords of council in August 1515 and swear not to give aid to Lord Home but rather to pursue him at his utmost power.[111] This was clearly expedient but Home of Polwarth also gave the same oath and in the circumstances they had little choice. This growing crisis amongst the Homes may have been the trigger that led to Galbraith's return. It is noticeable that in April, 1516, he acted before the lords on behalf of David Home of Wedderburn, his father's landlord and the earl of Angus's brother-in-law. Although Lord Home and his brother William were not executed until the following October, it seems that Home of Wedderburn had done enough to distance himself from them, albeit temporarily. Galbraith's career does not ultimately appear to have suffered. Indeed the events of 1515 and 1516 may have helped him in that the support for Queen Margaret among the Homes in 1515 may have influenced her in his favour when looking for an

---

[109] CS 5/27 fo. 54r: 17 Aug. 1515; CS 5/27 fo. 135r: 11 Jan. 1516; Emond, 'Minority of James V', 81.
[110] Emond, 'Minority of James V', 88-9.
[111] CS 5/27 fo. 56v: 27 Aug. 1515.

advocate in 1517. By the time of the revenge killing of Albany's deputy, Seigneur de la Bastie, by Home of Wedderburn in September, 1517, Galbraith was already acting for Margaret Tudor and indeed Margaret was even prepared to defend Home's involvement in the murder.[112] In the difficult circumstances of the following years Galbraith may have kept in touch with Home of Wedderburn. After his death, George Home, his son and heir, was represented by Galbraith early in 1525 in a sheriff court of Berwick held in Edinburgh where Galbraith required the sheriffs *in hac parte* to appoint officers of the court for serving George as heir to his father. Amongst those appointed was Galbraith's nephew Simon Fortune as sergeant and John Galbraith, presumably another relative, as dempster.[113]

Within a year of his first appearance in Scotland after his return from France, Galbraith can be found as a witness to the transumpt made in St Giles by the commissary of St Andrews, Master Matthew Kerr.[114] This placed him in the company of three men destined to become leading lawyers and judges during the personal reign of James V: John Lethame, Henry Lauder and his former pupil, James Foulis. Like Leslie, Galbraith was made a burgess of Edinburgh. Although his name does not appear on the burgess roll, he was definitely a burgess by March, 1526.[115] A decade earlier he had been one of a number of people asked to convene in the tolbooth to advise the council of Edinburgh concerning certain leases and his admission as a burgess may have been for this, and perhaps similar services to the burgh, and may date from soon after his return to Scotland.[116]

Although designed as a chaplain in 1526, it was not until around 1528 that Galbraith held an ecclesiastical position which can be more closely identified.[117] From this time he was treasurer of the chapel royal in Stirling, a post which his relationship with the queen mother was no doubt instrumental in securing since Stirling castle was part of Margaret's tocher. By the time he was made a lord of session, in November 1537, Galbraith had become parson of Spott. This latter appointment probably reflects the fact that for some time he had been acquiring land in East Lothian. In 1523 he purchased the lands of East Windshiel in Berwickshire from David Renton of Billie, an in-law (*genero*) of Galbraith's client, Sir William Sinclair of Hermiston

---

[112]   Kelley, 'Douglas Earls of Angus', 292. On Galbraith as advocate for the queen, see J. Finlay 'Robert Galbraith and the role of queen's advocate' (1999) *JR* 277-290.

[113]   *HMC, Milne-Home*, 34-5.

[114]   *Midlothian Chrs.*, 87*ff*: 16 Aug. 1516.

[115]   *Yester Writs*, no. 424: 8 Mar. 1526.

[116]   *Edin. Burgh Recs.*, i, 150: 18 Apr. 1516. Galbraith's name follows that of Adam Otterburn, common clerk of the burgh, and Thomas Hamilton, both noted lawyers.

[117]   *Prot. Bk. Foular*, ii, no. 668: 28 Feb. 1526; Watt, *Fasti*, 339.

('Hirdmanston').[118] Five years later he purchased the neighbouring estate of Mid Windshiel from Thomas Redpath.[119]

Galbraith acquired land not only through purchase but also through gift and distraint. Already by 1520 he can be found taking an annualrent from a large house in Edinburgh from Margaret Whitehead as security for a debt. Galbraith signed a reversion under which Margaret could redeem the annualrent on payment of £160.[120] Margaret was clearly in financial difficulties because the previous year she had resigned a tenement to Janet Paterson in return for a loan, a transaction which Galbraith witnessed.[121] Margaret's financial position did not improve because in 1521 the large house from which Galbraith enjoyed an annualrent was conveyed to him, again under reversion of £160.[122] A few months later Margaret redeemed an annualrent held in another property by Andrew Touris, only to transfer it to Galbraith.[123] Things must have looked bleak for her, because the next month Galbraith purchased from John Craik some waste ground neighbouring the large house which he held as security for one of Margaret's debts.[124] Four years later, Margaret named Galbraith as one of her procurators to resign a small annualrent on her behalf although there is no indication that she did so in security of a debt. Margaret was dead by September 1529, when one of her four daughters, Agnes Liddel, used Galbraith as her attorney to obtain sasine of her part of an annualrent in yet another property.[125] Shortly after this, their mother's debts caught up with them and, for unpaid rents of lands in Ettrick Forest held of the queen, their property was apprised.[126] Queen Margaret resigned an annualrent worth 2 merks from the proceeds in favour of her advocate Galbraith.[127] Unlike the queen, there is no evidence that Margaret Whitehead was ever one of Galbraith's clients. Consequently it must be presumed that the debts she owed to him—as to others—were pure money debts and that, like other men of law, he was involved in money-lending. In 1527 Galbraith purchased land next to the tenement which he had obtained as Margaret's creditor on the north side of the High Street.[128] This augmentation replicated his behaviour with the estates of East and Mid Windshiel in Berwickshire. To these he could add in 1539 the gift of the lands of Worcley in Berwickshire, which had fallen

---

[118] *RMS,*, iii, no. 833: confirmation, 3 Sep. 1529.
[119] Ibid., iii, no. 605; NAS, Cockburn of that ilk, GD 216/1: 5 July 1528.
[120] *Prot. Bk. Foular*, ii, nos. 136, 137: 17-18 Nov. 1520.
[121] Ibid., ii, no. 5: 5 July 1519.
[122] Ibid., ii, no. 183: 4 Mar. 1521.
[123] Ibid., ii, no. 249: 9 Nov. 1521.
[124] Ibid., ii, no. 257: 31 Dec. 1521.
[125] Ibid., iii, no. 154: 27 Sep. 1529.
[126] *RMS,*, iii, no. 869: 24 Dec. 1529.
[127] *Prot. Bk. Foular*, iii, no. 221: 12 Apr. 1530.
[128] Ibid., iii, no. 791a: 6 Mar. 1527.

to his client Patrick, earl Bothwell, through nonentry, and which Patrick gifted to Galbraith.[129]

Further gifts came to Galbraith from the king. In 1529 he received the nonentry of certain lands in Edinburgh and two years later the king granted him the wardship of Hermiston in Haddington following the death of William Sinclair which occurred at Candlemas (2 February), 1531.[130] These may have been in appreciation of services performed by Galbraith on behalf of the king's mother, or as treasurer of the chapel royal, or even for services on behalf of the king himself since he did act briefly as substitute for the king's advocate.[131]

It is clear that Galbraith had property in Edinburgh well placed for attendance in the tolbooth and also for carrying on business. There are several references to legal transactions taking place in his chamber.[132] In 1524 he received sasine of another tenement on the north side of the High Street which, a year later, he granted to another man of law, Master Abraham Crichton, reserving to himself a small annualrent.[133] Galbraith had known Crichton at least since the summer of 1517, when he acted for John Crichton, the nephew and heir of the late Adam Crichton of Ruthvenis, when Abraham was John's tutor.[134] All the signs indicate that Galbraith's career and finances were prospering. Then suddenly in 1536 there is a reference to a fee being paid to the royal messenger Alexander Hutton for arresting Galbraith's goods.[135] This arrestment should not be taken as an indication of financial difficulties. It was probably made by Abraham Crichton, by then parson of Chirnside in Berwickshire (and, from 1540, official of Lothian), since the two were involved in a dispute concerning the teinds of Hermiston and Salton in East Lothian which Crichton alleged were assigned to him by the abbot of Dryburgh.[136] The matter came to an end when Crichton put the value of the teinds to Galbraith's oath and Galbraith swore to a certain valuation.[137] Presumably the arrestment was then removed. Certainly it did not prevent Galbraith being sworn in as a lord of session on 7 November the following year.[138] Although this appointment did not necessarily mean the end of his activity as an advocate, it is the date from which Galbraith should more

---

[129] CS 6/11 fo. 150r: 16 Feb. 1539.
[130] *RSS*, ii, no. 414: 2 Nov. 1529; *RSS*, ii, no. 820: 10 Feb. 1531. For Sinclair's death, see CS 5/43 fo. 67v: 9 Nov. 1531.
[131] See chapter seven.
[132] E.g., NAS, N.P. 1/2A fos. 35r-v: 16 May 1532.
[133] Prot. Bk. Foular, ii, nos. 506, 643: 8 Oct. 1524; 20 Oct. 1525.
[134] CS 5/30 fo. 120v: 28 July 1517.
[135] *TA*, vi, 266.
[136] CS 6/7 fo. 172v-174v: 29 Mar. 1536; CS 6/8 fo. 25r: 24 May 1536. In July 1527, Crichton was designed parson and vicar of the kirk of Crawfordjohn: CS 5/37 fo. 145v: 9 July 1527. At some point after 1536 he became provost of Dunglas.
[137] CS 6/8 fo. 41r: 31 May 1536.
[138] CS 6/9 fo. 2r: 7 Nov. 1537.

properly be seen as a judge and no attempt has been made to continue to compile his client list during his years as a senator of the college of justice.

Robert Galbraith was murdered by John Carkettle of Finglen and his accomplices in the kirkyard of the Grey Friars, on the morning of 27 January 1544, at the time of divine service.[139] Allegedly the murder was in revenge for favour shown by him to Sir William Sinclair of Hermiston in a legal action.[140] Since there is a gap in the record at the time of the killing, it is not possible to confirm whether such an action took place nor whether the accusation had any basis in truth. But the pre-existing relationship between Galbraith, his nephew Simon Fortune, and their family with the Sinclairs of Hermiston, which may have stretched back several generations, at least makes it plausible.[141] The murderer was certainly Carkettle who was himself, as a burgess of Edinburgh, certainly not unknown to Galbraith; for instance, both were executors of Janet Paterson in 1534.[142] The killing provoked fear amongst the members of the college of justice which prompted the governor, Arran, to order that the killers be pursued with all rigour of law and to declare that henceforth anyone who killed a judge, advocate or scribe of the college committed lèse majesté.[143] Carkettle and his accomplices, William Ken, James Gibson and Alexander Thomson, were threatened in March, 1544, with escheat for the 'treasonable slaughter'[144] Less than two months later, however, they received a remission.[145] They had bought their way out of trouble by offering to pay assythment to Galbraith's heirs. In January 1549, Carkettle and Gibson were ordered to relieve cautioners found on their behalf before the justice court.[146] His executor, his cousin Master Adam Galbraith, devoted £20, from the assythment of £500, to provide a chaplain to pray for Robert's soul in St Giles. Galbraith's house on the High Street became the property of Master Adam who by the mid-1550s was rector of Mordington in Berwickshire.[147] Another of his heirs was his nephew, Robert Galbraith, probably the son of his brother Simon. As assignee of the late Robert, this nephew was involved in an arbitration with Sir James Stirling of Keir in 1551 concerning the lands of Ballindrocht which must have been held by the judge

[139] CS 7/8 fo. 386v: 31 Jan. 1553.
[140] Hugo Arnot, *Criminal Trials* (Edinburgh, 1785), 155.
[141] In 1379, John Sinclair of Hermiston was granted the lands and village of Kimmergame, later held by David Galbraith: Kelley, 'Douglas Earls of Angus', 150-3, citing NAS, RH 1/2/141. The Sinclairs retained the land until 1467, when the laird, John Sinclair, died and his daugthers married George Home of Wedderburn and Patrick Home of Polwarth who each took over as vassals of the earl of Angus in Kimmergame. As was mentioned above (p. 146), David Galbraith was a tenant of the Homes of Wedderburn.
[142] NAS, N.P. 1/2A fo. 63r: 24 June 1534.
[143] *ADCP*, 537.
[144] *RMS,*, iii, no. 668: 22 Mar. 1544.
[145] *RSS*, iii, no. 752: 3 May 1544.
[146] *ADCP*, 638.
[147] *Prot. Bk. Alexander King*, no. 16: 11 July 1555.

during his lifetime although there would appear to be no contemporary record of this.[148] Robert subsequently became a monk at the abbey of Glenluce, perhaps through connections gained by his uncle who had acted for the abbey on several occasions.[149] It might be thought that Galbraith was then forgotten. But he still had a contribution to make to Scottish legal history because a manuscript which he compiled, was later used by James Balfour in compiling his Practicks. This manuscript, in excess of six hundred folios in length and containing a version of the treatise *Regiam Majestatem* as well as varous statutes and other conventional legal material, was not only subscribed by Galbraith but bears evidence that it belonged after his death to Robert Reid, bishop of Orkney and the second lord president of the college of justice.[150] Despite Reid's ownership, Balfour referred to the manuscript as the *Liber Galbraith* and this suggests that Galbraith's reputation as a lawyer survived him for at least a generation.[151]

Galbraith and his clients

It is proposed to analyse Galbraith's client list using the same approach with which that of Leslie was considered above. From 17 August 1515 to 9 March 1517 Galbraith represented thirty-three clients of which twenty-five can be placed geographically. Of these first 25 clients, 23 (92 per cent) came from south of the Forth. Ten came from the Marches, primarily the east March, 4 each coming from the sheriffdoms of Berwick and Roxburgh, and 1 each from Dumfries and Wigtown. The rest came from Edinburgh (2), Haddington (2), Linlithgow (1), Ayr (3), Lanark (3) and Renfrew (1). The two northern clients were the parishioners of the subdeanery of Brechin, and John, Lord Drummond, who was steward of Strathearne. The balance lies towards the south-east and the importance of Berwick and Roxburgh in particular should be noticed. Although his home area was not quite so productive as Fife and Perthshire was for Leslie in his early years, clients from the Borders were certainly important for Galbraith. Political factors during this period may have resulted in fewer clients from Berwickshire than might otherwise have been the case.

Unlike Leslie, Galbraith did not represent any major magnates in this early phase of his career. The first time he represented an earl, it was the earl of Angus in 1518; indeed it took him a decade until the number of earls he had represented reached four, whereas Leslie achieved this target in just over four years. His three most notable initial clients were the abbot of Melrose, John,

[148] Fraser, *Stirlings*, 403: 7 May 1551.
[149] *Prot. Bk. Alexander King*, no. 88: 10 Mar. 1556.
[150] This manuscript is now known as the Cambridge MS.: *APS*, i, 192-3.
[151] Balfour, *Practicks*, introduction, lx.

Lord Drummond, and Margaret Tudor. But generally he began by dealing with lairds, burgesses, and tenants; in short, the middling sort, rather than those who might have offered him patronage and introductions to other clients. This might be put down to his own modest birth and his lack of personal ties with the nobility although, on the other hand, it was his relationship with the Homes and the earl of Angus which probably brought his name to the attention of Margaret Tudor.

Looking more widely at Galbraith's client list as a whole, out of 258 clients the designations of only 212 can be placed geographically. These were divided more evenly throughout the realm than the clients of Robert Leslie. Edinburgh was the sheriffdom from which he attracted the most clients, 20, with 4 from Linlithgow, 2 from Leith and 15 from the constabulary of Haddington. All of these together represent less than 20 per cent of his clientele. Ayr (16 clients), Dumfries (14), Perth (14), Fife (11), Roxburgh (10) and Aberdeen (10) were the other main sheriffdoms which provided him with clients. Sheriffdoms such as Galloway (3), Kirkcudbright (5), Wigtown (2), Selkirk (1), Inverness (7), Nairn (1), Forres (1), Forfar (9), Renfrew (5) and Lanark (6) illustrate how diverse his client-base was. This confirms the impression given by looking at Galbraith's earliest clients, and strongly suggests that he built up his practice in Edinburgh, predominately on the basis of his reputation, rather than from extensive local patronage although, of course, that was also an element.

i) *Geographical proximity*

Although Galbraith's clients were less geographically concentrated than was the case with Robert Leslie, the same percentage (58%) of Galbraith's clients came from south of the Forth as, in Leslie's case, came from the north.[152] Galbraith represented two of the five sheriffs in the Borders: Patrick, third earl Bothwell (sheriff of Berwick) and John, third lord Yester (sheriff of Peebles). Although he did represent Robert, fourth lord Sanquhar (who was the hereditary sheriff of Dumfries) this was during his minority, when the duties of sheriff were carried out by Ninian Crichton who was mentioned earlier as one of Leslie's clients.[153] The sheriff of Selkirk, James Murray of Fallahill, was represented by Henry Spittall, and the sheriff of Roxburgh, James Douglas of Cavers, although he did constitute Galbraith as one of his procurators in 1519, was never represented by him.[154] From Galbraith's point of view, this is not a bad showing particularly when added to other court holders such as the earl of Buchan (sheriff of Banff), Lord Drummond (steward of Strathearne),

---

[152]   See Figure 6.4.
[153]   Rae, *Frontier*, 234.
[154]   In 1532, Douglas of Cavers named Spittall as his only procurator.

Campbell of Loudoun (sheriff of Ayr), Lord Gray (sheriff of Forfar), Lindsay of Byres, (sheriff of Fife), John, Lord Erskine (sheriff of Stirling), William, master of Ruthven (sheriff of Perth) and Archibald Dunbar (bailie of the regality of Glasgow), to name just a few of those whom he represented.[155] It is not to be expected that Galbraith attended the courts held by his clients with any regularity, given the demands on his time this would have created. The large number of cases involving accusations of improper procedures being used by sheriffs for whom he acted indicates that he was rarely, if ever, on hand to offer advice when sheriff courts were being held.

The five burgesses for whom Galbraith acted were drawn from Ayr, Dumfries, Edinburgh, Haddington and Montrose and offer no geographical pattern. In terms of ecclesiastical foundations, however, patterns do emerge. This is most notable in the diocese of Ross, where he acted for the archdean, subdean and chanter.[156] At a higher level, he represented important abbots in the south of Scotland from the abbeys of Melrose, Kelso, Newbattle and, in the west, Glenluce. In the north-east he also acted for the abbeys of Deer and Scone. His reputation locally in the Borders may have helped him at Melrose and Kelso, and also with Christian McDowall, prioress of Eccles in Berwickshire, for whom he acted in 1529. It is somewhat surprising that he did not act for John Home, abbot of Jedburgh, given his family background. He did however act for several influential figures, such as John Hepburn, prior of St Andrews, Elizabeth Swinton, prioress of Elcho and Elizabeth Hepburn, prioress of Haddington.

The pattern of his activity for the prioress of Haddington is interesting since Galbraith was acting for her against another of his clients, John, Lord Hay of Yester. Elizabeth secured his services first, in a case in 1526 involving the perambulation of various lands bordering the estates of Lord Hay, a dispute that quickly went to arbitration and which shall be mentioned again later. In 1528 and 1529, Lord Hay used Galbraith as his procurator in two actions.[157] Then in 1533 Elizabeth brought a further action against Hay, claiming that she had again been impeded in using a common passage and that Lord Hay and his accomplices had stopped a cart full of wood for fuel being carried from Nunhope to the priory. Nunhope was one of the lands in dispute in 1526. Hay on this occasion was represented by Henry Spittall. It is likely that he

---

[155] To this should be added earl Bothwell who was also hereditary sheriff of Edinburgh; his son, Patrick, master of Hailes, as sheriff-depute of Edinburgh was twice represented by Galbraith in 1527. In that year he also appeared, albeit on only one occasion, for Henry Stewart, sheriff-depute of Banff. He also acted for earl Marischall, sheriff of Kincardine, and the earl of Huntly (sheriff of Aberdeen); and Lord Somerville (baron of Carnwath).

[156] CS 5/33 fos. 65v, 67v: 5 Dec. 1522; CS 5/34 fo. 169v: 25 May 1524.

[157] One of these was against Elizabeth Cunningham, lady Belton, his grandmother. Lord Hay had been factor of her estates. Cameron, *James V*, 101-5, assesses the significance of this case, and Lord Hay generally.

could not use Galbraith because Galbraith was bound to act for Elizabeth on the basis that she had constituted him first and that any subsequent agreement to act for Lord Hay would doubtless have excepted her. The basic idea seems to have been *prior tempore potior iure*, although that phrase was not used. Galbraith may have acted for the prioresses of Eccles and Haddington through his connection to other members of the McDowall or Hepburn families for whom he acted. There is no obvious connection between these foundations and any of his other clients in their locality.

Galbraith's career suggests that family and political connections might repel clients as easily as they attracted them. For example, Leslie's client Ninian Chernside of East Nesbit, would never have dreamed of employing Robert Galbraith to act for him against Lord Home in 1524. This was not merely because Galbraith had traditional links with the Homes, but because Chirnside was one of those responsible for the murder of David Home, prior of Coldingham, in the winter of 1517.[158] Similarly, Galbraith acted as curator to the heiresses of Blackadder because Home of Wedderburn had strongly asserted his claims to their wardship and marriage and had by 1516 seized Blackadder castle. Patrick Blackadder of Tulliallan claimed to have a royal gift of these lands, but family loyalty determined which side Galbraith should take. Margaret and Beatrice, the heiresses of Robert Blackadder (who had died at Flodden), were the daughters of Angus's sister, Alison Douglas. Her marriage to David Home of Wedderburn involved Galbraith in the legal aspects of a feud that was to last for a decade.[159]

It was not the only such matter in which he found himself involved. On the West March, in the serious feud which developed between (or, rather, was inherited by) James Douglas of Drumlanrig and Robert Crichton of Sanquhar, Galbraith represented Douglas. Crichton, as sheriff of Dumfries, allegedly tried to arrest James who claimed that his father, and all of his kin and servants, had been exempted from the jurisdiction of Crichton's father when he was sheriff because of the feud. Galbraith successfully argued Douglas's case before the lords who confirmed the exemption and named sheriff-deputes to hear all actions concerning Douglas, his tenants and household, within the shire of Dumfries.[160] A year later Douglas brought another action against Crichton of Sanquhar, on behalf of Thomas Ferguson of Craigdarach, his 'kynsman servant and part takar', whose father had been killed during the feud with the Crichtons, and successfully asserted Ferguson's right to exemption from all courts held by Crichton.[161] Douglas and Ferguson again used Galbraith as

---

[158] Emond, 'Minority of James V', 173.
[159] On the Home/Blackadder feud, see Kelley, 'Douglas Earls of Angus', 289-292.
[160] CS 5/29 fo. 12r: 17 Feb. 1517.
[161] CS 5/31 fo. 128r: 19 July 1518. In 1516, Ninian Crichton received a remission for the 'forethocht felony' of Robert and Alexander Ferguson: *RSS*, i, no. 2703: 8 Feb. 1516. If this Ninian, described as

procurator. Ferguson was involved in further litigation late in 1518 and early the following year against Margaret Moncrieff, widow of Laurence Crichton of Rossy, and Robert Crichton of Sanquhar and, again, he used Galbraith.[162]

Feuding and local disturbances were an unavoidable part of the political background of the minority. In resuming his relationship with Sir Hugh Campbell of Loudoun, the man responsible for killing Gilbert, earl of Cassillis, in August 1527, Galbraith would probably have had to accept the antipathy of the Kennedys, and after the date of the killing they do not feature as his clients.[163] Campbell, on the other hand, was a client of his early in 1527 and again in the early 1530s once Angus, Glencairn's nephew, was (from Galbraith's perspective) safely out of the way and Campbell enjoyed royal favour. Campbell's initial relationship with Galbraith may have come about because of the fact that he was bailie for the abbot of Melrose in the lands of Kylesmuir in Ayrshire and Galbraith had in the past acted for the abbey.[164] More directly, Campbell of Loudoun was the nephew of another of Galbraith's clients, James Wallace of Craigie, through James's sister Isobel.[165]

ii) Kin relationships

There are several instances of Galbraith's clients belonging to one surname. The most direct examples concern fathers and sons, such as William, earl Marischall, and his eldest son and heir Gilbert Keith of Troup, or Sir Gavin Kennedy of Blairquhan and his successor James.[166] Galbraith also appeared for John Lockhart of Barr and his daughter Margaret in separate actions.[167] He also acted for siblings. The Sinclair family alone provides two examples of this: the brothers Sir John Sinclair of Dryden and Patrick Sinclair of Spott and, in the main line, Elizabeth Sinclair, daughter of Henry, Lord Sinclair, and her brother William.[168] Robert Gordon of the Glen and James Gordon of Lochinver were also brothers, their father being John Gordon of Lochinver,

---

brother of the late Robert Crichton of Kirkpatrick, was Ninian Crichton of Bellibocht then he was a client of Robert Leslie.

[162] CS 5/32 fos. 39r, 144r, 165r.
[163] Earlier in 1527 Galbraith had acted for James Kennedy of Blairquhan, a man who certainly claimed kinship with the earl: CS 5/37 fo. 82r: 4 Apr. 1527. Campbell was put to the horn on 6 Oct. 1527: CS 5/37 fo. 241r.
[164] Sanderson, *Ayrshire and the Reformation*, 18.
[165] *Scots Peerage*, v, 494. Galbraith's father witnessed a discharge by Wallace to David Home of Wedderburn on 18 Oct. 1498: *HMC*, Milne-Home, 29.
[166] *RSS*, i, no. 3265; CS 5/35 fo. 81v (William, earl Marischall); CS 5/38 fo. 113r (Gilbert Keith); CS 5/28 fo. 211v (Sir Gavin Kennedy); CS 5/37 fo. 82r (James Kennedy).
[167] C.S 5/37 fo. 67r: 30 Mar. 1527 (John Lockhart v Poor tenants of Calston); CS 5/36 116v: 3 Dec. 1526 (Margaret Lockhart v John Campbell).
[168] That the Sinclairs were brothers is clear from Patrick being described as John's brother in 1516: CS 5/27 fo. 172r: 12 Feb. 1516.

while Alexander Elphinstone, canon of Aberdeen, was the brother and heir of tailzie of Andrew Elphinstone of Selmes.[169]

But a kin relationship did not necessarily mean political agreement or a harmonious personal relationship. In 1516 Galbraith acted for John Somerville of Cambusnethan. This is his only recorded appearance for a man who in 1520 was to take a significant role, along with David Home of Wedderburn and others, in the 'Cleanse the Causeway' affair in Edinburgh for which he was duly forfeited. Although Cambusnethan was a strong Angus adherent, Galbraith did not act for him again. Even in August 1525 when, with Angus in control of government, Cambusnethan sought to have his forfeiture reversed in Parliament, Galbraith did not appear on his behalf.[170] The next occasion on which Galbraith did come into contact with Cambusnethan was when he acted on behalf of the latter's kinsman, Hugh, Lord Somerville, against him. Somerville had signed the 'great aith' of November 1528, against Angus and was clearly inimical to Cambusnethan. In December 1528, Somerville brought an action against Cambusnethan for the sum of 957 merks allegedly owing to him. Moreover, he alleged that he had lawfully redeemed certain lands in Carnwath, a claim that Cambusnethan disputed through his forespeaker, James Foulis. In pursuance of the sum allegedly owed, Somerville sought to have all Cambusnethan's lands apprised before the sheriff-deputes of Lanark, whose impartiality was questioned by Cambusnethan. Cambusnethan also claimed that he would be risking his life in going to Lanark and asked that the matter be decided in the tolbooth of Edinburgh with some of the lords of session present.[171] Despite their kinship, the argument between Somerville and Cambusnethan was a fierce one.[172] It is possible that his failure to act for Cambusnethan indicates that Galbraith had disregarded his natural political allegiance to the Douglases and Homes in favour of Somerville who was close to the king.[173] This may reflect the realpolitik of a situation in which Galbraith benefited from the fall of Angus because of his relationship with Margaret Tudor, and, having recently been given a position in the chapel royal, he may have been expecting future royal patronage. The Somervilles provide a useful reminder of something that must have been obvious to Galbraith: that political considerations, particularly during a minority, could occasionally outweigh the traditional bonds of family relationships.

---

[169] CS 5/27 fo. 217v: 6 Mar. 1516: Robert Gordon as procurator for John his father; CS 5/40 fo. 135r: 5 Nov. 1529.

[170] *APS*, ii, 298: 3 Aug. 1525; CS 5/38 fo. 187v: 6 Nov. 1528; Emond, 'Minority of James V', 261-2.

[171] CS 5/39 fo. 33v: 12 Dec. 1528. See also Cameron, *James V*, 55-6.

[172] Somerville appears to have operated something of a vendetta against Cambusnethan in his barony court of Carnwath: *Carnwath Court Bk.*, 124, 143, 144, 160, 164, 194, 205, 207-8; *Acta Sessionis (Stair)*, 58-9.

[173] In December 1528 Angus was leaving for exile and his return during Galbraith's lifetime must have seemed unlikely although in fact he did return the year before Galbraith died. On Galbraith's relationship with Angus, see below.

But those bonds were always important and the most striking example of the effect of marriage on Galbraith's client list concerns the sisters of the earl of Angus all four of whom married men who became clients of his. Elizabeth Douglas was married to John, Lord Hay of Yester, Alison to David Home of Wedderburn, Margaret to Sir James Douglas of Drumlanrig and Janet to John, Lord Glamis.[174] Home and Douglas were clear Angus adherents; Hay and Lord Gray were figures for whom Galbraith first acted in 1527 and 1528 respectively. The marriage link was not in all cases coincidental. Galbraith was already close to Home of Wedderburn although in respect of Douglas of Drumlanrig and Gray the Angus connection may have opened doors. But Lord Hay only became a client during the personal reign of James V when Angus was a fugitive and only after he had come into contact with Galbraith in the arbitration involving the prioress of Haddington mentioned earlier.

It was possibly as a result of marriage that Robert Galbraith came to represent Elizabeth Swinton, the erstwhile prioress of Elcho, against Robert Leslie's sister in litigation also mentioned earlier. Like the Galbraiths, the Swintons were very close to the Homes of Wedderburn. When Sir John Swinton (d. 1493) was a child, William de Wedderburn was his *scutifer* (esquire).[175] His grandson, also named John (d. 1521), was married to Katherine Lauder, one of the Lauders of Bass. In 1518 this John's son married Margaret, daughter of David Home of Wedderburn, thus strengthening further the link between the two families at what was certainly a difficult time for the Homes. Elizabeth Swinton was the great-aunt of David Home's son-in-law. To this tenuous link can be added the fact that Galbraith's father held lands in the barony of Coldingham, Berwickshire, of which John Swinton of that ilk was the superior.[176] Moreover in 1519 Robert and his brother Simon were witnesses to a letter of reversion made by their father in favour of John Swinton concerning these lands.[177] Galbraith certainly acted for Robert Lauder of the Bass whose family, already linked to the Swintons, became even closer to them by the marriage of his daughter to her cousin Sir John Swinton, the son of John and Margaret Home. Moreover, Lauder of the Bass was close to David Home of Wedderburn, and, during Angus's ascendancy in 1526, he received a respite for having assisted him during Albany's governorship.[178] In 1532 Eufame Leslie appears to have bought off Swinton's interest in the Elcho matter by granting him a letter of tack, and giving him a discharge in respect of all past debts.[179]

[174] *Scots Peerage*, i, 189–90.
[175] Douglas, *Baronage*, 127.
[176] NAS, Bruce of Kennet, GD 11/73: 2 July 1508.
[177] Ibid., GD 11/88: 15 Apr. 1519.
[178] *RSS*, i, 3404: 28 June 1526.
[179] NAS, Swinton Charters, GD 12/108: 8 July 1532; GD 12/109: 31 July 1532.

Galbraith had a small group of clients, only four in number, in the sheriffdom of Renfrew. The group can be explained on the basis of affinity by marriage alone. The main line of the Sempill family descended after the death of John, Lord Sempill, at Flodden to his eldest son William. William's younger brother, Gabriel Sempill of Cathcart, married Janet, the daughter of John Spreule of Coldon (or Cowdin), also in Renfrewshire.[180] Galbraith acted for John Spreule in 1524, and for William, Lord Sempill, in 1526. In 1517 Galbraith had acted against the latter in a dispute with Margaret Crichton, lady Sempill. Presumably Margaret was William's step-mother.[181] It seems that William's father, prior to Flodden, had given him a box of money and jewellery that Margaret possessed but refused to hand over. Margaret obtained letters of cursing against William, and alleged that he was being obstructive and was preventing her land from being worked.[182] His fourth identified Renfrewshire client was Ninian, Lord Ross. In 1523 Ninian married Elizabeth, sister of William, master of Ruthven who can be linked to Galbraith from 1519.[183]

Despite the importance of marriage bonds, they were sometimes insufficient to prevent a dispute going to law. For example, in 1517 David Home of Wedderburn brought an action against Sir Ninian Seton of Tullibody, one of Robert Leslie's Perthshire clients.[184] Seton, through his mother, was the grandson of Alexander, Lord Home. But a family connection had the potential to cause a conflict of interest and it could destroy as well as create a link between a lawyer and client. Galbraith's relationship with Sir William Sinclair of Hermiston has already been described. In 1531 Sinclair died naming Galbraith in his last testament as tutor to his two daughters Margaret and Elizabeth. Nine months later Sinclair's widow, Beatrice Raiton, and her new husband William Crichton of Drylaw, removed these children from the convent at Haddington where they were being educated at Galbraith's expense (although Galbraith would have more than recouped his expenditure from the wardship of their lands granted to him by the king).[185] Galbraith brought an action to have the girls returned and their mother was prompt in complying with the lords' decreet ordering their deliverance.[186] The interesting aspect of the case in the present context is that William Crichton

---

[180] Douglas, *Baronage*, 467.
[181] According to Douglas (*Baronage*, 467), followed by the *Scots Peerage* (vol. vii), John, first Lord Sempill was married to Margaret Colville, daughter of Robert Colville of Ochiltree. Margaret Crichton is not mentioned but entries in the *acta* suggest she was John's second wife.
[182] CS 5/29 fo. 151r: 26 Mar. 1517; CS 5/31 fo. 33v: 22 June 1518. On both occasions William was personally present and there is no indication of a forespeaker acting for him.
[183] *Scots Peerage*, vii, 252; CS 5/32 fo. 142v: 17 Mar. 1519.
[184] CS 5/30 fo. 119
[185] The prioress of Haddington was one of Galbraith's clients and the convent was situated not far from where he held the majority of his lands.
[186] CS 5/43 fos. 66r-66v; 82v: 9 and 18 Nov. 1531.

was a relative of George Crichton, bishop of Dunkeld. In 1527, when George had not long been in office, Galbraith acted for him before the lords of session.[187] Now George stood against him at the bar with the laird of Drylaw and his wife, Lady Hermiston. Galbraith therefore stated that as he was the pensioner of the bishop, and had 'maid his band to him', it was incumbent upon him to discharge the bishop from this obligation since they stood opposed to each other. In response the bishop discharged Galbraith from any obligation entered into towards him under the bond. The terms of the obligation were not stated. Certainly Galbraith, since the summons in the case ran in his name as principal, was acting directly against the bishop and his kinsman and no bond then in existence would have countenanced the bringing of such a direct personal action. It is a moot point whether it would still have been necessary to discharge the bond had Galbraith merely been acting as a procurator and if someone else had been the children's tutor. Although in 1519 he acted for William Ruthven against Gavin Douglas, the previous bishop, he never acted against George Crichton and so there is no way of telling for certain whether their agreement entirely precluded him from doing so. It was, however, standard practice for men of law when making bonds to reserve the right to act for clients to whom they had previously become bound. Whatever the precise nature of the restraint under which he had placed himself in relation to the bishop of Dunkeld, once the bond was discharged it disappeared together with, no doubt, his pension. Galbraith never again appeared for the bishop and this case stands out as an example of a lawyer-client relationship that broke down because of a conflict of interest.

iii) Consensual relationships

Mention has already been made of the bonds entered into by Lord Maxwell with other clients of Galbraith. Galbraith was also witness to a bond of manrent given in November 1526 by Leslie's client, Ninian Crichton of Bellibocht, to his own client, James Douglas of Drumlanrig.[188] Ninian promised to support Douglas, excepting his allegiance to Lord Crichton of Sanquhar although promising not to support Crichton if he wrongfully molested Douglas. This was in the context of a local feud. On a national scale, Galbraith's principal client, Margaret Tudor, was so involved in the politics of the period between 1513 and 1528, and wavered so much in her friendships and alliances, that anyone directly connected to her must have found it difficult to adopt a consistent position. Certainly Galbraith can be linked to the

---

[187] CS 5/37 fo. 158r: 13 July 1527.
[188] NAS, Crown Writs, AD 1/91: 24 Nov. 1526; Wormald, *Lords and Men*, 261.

Homes who gave her support against Albany. But the political complexity is such that no attempt can be made here to assess the impact on Galbraith's career of the political ups and downs of the Queen Dowager. The fact that Albany could probably rely on the support of the earls of Crawford and Erroll and Lords Glamis and Saltoun in 1516, all of whom were clients of Galbraith during different political circumstances later in his career, shows how difficult it would be to find in his client list evidence of a party that was consistently 'pro-Margaret' (over a period during which Margaret herself was at some points 'pro-Albany').[189]

Moreover, there is less evidence of bonds entered into by some of the earls for whom Galbraith acted (notably, Buchan, Erroll and Sutherland). This makes it more difficult to trace their supporters and part-takers. One example of (presumably consensual) conduct occurred when two of Galbraith's clients, James Douglas of Drumlanrig and James Gordon of Lochinver, co-operated in the murder of Thomas MacLellan of Bombie in Edinburgh in 1526.[190] The killing occurred in the context of a dispute, in which Galbraith was active, concerning James's mother who had married MacLellan after her first husband's death.

Conclusion

As men of law Robert Leslie and Robert Galbraith had much in common and essentially their careers developed along similar paths. Using local contacts initially, each built up a considerable number of clients. The income that this brought in was lent at interest or used to purchase land, Leslie obtaining lands in Perthshire and Galbraith in Haddington and Berwickshire. Both rose from relatively modest origins to mix with important figures and to hold offices in royal service. A similar picture applies equally to many of their contemporaries with whom they interacted and with whom, as with each other, they competed and co-operated as circumstances demanded.

During the period January 1517 to January 1536 Leslie and Galbraith were recorded confronting each other before the lords 62 times in 42 different cases.[191] Both were named together as procurators, either the pair of them alone or along with others, on 131 occasions. In theory, these constitutions might, but need not, have resulted in either Leslie or Galbraith acting for the party making the constitution. They need not indicate close co-operation between them. Yet it would be surprising if such co-operation did not exist, at least in some cases. After all these two advocates between them shared a considerable proportion of the court business of their generation. So, for

---

[189]   Emond, 'Minority of James V', 105.
[190]   *Scots Peerage*, v, 261; CS 5/36 fo. 18r: 26 June 1526; CS 5/38 fos. 171v; 173r: 25 and 30 Sept. 1527.
[191]   Finlay, 'Professional Men of Law', Appendix 11.

instance, where one of Leslie's clients called upon one of Galbraith's to act as warrantor, it is likely that the two advocates would co-operate in finding the best approach to defend the matter in question. Galbraith can be found working in conjunction with Thomas Hamilton and Thomas Kincraigie as well as, on one occasion, with Leslie when they were both named as procurators for Ninian, Lord Ross.[192] They also co-operated as arbiters on several occasions.

But there were cases where co-operation was less than might have been expected. An example occurred when Galbraith's client, Margaret Tudor, was called upon by Leslie's client, David Learmonth, provost of St Andrews, to warrant him in the lands of Balgony in Fife which were claimed by James Lundie. Learmonth's title was based upon a lease granted by Margaret in 1513 when she was tutor to James V.[193] Lundie's allegation was that the lease, purporting to last for thirteen years, was invalid because it was alleged that Margaret lacked the power to set lands beyond the term of her office. Beyond this *ultra vires* argument, it was also alleged that the queen granted the lease in her own name, instead of the king's, and did so under her signet.[194] Leslie's attack on Lundie's title to sue fell flat when Lundie produced his own lease, dated February, 1516, and given by Albany under the privy seal.[195] In the face of what appears to have been a lack of co-operation from Galbraith, Learmonth then had to raise an action against the queen relying on the warrandice clause of his lease.

Clients

Dividing Scotland (albeit rather unevenly) into four quarters, and matching this division to the client lists of both Leslie and Galbraith (insofar as clients' origins are known), produces predictably different results (see Figure 6.4).

[192]   CS 5/37 fo. 62v (Kincraigie): 29 Mar. 1527; CS 5/43 fo. 74v (Hamilton): 15 Nov. 1531; CS 5/41 fo. 71v: 7 Apr. 1530.
[193]   CS 5/33 fo. 28v: 20 Nov. 1522.
[194]   CS 5/33 fo. 96r: 15 Dec. 1522.
[195]   CS 5/33 fo. 94v: 15 Dec. 1522.

Leslie			Galbraith		
North-east[196]:	148	(56.5%)	North-east:	73	(34.0%)
North-west[197]:	5	(1.9%)	North-west:	8	(3.7%)
South-east[198]:	50	(19.1%)	South-east:	66	(30.7%)
South-west[199]:	57	(21.7%)	South-west:	6	(27.9%)
Foreign[200]:	2	(0.8%)	Foreign:	8	(3.7%)
Total:	**262**	(100%)	**Total**:	**215**	**(100%)**

Figure 6.4

As a source of clients the north-west is negligible. More than half of Leslie's clients came from his own area, the north-east. In Galbraith's case, almost a third were from the south-east although the Borders produced far fewer litigants than Fife and Perthshire. Both show a clear east coast bias but, again, this can be explained simply on the basis of demographics. In terms of foreign litigants, Leslie attracted only 2: a merchant from Avignon and the master of a ship from Dieppe. Galbraith had 8 clients who were resident abroad although 3 of them, Master Alexander Fotheringham, chaplain of St Ninian's church in Bruges, John Moffat, conservator in Flanders, and Marion Frog (living in England), were Scots. Of the rest, 2 were French merchants, 1 was an Englishman, 1 was a servant to the king of Denmark, and 1 is unidentified. To add to the international flavour, both the Frenchmen (1 of whom, Guillaume Besselaw, was the factor of a Piedmontese merchant) were in dispute with other Frenchmen and the Dane was involved in an action with Hans Grail, a 'ducheman' (who may therefore have been Dutch or German). Most of the cases involving these litigants were straightforward debt actions or involved spuilzie of ships. There is no indication that Galbraith was able to benefit particularly from contacts he might have made whilst living in France nor can it be said that he or Leslie specialised in cases involving foreigners since such cases were common and various procurators were involved in them. The most that can be said is that both Leslie and Galbraith must have been at least

---

[196] Sheriffdoms of Aberdeen, Banff, Clackmannan, Elgin, Fife, Forfar, Forres, Nairn, Perth, Kincardine, Kinross; regalities of Arbroath, Dunfermline and St Andrews; burgh of Dundee. As is obvious, 'north-east' is taken to mean here the eastern half of the country north of the Forth.
[197] Sheriffdoms of Argyll (including the Isles) and Inverness.
[198] Sheriffdoms of Stirling, Edinburgh, Haddington, Linlithgow, Peebles, Lauderdale, Berwick, Roxburgh; port of Leith.
[199] Sheriffdoms of Ayr, Dumfries, Dumbarton, Renfrew, Galloway, Kirkcudbright, Wigtown; bailiary of Cunningham.
[200] From France, England, Denmark and Flanders.

competent exponents of the sea laws to have agreed to act in cases involving shipping.

Attendance

Numerous factors affected the amount of time the lords would sit in any given year and might also affect in which parts of the year the court sat. Internal political upheaval (particularly during the minority), and bouts of plague, were the major factors. On average, taking the surviving record for the period 25 March 1515 to 24 March 1536, the court sat only on 100 days *per annum* and it is impossible to prove that any particular advocate was in attendance for more than a fraction of this time. On average, Leslie was mentioned as present on 26.4 days per year, while Galbraith's presence can only be proven on 23.2 days.[201] The high points of attendance for both Leslie and Galbraith came in 1528, the year of James V's escape from the custody of Angus. In that year Leslie was named as appearing before the lords on fifty-one days, and Galbraith on sixty-five days (out of a possible ninety-two). This year was something of a crossover point. Before and during 1528, Galbraith was more regularly in attendance than Leslie. Afterwards, however, Leslie begins to appear more often than Galbraith. This was probably due to Galbraith becoming treasurer of the chapel royal in that year. It is essential to remember that these figures are only approximate and represent the minimum number of possible appearances. This is due to the fact that the clerks of council did not bother to record the attendance of forespeakers when the parties themselves were present unless the forespeaker in question specifically did something that it was necessary to record.

Moreover, the factors that affected the number of days on which the lords met could affect the attendance of particular advocates to an even greater degree. The lords sat in Edinburgh primarily because of its importance as the centre of government and finance within the realm. But if Edinburgh became unsuitable, due to war or plague, they were better able to move elsewhere than the advocates who practised before them. For example, in the autumn of 1529 there was a serious outbreak of plague in Edinburgh. A proclamation was issued punishing with death anyone dwelling in Fife who repaired south of the Forth. This placed an advocate like Leslie, with his numerous Fife clients, in a difficult position. In one case, he claimed that evidence belonging to a client was lying in Fife and could not be brought to Edinburgh for his defence.[202] From 7 April to 10 November 1530 there is no sign of Leslie appearing before the lords. During that time the session was itinerant, meeting in Stirling on 22

---

[201] See Finlay, 'Professional Men of Law', Appendix 10.
[202] CS 5/40 fo. 134r: 5 Nov. 1529.

April and for several days in May and a day in June; then in Edinburgh briefly on 1 July before moving south to Peebles. By 19 July the lords of the exchequer were sitting in Linlithgow where they remained until September. Having convened again at Peebles on 11 September, the lords ordered the session to convene in Edinburgh if it was free of the plague, otherwise to meet in Linlithgow. Circumstances must have necessitated a change because on 8 and 10 October the lords of session met in Dundee and, at the end of the month, in Stirling. On 7 November they were in Perth. It was not until 10 November that Leslie made an appearance, acting in two cases, one for Paul Dishington of Ardross and the other for George, earl of Rothes. If the record is accurate, then in total he had missed forty days for which a sederunt was recorded. Nor was he unique. Adam Otterburn, as provost of Edinburgh, remained in the burgh during this period to carry out the functions of his office.[203] Robert Galbraith, apart from one appearance at Stirling in May 1530, did not appear again until February 1531. Galbraith was certainly in Edinburgh in September and December 1530.

In more normal times, there is much room to speculate on how advocates occupied themselves when the lords were not in session. There were, of course, other courts before which they might plead. Galbraith appeared in Berwick sheriff court (which routinely sat in the tolbooth of Edinburgh), and Leslie can be found, albeit rarely, in Fife sheriff court and in Dunfermline regality court. The court books of the latter two survive during part of his career and they reveal that Leslie did not act regularly in those courts although once again there is no way of saying how often he was in attendance. There is evidence that both Galbraith and Leslie were notaries public. The protocol books of neither have survived, and in Leslie's case the evidence for his status as a notary is limited to one reference. This document, mentioned in Dunfermline Regality court book, was drawn up by Robert Leslie 'notar of Aberdeyne dioces'. It might have been expected, if this was Robert Leslie the man of law, that he would have been a notary of St Andrews diocese. Nonetheless the document was an assignation made in Fife of the lands of Melgun by Patrick Wemyss of Pittencreiff to Master Thomas Wemyss and Leslie, complete with the designation 'of Innerpafray', later acted as an arbiter in a dispute concerning the same land between Thomas Wemyss and Andrew Wood of Largo.[204] This is not conclusive evidence that the arbiter and the notary were the same man and, indeed, one document is slim evidence of a notarial career. It is perhaps best left an open question whether Robert Leslie the advocate was also a notary until further evidence can be found. In Galbraith's case, the evidence of his status as a notary also consists of a single

---

[203] Inglis, *Otterburn*, 42.
[204] *Dunfermline Regality Ct. Bk.*, 121.

document so far discovered, an instrument of sasine dating from 1529 which bears to have been drawn up by him and contains his elaborate notarial mark.[205] It narrates a ceremony of sasine in the hands of himself and Simon Fortune, his nephew, another notary, by Isobel Hoppringle, prioress of Coldstream, of lands near the convent held by the queen dowager in liferent. The circumstances are entirely consistent with the notary, who describes himself as '*artium magister clericus Sanctiandrois diocesis publicus sacra apostolica*', being Robert Galbraith the advocate.

Arbitration

Leslie was involved as an arbiter in at least eight arbitrations all of which belonged to the second half of his career while Galbraith was involved in at least eleven over a longer period. In three arbitrations both were involved. Such activity was by no means unusual since men of law were often selected as arbiters generally because of their learning and impartiality. In one of the arbitrations involving both Leslie and Galbraith, the arbiters were chosen by the lords—rather than the parties—specifically on the basis that they were 'neutrale and discrete men'.[206]

Sometimes the parties agreed to submit their dispute to the lords as a body who would decide the matter as arbiters. In one case, a client of Galbraith's agreed to this mode of resolution 'for stanching of pley and to leif in rest & quiete in tyme tocum' even though he believed his case was just and good in law.[207] More often, the parties themselves selected the men who were to act as arbiters and, as well as leading churchmen and lords of session, they selected professional advocates. From the point of view of men such as Leslie and Galbraith, it was often the case that a party who selected them to act as an arbiter already had a pre-existing relationship with them as one of their clients. For example, Ninian, Lord Ross, was an established client of Leslie's who then selected him as one of the arbiters in a dispute with Adam Whiteford.[208] The same thing happened in relation to both Leslie and Galbraith in a dispute that came before the lords in June 1526. The matter concerned spuilzie by George, Lord Seton, which was alleged by Alexander, Lord Elphinstone. As so often, spuilzie appears to have been merely the tip of a deeper dispute. Leslie appeared for Seton, and Galbraith for Elphinstone.[209] The matter was eventually submitted to arbitration, and the 'compromise' or submission,

---

[205]   NAS, RH 6/1039: 22 Apr. 1529.
[206]   CS 5/42 fo. 123r: 17 Mar. 1531.
[207]   CS 5/37 fo. 64v: 29 Mar. 1527.
[208]   CS 5/41 fo. 150v: 28 Mar. 1531; CS 5/41 fo. 71v: 7 Apr. 1530.
[209]   CS 5/36 fo. 21v: 30 June 1526.

dated 5 December, was registered in the books of council two days later.[210] For the arbiters on his side, Seton selected Master John Campbell of Lundie, Robert Leslie and Richard Maitland of Lethington, or any two of them; Elphinstone selected the treasurer, Archibald Douglas, Master James Lawson, and Robert Galbraith, or any two of them. There were two 'overmen & odmen', George Douglas, brother of the earl of Angus, and Sir William Cunningham, feuar of Glencairn. The degree of impartiality expected of either Leslie or Galbraith is questionable. Their inclusion was perhaps seen as useful in helping the process of finding an accommodation between the parties since they were no doubt thoroughly versed in the affairs of their respective clients.

As well as an antecedent relationship with one of the parties to an arbitration, Leslie also appeared for parties with whom his initial point of contact was an arbitration. For example, the first time he can be connected to Adam Dundas was when the latter selected him as an arbiter in a dispute with Andrew Murray concerning the escheat of Archibald Douglas in Ballincreiff, the former treasurer and, as has just been seen, erstwhile amicable compositor. The submission to arbitration was made on 26 November 1528.[211] Evidently the decreet arbitral, if one was made, did not end the matter because the following July Leslie was acting for Dundas against Murray who had allegedly impeded him from harvesting corn from the disputed land.[212] There is nothing to link Leslie with Dundas prior to the arbitration. This is relatively unusual. While some of the arbitrations in which they were involved concerned parties who were not, and did not become, clients, generally speaking, there was often a pre-existing link between Leslie or Galbraith and one of the parties when they acted as arbiters.

Criminal cases

It is difficult to tell whether Leslie routinely attended criminal courts. These were often held by justices, most often William Scott of Balwearie and Patrick Baron of Spittalfield, deputed by the justice general, the earl of Argyll.[213] Since they generally met in the tolbooth of Edinburgh it would have been convenient for men of law to attend or to represent accused persons, although the justiciary record is not sufficiently detailed to indicate their presence. Leslie

---

[210] CS 5/36 fo. 127r: 7 Dec. 1526.

[211] CS 5/39 fo. 7v: 26 Nov. 1528.

[212] CS 5/40 fo. 62r: 16 July 1529.

[213] The presiding justices recorded during this period, either as deputes of Argyll or justices *in hac parte*, were as follows: William Scott of Balwearie; Patrick Baron of Spittalfield; Archibald Douglas, provost of Edinburgh; Sir John Stirling of Keir; Master John Campbell of Lundie; Robert Barton of Over Barnton, Treasurer; James, earl of Moray; Patrick, Lord Gray; Andrew Auchinleck and Henry Wardlaw of Kilbarton: NAS, JC. 1/4: 25 June 1526-11 Oct. 1531.

certainly had the opportunity to attend and definitely did so on three occasions when he appeared to give caution for the later appearance of persons (presumably clients) charged with offences.[214] From 25 June 1526 to 11 October 1531 justice courts sat mainly in Edinburgh but also in Linlithgow, Perth, and Stirling, on seventy-six separate days under a variety of justice-deputes.[215] On eight of those days Leslie's whereabouts are known because he was appearing before the lords of council in Edinburgh.[216] On each of those days the justice court was also held in the tolbooth of Edinburgh and so Leslie may have attended both courts. On a further occasion it is known that Leslie was rendering accounts in the exchequer but, again, Patrick Baron was holding his justice court in the same place on the same day and so Leslie's attendance is not precluded.[217] In terms of justice ayres, once again Leslie's attendance can be neither proven nor disproved with one exception. On 11 November 1529 the justice ayre at Kirkcudbright commenced.[218] The very next day Leslie was in Edinburgh appearing before the lords and so he certainly did not attend the ayre. He may have attended the Perth justice ayre, which began on 22 November 1530, even though he appeared before the lords on 26 November because the lords were sitting in Perth at the time. In 1535 even though he appeared in Edinburgh on 15 November and 7 December it is possible that he attended the Dumfries justice ayre that began on 21 November. If he did, then as usual his presence went unrecorded.

As a cleric Robert Galbraith was much less likely to involve himself in criminal cases since churchmen refused to have anything to do with matters of blood and criminal courts had authority to punish corporally and capitally. No instance of him appearing in a criminal court survives. On ten of the seventy-six days when justice courts were being held, he was busy on civil business before the lords and on some of those days he appeared more than once.[219] More definitely, he certainly could not have attended the Dumfries justice ayre that began on 19 October 1529 because the next day he was active in Edinburgh again appearing before the lords of council. The following month the Kirkcudbright justice ayre began on 11 November but once more Galbraith was in Edinburgh, witnessing an indenture, the next day.[220] The case is similar with the Dumbarton justice ayre in October 1531 and the Perth ayre

---

214 NAS, JC1/3: Stirling, 25 Oct. 1526; Edinburgh, 19 July 1527; Edinburgh, 30 Nov. 1528.
215 This figure has been taken from the earliest justiciary court book, NAS, JC. 1/4, by counting each day on which a justice court was recorded. The court book has no pagination.
216 The dates are as follows: 7 July 1526; 8 Aug. 1527; 18 Dec. 1527; 16 Dec. 1528; 23 Feb. 1529; 24 Mar. 1530; 26 Jan. 1531; and 1 Feb. 1531.
217 ER, xvi, 84: 25 Aug. 1531.
218 RSS, ii, appendix, 766–771, gives the commencement dates of these justice ayres.
219 The dates are as follows: 7 July 1526; 4 Dec. 1526; 29 July 1527; 16 Aug. 1527; 23 Nov. 1527; 18 Dec. 1527; 7 Sep. 1528; 16 Nov. 1528; 23 Feb. 1529; and 4 Mar. 1529.
220 The Binns Papers 1320–1864 eds. J. Dalyell of Binns and J. Beveridge (Scottish Record Society, 1938), no. 32: 12 Nov. 1529.

in December 1530, although in the latter case some four days elapsed between the beginning of the ayre and definite proof that Galbraith was in Edinburgh involved in a ceremony of sasine.[221] Nonetheless, the evidence is clearer in the case of Galbraith than it is in the case of Leslie and it strongly suggests that he never involved himself in matters that were subject to criminal jurisdiction.

---

[221] *Prot. Bk. Foular,* iii, no. 273: 9 Dec. 1530.

Chapter Seven

The Office of King's Advocate

Little attention has been paid in the past to the early development of the office of king's advocate. The term first appears during the reign of James III and this has led to the suggestion, misleading in my view, that the earliest holder of the office was John Ross of Montgrennan.[1] In part confusion may have resulted from the suggestion that in the early sixteenth century the word 'advocate' was used exclusively to refer to His Majesty's Advocate.[2] Although normally the case this is not invariably true. At least two fifteenth-century statutes use the term 'advocate' in a more general sense.[3] There is also evidence from the fifteenth-century protocol book of James Darow, from contemporary literary works and from other sources where the word 'advocate' was used but not in relation to the king's man of law.

Looking at the substantive role involved in representing the king in litigation, the evidence suggests that the origin of the office should be placed during the early part of the reign of James IV and that the first incumbent was Master James Henryson of Fordell. During the king's minority several people appeared on his behalf in litigation, although only three were identified by name in the record: David Balfour of Caraldston (Careston), Alexander Inglis, the comptroller, and William Knollis, Lord of St Johns, the treasurer.[4] Of these, Balfour alone was described as forespeaker and advocate to the king albeit only very rarely.[5] Normally those acting for the king are not identified and there is no way of knowing even if they were men of law or treasury clerks. What is clear is that the position of Balfour, who was a man of law, was an interim one. Following Henryson's first appearance on the king's behalf in October 1493, Balfour only appeared for the king on two occasions and these were in Henryson's temporary absence.[6] On one of these occasions, he was described as 'comperand on the behalf of the kingis hienes his advocate *as he*

[1] See J. Finlay, 'James Henryson and the origins of the office of king's advocate' (2000) *SHR* 17–38.
[2] J. Inglis, *Sir Adam Otterburn of Redhall, 1524–1538* (Glasgow, 1935), 4.
[3] *APS*, ii, 8 c. 24; *APS*, ii, 19 c. 16.
[4] Inglis (*ADC*, i, 96); St John (*ADC*, i, 27). William Knollis, Lord of St John is described at this time as master of the king's household and treasurer: *Rot. Scot.*, ii, 505. See also Macdougall, *James IV* (Edinburgh, 1989) 208; *The Knights of St John of Jerusalem in Scotland*, (Scottish History Society, 1983), eds., I.B. Cowan *et al.*, 199.
[5] *ADC*, i, 190, 212, 262, 292.
[6] *ADC*, ii, 308; 21 Jan. 1499; *ADC*, ii, 472; 7 Dec. 1500.

allegit'. It is clear from this that Balfour's title to appear for the king was not generally recognised and there is no evidence to associate his earlier appearances with a distinct office of advocate for the king.

Henryson's first appearance for the king came three months after a royal act of revocation in June 1493 and may conceivably be connected with it. Whether or not this was the case, the difference in status between Henryson and Balfour quickly took tangible form in the fact that Henryson began to receive a fee of £40 from the king, first paid in 1494-5.[7] This amount was regularised as an annual pension in October 1498 to last for his lifetime or until the king provided him with lands to the same annual value.[8] This pension was consistently paid to Henryson and his successors.

No record survives of Henryson being sworn into office. His successor, Master James Wishart of Pittarow, took the oath as king's advocate at the end of September 1513, following Henryson's death during the Flodden campaign.[9] At the same time he was sworn in as justice-clerk, an office which Henryson had held since the death of the previous incumbent, Richard Lawson, in 1507. After Wishart these two offices were never held simultaneously by the same person, and the appointment of 1513 seems to have been made hurriedly. Nonetheless the fact that it was made so formally adds weight to the idea that a new development had occurred during the reign of James IV.

But the king in the early sixteenth century did not enjoy a monopoly of his advocate's services. Indeed the same is true of his other officials with legal skills. There are many instances of the clerk register, the justice-clerk and the king's advocate all representing private clients before their fellow judges in the reigns of both James IV and James V and this was an acceptable practice.[10] But although it is clear that the advocate was prepared to step from bench to bar to represent the king and others, the date at which the king's advocate became *ex officio* a lord of council is less clear.

Prior to becoming justice-clerk in 1507, James Henryson did appear as a lord of council and latterly was appearing in this capacity almost as often as Richard Lawson.[11] Despite this, there is no evidence of a link between

---

7   *TA*, i, 237.

8   *RSS*, i, gives £50 but this is wrong. A payment was made in 1497 of £23 6s 8d in part payment of his 'pension': *TA*, i, 370. The word 'fee' is used the following year but thereafter 'pension' is the usual term used to describe his annuity.

9   CS 5/26 fo. 6v: 30 Sep. 1513. There is no record of James Henryson performing a similar ceremony and the absence of such evidence lends weight to the suggestion made below that the office of king's advocate developed only during the personal reign of James IV.

10   On one occasion James Henryson's name appears on the sederunt followed by '*non debet poni [pro] [Ducissa] de Montros, quia procurator eius*'. On the day in question he did appear as the procurator for the duchess of Montrose: *ADC*, iii, 164 (17 Jan. 1503).

11   From Martinmas 1505 to Martinmas Eve 1506 Henryson appeared in the sederunt on 37 occasions, Lawson on 40 occasions. On the earlier period see T.M. Chalmers, 'The King's Council: Patronage

Henryson becoming king's advocate and his becoming a lord of council, even though the former pre-dated the latter by less than two years.[12] A list at the beginning of an early volume of the *acta* of the lords of council does include Henryson as one of the lords, designing him *advocatus*.[13] However, that is not in itself decisive because after 1494 this quickly became his general designation. In a similar list of the lords of session given in October 1514, James Wishart is listed only under the designation justice-clerk.[14] Nicol Crawford, his successor in that office, appears with the same designation in a list of the lords ordained to sit continually upon the session in November 1528.[15] The latter list also includes Adam Otterburn who was given no designation despite his status as king's advocate. Otterburn, who regularly appeared on council sederunts throughout the 1520s, rarely did so with a designation although it is clear from his position on the sederunt that his position was elevated to some extent following his admission as king's advocate.[16] This contrasts with Crawford, whose appearances are recorded either by giving his name, his designation, or both. The earliest indication that the king's advocate as a distinct office holder should have a seat on the bench as of right does not occur until 14 February 1531 when the chancellor presented a list detailing those who had the right to vote on the session.[17] Included with the temporal lords were the treasurer, secretary, keeper of the privy seal, justice-clerk, advocate and the clerk of chancery.

The fact that Otterburn sat on the bench does not appear to have hindered him in acting as advocate for the king.[18] Mention was made earlier of the vulnerability of the advocate to charges of partiality as a judge, but wider controls existed to ensure that the advocate could not take unfair advantage of his position on the bench.[19] Therefore, when Adam Otterburn brought an

---

and the Governance of Scotland, 1460-1513', (Ph.D. thesis, Aberdeen University, 1982), 460 [(tables 4.2.2.2(b) and 4.2.4.1(b)].

[12] The first occasion Henryson appears on a sederunt of the lords of council is on 15 June 1496: *ADC*, ii, 2.

[13] CS 5/7 fo. 1Av.

[14] CS 5/26 fo. 168r: 24 Oct. 1514.

[15] CS 5/39 fo. 1r: 16 Nov. 1528.

[16] Normally only Otterburn's name is listed, however he is designed at CS 5/36 fo. 19r and at CS 5/37 fo. 13r (27 June 1526 and 13 March 1527; see also Hannay, *College of Justice* 206). When he became king's advocate Otterburn began to be named earlier in the sederunt. He was always named after Wishart (whose presence was normally indicated by the designation *clericus justiciarie*). However following Wishart's death Otterburn's name virtually always appears before that of Nicol Crawford, the new justice-clerk. In line with this Otterburn's name (without any designation) appears before that of Nicol Crawford (who is designed) in a list of the temporal lords of session in Nov. 1528: CS 5/39 fo. 1r. But Otterburn also had precedence in the sederunt over Crawford during Wishart's lifetime as can be seen from a list of the lords in Sep. 1524: CS 5/34 fo. 204v.

[17] CS 5/42 fo. 52r: 14 Feb. 1531.

[18] Nor is there any reason why it should have done. James Foulis, one of the busiest advocates of the late 1520s, can be found sitting as a lord of session on days when he appeared for private clients.

[19] See, above, pp. 106-7.

action against John Thornton for contravention of statutes prohibiting barratry (the unauthorised buying and selling of benefices), Thornton was successful in having the decreet against him annulled for procedural irregularities.[20] Otterburn had obtained the decreet 'privatlie' in the presence of only three lords, an insufficient number for that purpose.[21] Although the allegation of the presence of an inadequate quorum of lords is not a particularly rare one, the suspicion is that it was easier for Otterburn to use his office as king's advocate to obtain a decreet in these circumstances than it would have been for other litigants.[22] In an arbitration, the fact that Otterburn was involved as one of the arbiters sufficed to disqualify him when one of the parties reclaimed from the decreet arbitral to the lords of session.[23] The arbitration, between Robert, abbot of Balmerino in Fife on the one hand, and Sir William Scott of Balwearie, William Scott his son, Hugh Moncreiff and Thomas Scott, on the other, concerned the lands of Petgorno. Otterburn must have presumed the king had no interest in the matter, otherwise it is unlikely he would have agreed to help adjudicate in the dispute. The king, alleging that he did have an interest, took the remedial step of issuing letters of inhibition to stop the arbitration and restore the matter to the session. These letters were allegedly presented to the arbiters before they pronounced their decreet and, by being party to such a breach of a royal inhibition, Otterburn could not represent the king in the matter once it returned to the session. He had already, with his fellow arbiters the bishop of Galloway, the official of Lothian and Peter Carmichael, decided in the abbot's favour.[24] Robert Leslie took his place as the king's representative, albeit appearing as 'advocat for oure soverane lord' rather than 'oure soverane lordis advocat' which was the regular designation for the king's advocate.[25]

In terms of procedure, although a specific day was assigned to the hearing of actions directly involving the king, there were less obvious cases over and

---

[20] On barratry generally see R. Nicolson, *Scotland: The Later Middle Ages* (Edinburgh, 1974), 294-5; 557. On Thornton, see I.B. Cowan 'Patronage, provision and reservation: Pre-Reformation appointments to Scottish benefices', *The Renaissance and Reformation in Scotland,* eds. I.B. Cowan & D. Shaw (Edinburgh, 1983), 83-4, 87.

[21] CS 5/38 fos. 8v-9r: 8 Nov. 1527; also CS 5/37 fo. 239v: 25 Sept. 1527. The major ground of nullity in favour of Thornton was that 'the said decrete was gevin privatlie be thre of the lordis of counsale with the chancellar allanerlie quhilkis be the law and practik of the sessioune war nocht sufficient in novmer to deliver ane complant and mekle less to gif ane decrete or sentence diffinitive in ony actioun movit in the sessioune'.

[22] On the plea of 'lack of nomer' amongst the lords, see chapter five. Otterburn was undoubtedly aware of the fact that the procedure was illegal but it is conceivable that he hoped to get away with it. Certainly he did not anticipate Thornton's action to annul the decree which was, at most, a delaying tactic.

[23] CS 5/37 fos. 161r, 164r, 194r, 199v, 214v, 222v, 226v, 237r; CS 5/38 fo. 83v; CS 5/39 fos. 52v, 53v, 54r.

[24] CS 5/37 fo. 237r: 4 Sep. 1527.

[25] CS 5/37 fo. 226v: 30 Aug. 1527. This subtle difference in terminology was significant. Compare this phraseology with Robert Crichton's admission as advocate in 1581 mentioned below.

above these from which issues affecting the king's interest might emerge.[26] Whilst the use of the 'king's table' permitted the advocate to manage conveniently the majority of cases with which he had to deal, he still faced difficulties when cases were heard in his absence.[27] These potential difficulties were augmented by the fact that the advocate *per se* did not have the right to be admitted to the council chamber and so in theory had no right to hear all the cases and decide whether or not any of them raised issues affecting the crown. In practical terms, however, these were not serious problems. To assist him, the advocate could rely on the rule developed by the lords that no judicial deliverance prejudicial to the king was valid unless the king's advocate had been warned to compear for the king's interest.[28] Warning was generally given by the opposing party, but the lords themselves could warn the advocate to appear.[29]

Moreover, in practice the early crown advocates were also lords of session who thereby had no difficulty gaining access to the council chamber. A problem only emerged when Henry Lauder, who was not a lord of session, was thrust into the office late in 1538 after Otterburn's sudden fall from grace.[30] This was partially remedied in January 1539 by the intervention of the king, who ordered the lords to admit:

> oure lovit familiar clerk maister henry lauder our advocat to sett
> and remane in oure counselhous to heir and se delivering of billis
> geving of interlocutouris decisiounis and determinaciounis of all
> causis and actiounis sua that he may heir and knaw sik thingis as
> sal happin to occur that concerns ws exceptand alwayis the
> actiounis and causis for the quhilkis he beis advocat and speikis
> for at the bar alanerly.[31]

---

[26] The advocate, of course, was also instructed directly by the king, or, during a minority, by the governor, to act in a particular case or adopt a specific line of conduct. Surviving correspondence between the king and his advocate is rare. See, for example, HMC, 4th Rep. (countess of Rothes), Appendix, pages 503*ff.*, nos. 97 and 98; for Albany instructing the advocate to act, see CS 5/28 fo. 85v. A letter from the king to Otterburn is recorded in the *acta* in 1536: CS 6/7 fo. 150r.

[27] For the use of this table see chapter five. The 'king's table' was a table containing privileged summonses affecting the king's interest.

[28] CS 5/27 fo. 164r; CS 5/43 vol. 8v. For an example of the lords refusing to admit a protest in an action because it involved the king, see CS 5/39 fo. 42r (*King v John Grahame of West Hall*). The king's advocate was present and stated that no procedure should be had in this case until he was warned to appear.

[29] CS 5/18/2 fo. 11v: 2 Dec. 1506. The lords warned James Henryson to wait until the next warning regarding the matter between the king and the abbot of Dunfermline concerning the superiority of Cluny.

[30] Lauder was the obvious candidate to replace Otterburn having acted as his depute on several occasions in the 1530s. See below.

[31] CS 6/11 fo. 82r: 20 Jan. 1539.

In any action in which Lauder spoke at the bar for the king, he remained under the same obligation as any other man of law to retire and allow the lords to deliberate in secret.[32] This position was only temporary because Lauder was within a few months admitted to a vacancy on the bench.[33]

The role of the advocate-depute

If anything, the role of lord of session added to the burden of political and administrative duties which the king's advocate had to bear and which might lead to periods of enforced absence. Such absences—especially at justice ayres or on foreign embassies—did not commonly fall when the lords of session were sitting, but when they did it was the practice to appoint in advance one or more substitutes to appear on the king's behalf.[34] As already noted, David Balfour twice represented the king, in 1499 and 1500, on occasions when there is no indication of Henryson being present.[35] In December 1509 Adam Otterburn appeared for the king during Henryson's absence,[36] while Robert Galbraith represented James V in 1528 during Otterburn's absence.[37] Other substitutes for Otterburn during the reign of James V were Thomas Scott,[38] James Foulis,[39] Henry Balnavis,[40] Henry Lauder,[41] and Thomas

---

[32]   ADCP, 377. See chapter five for examples of instances when Lauder, having become a lord of session, was required to pass from the bench to the bar and not vote due to suspected partiality. By the terms of the oath *de fideli administratione* Lauder, as a lord of session, was bound to keep secret those deliberations of the lords to which, as one of their number, he was privy.

[33]   Lauder first appears on the bench on 2 Mar. 1540: CS 6/12 fo. 57v.

[34]   In a letter dated at Stirling on 12 Mar. 1536 James V instructed Adam Otterburn, who was about to leave the realm on the king's 'erandis', to ensure that nothing was done in relation to a case concerning the sheriffship of Tweeddale until Otterburn's return because 'ye have our defencis of the samin': CS 6/7 fo. 150r: 15 Mar. 1536. Otterburn then left to pursue political negotiations in London: Inglis, *Otterburn*, 62. He had returned by 13 July: CS 6/8 fo. 103r: 13 July 1536.

[35]   ADC, ii, 308; 21 Jan. 1499; ADC, ii, 472; 7 Dec. 1500.

[36]   CS. 5/21 fo. 49r: 6 Dec. 1509. Otterburn's full designation was 'advocat for our soverane lord for the tyme'. He appeared again with a similar designation in Feb. 1517: CS 5/39 fo. 20v. It should be noted that the examples given in the text are not exhaustive.

[37]   CS 5/39 fo. 20r: 7 December. This was a special constitution further details of which are given below.

[38]   In May 1530: CS 5/41 fos. 74r, 81v; and July 1532: CS 6/2 fo. 223r. Scott, the son of William Scott of Balwearie, was named as one of those who had a vote on the session in Feb. 1531: CS 5/42 fo. 52r. He can be found in the king's service as one of the king's squires and gentlemen in Feb. 1529 (RMS, ii no. 4073) and was active in diplomatic affairs (TA, v 409, 441; vi 43, 270). In 1536 he replaced the late Nicol Crawford as justice-clerk: RMS, ii no. 2004.

[39]   From August to December 1530 in Dundee and Perth: CS 5/41 fos. 97v, 117v, 119v, 135v. Inglis plausibly explains Foulis's appearances on the basis that the king's advocate Otterburn was unable to leave Edinburgh, where he was provost, when the court vacated the burgh in time of plague: Inglis, *Otterburn*, 25 n.2. This convincingly disposes of the idea, found in the *Dictionary of National Biography* and since repeated elsewhere, that Foulis was joint king's advocate from 1527.

[40]   CS 6/10 fo. 106r: 5 June 1538.

[41]   In December 1533 and May 1534: CS 6/3 112v; CS 6/4 fo. 141v; *Yester Writs*, no. 501. This last reference mentions a letter from the king instructing the lords of session to delay a matter and continue the summonsing of the advocate until his return from England where he was to pass in the king's service. The letter was presented to the lords by Henry Lauder, king's advocate in Otterburn's absence.

Marjoribankis.[42] During the minority of Mary (1542-54) Thomas Kincraigie[43], James McGill (described specifically as procurator to Lauder in his absence)[44], Hugh Rigg,[45] Thomas McCalzeane,[46] David Borthwick[47] and Adam Otterburn[48] all appeared as substitutes for Henry Lauder. The earliest reference to an 'advocate depute' was made in November 1533 when the term was applied to Henry Lauder.[49] Conversely Lauder was described as 'principale advocat' in November 1544 when, during his absence, the king was represented by Thomas Kincraigie.[50] It would appear that deputes or substitutes had the same competence as the king's advocate and might do anything that was judged to be to the advantage of the crown provided that the king's advocate might do the same were he present.[51]

The use of deputes reflects the fact that the king, like any other litigant, could constitute one or more advocates to represent him either specially or generally.[52] In the examples above it is often impossible to tell from the context which type of constitution is involved. However at least three definite

Lauder also appeared 'in absence of' Adam Otterburn in June 1532 when Otterburn was negotiating a truce with England: *ADCP*, 405; CS 6/2 fos. 209v, 223v. He also did so late in 1533 during Otterburn's absence (CS 6/3 fos. 95r, 111v, 112v, 170v) and again in 1536 when Otterburn was in London: CS 6/7 fo. 165v. See above fn. 34. Other appearances at this time may be found at CS 6/7 fos. 167v, 178r, 182r, 183r, 184r; CS 6/8 fos. 11r, 14r, 26v.

42   CS 6/7 fo. 173r: 29 Mar. 1536; CS 6/8 fo. 17v: 19 May 1536. This was also during Otterburn's time in London.

43   In Nov. 1544: *APS*, ii, 447-8.

44   21 June 1547: CS 6/23 137r. Lauder was absent because in May along with Master John Scrimgeour he had been commissioned to go to Dundee to hold courts and take cognition concerning spuilzie and to make a retour on 15 June (CS 6/23 fos. 80r-v). Evidently Lauder was late in returning. He had certainly left by 10 June when Master Thomas McCalzeane his 'substitute' appeared as the queen's advocate: CS 6/23 fo. 125v. This suggests a multiple constitution similar to that of Nov. 1546 mentioned below (see fn. 86).

45   In Dec. 1546: CS 6/28 fo. 62r.

46   In Nov. 1543: *The Scottish Correspondence of Mary of Lorraine 1543–1560*, ed. A.I. Cameron (Scottish History Society, 1927) no. 36. Also (as mentioned above, fn. 44) in June 1547: CS 6/23 fo. 125v.

47   In Dec. 1548: CS 6/28 110r.

48   *RMS*, no. 2885: 18 Mar. 1543. This entry describes Otterburn as '*regis pro tempore advocatum*'. Unfortunately this cannot be amplified by reference to the *acta* of the lords of council and session because there is a gap in the record at this period. Lauder as king's advocate brought an action against Otterburn, his wife Euphemia Ramsay and his son John, in 1541, seeking to reduce the alienation to them of the lands of Gorgie made by the late Sir James Hamilton of Finnart and James Colville of East Wemyss: CS 6/16 fo. 84v-85r. This does not appear to have affected Lauder's relationship with Otterburn however, since Otterburn agreed to Lauder acting as one of the arbiters in an arbitration between John Stanehope and him: CS 7/1/2 fo. 412r: 20 June 1543.

49   CS 6/2 fo. 111v: 10 Mar. 1533. Lauder appeared in the same capacity in Jan. and May 1534: CS 6/3 fo. 170v and 6/4 fo. 141v. He also appeared as 'advocate depute to the kingis grace' in May and June 1536: CS 6/8 fos. 14r, 34v, 67v.

50   *APS*, ii, 447-8.

51   This is evident from the terms of a judgement given in December 1546. The lords stated that Hugh Rigg, as advocate in Lauder's absence, had the right to renounce a criminal action which had already been raised by the queen's advocate without requiring a special mandate: CS 6/28 fo. 62r.

52   *RSS*, ii, no. 1345. A 'special constitution' means that the advocate was mandated to represent his client in a particular case only; a 'general constitution' indicates a mandate to deal with any cases which may arise affecting that client, perhaps during a specified time.

examples of special constitutions can be identified. The first is the most striking. In September 1528 Robert Galbraith was specially constituted by the king to represent him in a dispute which had been ongoing since the early 1520s concerning the lands of Nether Loudoun and Stevenston in Ayrshire.[53] Galbraith had earlier represented the king's brother, James, earl of Moray, in the same dispute and was the natural choice when, in the absence of the advocate, the king in conjunction with his brother sought to bring an action of error to overturn the verdict of an inquest which had served Marion Campbell as heiress to the lands in question.[54] Galbraith's authority to act seems to have expired at the conclusion of the action of error. Three years later a new phase to the dispute arose in which William Cunningham brought an action against Moray and Hugh Campbell to have the lords' decreet of 1528 'retreted' (annulled).[55] This time Galbraith was prelocutor for Campbell and stated that although he had been advocate for the king when Marion's retour had been reduced: 'that office was now deid in him and he had na powar therein and als the kingis grace had uther advocatis'.[56] Galbraith went on to argue explicitly that his 'advocation' had expired. He simply no longer had authority to function as king's advocate.

Galbraith was chosen to act in this case probably because he was already familiar with the complexities of its earlier phase at which time the king's advocate involved was James Wishart (who had since died). In 1528 Adam Otterburn, his successor, was about to set off on an embassy when the case arose and it may have seemed desirable to constitute Galbraith to see the matter through.[57] The other two examples of special constitutions occurred when for some reason the king's advocate could not act on the king's behalf. The first of these has already been mentioned: Robert Leslie acting for the king when Otterburn was involved in an arbitration that was reclaimed to the session.[58] The other instance is similar and occurred in 1530 when Thomas Scott represented the king in an action of error against the provost and bailies of Edinburgh and an inquest which they had summoned. Otterburn, as

[53] CS 5/38 fos. 162r-163r; CS 5/39 fos. 20r-v. The major references to the dispute are: CS 5/33 fos. 37v-39v, 40r-40v, 115r, 166r,191r-194v; CS 5/38 fos. 162r-163v; CS 5/39 fos. 20r-v; CS 5/42 fo. 64v; CS 5/43 fos. 84v, 103r-v, 106r-v, 150r, 157r-v, 197r.

[54] The facts are complex and confusing. The basic dispute involved Hugh Campbell, sheriff of Ayr and William, master of Cunningham. However, the king assigned his rights to nonentry in the land to his brother (CS 5/33 fos. 191r-194v) and so provided him with an interest in the dispute. Although Galbraith represented Moray at the serving of the brieve in 1528 (Laing Chrs. no. 365), seven years earlier he was Marion Campbell's forespeaker (CS 5/33 fo. 37v) and in 1531 (CS 5/43 fo. 106r) he was to act in the same capacity for Hugh Campbell in a separate action connected with the same dispute.

[55] CS 5/43 fo. 106r: 4 Dec. 1531.

[56] CS 5/43 fo. 103v: 1 Dec. 1531.

[57] There may also have been a political motive since Hugh Campbell was one of those instrumental in the king's escape from Angus's custody and Galbraith may have been his choice.

[58] See above, text at fn.24.

provost of Edinburgh, was again disqualified from representing the king in this case, although he did so in all other cases at the time.[59]

To complement these examples, there are at least two definite instances of the general constitution of an advocate-depute. In November 1533 Adam Otterburn named Henry Lauder as his depute 'in all our soverane lordis materis', an office which Lauder accepted.[60] When Lauder himself was the queen's advocate in November 1546, he constituted at St Andrews Marjoribankis, Rigg, McGill, McCalzeane and Borthwick as his substitutes in all actions and business concerning the queen until his return.[61] The wording of this latter constitution clearly gives the impression that Lauder was responsible for selecting his own replacements.[62] In Lauder's absence during December 1546 the cases concerning the queen appear to have been divided between only Rigg (who appears twice) and McGill (one appearance). This is in line with general practice where only a minority of those named in a multiple constitution actually appeared in court.[63] In 1525 the lords auditor of the exchequer had been adamant that they had no power to make or discharge a comptroller.[64] The same was probably true where the lords of session and the office of king's advocate, or even advocate-depute, was concerned. Nevertheless, it would appear that the initiative to name deputes or substitutes for the advocate was not solely the preserve of the king, although any discretion the advocate exercised to name his own deputes would have been without prejudice to the king's ultimate right to make or discharge the principal advocate.[65]

In his nineteenth-century biographical work *The Lord Advocates of Scotland*, G.T. Omond claimed that there were, in the period before 1532, two king's

---

[59] CS 5/41 fos. 74r, 81v (7 Apr. and 22 May 1530). See above, pp. 175-6.

[60] CS 6/2 fo. 111v: 10 Mar. 1533. It should be pointed out, however, that two actions involving Otterburn as king's advocate were suspended, by a letter from the king, until his advocate's 'hamecuming furth of Ingland': CS 6/2 fo. 112v: 11 Mar. 1533. On the reason for Otterburn's absence, see Inglis, *Otterburn*, 49.

[61] CS 6/28 fo. 75v; *ADCP*, 559. Lauder was in St Andrews when the court began sitting there on 16 Nov. (CS 6/22 fo. 1r) but where he went when he left is unknown, although his destination was probably Edinburgh. At the end of December Arthur Hamilton was paid four shillings to carry writings from St Andrews to him (*TA*, ix, 47). On 17 Jan., after the Christmas vacation, he was back in St Andrews (CS 6/22 fo. 71r).

[62] This constitution appears in a writ found together with the *acta*; the entry for Nov. 26 does not indicate that it was recorded on that day. No doubt the constitution would have been recorded in the book of procurators, if it was still being maintained, and presumably constitutions of a similar type were also noted there.

[63] Rigg appears in three separate cases: CS 6/22 fo. 32r: 3 Dec.; CS 6/28 fo. 62r: 10 Dec. and CS 6/22 fo. 48r: 11 Dec. McGill also appears, but again dealing with a separate matter, on 11 Dec.: CS 6/22 fos. 46r-v.

[64] CS 5/35 fo. 148r: 13 Aug. 1525.

[65] In Nov. 1544 Thomas Kincraigie was deputed by the governor to act as queen's advocate in the absence of Lauder. Although the wording refers to this happening 'in tyme tocum quhen tyme requiris' the appointment was only a short-term measure: *APS*, ii, 447-8.

advocates at any one time.[66] While it is certainly true that the phrase 'oure soverane lordis advocatis' does appear in the *acta* of the lords of council in the fifteenth century, this is ambiguous and need not be a reference to two (or, indeed, more than two) advocates working simultaneously. The only other direct evidence in favour of Omond's view is a reference to the pursuit of a summons of error by Adam Otterburn and James Foulis 'as advocatis to oure soverane lord'.[67] These were the 'uther advocatis' to whom Robert Galbraith referred in 1531 and the summons of error in question related to the long series of disputes concerning the lands of Nether Loudoun. But the significance of this reference is not, as has sometimes been claimed, that Otterburn and Foulis were joint advocates. It indicates that, like Galbraith, both had been involved in representing the king, perhaps even at different stages in the same litigation, but separately rather than jointly. Foulis had been appointed advocate-depute when the court moved out of the capital to avoid the plague at a time when Otterburn, not only king's advocate but also serving as provost of Edinburgh, was obliged to remain behind.[68] Standing against this evidence is the regular practice of appointing substitutes for the advocate to represent the king. This strongly indicates that the office of advocate was generally not held jointly at least prior to Mary's reign.[69]

For the wider picture it is necessary to investigate briefly how the office was held later in the century. The earliest unambiguous reference to two advocates holding office at the same time does not occur until 1555 when Master John Spens of Condie was granted a pension, and the queen's special and general mandate, in the same terms as that held by Henry Lauder, queen's advocate, to be held jointly with him.[70] No reason for such an appointment was given although Lauder's regular appearances in the late 1550s indicate that he was in robust health. While Lauder was certainly the senior man in terms of age and experience, both he and Spens in practice appear to have enjoyed the same functional competence. To complicate matters, a third advocate, Robert

---

[66] Omond, *Lord Advocates,* i, 8 n.3. Omond gives no contemporary evidence to substantiate his assertion.

[67] CS 5/43 fo. 106r: 4 Dec. 1531.

[68] Inglis, *Otterburn,* 25. See fn. 39. Confusion concerning Foulis may occur because from 1527 he is found acting as a lord of session in his own right. His legal activities do not suggest that he was acting in this capacity *ex officio* as joint king's advocate as some scholars have claimed.

[69] It is interesting to note that when the office of king's attorney emerged in England in the thirteenth century it was likewise not held jointly. As in Scotland, there is no record of the man said to have held the office first (Lawrence de Brok) actually being sworn into it. Lawrence first appeared in 1243 acting for the king and was paid a regular fee, but it was not until William Langley in 1315 that there is evidence of appointment by letters patent and swearing into office; even so, it was not until 1527 that the title 'king's attorney' became a regular designation: J. Sainty, ed. *Law Officers and King's Counsel* (Selden Society supplementary series, 1987), 41; G.O. Sayles, ed., *Select Cases in the Court of King's Bench,* v, (Selden Society, 1958), xxx-xl; G.O. Sayles, ed., *Select Cases in the Court of King's Bench,* vi, (Selden Society, 1965), xxviii-xxx. Provision was made, however, for the king's attorney to appoint his own deputy or deputies: W. Holdsworth, *A History of English Law,* vi, (London, 1937), 460, n.3.

[70] *RSS,* iv, no. 3059: 21 Oct. 1555.

Crichton, was appointed by the regent, Mary of Guise, in February 1560 to act as 'ane of oure soveranis advocattis'.[71] Both Spens and Crichton retained their positions following Lauder's death in July 1561.[72]

It is likely that Spens replaced Lauder as the principal advocate with Crichton, except for a brief hiatus following his escheat for participation in the battle of Langside in 1568, acting as his depute.[73] Crichton regularly appears in the 1560s under the designation queen's advocate, reappearing in the early 1570s designed as king's advocate.[74] However, it was Spens who held the position on the bench that the advocate had come to hold *ex officio,* a position which on his death in 1573 was given to Master David Borthwick, his successor as king's advocate.[75] The stated reason for favouring Borthwick over Crichton was his many years of experience of the laws and practick of the realm: like Spens, he was simply the more experienced man.[76] This reinforces the view that after his initial appointment in 1560 Crichton was intended to function under the instructions of the advocate and as his depute. His inferior position is reflected in the fact that it was not until the day after Borthwick was actually buried in 1581 that Crichton was at last admitted to a seat on the bench as king's advocate.[77] It seems incongruous that Crichton, described in the record as 'advocat to our soverane lord' should appear clutching privy seal letters which constituted him 'our said soverane lordis advocat'.[78] The difference, however, is clear: this was promotion from advocate–depute to principal advocate. Indeed, Crichton had received his appointment in January 1580 to take effect immediately on Borthwick's death and had produced his letters of appointment on 19 December presumably with Borthwick's demise

[71]   *RMS,* v, no. 749.
[72]   Lauder's death on 19 July 1561 is indicated by a marginal entry next to the sederunt on that day: CS 1/2/1 fo. 28r.
[73]   For Crichton as a fugitive after Langside, see *RSS,* vi, no. 301: 8 June 1568. Apparently he returned to office quickly: see *RMS,* iv, no. 2137 and *RSS,* vi, no. 1271 (Spens and Crichton, king's advocates, 1571). It was Spens rather than Crichton who appeared on the sederunt of the privy council in Nov. 1561: *R.P.C.,* i, 188.
[74]   For example: *ER,* ixx, 489 (1562); *RSS,* vi, no. 1271 (Spens and Crichton, king's advocates, 1571).
[75]   *RSS,* vi, no. 2155: 15 Oct. 1573. There is a gap in the CS series at this period, however there is reference in the reliable EUL MS La. III 399 fo. 69 to Borthwick's admission on 20 Oct. to the place on the session held by the recently deceased Spens. Spens in fact died during the last two weeks of June 1573. His last will and testament was dated 16 June of that year: CC 8/8/3 fos. 54v-55r.
[76]   Borthwick, a student at St Andrews in 1525, was made a burgess of Haddington as early as July 1531: NAS, GD 1/413/1; see also NAS, B30/1/2 fo. 25r (*Prot. Bk.* Alexander Symsoun of Haddington). As a servant of the king's secretary, Sir Thomas Erskine of Brechin, he went to France late in 1535: CS 6/7 fo. 13r. Moreover he was named as a potential substitute to Henry Lauder as early as 1546: see above, p. 178. Crichton's third wife was Isobel Borthwick, perhaps a relative of Master David: *RMS,* iv no. 2817: 24 Nov. 1578.
[77]   It is clear from the confirmation of his testament that Borthwick died on 30 Jan. 1581: CC 8/8/10 fos. 239v-241v.
[78]   CS 1/3/1/ fo. 142r: 1 Feb. 1581.

in prospect.[79] It was not until some six weeks later, when Borthwick was actually dead, that Crichton was admitted into office.

A year after his admission Crichton, now principal advocate, appointed Alexander Chene advocate-depute.[80] This appointment recalled earlier practice in that it did not bear to have been made directly by the crown (although it could hardly have been made without royal approval). Chene was to pursue or defend all the king's matters as if the principal advocate were himself present to do so, but he was clearly subordinate: it was made plain that he was to hold office during Crichton's will and provided he did not prejudice his honour.[81] Crichton did not long enjoy tenure of the office of principal advocate. After his death he was replaced in June 1582 not by Chene but by David McGill of Nesbit who also took Crichton's place on the session.[82] McGill had already been recognised as the advocate's substitute in a royal letter of March 1582.[83] Moreover, he had brought himself to official attention in 1580 by proposing to the king articles for reform of procedure before the court which prompted the king and his council to instruct the judges to admit him to their presence that he might explain his ideas.[84] Shortly prior to Crichton's death, the king and his ministers declared themselves satisfied with McGill's previous service as Crichton's substitute and appointed him generally to 'supplie the place of our Advocate in his absence' in all causes due to Crichton's current infirmity.[85] Two weeks later Crichton was dead.[86] Master John Shairp represented both the king's advocate and the comptroller in an action on 23 June and then, on 26 June, in a case of nonentry brought at the instance of both Borthwick and Crichton, McGill appeared for the king 'the

---

[79]   The exchequer rolls only mention Crichton as king's advocate in the compt of William Murray of Tullibardine in 1580 (*ER*, xx, 549) whereas Borthwick and Crichton are recorded as advocates to the king in 1575 (*ER*, xx, 467).

[80]   CS 1/3/1 fo. 164r: 30 Jan. 1582. This can be compared with Lauder's nomination of substitutes in 1546 although that was a purely temporary measure.

[81]   Although Chene had connections to Aberdeen (see *RMS*, viii, no. 1920), where he was commissary in 1585, the terms of his appointment are clearly general and not simply regional.

[82]   26 June 1582: CS 1/3/1 fos. 174r-v. David McGill was the brother of James McGill, the late advocate and clerk register: *Prot. Bk. King*, no. 123: 12 June 1556; NAS, CC 8/8/11 fo. 151v: 15 Oct. 1579. There is some evidence that David had been a substitute advocate during Mary's minority: *Prot. Bk. King*, no. 225: 16 Mar. 1557.

[83]   *RSS*, viii, no. 720: 13 Mar. 1582. Possibly McGill was the king's choice as advocate-depute as opposed to Chene who was Crichton's choice. In 1579 both James and David McGill had been overlooked as successor to their father as clerk register although the latter in his will had hoped, through his influence with the earl of Morton, to have one or the other succeed him: CC 8/8/11 fos. 146v-152r: 16 Oct. 1579.

[84]   CS 1/3/1 fos. 118r-v. The king's letter to the court described McGill as a man of a 'zelous mynd' but did consider his 'overtures sumquhat dowtfull' and required an explanation of their meaning to be given to the lords of session.

[85]   Pitcairn, *Criminal Trials*, i, 101. This letter is dated at Dalkeith, 12 June 1582.

[86]   Crichton appeared personally on behalf of the king on 20 June (CS 7/90 fo. 259r) and 22 June (CS 7/90 fos. 275r-v). It would appear that he died suddenly certainly before 26 June, possibly on the evening of 22 June.

utheris twa advocatis being decessit'.[87] The next day he was formally admitted by the lords as king's advocate and an ordinary lord of session.[88] Three years later his son, Master David McGill younger, was appointed for life as substitute and depute to his father who was described as 'his maiesties privat advocat'.[89] McGill younger was to enjoy all the powers which had pertained to the office of advocate substitute by the law or practick of the realm at any time in the past. These powers were by then well understood, although their exercise prior to 1560 appears to have been less formal than it afterwards became. The picture is certainly one in which a single figure dominates: that of the principal advocate.[90] This is in line with recent research indicating that by the end of the sixteenth century the advocate, when pursuing criminal matters, normally exercised his office personally, but, when a depute did occasionally appear in his stead he did so as an aid rather than a substitute.[91]

Arguably the appointment of Spens as joint advocate with Lauder in 1555 is not as revolutionary as it appears. In practice he was fulfilling the same basic function as had other men of law in the past whenever the advocate was absent or otherwise unable to act. The only differences were that Spens was formally installed by the queen as one of her advocates in his own right, he was in receipt of a pension, and his appointment was not merely temporary. Moreover, Spens's appointment coincided with a period when the regent, Mary of Guise, was seeking to restore order in the country.[92] That she was prepared to experiment is clear from her willingness, under the influence of French humanist ideas, to set up royal lectureships, one of which was in law.[93] More generally, the promotion of Spens also occurred at a time when the legal profession was beginning to expand significantly. In 1549 the number of general procurators before the college of justice was still only nine.[94] Six years

---

[87] CS 7/90 fos. 280r, 301r-v. McGill's appearance in this case was probably still in the capacity of substitute advocate. On the career of Shairp see M.H.B. Sanderson, *Mary Stewart's People* (Edinburgh, 1987), 22-33.

[88] CS 1/3/1 fos. 174r-v. McGill was admitted on 27 June although the royal letters by which he was admitted were subscribed the day before. Unlike Crichton, McGill does not appear to have waited until his predecessor was buried before replacing him.

[89] NAS, PS 1/53 fo. 59v: 31 Oct. 1585. I am indebted to Dr Robin MacPherson, for this reference.

[90] Examples of substitutes for the king's advocate in the early seventeenth century are given in Pitcairn, *Criminal Trials*, where in place of Master Thomas Hamilton can be found Master Robert Linton (Jan. 1601) and Master Robert Foulis (July 1611): Pitcairn, *Criminal Trials*, i, 337, iii, 201.

[91] Wasser, *Central Criminal Courts*, 106. It is difficult to be certain what the distinction between an aid and a substitute means in this context. 'Aid' may connote a subordinate rather than merely a replacement and this would appear to fit the general trend in appointing advocates-depute even though the phrase 'substitute advocate' was still used in James VI's reign.

[92] Wasser, *Central Criminal Courts*, 127.

[93] *RSS*, iv, no. 3144; J. Durkan, 'The Royal Lectureships under Mary of Lorraine', (1983) *SHR* 73-8. The first lecturer was Master Alexander Sym for whom the town council of Edinburgh constructed a 'powpet' (lectern) in the Magdalene chapel: *Edin. Burgh. Recs.*, ii, 251.

[94] *ADCP*, 584.

later the number had increased to fourteen.[95] The Edinburgh tax-roll of September 1565 mentions twenty-six men of law who were burgesses, although this includes Writers to the Signet.[96] By 1586 there were fifty advocates in the Court of Session and in July 1590 the lords declared that they would only allow new admissions of advocates upon the death of one of those fifty.[97] This expansion began in the 1550s when the rate of admission of qualified candidates significantly increased; the old system of the king's advocate simply constituting his own substitutes before leaving Edinburgh may have been less well suited to circumstances in which there was a proliferation of advocates plying their trade.[98] Moreover, although difficult to quantify in absolute terms, the business of the courts and that of the king's advocate appears to have grown significantly as the sixteenth century progressed and it is against this background that the change of practice during the minority of Queen Mary should be seen.[99]

Co-operation with financial officers

It was not unusual for both the comptroller and the treasurer to represent the interests of the crown in judicial matters during the minority of James IV. In 1532 the 'tabular' was ordered to table all summonses pertaining to the king's profit as required by the treasurer and the advocate.[100] Financial officials often appeared on the king's behalf in litigation relating to their area of fiscal responsibility.[101] Such appearances normally coincided with sittings of the lord auditors of the exchequer (usually held in June, July and August) but this was

---

[95] CS 6/29 fo. 4v: 13 Nov. 1555.

[96] M. Lynch, *Edinburgh and the Reformation* (Edinburgh, 1981), 377.

[97] *Scottish Notes & Queries* (1st series), x, 140; EUL La. III.399 fo.116. The list from 1586 contains 55 names. Two of the advocates mentioned were dead, two were commissaries and one had become a bishop, leaving 50 potentially active advocates.

[98] There are numerous examples of admissions in the 1550s: Alexander Sym was admitted on 13 Nov. 1555 (CS 6/29 fo. 4v), John Moscrop on 20 Nov. 1555 (CS 6/29 fo. 6v), Master John Dunbar in July 1557 (CS 6/29 fo. 50r), in Nov. 1557 Master George Crichton (CS 6/29 fo. 55r).

[99] The increase in business can be demonstrated in several ways. The increased size of the records of court cases—over and above changes that may have occurred in the detail in which the clerks recorded them— is the most obvious sign. The increased tendency for courts to spend days at the end of each session simply continuing cases to be heard at the next session indicates how busy they were. Thus in December 1540 the lords continued a summons of error at the instance of the king's advocate until after Christmas and ordered that it 'run our [over] becaus of gret besynes now ado quhill thai mycht gett oportunitie to discuss the samyn in the next sete of sessioun': CS 6/14 fo. 55v.

[100] *ADCP*, 378. The tabular (see chapter five), was the person responsible for arranging summonses in a table for administrative convenience.

[101] On the treasurer generally at this period see A.L. Murray, 'Financing the royal household: James V and his comptrollers, 1513-1543', *The Renaissance and Reformation in Scotland*, eds. I.B. Cowan and D. Shaw (Edinburgh, 1983), chapter three.

not always the case.[102] Thus in July and August 1516 the comptroller, Sir Alexander Jardine of Applegarth, appeared several times on the king's behalf.[103] In December of the same year Jardine's successor, Robert Barton of Over Barnton, represented the king in a case concerning the withholding of the burgh customs of Elgin and defrauding of the Perth customs.[104] The treasurer, Master John Campbell, appeared for the king in March 1524.[105] The following day, in a case concerning unpaid fines imposed in a justice ayre, the treasurer's clerk, Master James Currour, appeared for the king.[106] In December 1527 Barton appeared together with the king's advocate against John Moncur and his wife.[107] This action concerned a claim by the latter to land held in ward and nonentry by the king. Otterburn appeared for the king whereas Barton appeared in his own right as comptroller. In July, 1540, Master Henry Balnavis appeared as advocate to the king in an action concerning the escheat of goods which had belonged to a man who had died without being legitimated.[108] The goods in question, having been inventoried, were delivered to Balnavis as treasurer's clerk. This case arose on a day when Lauder, the king's advocate, was present in court and Balnavis was clearly not usurping his role: his presence, despite the misdescription of him in the record, may be attributed solely to his role as clerk to the treasurer.[109] John, abbot of Paisley, Queen Mary's treasurer, represented her in an action against Patrick, earl Bothwell, concerning one of the queen's ships.[110] David Wood, the comptrollar, was present together with Lauder, the advocate, and Master

---

[102] As A.L. Murray points out ('Exchequer and Crown Revenue', 35), the audit customarily occurred at this time, following the Whitsunday term in mid-May, however practice was not always consistent. In 1520, for example, the audit was undertaken from October to December.

[103] CS 5/28 fos. 4r, 21v: 17 July and 13 Aug. 1516. Jardine is recorded as comptroller in Mar. and Aug. 1516, and accounted on 26 Sept.: Murray, 'Exchequer and Crown Revenue', Appendix, 103.

[104] CS 5/28 fo. 53v: 1 Dec. 1516. Just four days later Barton appeared in his own right in an action against Philip Galteret, a merchant of Florence, challenging the judges' competence to hear the case between them. The lords ordained that the case continue with the admiral in attendance on the bench: CS 5/28 fo. 57v, 59r: 5 Dec. 1516.

[105] CS 5/34 154v: 19 Mar. 1524. This appearance may be in the context of the exchequer. It is clear that the lords auditor of the exchequer were sitting on 4, 5 and 7 Mar. The exchequer was also sitting on 13 Apr. These sittings were all *in domo cancellarii* but it is unclear whether other sittings around this time were of council or of exchequer: on the difficulties of making this differentiation, see A.L. Murray, 'Exchequer, Council and Session, 1513–1542' in *Stewart Style 1513–1542: Essays on the Court of James V*, ed. J. H. Williams (East Linton, 1996), 100–101.

[106] CS 5/34 fo. 156r: 19 Mar. 1524. Currour, custumar of Banff (*ER*, xiv, 341; xv, 275) was described as a treasury clerk in 1522 (*TA*, v, 241). He also appeared in the king's name in Feb. 1523: CS 5/33 fo. 174v.

[107] CS 5/38 fo. 62v: 13 Dec. 1527.

[108] CS 6/13 82v: 14 July 1540. The dead man was William Hume, alias 'sueit will'. This is not the only reference to Balnavis appearing 'in our soverane lordis name': e.g. CS 6/11 fo. 215r: 13 Mar. 1539.

[109] For Balnavis, man of law, judge and leading Protestant, see *The Works of John Knox*, ed. D. Laing, vol. 3 (Edinburgh 1846-64) 405, and also pp. 65-6 above. The position of treasurer's clerk was obviously a solid foundation for success in later life with Thomas Marjoribankis being an earlier incumbent: *TA*, vi, 327: 4 June 1536.

[110] CS 6/28 fo. 52r: 26 June 1546.

David Ramsay, the custumar of Edinburgh, in an action before the lords auditor of the exchequer in August 1541 which concerned, amongst other things, the burgh customs of Dundee.[111]

Although these financial officials did appear on the king's behalf, their authority to do so appears to have been circumscribed. Only matters affecting their responsibility, actions arising directly from the audit or, at other times, indirectly from the general administration of their offices, appear to have come within their competence.[112] For example, in 1532 the widow of John Ayton, the king's master mason, brought an action against the treasurer, Robert Barton, which led to her obtaining payment of £20 owing to her late husband's estate.[113] The comptroller in 1541, David Wood, brought an action against Thomas Davidson who was importing English cloth and other goods at the port of Leith without paying customs to the custumar of Edinburgh. He was also engaged in sending merchandise the other way 'uncustumat & als without coquete'.[114] Moreover, it was the then comptroller, Robert Barton, together with John Beaton of Creich, the king's chamberlain in Fife, who brought an action against the aptly named John Gardner in 1523.[115] Gardner was pursued for repayment of his fee paid to him for tending the yards at the royal residence at Falkland and for non-payment of duties which he owed the crown as a concomitant to the 'office of gardnarschip' which he held and which, it was held, he had failed to fulfil.

Although in theory their roles were different, it can occasionally be difficult to distinguish from the record why the treasurer appears in some cases and the comptroller in others. In an action to recover maills and duties owing to the king but wrongfully detained, the advocate and the comptroller both appeared on the king's behalf.[116] The following month a lease of certain lands held by Adam Reid during their nonentry, which had not been validly assigned by a previous treasurer, was reduced by the current treasurer. A previous decreet, by which Adam had prevented Thomas Corry from taking the maills of the said lands, was reduced. The distinction to be drawn must be that the latter

---

[111] CS 6/16 fos. 134r-136r: 25 Aug. 1540. The clerk of the coquet of Dundee was also involved in this case in regard to a complaint made to the king that the burgh had been 'hevely done to & heryit'.

[112] Murray, ('Exchequer and Crown Revenue', 205), states that the comptroller acted as pursuer in cases before the council affecting the crown revenue. To a certain extent this would overlap with the advocate's competence in, for example, actions of error, which were normally brought by the advocate but not always or, at least, not exclusively. This is developed *infra*. The advocate by himself could bring actions relating to economic matters, for example, importing salt from France against the king's inhibition and selling it to the lieges in contempt of royal letters: CS 6/16 fo. 136v. It is possible to find cases where the comptrollar pursued actions of deforcement in the king's name where the officer deforced was seeking to collect the king's maills: e.g. CS 5/28 fo. 21r-v: 12 Aug. 1516.

[113] CS 6/1 fo. 87v: 27 July 1532.

[114] CS 6/15 fo. 143r: 30 May 1541. There are numerous examples of actions involving both the treasurer and the comptroller.

[115] CS 5/34 fo. 37r: 19 Dec. 1523.

[116] CS 5/32 fo. 2r: 18 Nov. 1518.

case involved nonentry, which was the treasurer's responsibility, whereas the earlier case must have related to sums payable directly to the comptroller by crown tenants.[117] There are also hybrid cases in which the king's advocate was involved along with the comptroller or treasurer.[118] Sometimes in such cases the advocate acted specifically as procurator for the financial officers, at other times they functioned independently.[119] There appears to be no reason in the majority of cases why both the advocate and the comptroller or treasurer should appear together. However, it was possible in some cases that both the treasurer (or comptroller) and the advocate might have separate interests in the same action. For example, in July 1546 the advocate appeared and desired that he be summoned to appear along with the treasurer in an action that had been brought by John, Lord Glamis against James Kirkcaldy of Grange (himself a former treasurer) concerning the reduction of private contracts between them. The queen's legal and financial interest in the matter rested on the fact that Kirkcaldy was under summons for treason, having been involved in the murder of Cardinal Beaton.[120] In spite of this clear interest, however, the lords ordered that Glamis should be permitted to pursue his action on his own even though the advocate had claimed it was prejudicial to the queen's interest.[121] Glamis, having raised his summons first, was permitted to continue with his action on his own because it had already commenced and pre-dated the summons for treason. There is some irony in Kirkcaldy's position. When he was treasurer in 1539 the former advocate Adam Otterburn, then warded in Dumbarton castle, found himself in debt to him having been forced to pay a large fine to the crown.[122] Otterburn himself had pursued the treasurer, Archibald Douglas of Kilspindie, for treason in 1528 and with Kirkcaldy now accused of treason events had come full circle.

Generally co-operation between the crown advocates and crown financial officials appears to have been close.[123] This reflects the fact that the advocate

---

117 CS 5/32 fo. 37v: 3 Dec. 1518. Murray, 'Exchequer and Crown Revenue', 206.

118 See also the supplication by Walter Gourlay mentioned in chapter five, fn. 245.

119 The comptroller often brought actions in which he was represented by a man of law other than the advocate in court: e.g. where Master John Chisholm represented Robert Barton in an action brought against the custumar of Cupar in relation to a debt of £50 owed to the comptroller in the king's name: CS 5/34 fo. 174r: 1 June 1524.

120 CS 6/21 fo. 17v: 5 July 1546. On Kirkcaldy of Grange and the assassination of Beaton, see Sanderson, *Cardinal of Scotland* (Edinburgh, 1986), 184, 223. Grange's son, William, was directly involved in the murder.

121 Presumably the prejudice was financial; if Kirkcaldy stood to lose financially against Glamis, then the queen would lose financially in the event of his forfeiture.

122 CS 6/11 fo. 142r: 16 Feb. 1539. Nicol Cairncross, burgess of Edinburgh, granted caution that Otterburn would pay £1000 to Kirkcaldy of Grange, the treasurer. Otterburn was then put to liberty on condition he passed to Fife and remained there at the king's pleasure. See also Inglis, *Otterburn*, 69.

123 In 1508 James Henryson was even commissioned and sworn to the office of 'balzery' to the treasurer: CS 5/19 fo. 327v. It is not clear what this position of 'bailie' entailed although there is no evidence that it was anything other than temporary.

was the obvious source of advice on the law and legal procedure for those seeking to uphold the king's lawful interests in the economic sphere. By giving such advice the advocate could, indirectly, even help line his own pockets. In January 1499 James Henryson brought an action against the sheriff of Stirling in respect of a sum owed by the latter to the treasurer which had been assigned to the advocate in part payment' of his yearly pension.[124] The relationship between advocates and accountants also manifested itself procedurally. In Balfour's time it was a rule of law that in any case where the king had special interest lawful warning to the king's advocate was sufficient and the comptroller need not be warned separately.[125] It is probable that this was a rule of long standing. In 1525 the comptroller complained to the lords that since neither he nor the advocate had been lawfully summoned to an action no process should be led against them; the implication is that warning to one would suffice as warning to the other.[126] On the other hand in raising an action against the king it would appear that pursuers were at liberty to bring their case against both the advocate and the comptroller. Thus, by a general act at the beginning of Mary's reign, the lords ordered that any party who had been dispossessed of their heritage, tacks or steadings by royal officers or servants during the time of James V should, for the benefit of the late king's soul, have privilege in the calling of any summons they raised against the king's comptroller and his advocate.[127]

Close co-operation between the advocate and the crown's financial and administrative officials was essential because of the matters that the advocate was required to investigate and pursue on the crown's behalf. The clearest general example of this co-operation was the search conducted into records of heritable titles during the reign of James IV which formed the necessary background to the large number of actions of recognition brought on the king's behalf during his reign.[128] Recognitions tend to arise more rarely in the reign of James V, but actions relating to the casualties of nonentry and ward were increasingly common and also required familiarity with government records.[129] Co-operation was such that in 1540 the advocate was in a position to bring actions for debts owed to the crown which had been incurred over fifty years earlier. For example, the successor of Alexander Dunbar of

---

[124] *ADC*, ii, 324. No doubt this was administratively convenient for the treasurer who did not himself have to pursue the matter legally.

[125] Balfour, *Practicks*, ii, 296.

[126] CS 5/35 fo. 111v: 27 July 1525.

[127] CS 7/1/1 fo. 177v: 15 Jan. 1543.

[128] According to Nicolson there were at least 149 such actions during the personal reign of James IV: R. Nicolson, 'Feudal Developments in Late Medieval Scotland' (1973) *JR* 17.

[129] On nonentry and ward see the summary by G.L. Gretton, 'The Feudal System', *The Law of Property*, ed. K.G.C. Reid (Edinburgh, 1996), paras 75, 81. That the right to nonentry or ward was viewed as a commercial commodity is clear from the fact that normally the advocate represented the king and also spoke on behalf of the king's donatar and both the king and his donatar appeared in the libel.

Cumnock, sheriff of Elgin and Forres, who had rendered his accounts in July 1489, was pursued by the advocate on the treasurer's behalf for sums owing and unpaid since that time.[130] Shortly thereafter the successor of Thomas McClellane of Bombie, custumar of Kirkcudbright and Wigtown, was pursued for the arrears which his predecessor had owed to the comptroller in 1506.[131] In order to bring actions for what in fact were modest amounts of money, careful scrutiny of the exchequer rolls was required and the treasurer and his clerks no doubt did this. That such care was taken not only indicates the king's perennial need for money, but also that such cases functioned as deterrents to those tempted to delay rendering accounts.[132]

It would be misleading, however, to obscure the primary activity of the advocate by considering only its financial consequences, particularly because the king's interest in most cases could be defined in monetary terms. A good example of this distinction occurred in 1518 in the context of an action brought by the king and his mother against James Murray of Falahill.[133] The charge concerned the alleged convocation of lieges by Murray in contempt of the king's authority.[134] There seems to have been some question as to who was Murray's principal adversary. From the defender's viewpoint, the standing of witnesses produced by the queen could be questioned if she were the principal pursuer. To counter this, the king's advocate argued that the action properly belonged to the king rather than the queen. This, he argued, was not due to the contempt but because if the action were successful the profit would accrue to the king and not to the queen. The rationale was financial; yet clearly the financial aspect of the case was secondary. Regardless of potential profit to the crown, it was incumbent on the advocate to act subject to law and he could not issue a summons without legal cause. The legal rationale on which the advocate grounded his activities varied. The majority of cases, however, fell into three broad categories: the defence and vindication of the king's economic rights (most readily understood by reference to the crown's interests in land); the defence of royal authority; and oversight of the administration of justice.

---

[130]   CS 6/14 fo. 53v: 10 Oct. 1540. The debt in question was alleged to be £32 15s. Compare *ER*, x, 84–5, where the sum of the debts in question actually amount only to £32.

[131]   CS 6/14 fo. 62v: 10 Oct. 1540. The arrears sought amounted to £60 3s 4d. This was the level of arrears in 1507 (*ER*, xii, 472); however, the clerks appear not to have noticed that the arrears actually increased the following year to £90 13s 4d (*ER*, xii, 598).

[132]   The descendants of higher officials such as the comptroller or treasurer were not exempt from such actions; e.g. George, the son and heir of George Robison, erstwhile comptroller, was pursued for debts owed to the king by his late father: CS 5/17 fo. 15v: 17 Nov. 1505.

[133]   CS 5/30 fos. 185v–186v: 10 Feb. 1518.

[134]   It was alleged that Murray and two hundred others beset the way armed for war doing all that they could to slay a local laird whom the queen had appointed captain of her castle of Newark. Murray alleged that his actions were consistent with his duties as sheriff of Selkirk. He objected to certain witnesses brought by the queen, whom he alleged was the principal party against him, because they were her tenants.

Deforcement and barratry

In terms of upholding royal authority, the two most common types of action were those concerned with deforcement of royal messengers and barratry. The complaint by messengers that they had been deforced, normally in the context of a poinding, was relatively common. In practice, once deforced, the messenger would break his wand and seek witnesses whom the advocate would later call to prove his case.[135] For example, from November 1528 to November 1529 there were eleven separate instances of the advocate bringing an action for deforcement.[136] The sentence on being found to have deforced the king's officers was mandatory: escheat of all moveable goods and imprisonment for a year and a day and further upon the king's will.[137] The significant point about deforcement was not the degree of violence used, or indeed the degree of deforcement whether partial or whole: it was the 'contemptation' done to the king's 'auctorite riale' which mattered.[138] The messenger, whether herald, macer, *nuncius* or sheriff *in hac parte*, represented the king and an affront to the king's representative was an affront to the king which the advocate was required to pursue.

Purchasing benefices at Rome without the king's licence damaged the crown in two obvious respects: firstly, it meant the transfer of a large sum of money out of the realm and, secondly, it directly challenged the royal privilege of nominating someone to hold the benefice.[139] Legislation against

---

[135] For example, CS 5/39 fo. 124r: 27 Feb. 1529. The messenger at arms carried a red wand of office at least three quarters of a yard long, as well as a horn: *APS*, ii, c. 11 (1432). See M.B. Wasser, 'Violence and the Central Criminal Courts in Scotland 1603-1638' (Ph.D thesis, Columbia University, 1995), 105-6. For an example of a process of deforcement led before the regality court of Kilwinning, see CS 6/14 fo. 111r.

[136] CS 5/39 fo. 10v: 26 Nov. 1528 (Thomas Nevin, messenger, deforced); 79v: 8 Feb. 1529 (Andrew Mercer, messenger, deforced); 93v: 15 Feb. 1529 (John Adamson, messenger, deforced); 124r: 27 Feb. 1529 (Andrew Mercer deforced); 125v: 1 Mar. 1529 (John Adamson deforced); CS 5/40 fo. 9v: 15 Apr. 1529 (Robert Champnay, deforced); 13v: 23 Apr. 1529 (Robert Champnay, deforced); 16v: 5 May 1529 (William Duncan deforced); 45v: 24 May 1529 (Robert Champnay and John Langlands deforced); 46r: 24 May 1529 (John Langlands deforced); 137r: 10 Nov. 1529 (John Gourlay deforced). In the following year, to Nov. 1530, there were no actions for deforcement.

[137] When James Henryson prosecuted John Lindsay of Wauchop for the slaughter of a messenger at arms the sentence was death: Pitcairn, *Criminal Trials*, i, *49.

[138] The phrase 'contemptation done ... to his auctorite riale' is standard in the decreet of the lords whenever they find deforcement established. There were variations in the degree of physical harm done. The allegation might be one of violent and masterful deforcement where violent hands were placed upon the officer (e.g. CS 6/1 fos. 35v-36r) or simply wrongful deforcement where the officer was prevented from carrying out his assigned task (e.g. CS 5/39 fo. 124r). The sentence was the same in either case because the same level of contempt for royal authority was exhibited.

[139] The cost and time involved in appeals to the Roman curia were acknowledged by Sixtus IV in the bull, *Triumphans pastor eternus,* which raised St Andrews to a metropolitan see in 1472: L.J. Macfarlane, 'The primacy of the Scottish church 1472-1521', *Innes Review*, xx (1969), 112. In England the right to nominate a clerk to a benefice was a temporal right (an 'advowson') justiciable in the king's courts: J.H. Baker, *Introduction to English Legal History* (London, 1985) 149. The issue does not appear to have been

clerics negotiating directly with Rome in the purchase of benefices had existed since the reign of James I. The royal privilege of nomination does not appear to have been formally settled until a papal indult issued to James III in 1487. This confirmed that the pope would delay, for at least eight months, making provision to fill vacancies worth more than two hundred gold florins of the camera. The king (and his successors) were thereby given time to make supplications on behalf of their nominees.[140] This privilege appears to have hardened into a right by 1526 when the estates asserted that the king had the power to nominate, rather than merely recommend, a candidate.[141] This may have been a further response to the practice of churchmen naming those to be promoted in Rome as their successors; the privy council had tried to end this in November 1525 because of the great damage it was doing to the king's interests.[142]

Although there was a degree of tension in the relationship, especially where issues such as barratry were concerned, the balance of power between the church and the crown in Scotland during the reign of James V was increasingly in favour of the king.[143] In a supplication which he made to the lords in December 1529 the king's advocate took it for granted that the king and his predecessors had had the right of granting provision to all vacant benefices in any diocese of the realm.[144] It was precisely the king's desire to protect both his income and his rights *vis-à-vis* Rome which explains why disputes concerning benefices so rarely appeared before the courts of the official but were so regularly raised by the king's advocate before the lords of council.[145] The rights of the king's nominee were subordinated to the interests of the king in stamping out barratry and that is why such actions proceeded at the king's instance in the king's court.[146] Moreover, there is evidence that the parties, left to themselves, were keen to avoid litigation if possible.[147]

---

controversial; the church seems to have acquiesced in royal claims to have jurisdiction in the matter: Helmholz, *Canon Law and the Law of England* (London, 1987), 83.

[140] I.B. Cowan, 'Patronage', 75; Macdougall, *James III*, 229. For lay patronage see Macfarlane, *Elphinstone*, 211–14. See also *ADCP*, introduction, xlviii–lv.

[141] W.C. Dickinson, *Scotland from Earliest times to 1603*, ed. A.A.M. Duncan (Edinburgh, 1977), 274; Cowan, 'Patronage', 76. According to Macfarlane, 'Primacy', 115, James III by 1478 was able to over-ride papal provisions at will and that the privilege granted in 1487 soon became a right.

[142] CS 5/35 fo. 165r: 23 Nov. 1525.

[143] The concessions granted to the crown in relation to the endowment of the college of justice are one indication of how the balance of power lay during the reign of James V. The papacy certainly feared an attack on church property in Scotland and preservation of the liberty of the church was in Cardinal Beaton's view a paramount consideration: Sanderson, *Cardinal of Scotland*, 86.

[144] CS 5/40 fo. 150v: 3 Dec. 1529. It must of course be remembered that statements by the king's advocate are nowhere free of political propaganda on behalf of the crown.

[145] Ollivant, *The Official*, 83–4; 126.

[146] There is a parallel with the situation in England where from the end of the fifteenth century an increasing number of cases based on the Statute of *Praemunire* of 1353 were being brought. This statute primarily sought to deter litigation affecting the king from being heard in church courts and the actions based upon it have been interpreted as an attack on ecclesiastical jurisdiction: Helmholz, *Canon Law*,

As a symptom of the tension between crown and papacy, barratry had the potential to divide the loyalties of the spiritual lords of session. In 1522, for example, there was a dispute between Master John Sauchy and the king's secretary concerning the fruits of the parsonage of Eddleston in Tweeddale. Sauchy had obtained executorials in Rome which he sought to exercise; however, the secretary questioned his right to do so and alleged that he himself had been provided to the benefice. The bishop of Aberdeen, although as president of the court he had read out the summons, refused to question Sauchy's executorials and dissented from all things that were in prejudice of his conscience or that may have incurred any legal process against him from the pope.[148] Such reticence from a lord of session was unusual. Just as unusual was the fact that the secretary then brought the official of St Andrews before the lords to reinforce his case. The official stated that he had convened in the archdeanery of Lothian with 'certaine advocatis & men of law' and that together they had considered Sauchy's executorials and were of the opinion that the secretary had been justified in appealing from them and that they were willing to have this opinion added to the end of his appeal.[149] The most singular aspect of the case is that although Sauchy was alleged to have contravened the acts of parliament against barratry, the king's advocate does not appear from the record to have been involved at any stage.

The record, however, does display a regular stream of actions brought to enforce the statutes against barratry.[150] A good example is the action raised by the king's advocate in October 1528 against the sub-prior and convent of Holyrood and dean John Lamb, canon of the same, for their 'hie presumptioune' in attempting to present the latter as prior of St Mary's Isle in Kirkcudbrightshire, contrary to the king's nomination and in prejudice to the privilege of his crown.[151] Three months later an action was concluded against Dean David Murray for purchasing the priory of Beauly in Rome after the

317 and, ibid., *Roman Canon Law in Reformation England* (Cambridge, 1990), 25-7. At the period of this study *praemunire* was the live issue in England and, indeed, was the means by which Wolsey was removed from power: J. Baker, *The Reports of Sir John Spelman* (Selden Society, 1978), 2 vols, ii, 66-70; Richard Marius, *Thomas More* (London, 1984), 126-7; Peter Gwynne, *The King's Cardinal* (London, 1990), 623*ff*.

[147] Cowan, 'Patronage', 86-7.

[148] CS 5/33 fos. 85v-86r: 12 Dec. 1522. Sauchy also features in a barratry case pursued by James Wishart early in the reign of James V: *ADCP*, 29*ff*.

[149] CS 5/33 fos. 93r, 101r: 15 and 18 Dec. 1522.

[150] It has been suggested that the fifteenth-century statutes against barratry were motivated by concern about papal reservation of benefices, a matter that was not affected by the indult of 1487: Cowan, 'Patronage', 82; see also MacFarlane, *Elphinstone*, 212. Nonetheless in 1488 the purchasing at Rome of a benefice which belonged to the crown through the king's right of presentation *sede vacante* was brought within the statutory offence of barratry: G. Donaldson, 'The rights of the crown in episcopal vacancies' reprinted in *Scottish Church History* (Edinburgh, 1985), 38. The actions before the lords of session tend simply to refer to contravention of the acts against barratry and the precise ground is not always evident from the record.

[151] CS 5/38 fo. 184r: 20 Oct. 1528.

king's familiar chaplain, Master James Haswell, had been provided to the same
by the king who had sent the pope 'his effectuiss writingis for his [i.e.
Haswell's] promotioune to the said priorie be vertu of rycht and privelege of
his croune'.[152] The temporal lords of council declared that Murray and his
accomplices were traitors who had broken the acts concerning barratry and
should be put to the horn and banished, never again to 'use worschip' within
the realm. The drain of resources abroad through the purchasing of benefices
in Rome was condemned in one case because it hurt the 'ordinaris that may
nocht benefice lordis sounis and thir awne servandis for pley of sik
barratouris'.[153] This was a reference to the financial damage created by disputes
between the king's nominee and other claimants to ecclesiastical vacancies:
such disputes might engender delay in the receipt of the fruits of the benefice
by its lawful holder.

The administration of justice

The king's interest in the administration of justice required that his advocate
became involved in pursuing those guilty of improper conduct in the king's
courts. In terms of volume, the most common case of this type involved the
pursuit of a summons of error based upon the allegation that a sheriff and
inquest had improperly served a brieve of inquest (also known as a brieve of
succession), but such summonses were also brought against other retourable
brieves such as the brieve of tutory.[154] In proceeding upon such brieves it was
the responsibility of the sheriff and local inquest to make a retour to the king's
chancery answering the points of the brieve.[155] In the case of the brieve of
succession, this involved indicating whether the last holder died vest and saised
as of fee in the lands in question at the faith and peace of the king and, if so,
who the nearest lawful heir of that person was and what the value of the lands
was. The summons of error might be raised by the king's advocate alone or,
more usually, by the advocate in conjunction with the party who felt
aggrieved by the decision of the sheriff and the inquest.[156] The allegations

---

[152] CS 5/39 fo. 63r: 27 Jan. 1529.

[153] CS 5/37 fo. 239v: 25 Sept. 1528.

[154] On the topic of wilful error, see I.D. Willock, *The Jury in Scotland* (Stair Society, 1966), chapter xii. For
the brieve of inquest, see *Fife Ct. Bk.,* 312.

[155] It would appear that the king's advocate was warned in advance of the service of brieves of inquest. In
an apparently isolated judgment in 1524 the lords decerned that, notwithstanding an act of parliament
produced by Wishart, the king ought not to be warned forty days before the serving of such a brieve:
CS 5/34 fo. 115v: 24 Feb. 1524. Two years later in another case involving a brieve of inquest the lords
mentioned that the advocate should be lawfully warned to the action upon forty days notice: CS 5/36
fo. 7v: 13 Mar. 1526.

[156] The original authority for bringing the action lay with an act of parliament of 1471 which allowed a
party aggrieved by the malice or ignorance of an assise or inquest to bring an action to have the
determination of that inquest reduced: *APS,* ii, 100 c.9. The statute does not mention the king's
interest and apparently took it for granted. However it does mention that the inquest should be

raised in the summons varied but might include an accusation against the sheriff of partiality or inordinate procedure and a complaint against the inquest of manifest, wilful and/or ignorant error.[157] Sometimes the distinction between alleged procedural irregularity and bias was negligible and the underlying assumption in some cases appears to have been that if the judge permitted an obvious irregularity then he must have been partial and both grounds were entered in the libel.[158] However, there are certainly examples in which a kin relationship between the sheriff and the party seeking to have the brieve served can be demonstrated.[159]

Allegations of inordinate procedure might concern the judge himself, for instance that he was not of age or that he lacked a proper commission to serve the brieve,[160] or they might relate to the manner in which the brieve was executed. A properly executed brieve was lawfully proclaimed on a market day at the market cross of the principal burgh of the sheriffdom[161] fifteen days in advance of the service of the heir,[162] provided that this did not occur during 'feriat' (vacation) time.[163] The brieve had to be served by a properly constituted inquest of the worthy men of the sheriffdom who best knew the truth of the matter in question,[164] and the seals of the majority of them had to be affixed to the retour to make it valid.[165] By statute the summons of error

punished after the form of the king's laws in *Regiam Majestatem*. Arguably the king's major interest in most summonses of error lay in the fact that he was feudal superior of the lands which the summons brought into question. In so far as irregular proceedings in the king's courts were alleged, his interest lay in ensuring the correct administration of justice.

[157] 'Sheriff' includes here the sheriff-depute, or sheriff *in hac parte* commissioned for the purpose of serving the brieve, stewart or president of the burgh court and his bailies. Even the justice-clerk Nicol Crawford, as sheriff depute of Linlithgow, was not immune from having a summons of error raised against him by the advocate: CS 5/36 fo. 102r: 28 Nov. 1526.

[158] For example, it was alleged in one case that the heir who sought to be served was within the third degree of consanguinity to a member of the inquest which had been proven by a notarial instrument on the day of the sheriff court: CS 5/39 fo. 20r: 7 Dec. 1528. Partiality was much more often alleged than given as a ground of judgment.

[159] E.g. John, Lord Lindsay, sheriff principal of Fife and Master John Spens were allegedly related in that the sheriff's grandmother and John's mother were sisters: CS 5/39 fo. 122r: 27 Feb. 1529.

[160] CS 5/39 fo. 164v, 12 Mar. 1529; allegation that William Edmonstone of Duntreath, steward of Menteith, was not old enough to be a judge; CS 5/33 fo. 204r, 20 June 1523; allegation that William Abernethy, alleged sheriff of Aberdeen *in hac parte* by the king's commission was not sworn and did not have a lawful commission.

[161] CS 5/39 fo. 20r: 7 Dec. 1528.

[162] CS 5/39 fo. 170v: 10 Feb. 1529. In one case (CS 5/39 fo. 164r) it was alleged that the proclamation of the day on which the brieve was to be served followed the date of the service.

[163] CS 5/39 fo. 80v: 8 Feb. 1529.

[164] E.g. CS 5/39 fo. 80v: allegation that the inquest chosen by the sheriff depute were 'sempill persounis' and that he had 'left out barons and worthy men that best knew the verite in the said mater'.

[165] CS 5/33 fo. 27r: 19 Nov. 1522; allegation that there were only six seals on a retour and therefore it should be annulled.

had to be raised within three years of the service of the heir;[166] however, the lords in certain circumstances relaxed this requirement.[167]

In cases where there was no lawful heir the crown took the lands as ultimate heir. An example of the king's advocate arguing (albeit unsuccessfully) that a tenement was escheat to the crown through lack of heirs occurred in December 1522 when James Wishart argued that the tenement in question was the conquest of a foreigner whose 'haile blud' had been destroyed by the death of his last descendant.[168] Such an argument is rarely found.[169] Equally rare are parties technically ineligible to be served as heirs because of their personal status.[170] In a case concerning a brieve of tutory, Thomas, abbot of Balmerino, was not served as tutor allegedly because 'he is ane monk and deid to the warld and is nocht able thirfor'.[171] It was argued that Thomas, as nearest agnate, should have succeeded as tutor because by the consuetude (custom) of the realm abbots were not precluded from succeeding to the office of tutory and, further, anyone served as tutor at law could not transfer the office to another. This was still the law in Balfour's time.[172] Finally, confusion might exist concerning the nature of the interest held by the last occupier of the land.[173] Thus in one case an inquest was declared to have erred when it retoured that the lands in question were held of the king in blench ferme, although no evidence to support this had been produced.[174] This particular record, however, was amended when the party who had sought to have the brieve served produced a charter bearing that the lands were indeed held blench and the inquest was thereby assoilzied.

Indeed, the consequences of getting the retour wrong were potentially devastating for the members of the inquest: escheat of moveables and imprisonment for at least a year.[175] There are regular instances of men coming

---

[166]　CS 5/33 fo. 113r: 19 Dec. 1522.

[167]　E.g. CS 5/33 fo. 137r: 29 Jan. 1523; where the party who had raised the summons in conjunction with the advocate had been out of the country.

[168]　CS 5/33 fo. 77r: 9 Dec. 1522. 'Conquest' here is meant in its technical sense of land acquired by purchase and not inheritance. See Gretton, 'Feudal System', para 54.

[169]　There is an example of a successful case brought by the advocate in which the king gained the escheat as ultimate heir: CS 5/17 fo. 225v: 20 Jan. 1506.

[170]　For instance, friar Thomas Sleich of the order of the friars preachers who, as a religious man, was 'deid to the warld' and so could not be served as the nearest lawful heir: CS 5/33 fo. 77r: 9 Dec. 1522.

[171]　CS 5/39 fo. 167r: 12 Mar. 1529. This action was brought by the advocate and the tutor-dative of George Forrester against Alexander Forrester who had been served tutor at law, together with the sheriff deputes of Fife and the inquest who had served him.

[172]　Balfour, *Practicks*, i, 117.

[173]　E.g. was that interest infeftment or merely liferent?: CS 5/33 fo. 10r: 12 Nov. 1522.

[174]　CS 5/40 fo. 40r: 21 May 1529. There are several similar cases together in the record at this point.

[175]　The knock-on effect of having a retour reduced was normally the casualty of nonentry and escheat of anyone who had wilfully erred. In 1530 the king's advocate, acknowledging numerous reductions of such retours in the current session, stated with the treasurer's assent 'that every man sall have the nonentres of thir saidis landis and eschetis of thir gudis': CS 5/41 fo. 10v. This appears to mean that the crown, perhaps in the face of protest, was prepared to renounce (at least temporarily) the major

forward before the lords to distance themselves from the final verdict of the inquest in the hope of avoiding the consequences of being found to have acted wrongly.[176] In one case two members of an inquest appeared with a notarial instrument as proof that they had refused to serve a brieve and that their names should therefore be removed from a subsequent decreet of error.[177] The king's advocate immediately offered to prove that the instrument in question was a forgery. A similar case is revealed in a supplication to the lords made by Charles Thornton who had been warded having been convicted of error whilst acting on an inquest.[178] His warding occurred despite the fact that his procurator had produced a notarial instrument stating his refusal to serve on the inquest because of his belief that the party seeking to serve the brieve was too young to be validly retoured as heir. Thornton had been escheated despite the fact that his procurator, Henry Spittall, had not had an opportunity to prove his allegation. The lords suspended this escheat, however, when another procurator for Thornton, Robert Galbraith, produced the instrument before them. The treasurer, John Campbell, who had originally claimed that the instrument was forged, then backed down and admitted that he had no reasonable cause to persist in that claim. So high were the stakes that inquests, or some members of them like Thornton, sometimes had a man of law to represent them.[179] Thus Thomas Marjoribankis, procurator for bailies and an inquest who had been summoned for error, asked for the formal recording of a concession made by the treasurer and the advocate to the effect that if he could prove within a week that his clients had not erred then they would incur no danger.[180]

The potential consequences of error were equally serious for the sheriff. It was the responsibility of the sheriff to maintain an adequate record of processes led before him so that he might answer for his conduct.[181] The leading action of this period was that raised by the king's advocate against John, Lord Lindsay of the Byres, sheriff principal of Fife and his deputes for alleged inordinate

economic benefit which such actions brought. However, in the cases which follow this announcement wilful error appears to be punished as normal by escheat to the crown.

[176] E.g. CS 6/14 fos. 92r-v, 111r: Patrick Maxwell, alleged to have been a member of an inquest, claimed that he was not present when a retour was made, that his seal was not affixed to it, and that it had been iregularly issued from the chancery. However the majority of the seals of the inquest were on the retour and and lords found it adequate, although ignorantly arrived at by the inquest.

[177] CS 5/40 fo. 65v: 23 July 1529.

[178] CS 5/36 fo. 84v: 16 Aug. 1526.

[179] Generally speaking the sheriff or sheriff-depute would appear personally, or employ a man of law to act for them, to defend themselves against a summons of error whereas it was much rarer for members of the inquest to appear or be represented. Presumably they left it to the presiding sheriff to vindicate the retour before the lords of session.

[180] CS 5/40 fo. 87r: 4 Aug. 1529.

[181] CS 5/33 fo. 124r: 23 [Jan.] 1523; dispute re the court books, seal of office and signet of the sheriff principal of Perth, William, master of Ruthven, who was responsible for answering for all processes led by himself or his deputes.

proceeding in sheriff courts held on 19 October 1526 and 28 March 1528 in the refusal to serve Robert Orrock to the lands of Orrock.[182] Orrock had obtained letters charging the sheriff to serve him as heir under the threat of losing his office.[183] Both Lindsay and his deputes lost their offices perpetually during the king's will, according to the terms of an act of parliament which defined the penalty for those guilty of the partial administration of justice.[184] The sheriff principal was ordered to deliver his court books, rolments and seal or signet of office within three days on pain of rebellion[185] and, once delivery was made, the king's advocate made it clear that no value should be ascribed to any books other than those delivered.[186] The following day the lords ordered that the court books be handed over to the king and delivery to the advocate in his name then took place.[187] Lindsay was replaced by the earl of Rothes.[188]

An interesting, albeit less serious, dispute arose in 1523 concerning the sheriff clerkship of Perth.[189] In pursuit of his claim to hold this office Alexander McBrek purchased royal letters seeking delivery from the sheriff, William, master of Ruthven, of the court books, seal and signet of office. The lords annulled these letters because they had been purchased without cognition; nonetheless the significant aspect of the case is that McBrek requested the king's advocate to procure for him because he had the king's letters and Ruthven stood opposed to him. The advocate, although present, was not drawn into the case but it is nonetheless instructive in demonstrating how a man who believed himself to be an office holder clearly thought it was his right to be represented and defended by the king's advocate simply on the strength of letters purchased from the king's chancery. In this context it is worth mentioning briefly that the advocate did sometimes appear for the officials and appointees of the king other than the treasurer and the comptroller. A good example occurred in 1541 when Henry Lauder appeared for Robert Orrock in the latter's capacity as depute to the king's master of work. Orrock was responsible for building a harbour at Burntisland in Fife and

---

182   CS 5/39 fos. 67v, 120r, 122r; CS 5/40 fos. 49r 50r, 55r , 68v, 69r, 70v, 129r, 155r. These references include some of the other complaints against Lindsay which occur at this period, especially following his loss of office.

183   CS 5/40 fo. 49r: 1 June 1529. Orrock also had other letters which the sheriff's deputes had refused to obey. For a list of the sheriff-deputes of Fife, see CS 5/39 fo. 122r: 28 Feb. 1529.

184   CS 5/40 fo. 50r: 2 June 1529.

185   CS 5/40 fo. 55r: 15 June 1529. Lindsay asserted that he used no seal or signet of office but used his own seal instead.

186   CS 5/40 fo. 68v: 23 July 1529.

187   CS 5/40 fo. 69r: 24 July 1529.

188   CS 5/40 fo. 155r: 12 Jan. 1530. This, at least, was subject to any appeal by Lindsay. However, Rothes was still exercising the office in 1541: CS 6/14 fo. 94v. Moreover, Cameron suggested that Lord Lindsay sought to win royal favour, and the return of the sheriffship, by serving on the assize which convicted Hamilton of Finnart of treason in 1540: Cameron, *James V*, 217.

189   CS 5/33 fo. 124r: 23 [Jan.] 1523.

his action was brought against two workmen ordering them to appear for work or else to be put to the horn.[190]

In November 1532 Adam Otterburn put the following proposition, that, as king's advocate:

> in all tymes tocum his taciturnite at the bar suld nocht be preiudiciale to the kingis actioun bot that his hienes may persew sic actiounis quhen his grace thinkis maist expedient.[191]

In other words the initiative in pursuing the king's matters was to lie with the king's advocate and parties could not rely on the argument that if the advocate were present and made no protest then he should subsequently lose any right to do so.

The point arose in the context of an action of error raised by the king and the master of Glencairn against Hugh Campbell, sheriff of Ayr.[192] William and Hugh had both consented to a continuation of the case without informing the advocate, as the latter declared to the king. In response the king wrote to the lords of session demanding that the summons, which should have been heard on the preceding Friday (the king's day), should be heard immediately and condemning 'collusion' between the other parties to the detriment of his interests.[193] The matter was heard and the advocate, having had his point upheld, then agreed to a continuation of the case.[194] That advantage had in the past been sought by litigants from the silence of the king's advocate is clear by reference to events in the sheriff court of Berwick, sitting in Edinburgh's Tolbooth in June 1518. A brieve of inquest was served and a retour made by the sheriff-depute in favour of William Manderstone in the presence of *inter alia* the earl of Arran, the treasurer and the king's advocate. William's prelocutor Robert Leslie, in making the specific point that the advocate produced no evidence to impede the service of the brieve, seems to have hoped thereby that personal bar might operate to prevent him from doing so in future.[195] Despite Otterburn's success in arguing his point in 1532, it was probably safer in general terms for the advocate to speak rather than remain

---

[190] CS 6/15 fo. 55v: 22 Mar. 1541. Orrock, as any official could, did appear for himself: e.g. CS 6/15 fo. 139v: 27 May 1541.

[191] CS 6/2 fo. 7r: 18 Nov. 1532.

[192] This is yet another stage in the dispute over the lands of Loudoun between the king, the earl of Moray, Hugh Campbell and his mother Isobel Wallace, and the master of Glencairn. The dispute appears to date back to the death of Isobel's husband Hugh Campbell in 1508. See further above, p.177.

[193] CS 6/2 fo. 6v. As was pointed out in chapter four, Friday was set aside in 1532 as the day on which were called summonses in which the king had an interest. Although this was the general rule, it was not always adhered to and such cases were called on other days particularly Wednesdays.

[194] CS 6/2 fo. 7v: 20 Nov. 1532.

[195] *Prot. Bk. Stathauchin*, no. 295: 29 June 1518. Adam Otterburn appears in the witness list. An objection to the brieve was made by a certain Philip Nesbit of that ilk for his own interest.

silent. Henry Lauder was certainly prepared to state that he was not willing to act, when invited by a defender to do so, until he had been further advised.[196]

In terms of the administration of justice the advocate may not only have been responsible for overseeing the king's judicial appointees; one case exists which suggests it was his role to enforce ethical standards within the legal profession. This was an action brought by Henry Lauder as king's advocate against his fellow man of law Master George Strang. Strang was an established lawyer having been appearing before the court since the mid-1530s. The accusation against him related to his conduct whilst representing John Ramsay of Dunure. Lauder alleged that Strang had stood with his client and sustained a false instrument and charter.[197] Strang consistently denied that he knew of the falsity of either document. Indeed he stated that 'he defendit na thing that is fals nor will nocht defend bot allanerly for defence of his client in his just actioun'.[198] Strang had alleged that a copy of the instrument in question was recorded in the protocol book of Sir John Galloway. Producing Galloway's protocol book, Lauder stated that no such instrument could be found inside it; Strang's response was that this proved nothing because Sir John had had more than one protocol book.[199] The conclusion of this action does not appear in the record, however it is likely that Lauder failed to make his charge stick because Strang soon re-appears acting for other clients.[200] More important is the fact that the action was brought by the king's advocate at all. It indicates a concern on the part of Lauder to ensure that professional ethics were maintained. Had Strang knowingly used falsified evidence on behalf of his clients clearly he would have broken the oath *de calumnia* as well as the act of sederunt laid down by the lords in May 1532.

The production and use of false notarial instruments is not often established in the record although allegations of such misconduct do appear regularly.[201] The king's advocate was required to summon notaries to appear before the lords to answer such allegations. In December 1540 an act of parliament warned that the traditional punishments would be applied rigorously to false notaries and to those who made or knowingly used false instruments.[202] This

---

[196] CS 6/14 fo. 105r: 25 Jan. 1541.

[197] CS 6/28 fo. 24v: 13 May 1549.

[198] CS 6/28 fo. 26r: 15 May 1549. To 'wittandlie' use a false document was a serious matter: *APS*, ii, 360.

[199] CS 6/28 fo. 34r. The dating of this entry is difficult to determine. It clearly belongs to 22 Feb. although the year is not given; the earlier entry belongs to 13 May 1549 (fo. 24v). Either folio 34r belongs to Feb. 1550 or it has been inserted in the wrong place in the volume and should be attributed to Feb. 1549 (thus placing it chronologically prior to folio 24). Whichever date, the sense of the entries is clear.

[200] CS 6/28 fo. 36r (procurator for Sir Simon Galloway); CS 6/28 fo. 57v (procurator for Agnes Strang and, separately, Sir John Rais) etc. Strang appears in the list of general procurators recorded in Mar. 1549 (*ADCP*, 584) underlining his status as a leading man of law at around this time. In May 1564 he replaced Thomas Kincraigie as one of the advocates for the poor: *RMS*, v, no. 1690. On the role of the advocate for the poor see above, pages 82–6.

[201] E.g. CS 5/17 fo. 151r: 19 Dec. 1505.

[202] *APS*, ii, 360.

last point is important: not all false instruments were made by notaries. In 1541 for example, Patrick Colquhoun confessed before the lords that he had induced 'an scolar' to forge a charter and to make a seal which he used as evidence in court.[203] Ironically the case in which Patrick used the forged document was one in which he and the advocate sought to reduce a decreet produced by the provost and bailies of Glasgow and the inquest of their baron court. Patrick and the advocate alleged that one of Patrick's tenants had been lawfully warned to remove prior to Whitsunday whereas the first instance court had found that no warning had been given. The lords of council assoilzied the defenders, presumably on the basis that Patrick had used false evidence, and the advocate then asked for Patrick's confession to be recorded in the *acta*, perhaps with a view to proceeding against him criminally.

The advocate was not only responsible for producing escheats for the crown but also had to secure the evidence of exactly what had been escheated. This follows from Henry Lauder's dealings with the Aberdeen notary James Young.[204] Following the execution and escheat of all the possessions, heritable and movable, of captain David Borthwick who had been convicted of heresy, Lauder required Young to extract from his protocol book the instrument of sasine by which Borthwick was infeft in the lands of Aberdour. Young refused—utterly, contemptuously and 'with iniureus wordis'. Having been charged to compear before the lords, he was eventually ordered to deliver a copy of the instrument to the advocate.

The royal demesne

A major part of the advocate's responsibility was the vindication of the king's rights to land and the preservation of crown estates. The act of annexation of 1455 had rendered considerable areas of land part of the king's patrimony and had forbidden their alienation without the formal consent of the three estates.[205] The enforcement of this act took a considerable amount of the advocate's time and also indicates the extent to which this, and subsequent similar legislation, was honoured in the breach. Lands in Banffshire held by John, earl of Atholl, were in 1506 decerned to pertain to the king as his property because according to the exchequer rolls the lands had been forfeited by John Douglas of Balvenie in 1455.[206] Similarly in 1541 a feu charter in favour of the late David Balfour of Burleigh was reduced because it related to

---

[203] CS 6/14 fos. 165v, 171r: 12 Feb. 1541.
[204] CS 6/15 fo. 168r: 21 June 1541.
[205] *APS*, ii, 42. For comment, see McGladdery, *James II* (Edinburgh, 1990), 93-5; Nicolson, *Later Middle Ages*, 378-9. The lands annexed to the crown in 1455 belonged to the Douglases. Other lands were added later (see Nicolson, Ibid., 455).
[206] CS 5/18/1 fo. 53r: 7 Feb. 1506; McGladdery, *James II*, 94. Cf. the earl of Huntly who admitted that lands in Strathearn which he possessed properly pertained to the crown.

'annext landis to the croune' and was made during the king's minority
without the advice or consent of the three estates; in modern terms, it was
ultra vires.[207]

Those occupying lands which were properly part of lands which pertained
to the king stood in danger of eviction. Alexander Calder, possessor of lands in
the earldom of Mar, found that the lands—as a pendicle (subordinate part) of
the earldom—were the king's property and had been illegally alienated from
the king's predecessors as earls of Mar.[208] They might also find themselves
charged with wrongful detention of maills and duties owing to the crown if
they could not establish a title to the lands.[209]

Criminal matters

As to the advocate's role in criminal matters, it is clear that the distinction
between criminal and civil actions certainly existed during the reign of James
V, indeed it was referred to by contemporaries, but its boundaries are
notoriously difficult to draw.[210] In some instances the same activity could have
been considered either a civil or a criminal wrong.[211] Thus there are references
to actions in which the advocate made it known that he intended to pursue
the case only as a civil matter and thereby renounced any criminal action.[212]
To the crown, the pursuit of criminal matters was not simply part of its
obligation to administer justice or to look to the internal security of the realm;
there were also financial benefits in terms of fines and escheats, as well as
indirectly from the purchasing of remissions.[213] Just as civil litigants sometimes
sought to ward off disaster by paying a composition to the crown, so those
convicted of crimes might be able to purchase a pardon. Legislation from the
reign of James IV recognised the problems posed by the regular use of
remissions in terms of general lawlessness, but throughout the sixteenth
century attempts to restrict the grant of remissions appear to have met with
limited success and regularly had to be repeated.[214] In April 1528 James V in

---

[207]   CS 6/14 fo. 162v: 11 Feb. 1541. Another similar case refers specifically to the king's lack of power 'to
set or dispone' lands that were 'part of the principalite or at least annexit thirto': CS 6/15 fo. 185v: 1
July 1541.

[208]   CS 5/17 fo. 66v: 3 Dec. 1505. The earldom had reverted to the crown in 1479 following the forfeiture
and death of John, earl of Mar, James III's brother: Macdougall, *James III*, 130-3.

[209]   CS 5/17 fo. 65v: 3 Dec. 1505.

[210]   *Fife Ct. Bk.*, 322.

[211]   E.g. breach of protection: A Harding, 'The medieval brieves of protection and the development of the
common law' (1966) *JR* 115; also deforcement, *Fife Ct. Bk.*, 322.

[212]   CS 6/28 fo. 62r: 10 Dec. 1546; see above, p. 176.

[213]   For instance the distinguishing feature of the developed action of contravention of lawburrows, which
was regularly pursued by the king's advocate, was that the caution forfeited was equally distributed
between the crown and the complainer: Clark, *Lawburrows* 18. In the early fifteenth century the forfeit
simply went to the crown: Clark, *Lawburrows*, 15; *Fife Ct. Bk.*, 331.

[214]   C. Gane, 'The effect of a pardon in Scots Law' (1980) *JR* 19.

presence of the lords promised 'to hald his handis fra geving of any respect or remissioune to ony persounis in tyme to cum without aviss of the lordis of counsale'.[215] A case early in Mary's reign illustrates the potential difficulties caused to the crown by the grant of remissions. A man named Alan Wilson was convicted for common theft before the bailie of Cunningham, his goods were escheat to the crown and he was put to the horn.[216] The bailie depute, Adam Montgomery, intromitted with Alan's goods which now belonged to the queen (i.e. to the treasurer) and it was the responsibility of Adam and the bailie to account for this property in the exchequer.[217] However, as the queen's advocate was informed, the fugitive Alan had received a remission for his crimes. Thereafter he had raised a summons before the sheriff of Ayr against Adam Montgomery, the bailie depute, accusing him of the spuilzie of the goods of which he had been escheated. The advocate, claiming collusion between Alan and Adam, succeeded in advocating the case from the sheriff court of Ayr to the session because the action concerned the queen's property. He clearly suspected Alan of bribing the bailie depute in order to get back his property in defraud of the crown; however, this had only been made possible in the first place by the crown's policy in granting remissions.

The most serious criminal offence dealt with by the advocate was treason. The main reason John Ross of Montgrennan is sometimes regarded as the first king's advocate was because of the role that he played in the major treason trials of the 1480s.[218] During the reign of James IV, the major treason trials were connected with government campaigns against the Isles and, in particular, those who supported and harboured Donald Dubh. James Henryson was closely involved in their prosecution.[219] In February 1506, for example, he oversaw the forfeiture of Torquil MacLeod of Lewis, the earl of Argyll's brother-in-law, for treasonably harbouring Donald and failing to hand him over to the king.[220] These proceedings were relatively straightforward in the sense that the personalities and issues involved were clear. This contrasts with the factional politics that characterised most of the minority of James V. From Angus's seizure of power, and his retention of control over the person of king in November 1525, his political opponents were faced with the very real problem that any armed resistance to Angus could be construed as a treasonable attack upon the king.[221] In the wake of such an attack, carried out

---

[215] CS 5/38 fo. 94r: 18 Apr. 1528. See also *APS*, ii, 287 c. 13 (1524).

[216] CS 6/22 fo. 78r: 22 Jan. 1547.

[217] The bailie was Hugh, earl of Eglinton, who was dead by the time the action reached the lords of council.

[218] Finlay, 'Professional Men of Law', 303.

[219] Macdougall, *James IV*, 177-190; Nicolson, *The Later Middle Ages*, 545.

[220] *APS*, ii, 264. Pitcairn, *Criminal Trials*, i, *49.

[221] As Emond points out ('Minority of James V', 493) it was generally believed that Angus was not afraid to bring the king to the battlefield. This explains the reluctance of the lords assembled near Linlithgow on 17 Jan. 1526 to launch an attack: they would have been liable to a charge of treason.

on 23 July 1526 at Darnick near Melrose by Walter Scott of Buccleuch and his supporters, those responsible were summonsed for treason.[222] The interesting thing about this summons was that the lords of council ordered that it 'be maid in dew forme as it pleisis our soverane lordis advocat to libell'.[223] That is, the king's advocate was personally to draw up the summons. Men of law did not generally draw up summonses, but it appears that it had become standard practice for the king's advocate to draft summonses for treason.[224] In November 1527 Angus's uncle, Archibald Douglas of Kilspindie, the treasurer, requested the lords to command 'the kingis advocat to libell a summondis of tresoun' against the earl of Moray.[225] That political events had come full circle, and that the advocate had a certain discretion in framing the summons, is evident from another entry in the *acta* made on 13 July 1528:

> Oure soverane lord with the aviss of the lordis of his counsale ordanis his advocat to mak summondis of tresoune apoun archibald erle of angus george douglas his brothir archibald douglas of kilspindy his eme and alex[ande]r drummond of carnok for sic punctis of tresoune as he can libell aganis thame to be summond to comper the ferd day of September nixt tocum and to speid the samin with diligence.[226]

According to Kelley, the trial of Angus was the first known case in Scottish history of legal defences being offered to a charge of treason.[227] It is interesting, if hardly surprising, to note that the first ground of defence was that Angus and his co-defendants could not obtain the services of a man of law to defend them.[228] The points of treason which Otterburn was able to libel were not

---

[222] Emond, 'Minority of James V', 508-9 (including footnote 104).

[223] CS 5/36 fo. 87v: 20 Aug. 1526. Lord Hay refused to consent to this unless it was done with the advice of the king or the three estates.

[224] Contrast actions of error in which the summons might not even be in the advocate's possession where another party was jointly involved with him in pursuit of the case: e.g. CS 5/30 fo. 208v, where Alexander Sutherland, co-pursuer with the king against a sheriff and inquest, was in custody of the summons when he failed to appear after his name was called at the tolbooth door.

[225] CS 5/38 fo. 30r: 26 Nov. 1527. The political background to this is briefly mentioned by Kelley, 'Douglas Earls of Angus', 383. Douglas was in possession of the castle of Spynie which Moray had taken from him. This was at a time when attempts were being made to have Douglas's illegitimate son, Alexander, raised to the vacant see of Moray following the death of Robert Shaw, the previous incumbent.

[226] CS 5/38 fo. 131v: 13 July 1528. The king is noted as being present on this day. Two days previously, parliament had been summoned to assemble on 2 September. The ground of revocation of Angus's forfeiture in Mar. 1543 rested on confusion in the record about the date of the summons of treason, given as 13 June in the parliamentary record. The summons was actually made on 13 July and the charges related to Angus's activities *after* 13 June: Emond, 'Minority of James V', 556.

[227] Kelley, 'Douglas Earls of Angus', 402. In 1587 treason was specifically excepted from the rule that no prosecution was competent in the absence of the accused: *APS*, iii, 457-8.

[228] *APS*, ii 322. In 1539 Hugh Rigg only agreed to represent James Colville in a treason case on condition that he himself 'incur na cryme nor uthir displessyr throw his procuratioun': *APS*, ii, 353.

particularly impressive and Emond is correct to conclude that they could never have secured a death sentence.[229]

The substantive law of treason was described briefly, including details of some leading cases, by James McGill and John Bellenden in the *Discours Particulier* in 1560.[230] The major treason trials of James V's reign however are not mentioned. These are the actions brought in the years following James's return from France, most notably against the master of Forbes, Lady Glamis, James Hamilton of Finnart, James Colville of East Wemyss and the posthumous action against Master Robert Leslie. Cameron has suggested that James, rather than lashing out indiscriminately in his paranoia over the Douglases, was willing to wait patiently to revenge himself on particular targets who had actively supported Angus's minority government.[231] If this interpretation is correct, then the legal attack upon the dependants of the late Robert Leslie in 1540 can only be understood as motivated by the king's desire to gain financial profit from the escheat of his estate. Leslie was not a significant enough political figure to warrant prosecution; it may only have been bad luck that his name became associated with Finnart's alleged plot to kill the king in 1529. Indeed Leslie only became implicated after Finnart's execution. It is entirely consistent with the king's policy in legal matters that he should require Henry Lauder to prosecute the family of a man who had long been a legal colleague of his in order to get his hands on the escheat.

A supplication before the lords of the articles and council in February 1541 brings to life the fearful atmosphere of this period.[232] It had been alleged by William Geddes that John Ross had clandestinely spoken with James Geddes, knowing him to be a servant of Archibald Douglas of Kilspindie, the earl of Angus's brother. William failed to prove his allegation and was condemned to death for leasing-making.[233] This, however, was not enough to assuage John's fear and he wanted the secretary to demonstrate what the king's will was in the matter. The king, as sought, granted a declaration of John's innocence under the great seal. With the potential of the use of torture to obtain evidence of guilt at a later date John was probably wise to take this precaution. The following year Lord Glamis had his sentence of forfeiture reduced

---

[229] Emond, 'Minority of James V', 557. The basic charge was that Angus had raised an army against the king and had sought to hold Tantallon and Newark against him: *APS,* ii, 324-6. There was certainly no question of conspiring to kill the king; the most that could be alleged was that Angus had exposed him to danger.

[230] P.G.B. McNeill, 'Discours Particulier d'Escosse, 1559/60', in *Miscellany II,* ed. W.D.H. Sellar, (Stair Society, 1984), 123-131.

[231] Cameron, *James V,* 215.

[232] CS 6/14 fo. 201v: 21 Feb. 1541.

[233] On which see Hume, *Crimes,* i, 344ff. Hume accepts that contemporary leasing-making involved the notion of 'calumny carried to the king against a subject'.

because his conviction was based on the use of a confession extracted under torture. Such evidence was, however, generally admitted.[234]

The consequences of many treason convictions in the latter part of James V's reign were reversed early in the reign of his daughter when political circumstances were very different. The most notable beneficiary of this was the earl of Angus.[235] But, as was seen with Adam Otterburn, the holder of the office of king's advocate had to be prepared for sudden changes in political fortune and Henry Lauder does not appear to have suffered for his role as James V's prosecutor. He avoided the fate of Henry VII's agents, Empson and Dudley, although it is a moot point whether James Henryson would have done so had he survived beyond James IV's reign.[236]

Henryson was not greatly occupied in the prosecution of treason. However in the pursuit of more mundane cases, both criminal and civil, he and his successors were at times required to leave their Edinburgh residences and go further afield. In the years prior to his appointment as justice-clerk in 1507, Henryson can be found in justiciars' courts throughout the realm. His name appears after that of Richard Lawson on a witness list in an instrument drawn up in the tolbooth of Ayr during a justice ayre in June 1505.[237] The following year he again appears on a witness list with Lawson witnessing a transumpt made in the tolbooth of Lauder by the justiciar, Lord Gray, during another ayre.[238] He received expenses for his attendance at the ayres of Perth and Stirling in July 1507.[239] In October 1511, at a justice court in Ayr, he witnessed as John Muir produced a remission for alleged oppression in the poinding of bestial pastures and promised to satisfy the complaints of others against him.[240] It was asserted in chapter four that most men of law were well known in the major tolbooths of sixteenth century Scotland; this was nowhere more true than in the case of the crown's advocates.

Conclusion

The substance of the role of the king's advocate developed during the reign of James IV when, under financial pressure, the crown began a sustained programme of litigation against tenants and others who had not been sufficiently scrupulous in their legal affairs.[241] In the criminal sphere income

234 Willock, *The Jury in Scotland*, 199-200.
235 Kelley, 'Douglas Earls of Angus', 535, 541.
236 On Empson and Dudley see S.B. Chrimes *Henry VII* (London, 1972), 316-7; D.M. Brodie, 'Edmund Dudley: Minister of Henry VII' (1932), *TRHS* (4th ser.) 133.
237 NRA(S), no. 852 (Hunters of Hunterston) no. 4.
238 15 May 1506: NAS, Morton Papers, GD 150/269.
239 *TA*, iii, 329.
240 NAS, RH.6/775b.
241 See Macdougall, *James IV*, 156ff.

was drawn from the sale of remissions. By overseeing these activities, in close consultation with other officials, the early king's advocates grew in importance. The business in which these men engaged on the crown's behalf was extremely varied, ensuring that the king's interests in all spheres of legal activity were protected. When a group of men spuilzied royal letters from the king's sheriff *in hac parte* and then placed the purchaser of those letters in the king's 'irnis & stokkis', it was the advocate who brought a case against them.[242] When the earl of Huntly's brother was threatened and hindered from making his way to school, market and kirk it was the king's advocate who brought an action against his tormentors.[243] From economic matters, such as forestalling in burghs,[244] to 'law and order' issues such as the illegal convocation of lieges,[245] the advocate was the person with ultimate responsibility for raising actions to enforce the king's laws.

In terms of organisation, the king's advocate did not hold his office jointly in the period prior to Mary's reign but, although he nominally functioned as an individual, he was to a large extent reliant on the help of others. Without the co-operation of the financial officials of the crown and, prior to 1507 and again after 1524, the justice-clerk, he could not have obtained the evidence that in most cases was vital to the performance of his function. Moreover on those occasions when royal or burgh business prevented his attendance in court, the advocate required the co-operation of fellow men of law upon whom he could rely to represent the king's interests in his absence. Eventually such *ad hoc* substitution was regularised to some extent with deputes appointed on a permanent or semi-permanent basis. This worked so smoothly that by 1534 Adam Otterburn could spend six months abroad without seriously disrupting the administration of the duties of his office.[246] Over its first century of development the office of king's advocate showed steady growth and development, although it is true to say that many features of the advocate's activity and procedure were already evident by 1513.

---

[242] CS 5/17 fo. 107r–108v: 11 Dec. 1505.
[243] CS 5/36 fo. 11v: 2 May 1526.
[244] E.g. CS 6/13 fo. 193r: 13 Aug. 1540.
[245] E.g. CS 5/30 fo. 29v: 20 June 1517.
[246] From late Nov. 1533 to June 1534 Otterburn was in London.

CHAPTER EIGHT

The King's Men of Law, 1493–1561

Consultissimo viro Iacobo henrisoun serenissimi Scotorum
regis Iacobi quarti capitalium rerum quaestori tetrastichum

Dum licet & caelo miti spes ulla colonis,
Omnia continuo rura labore sonant.
Sic mihi si faveas studij pars maxima nostri,
Dulcis erit sudor tempore grana leges.[1]

This poem, published in Paris in 1510, was written by James Foulis, a young Scot following one of the by then traditional paths to wisdom by studying in the universities of France. It was dedicated to James Henryson, the poet's kinsman, who himself had studied in Paris in the 1480s.[2] Henryson's death in 1513 prevented the realisation of the sentiment expressed in the poem: he did not live to enjoy the great rewards of the poet's academic efforts. But the family connection is coincidental. Foulis was a man with ambitions to be a lawyer—he would soon be making his way from Paris to Orléans to join a number of his countrymen in the study of law—and the man to whom he dedicated his work had been for almost two decades the foremost man of law in Scotland.[3] The classical epithet *quaestor*, is not without significance because Henryson's legal career had been without precedent. By 1510, as the man charged with defending the king's rights in the courts of law, his importance was immense.

Hitherto, Henryson has been accepted as Foulis's grandfather, the father of his mother Margaret, who was married to an Edinburgh skinner also called

---

[1]   *Jacobo Follosii Edinburgensis Calamitose Pestis Elega Deploratio. Euisdem addivam Margaritam regi nam sapphicum carmen. Etc.* NLS, Hall 197d. (Paris, 1510).
      As long as hope may fall upon farmers under the gentle sky,
      and all estates continuously resound in work.
      If you favour me in this way the greatest part of our effort
      will be sweet perspiration; in time you will reap the harvest.

[2]   *Auctarium Chartularii Universitatis Parisiensis Tomus III: Liber Procuratorum Nationis Alemanniae in Universitate Parisiensis*, eds. C. Samaran & Ae. Van Moe (Paris, 1935), 542: Jan. 1484.

[3]   Kirkpatrick, 'Scottish Nation at Orléans', 81-83.

James Foulis.[4] In fact, Foulis was the son of another Edinburgh burgess, Henry Foulis. In one of Foulis's poems there lies the clue to his true relationship with James Henryson who, it appears, was the maternal uncle who took him into his household when plague had killed his sister, brother and, finally, his own parents.[5] This outbreak of plague in Edinburgh occurred in the late 1490s.[6] This makes sense of the chronology of Henryson's own early life. As an undergraduate at the University of Paris from 1484, and elected in December 1485, as proctor of the German Nation there, his own birth probably occurred in the late 1460s.[7] This would make him rather young to have been a grandfather in the 1490s. Indeed his first appearance as a procurator before the lords of council was not until 1490. The record of his name on the matriculation roll of St Andrews university in 1488 indicates that he may have spent some time there on his return from Paris before setting out on his legal career.[8]

The first reference to Henryson as king's advocate occurs in October 1493.[9] Less than two months later he was sworn in as a burgess and guild brother of Edinburgh.[10] This status he gained through his father, Robert Henryson, who was an Edinburgh burgess and, according to one later commentator, 'a man of distinction in the reign of King James III'.[11] Robert certainly seems to have been fairly wealthy. In 1461 he acquired an interest in some land in Inverkeithing, an interest which he immediately transmitted to his eldest son John whose early death by 1486 saw the land in turn fall into the possession of James's surviving elder brother George. Eventually the land fell into the hands of George's son Robert, James's nephew.[12] Throughout the 1470s numerous references to Henrysons appear in James Darow's protocol book which covers mainly the burgh of Stirling but also from time to time bears mention of dealings with land and property elsewhere in Stirlingshire and also in Fife.[13] One such transaction, witnessed by a Robert and William Henryson, occurred in 1476 and involved Elizabeth Airth of Plean and various lands of hers including those at Fordell in Fife which James Henryson, at the height of his power, was later to purchase.

---

4   *DNB*, vii, 510.
5   J. Ijsweijn & D.F.S. Thomson, 'The Latin poems of Jacobus Follisius or James Foullis of Edinburgh', *Humanistica Lovaniensia*, 24 (1975), 116, 143.
6   Ijsweijn and Thomson, 'Poems of James Foulis', 140.
7   Samaran & Van Moe, *Auctarium Chartularii Universitatis Parisiensis Tomus III*, 593.
8   *St Andrews Univ. Recs.*, 185.
9   *ADC*, i, 307:21 Oct. 1493.
10   *Edin. Burgh Recs*, 244: 7 Dec. 1493.
11   Sir Robert Douglas, *Baronage*, 518.
12   James himself had links to Inverkeithing: NAS, Henderson of Fordell Muniments, GD 172/108, GD 172/123.
13   NAS, B66/1/1/1. The NAS transcript has been used and compared, when required, with the original text.

More immediately, it is not until April 1494 that there is evidence for Henryson's marriage, to Helen Baty, daughter of the Edinburgh burgess John Baty, which may have occurred several years prior to this date.[14] Henryson was acting as executor of his late father-in-law's estate in July 1494.[15] At the end of the year he acted as forespeaker for Henry Foulis before the lords auditor of Parliament and it is likely that by this date Foulis was his brother-in-law.[16] Henryson's own immediate family tends to confirm the view that Henry Foulis was his contemporary rather than his son-in-law. Of his eldest son nothing is definitely known except that, according to a hitherto unnoticed reference to him in October 1508, his name may very well have been Patrick.[17] Douglas, and everyone since, has asserted that the eldest son died with his father at Flodden.[18] Having fought at that battle Patrick must have been born before 1495. The next son, George, was old enough to be at university in 1510 whilst the youngest, James, was definitely alive in 1508 and certainly dead by June, 1530.[19] Indeed George was also the subject of a dedication by James Foulis. The verses which Foulis devoted to his young cousin were published twice and have one variant reading: *puero* in the first version, is replaced by *iuvenis*, indicating that between 1509 and 1512 George had changed from a boy into a young man.[20]

The most significant aspect of James Henryson's career is not merely the fact that he was the first to hold the office of king's advocate; it is the fact that he held that office within the context of a career spent representing a large number of other clients. The king was a great deal more than *primus inter pares* amongst Henryson's clients, and acting for the sovereign accounts for much of his activity, but it did not preclude him from acting on behalf of others not all of whom by any means were connected to the royal administration. In part, this was due to the fact that the office of king's advocate was still embryonic. The king had legal interests to defend but for the first time his legal interests had begun to be properly exploited before his council. Driven by political

---

[14]   *Prot. Bk. Young*, no. 688: 1 Apr. 1494.

[15]   NAS, Henderson of Fordell Muniments, GD 172/171: 21 July 1494.

[16]   *ADA*, 204: 15 Dec. 1494. Henry and his wife had three children by the time they died in the plague outbreak dated to around 1499: Ijsweijn and Thomson, 'Poems of James Foulis', 140.

[17]   *Prot. Bk. Foular*, ii, no. 503, also no. 497; these make reference to Patrick as James's son but other evidence indicates that he must be the eldest son; see also D. Laing ed., *The Poems and Fables of Robert Henryson, now first collected* (Edinburgh, 1865), xlvii, who mentions Patrick but who does not make the connection with James. Henceforth it is assumed that the name Patrick is correctly ascribed to Henryson's eldest son.

[18]   Douglas, *Baronage*, 518; there seems to be no direct evidence for this but certainly after 1513 no record of a Patrick Henryson identifiable with the justice-clerk's family appears to survive and George is designed 'heir' of his father.

[19]   *Prot. Bk. Foular*, ii, no. 503: 20 Oct. 1508; William Stephen, *A History of Inverkeithing and Rosyth* (Aberdeen, 1921), xlvii.

[20]   Ijsweijn and Thomson, 'Poems of James Foulis', 132, 150. This is a further indication that James Henryson was Foulis's uncle, rather than his grandfather.

circumstances, coloured by an unwillingness to summon parliament in order to raise revenue by the unreliable means of direct taxation, a policy was adopted of taking stricter notice of the king's legal rights to augment the crown's finances. The most notorious means of achieving this goal was the use of the procedure of recognition which, although used during the reign of James III, was exploited in a much more rigorous and sustained way during his son's reign with correspondingly greater reward.[21] Henryson is the man most closely associated with this policy and may well have been its architect, working in close co-operation with the treasury. But the very fact that he succeeded Richard Lawson as justice-clerk general in 1507 indicates that not all of Henryson's time was taken up with his work as king's advocate.[22] It is noticeable, however, that significantly fewer private clients constituted him as their procurator after 1507 than had done so hitherto, and this must reflect his busier public duties which, of course, included acting occasionally as a lord of council.

Henryson, as well as representing private clients, discharged the office of town clerk of Edinburgh. He is first recorded holding this position in 1502. According to Inglis[23] this post was permanent but the evidence only points to Henryson holding it in two years, 1502 and 1507.[24] Nonetheless there appears to have been no new clerk named between Henryson in 1502 and Adam Otterburn in 1512; he possibly therefore held the post for up to a decade.[25] It was an unsalaried position but the common (or town) clerk drew fees for acting as notary in regard to ceremonies of sasine involving property within the burgh and indeed he may have held a monopoly of such business.

In terms of private clients, Henryson's business prospered although his allegiance to his principal employer, the king, naturally brought with it from time to time conflicts of interest. For instance, in 1501 Henryson acted for John, earl of Atholl.[26] Almost five years to the day later, he acted for the king against Atholl in relation to the lands of Bochrum and Kinninmonth in the sheriffdom of Banff which, Henryson claimed, belonged to the king by reason of the forfeiture of John Douglas of Balvenie in 1455.[27] But so far as it is possible to tell, Henryson was free to represent clients before the lords of council, or before ordinary judges, without his activities for the king imposing major restrictions upon him. Indeed, his position with the king could function

---

[21] Macfarlane, *Elphinstone*, 163–4; Ranald Nicholson, 'Feudal developments in late medieval Scotland', (1974) *JR* 16; Craig Madden, 'Royal treatment of feudal casualties in late medieval Scotland' (1976) *SHR, passim.*

[22] Lawson was dead by Aug. 1507: *Prot. Bk. Foular*, ii, no. 340: 25 Aug. 1507.

[23] Inglis, *Adam Otterburn*, 5; see also Elizabeth Ewan, *Townlife in Fourteenth Century Scotland* (Edinburgh, 1990), 50.

[24] *RMS*, ii, no. 2685; *Prot. Bk. Foular*, ii, no. 340: 25 Aug. 1507.

[25] *Edin. Burgh Recs.*, i, 272, 276.

[26] *ADC*, ii, 475: 28 Feb. 1501.

[27] CS 5/18/1: fo. 53r: 7 Feb. 1506; on this forfeiture see McGladdery, *James II*, 94–5.

as a means of creating business. The only surviving letter from James IV to Henryson, written just two months before Flodden, instructed him to 'stand with' William Leslie, brother and heir of the late earl of Rothes, in his pursuit of justice before the lords of council particularly in connection with the barony of Ballinbreich.[28] Henryson was to 'procure for the said Williame, sa fer as the actione concernis him self, and help him the best ye may thairin'. As to local courts, even before becoming king's advocate, Henryson had acted as prelocutor for the widow Marion Farnely before the sheriff-depute of Edinburgh in a case concerning her terce.[29] Despite his promotion, he continued as a regular attender of sheriff courts, appearing for example before John Hepburn, sheriff-depute of Haddington, in the tolbooth of that burgh in 1497.[30]

In addition to his yearly pension from the king for acting as his advocate Henryson was also given various additional gifts of land and revenue from the king in reward for his service. Much of this came from estates which had reverted to the king as *ultimus haeres* where landholders had died without legitimate heirs, as happened in the cases of Laurence Brown and John Henryson.[31] This latter individual, who died before December 1505, was himself illegitimate and was probably a relative of James, perhaps an illegitimate uncle. He can perhaps be identified with John Henryson who was sergeant of the barony of Fordell in Fife, not far from Robert Henryson's Inverkeithing interests, and it may have been gaining the gift of John's estate that encouraged James later to purchase the lands of that barony.[32] Henryson, particularly once he had become justice-clerk, also received incidental payments of an occasional nature from the king's treasury. Thus in March 1508, for his services on the justice ayre in Dundee he received £14 10s.[33] For comparison, the justiciar received 40s. per day while Henryson's daily rate was 18s. Given that the ayre lasted fifteen days Henryson in fact appears to have been overpaid by one pound, but there may be a reason why his expenses were slightly higher. The same rates were in force during an ayre in the south-west from October to early December 1511, earning Henryson £53 4s and again at Aberdeen the following spring bringing in £14 8s.[34] That same year (1512) brought in a further £12 for participation in the Chamberlain ayres of

---

28 *HMC*, 4th report (countess of Rothes), 503, no. 98: 7 July 1513.
29 *Prot. Bk. Young*, no. 553: 5 Nov. 1492.
30 Ibid., nos. 899, 900: 2 May 1497; cf. also, sheriff court of Edinburgh: NAS, Lothian Muniments, GD 40/4/99: 28 Apr. 1500; regality court of Broughton: *Prot. Bk. Young*, no. 1118, 20 Jan. 1501; sheriff court of Dumfries held in Edinburgh: *Yester Writs*, no. 278: 7 May 1504.
31 *RSS*, i, no. 305: 19 Dec. 1498; *RMS*, ii, no. 2451: 11 Sep. 1498; *RSS*, i, no. 1179: 16 Dec. 1505.
32 For John Henryson, see *RMS*, ii, no. 1818: 22 Jan. 1489.
33 *TA*, iv, 71. As was indicated in the previous chapter, Henryson, before becoming justice-clerk, also received money for his attendance at justice ayres. For example, in 1506: *TA*, iii, 329.
34 *TA*, iv, 319-20; see also NAS, RH6/775b.

Dundee, Perth and Cupar.[35] It is perhaps an insight into Henryson's relationship with the king that he should have picked up the equivalent of a day's expenses on the justice ayre in April 1501 by defeating the king 'at the butts'; although this appears to be his only recorded income through gambling.[36]

To complement this, Henryson also had a considerable income from private clients. He received a regular pension from the bishop of Dunkeld which, at least latterly, amounted to £10 annually.[37] From 1509 the abbey of Arbroath was also paying Henryson a pension of twenty merks, together with his expenses should he be required to leave Edinburgh on abbey business.[38] It was also in this year that he received a tack of certain lands in Peebles from Robert, abbot of Melrose.[39] Exactly how this was acquired is unknown although it was probably paid for rather than donated in return for service. As these clients, and others such as the abbot of Paisley and the archdeacon of Caithness, indicate, Henryson did not restrict himself to the secular courts.[40] Fairly early in his career, he appeared, in distinguished company, in St Giles before William Wawane, the official of Lothian, as a procurator for Arbroath abbey.[41]

Before he became a burgess of Edinburgh, let alone town clerk, Henryson had acted as its procurator in legal disputes.[42] Even a cursory acquaintance with his clientele indicates that Edinburgh was not the only burgh for which he acted nor were its inhabitants the only burgesses.[43] He also acted for several magnates, such as the earls of Angus, Caithness and Atholl and important lords of parliament as well as for much less illustrious clients.[44] The reference to him acting as advocate for the poor has already been discussed in a previous chapter. But, in an age and a reign noted for acts of personal piety, Henryson was not above acting for lepers as well as the poor.[45] The sheer scale and diversity of his private clients indicate clearly that Henryson was first and foremost a professional man of law, even though his services were primarily at the disposal of the king.

---

[35]   *TA*, iv, 320.
[36]   *TA*, ii, 102. This would seem to indicate a wager with the king.
[37]   *Dunkeld Rentale*, 248, 252, 258.
[38]   *Arbroath Liber*, ii, 388.
[39]   NAS, Henderson of Fordell Muniments, GD 172/177: dateable only to 1509.
[40]   *ADC*, i, 318: 26 Oct. 1493 (George, abbot of Paisley); Mr James Forrestor, archdeacon of Caithness: *ADC*, ii, 83: 4 Nov. 1497.
[41]   *Arbroath Liber*, ii, 298–9: 12 Dec. 1496.
[42]   *ADC*, i, 316: 25 Oct. 1493; *ADC*, ii, 38: 30 Aug. 1496; *ADC*, iii, 1: 23 Mar. 1500.
[43]   E.g., burgesses of Kintore: *ADC*, ii, 136: 3 Mar. 1498; burgesses of Dysart: CS 5/18/1 fo. 81r: 14 Feb. 1506.
[44]   E.g., *ADA*, 170: 1 June 1493 (Archibald, earl of Angus); *ADC*, ii, 111: 10 Feb. 1498 (William, earl of Caithness); *ADC*, ii, 475: 28 Feb. 1500 (John, earl of Atholl); George, Lord Seton, *ADC*, ii, 339: 30 Apr. 1499 (George, Lord Seton): *ADC*, ii, 423: 7 Nov. 1500 (John, Lord Somerville).
[45]   *ADC*, ii, 349: 17 Jan. 1500; *ADC*, ii, 427: 9 Nov. 1500.

The income from his legal activity had two primary outlets: it might be loaned out at interest, primarily to lairds and burgesses seeking capital, or it could be used to purchase land. In June 1493, along with Richard Lawson, he was acting against Alexander, Lord Monypenny, to recover the penal sum of 100 merks—which appears to have been twice the original debt—by having the lords auditor order Patrick Monypenny not to hand over rents and other sums in his possession which he owed to Alexander until the creditors' claim was satisfied.[46] The following April Henryson received notice from Archibald Forrester of Corstorphine that he was in a position to redeem his lands in Longniddry, which Henryson held in security, and that he required Henryson and his wife to resign the lands according to an earlier letter of reversion.[47] Thus it would seem that comparatively early in his career Henryson had begun what Ives identified as a favourite sideline of London lawyers: money lending.

But it is the acquisition of land that appears to have been Henryson's particular priority. This again invites parallel with leading English lawyers of his generation whose aspiration it was to acquire land and the status of gentility.[48] As a contemporary English adage put it, 'service was not heritage'.[49] In chapter five, it was seen that both Robert Leslie and Robert Galbraith purchased land with some of their income. Later advocates purchased considerable estates but Henryson and his erstwhile colleague Richard Lawson were perhaps the first to establish sufficient landed wealth to sustain the development and influence of their families over several generations. In September 1498 Henryson was granted a tenement and one built *domus* by the king at the southern end of the High Street.[50] This might have been the place where business, involving John, Lord Carlyle, was transacted in November 1500.[51] There is no evidence that Henryson was even present on this occasion although the action certainly took place 'on the stair of his hospice'.[52] In February 1505 further business was done, this time in Henryson's 'fore-room' in Edinburgh, involving the Sinclairs of Roslin and one of their vassals.[53]

---

[46]   *ADA*, 179: 18 June 1493.

[47]   *Prot. Bk. Young.* no. 688: 1 Apr. 1494.

[48]   Ives, *Common Lawyers*, 330.

[49]   Michael Bennet, 'Careerism in Late Medieval England', eds., J. Rosenthal and C. Richmond, *People, Politics and Community in the Later Middle Ages* (Gloucester, 1987), 34.

[50]   *RMS*, ii, no. 2451: 11 Sep. 1498.

[51]   *Prot. Bk. Young*, no. 1058: 20 Nov. 1500.

[52]   The word *hospicium* suggests that he held a lodging in Edinburgh in addition to the *domus* he received from the king and the tenement which he received from Cant in 1495 and possession of which was disputed with Fery. The same word was used of inns hired by masters for the giving of private instruction in the years prior to the founding of St Andrews university; see John Durkan, 'The Scottish Universities in the Middle Ages, 1412-1560' (Edinburgh University, unpublished Ph.D. thesis, 1959), 8.

[53]   *Prot. Bk. Young*, no. 1502: 25 Feb. 1505.

Henryson had already received the ward of the lands of Balbeithy in Fife, which had until his death belonged to the laird of Drumry, and £10 worth of land at Clifton in Roxburghshire given to him by the king out of singular favour and as a reward for good service.[54] This was land that had been recognosced into the king's hands following the alienation of the greater part of it by John Elemour of Clifton. Within a year the king, as a further token of affection, had promised to infeft Henryson in the lands of Kilquhinzie and Kilkerran in Carrick, again lands which had been recognosced into his hands.[55] At the beginning of 1507 this grant appears to have already been made.[56] In 1509 Henryson acquired the lands and barony of Straiton, again after the king had obtained them through the procedure of recognition.[57] At the same time he took on the designation Henryson 'of Stratonhall'.[58] He also appears to have received the annualrent of land lying on the north side of Edinburgh's High Street lately held by John Douglas and assigned to him by lord Maxwell,[59] as well as, the following year, the nonentry and ward of lands within the stewartry of Kirkcudbright. [60]

In addition to the lands which he received from the king and from other sources Henryson set about, in a short period in March and April 1511, buying up lands in and near Fordell in Fife. This was his only systematic purchase of an estate, which had obviously at some stage been divided between heirs portioners because the bulk of the land was purchased from various sellers in sevenths.[61] In May of that year the king literally gave his seal of approval to the enterprise by erecting the lands into the free barony of Fordell in Henryson's favour. [62] After this date, indeed to within three months of his death, Henryson continued to purchase, or at least to obtain tacks of, those parts of the barony which he did not yet possess.[63]

As the king's premier man of law, Henryson fulfilled a variety of tasks. As well as holding the post of justice-clerk general (and justice-clerk of the regality of Glasgow), he also acted as a lord of council.[64] It was in the latter capacity, for example, that he was sent by his fellow lords, together with the man of law and notary Master John Murray, to a woman named Janet

54   *RMS*, ii, no. 2982: 28 July 1506.
55   *RSS*, i, no. 1161: 21 Nov. 1506.
56   *RSS*, i, no. 1417: 25 Jan. 1507.
57   *RMS*, ii, no. 3309; NAS, Henderson of Fordell Muniments, GD 172/64: 21 Feb. 1509.
58   E.g. *Prot. Bk. Foular*, ii, no. 663: 9 Aug. 1510. See also note 184 below.
59   *Prot. Bk. Foular*, ii, no. 562: 25 May 1509; but this was disputed by Sir David Stevenson, chaplain of the collegiate church of Dalkeith ; Ibid., no. 564: 31 May 1509.
60   *RSS*, i, no. 2074: 26 May 1510.
61   See Laing, *Poems of Robert Henryson*, xlv.
62   NAS, Henderson of Fordell Muniments, GD 172/17/1: 1 May 1511.
63   Ibid., GD 172/18/1: 10 Jan. 1512, sasine; GD 172/20: 10 June 1513, tack.
64   As justice-clerk of the regality of Glasgow: *Glasgow Registrum*, 520: 6 Aug. 1509.

Edmonstone, in order to record her deposition.[65] The king also used him as a privy councillor and an ambassador. In the tense months preceding Flodden, Henryson was peripherally involved in the diplomatic manoeuvring between James IV and his brother-in-law Henry VIII; safe conducts were issued for him to go to England on several occasions but remained unused.[66] In one of his letters Henry's ambassador Nicholas West records a brief meeting with Henryson which illustrates how close he was to the king.[67] This was never in doubt. From the odd reference in the books of council, indicating that Henryson and other leading lords entered into the council chamber in the king's train, to that one item of personal correspondence which survives between James IV and his advocate, the evidence suggests a close working relationship.[68]

In many ways Henryson's career as king's advocate was paradigmatic. Although the first man to hold the office of king's advocate, his career has many similarities with those of his successors. Evidence of the rewards which acting for the king produced may easily be found in the careers of Wishart, Otterburn and Lauder. The same desire to purchase land outwith Edinburgh certainly animated the burgesses Otterburn, who acquired the estate of Redhall in Midlothian and Lauder, who became laird of St Germains in the constabulary of Haddington.[69] Regular and active involvement in arbitration, and also occasional missions of diplomacy, punctuate all of their careers to a greater or lesser extent.

It is James Wishart, Henryson's immediate successor, who does not quite fall into the pattern which Henryson's tenure of the office established. This is not surprising. Wishart is unique in never having had to take his instructions from an adult king. James V was eighteen months old when Wishart was sworn in to office and was still in his minority when the advocate died. This may explain why Wishart is the king's advocate about whom the least is known, although some details of his background have managed to survive. The son of John Wishart of Pittarrow, in the sheriffdom of Kincardine, James was probably named after his grandfather.[70] His mother may have been Janet Lindsay, who was John's wife in 1510.[71] He certainly had two brothers, probably both younger than him, John and William, and the suggestion has already been noted that the reformer, George Wishart, may also have been his

[65]   CS 5/19 fo. 127v: 30 Jan. 1508.
[66]   *Calendar of Letters and Papers Foreign and Domestic, Henry VIII*, i, 278 (n.d.)., 447: 24 July 1511; 731: 24 Jan. 1513.
[67]   Ibid., i, 792.
[68]   E.g., CS 5/25 fo. 37r: 27 Apr. 1513.
[69]   Otterburn purchased Redhall from William, master of Glencairn, in 1527: Inglis, *Otterburn*, 32–3.
[70]   James senior was a charter witness in 1481: *RMS*, ii, no. 1478: 28 May 1481; John is described as James's father in a charter dated 1512: *RMS*, ii, no. 3729: 30 Apr. 1512.
[71]   *Arbroath Liber*, ii, no. 504: 28 Oct. 1510.

brother.[72] James matriculated at St Andrews in 1496 as a member of the Angus nation there and became a licentiate in 1499.[73] It is not inconceivable that he then spent time studying abroad although he maintained his links with St Andrews, witnessing the confirmation of a charter there by Hugh Spens, provost of St Salvator's, in 1511 and marrying Elizabeth Learmonth who probably belonged to a prominent St Andrews family.[74] She may have been the daughter of David Learmonth who was at one time provost of the town since, in 1519, Wishart and his brother John witnessed lawburrows granted by Andrew Learmonth of St Andrews on behalf of the provost's son, David, in the sheriff court of Fife.[75] Interestingly, this was Wishart's only recorded appearance before the sheriff court despite his obvious connections to the region. Although he does not appear to have been constituted to appear before the lords of council until 1511, the early pattern of his constitutions indicates a slight bias towards Fife and the north-east.[76] Indeed the first party to name him as one of their procurators was John Melville of Carnbee, one of whose charters Wishart had witnessed at St Andrews two years previously.[77]

Rather than working as a professional advocate independently of the king, Wishart initially appears to have worked in the royal administration, probably as a clerk. In August 1511 he received a grant from the king of lands in the sheriffdom of Kincardine which had reverted to the crown because of nonentry.[78] In the charter he was described as '*regis clericus*'. The following year, he received another grant from the king, '*pro bono servitio et pro certa compositione thesaurario persoluta*', of the lands of Pittarrow (again in the sheriffdom of Kincardine) in free barony, specifying, as the *reddendo*, a pair of golden spurs.[79] He was appointed by James IV's widow, Margaret Tudor, during her regency following Flodden, presumably with the advice of the lords of her council.[80] His selection can only be explained on the basis of his pre-existing connection to the queen and the household of the late king. There were certainly more active and more experienced men of law to choose from, although it should be remembered that James Henryson had been a relative novice in 1493 when he was made king's advocate. Moreover Wishart was appointed hurriedly, in unexpected circumstances, and as a direct replacement; unlike Henryson, he held both the offices of king's advocate and justice-clerk from the beginning, a combination of roles never to be repeated.

[72] John appears with James junior in a contract dated 1509: *Arbroath Liber*, ii, 379; William appears in a grant of 1525: *Arbroath Liber*, ii, 451; for George Wishart, see Laing, *History*, vi, 669.

[73] *St Andrews Univ. Recs.*, 195; 87–8.

[74] SAUL, Cartulary 'A' b fo. 1v: 3 Oct. 1511.

[75] *Fife Ct. Bk.*, 138: 24 Mar. 1519.

[76] C.S: 5/22 fo. 155r: 9 Apr. 1511 (constitution by John Melville of Carnbee, in the sheriffdom of Fife).

[77] *RMS*, ii, no. 3355: 21 June 1509.

[78] *RMS*, no. 3619: 11 Aug. 1511.

[79] *RMS*, ii, no. 3729: 30 Apr. 1512.

[80] *ADCP*, 4: 24 Oct. 1513.

Yet prior to Flodden, Wishart does not seem to have practised extensively as a man of law. He did act, albeit occasionally, on behalf of others in legal and financial matters during that period. For example, in May 1512, he delivered a sum of money to the treasurer, Andrew, bishop of Caithness, on behalf of James Arbuthnot of that ilk, a neighbour of his in Kincardine.[81] Even so, his sudden promotion in 1513 must, to a certain extent, have thrown him in at the deep end. His private client-base appears to have remained comparatively insignificant and, outwith royal service, he had no major clients or patrons. In total, throughout his career he was only constituted as a procurator on thirteen occasions. This does not indicate a level of activity that could sustain the career of a professional man of law active before the lords of council.

Once king's advocate, it might have become dangerous for Wishart, as the king's legal representative during a troubled period, to become identified with one faction rather than another, and this may have limited his scope for increasing the number of his private clients, if that was ever his objective. Indeed his greatest asset, and perhaps the reason behind his appointment, was his neutrality and lack of damaging associations. Therefore, when in Albany's name he ordered John, Lord Hay of Yester, to enter Edinburgh castle in ward, it may be assumed that as justice-clerk he was merely fulfilling his administrative function, exhibiting the same political detachment as he did when signing acts of adjournal at the justice ayre of Dundee a fortnight later.[82] It is true that Albany rewarded his service in November 1516, with a grant of lands in Berwickshire which were part of the escheat of Alexander, Lord Home.[83] But on his own Wishart does not appear to have been especially politically active. The little that the record reveals about him indicates a civil servant rather than an outstanding man of law, and a figure whose survival in government probably depended upon his moderation, and willingness to accommodate the several masters whom, in the course of the minority, circumstance obliged him to serve.

The real inheritor of Henryson's mantle was Wishart's successor, Adam Otterburn. Having been the subject of a monograph in his own right, Otterburn is one of the better known figures of his generation.[84] Unlike Wishart, Otterburn clearly had a close association with Henryson dating from as early as 1503, and it is likely that for him Henryson was something of a role model.[85] Both men were notaries, and both had been educated abroad although it would appear that Otterburn, unlike Henryson, did not attend the

---

[81]   'Arbuthnot Papers', ed. J. Stuart, *Miscellany II* (Spalding Club, 1842), 106: 17 May 1512.

[82]   CS 5/29 fo. 59v: 4 Mar. 1516; CS 5/29 fo. 105v: 17 Mar. 1516.

[83]   *RMS*, iii, no. 110: 13 Nov. 1516.

[84]   J. Inglis, *Sir Adam Otterburn* (Glasgow, 1935).

[85]   The documented relationship between Otterburn and Henryson goes back to at least 1503: *Yester Writs*, no. 266; also, *Prot. Bk. Young*, no. 1429: 17 Apr. 1504.

university of Paris.[86] In 1508 Henryson and his wife appointed him, with others, to act as procurator when transferring land in the High Street to their son James.[87] During the following year Otterburn acted as king's advocate in Henryson's temporary absence and in 1512 he succeeded him as town clerk of Edinburgh.[88] Four years later Henryson's widow, Helen Baty, sold some land in Edinburgh to Otterburn.[89] The relationship between Otterburn and Henryson's immediate family appears to have been maintained until at least 1529 when Helen's son James acted as Otterburn's procurator when land was resigned to him by Lord Somerville.[90] Soon after Otterburn is found acting as Helen's cautioner in respect of a sum which Helen had received under the testament of her sister, Margaret, and which she was to pay to her daughter Janet.[91] George Henryson of Fordell can also be found, not long after, witnessing a transaction involving Otterburn.[92]

Otterburn's own family associations are less certain. He may well have been descended from the family which produced notable legal figures in the fifteenth century such as Master Nicholas Otterburn, the clerk register and Master John Otterburn, official of Lothian.[93] Unfortunately his parents have not been traced although it is possible that Marion Brown, the widow of Thomas Otterburn, in whose favour he resigned lands in 1515, was his mother thus making Thomas his father.[94] It is possible that Janet Otterburn, who was married to John Laing in 1528, was his sister although he had a daughter of the same name.[95] Otterburn himself had two wives, Janet Rhynd and Eufame Mowbray, although it was only by the latter that he had issue.

His pedigree as a man of law during the reign of James IV was certainly impressive when measured by the number of times he was constituted as a procurator before the lords of council. By this indicator, he appears to have increased his level of activity just at the time Henryson's decreased after he became justice-clerk.[96] This may have been more than coincidence and, whether or not he was apprenticed to Henryson, Otterburn's career was certainly boosted by his association with him. His professional activity certainly encompassed both the burgh court of Edinburgh and various sheriff

---

[86]   Inglis, *Otterburn*, 4.
[87]   *Prot. Bk. Foular*, ii, no. 497.
[88]   CS 5/21 fo. 49r.
[89]   NAS, GD 1/58/2: 8 Nov. 1516.
[90]   *Prot. Bk. Foular*, iii, no 75: 7 Dec. 1528.
[91]   Ibid., iii, no. 86: 28 Jan. 1529.
[92]   Ibid., iii, no. 159: 4 Oct. 1529.
[93]   NAS, GD 1/661/16: 1554; *RMS*, iii, no. 111.
[94]   NAS, B22/1/9 fo. 25: 3 Feb. 1515.
[95]   NAS, *Prot. Bk. Alexander Makneil*, B22/22/18 fo. 73v: 8 Feb. 1528. John Laing may have been related to Sir Neil Laing, the advocate and keeper of the signet during Mary's reign. Neil's first wife was Isobel Rhynd who probably belonged to the same family as Otterburn's first wife: *RSS* iv, no. 1219.
[96]   See Finlay, 'Professional Men of Law', Appendix 7.

courts. For example, he was present in 1518 when a court was held in Edinburgh by the sheriff-depute of Berwick.[97] As mentioned in a previous chapter, Otterburn himself was constituted one of the sheriffs-depute of Stirling by Lord Erskine in 1524 shortly before he was appointed king's advocate.[98] By this time he was also a lord of council and, in this respect, it is interesting to note that in 1523 he was authorised, in the absence of the justice-clerk, to subscribe all deliverances in criminal cases (provided he did so along with one of the regents).[99]

It is in the width of his diplomatic experience that Otterburn differs most markedly from Henryson, whose own efforts in this field were ended prematurely at Flodden. By the time of the king's escape from Angus in 1528, Otterburn had had significant diplomatic contact with England, and may have been in receipt of an English pension.[100] On 11 July, 1528, the king took advantage of Otterburn's experience by employing him as one of those charged to 'diviss (devise) ane letter of staite to the king of Ingland with instructionis and articlis as thai sall think expedient'.[101] Otterburn's connection to Angus (as recently as April he had acted as attorney to Archibald Douglas of Kilspindie, the king's erstwhile treasurer and Angus's uncle), did not disqualify him from James's service.[102] In this respect Otterburn was not alone. The best known associate of Angus to be tolerated, and indeed promoted, by James V was Sir James Hamilton of Finnart. Both men lost the king's favour suddenly, Otterburn in 1538 and Hamilton in 1540, although unlike Hamilton the consequences for Otterburn were not fatal. Otterburn was dismissed from office for communicating with the exiled earl of Angus. In the words of the English ambassador Sir Ralph Sadler, he was 'suspected to be over good an Englishe man'.[103] Yet his connections with members of Henry VIII's government are probably what saved him from Hamilton's fate, since they rendered him indispensable to James's foreign policy towards the end of his reign. Even though Otterburn was sent as an ambassador to London in 1542, by then his role as king's advocate was beyond resurrection.[104]

Otterburn was not only provost of Edinburgh but also the burgh's legal representative and appeared on its behalf in several cases, most notably in the major action against Leith in 1522-3.[105] Like Henryson he had the advantage of growing up in the place that was at the centre of the political, economic

---

[97]   NAS, Edinburgh Burgh Court Book, fragment, B22/23/1: 1500x1513; *Prot. Bk. Strathauchin*, no. 295: 29 June 1518.
[98]   CS 5/34 fo. 163v: 11 May 1524.
[99]   CS 5/33 fo. 199v: 15 May 1523.
[100] Inglis, *Otterburn*, 19-24.
[101] CS 5/38 fo. 131r: 11 July 1528.
[102] *Prot. Bk. Foular*, iii, no. 3: 22 Apr. 1528.
[103] *Hamilton Papers*, ii, 106; Inglis, *Otterburn*, 68-9.
[104] Inglis, *Otterburn*, 70.
[105] See chapter four.

and legal activity of the realm. Otterburn's successor, Henry Lauder, also came from this background. His father, Gilbert Lauder, was a man of substance; a leading burgess who in his time had acted both as bailie of the burgh and dean of guild. His mother, Gilbert's first wife Margaret McCalzeane, also belonged to an Edinburgh family and through her Henry was related to the advocate Thomas McCalzeane.[106] Gilbert's second wife, Elizabeth Hopper, also came from the burgh and was probably related to Janet Hopper, the wife of the advocate Hugh Rigg.[107] His third wife, Isobel Mauchane, also belonged to a family of burgesses, one that would later produce Master Alexander Mauchane, a leading advocate of the reign of Queen Mary.[108] Gilbert, as well as undertaking duties within the burgh, was also specially commissioned under great seal letters in 1525 to act with James Johnstone as a justiciar *in hac parte*.[109] The importance of the burgh of Edinburgh and its inhabitants in legal matters is further underlined by the fact that almost a year to the day before this the sons of both these men, Henry Lauder and William Johnstone, were sworn to uphold the office of sheriff of Linlithgow *in hac parte*.[110]

This appointment does not mean that the son had at last wholly eclipsed the father, and it seems clear that Gilbert Lauder remained a major influence on his son. A petition for interdict in 1540 is interesting in this respect. This very common procedure, known as sequestration of children, usually involved a young man, often a burgess, whose father was dead and who appeared before the lords seeking to be formally interdicted from alienating his heritage without the consent of a named individual, normally an elder relative or friend (and often a man of law), for a specific period.[111] In this case, Thomas Wycht, the twenty-seven year-old son of a deceased Edinburgh burgess, sought such an interdict against selling or wadsetting his lands for the period of three years without the 'speciall consent counsall and aviss of honorabill men and his truest frendis Gilbert Lauder and Maister Henry Lauder his sone burgesis of Edinburgh'.[112] Gilbert and Henry, chosen for their legal knowledge and practical experience, are not a surprising choice. But it is revealing that Henry, who had been an advocate in the college of justice for eight years, king's advocate for two; who had been constituted in 1531 a justice-depute by justice-general, the earl of Argyll, personally, and who had appeared before

---

[106] For Gilbert as dean of Guild, see CS 6/2 fo. 121v: 11 Dec. 1532. Margaret was married to Gilbert by 1506 and was still married to him in 1510: *Prot. Bk. Foular,* i, nos. 218: 10 Jan. 1506; 645: 2 May 1510. If Margaret was the sister of James McCalzeane, then Thomas and Henry would have been first cousins.

[107] Gilbert had remarried by Feb. 1517: NAS, Broughton and Cally Muniments, GD 10/47: 9 Feb. 1517; B22/1/9 fo. 150: 12 Feb. 1517.

[108] James Kirk, *Patterns of Reform: Continuity and Change in the Reformation Kirk* (Edinburgh, 1989), 29.

[109] NAS, JC. 1/3 (no pagination): 14 Aug. 1525.

[110] CS 5/34 fo. 183r: 21 July 1524.

[111] Balfour mentions the procedure, calling it 'interdictioun' rather than the modern term interdict: Balfour, *Practicks,* i, 186–7.

[112] CS 6/13 fo. 134v: 26 July 1540.

parliament as the Marischall's deputy, should still be associated with his father in a matter of this kind.[113]

Henry Lauder's early life appears to have followed a pattern familiar to men of law of his generation. He was a graduate by November, 1513.[114] There is no indication of where he studied, although it seems to have been outwith Scotland and France is a strong possibility.[115] By the summer of 1517 he had become a burgess of Edinburgh.[116] Unlike the king's advocate of the time, James Wishart, Lauder was very much part of the mainstream of legal practitioners of his day. By the time he himself took office as king's advocate, he had gained a great deal of legal experience. His first constitution was 17 July, 1517 although his first appearance before the lords came several months earlier, on 26 March, when he acted for a litigant from Haddington.[117] Fairly soon he could count amongst his clients several earls, including Patrick, earl Bothwell, David, earl of Crawford, and Cuthbert, earl of Glencairn.

Professional success over two decades as king's advocate brought with it extensive rewards in terms of gifts of escheat, nonentry and ward made by James V and during the minority of Mary. In 1540, Lauder received the nonentry of Ballindon in Fife, lands held directly of the king, and twelve years later he received the nonentry of lands in Lauderdale.[118] In tandem with grants of this nature, he also received the escheats of murderers such as Alexander Aldinston and John Scott, and of those who died without having been legitimated, such as John Thomson.[119] More importantly, by avoiding the fate of Adam Otterburn, who was obliged to pay a ruinous fine to avoid execution, Lauder managed both to enjoy his wealth and retain office until his death.[120]

Before concluding it is worth mentioning briefly the two substitute advocates used by Lauder during the 1540s who most merit attention, and who have not been mentioned in detail elsewhere: Thomas McCalzeane and David Borthwick.[121] These men were contemporaries at the university of St Andrews in the mid-1520s and, as noted in chapter two, both were assessors of Edinburgh in the 1560s. The comparison does not end there. Both were

---

[113] For Lauder as *deputato mariscalli*: *APS*, ii, 352: 26 June 1538.

[114] *Prot. Bk. Strathauchin*, no. 165: 19 Nov. 1513.

[115] See chapter three. He does not appear in the list of graduates of Paris university printed by W.A. McNeill, 'Scottish entries in the *Acta Rectoria Universitatis Parisiensis*', *SHR* (1964) 66.

[116] *Edin. Burgh Recs.*, 298: 14 Mar. 1517; *RMS*, iii, no. 173: 18 July 1517.

[117] CS 5/29 fo. 152v: 26 Mar. 1517. He was also named in a procuratory, by Master David Lauder, to resign certain lands in Feb. 1517: NAS, Broughton and Cally Muniments, GD 10/47: 9 Feb. 1517.

[118] *RSS*, ii, no. 3713: 7 Dec. 1540; *RSS*, iv, no. 2073: 24 July 1553. In 1549 he received the ward and nonentry of lands in Tranent after the death of his neighbour, George, Lord Seton: *RSS*, iv, no. 366: 20 July 1549.

[119] *RSS*, iii, no. 1655: 8 May 1546; *RSS*, iv, no. 2791: 4 Aug. 1554; *RSS*, iv, no. 971: 15 Nov. 1550.

[120] Otterburn was forced to pay £2000 for a pardon in 1539, and later often complained of his poverty: Inglis, *Otterburn*, 70.

[121] See chapter seven for the dates on which Lauder nominated them his substitutes.

burgesses: McCalzeane was the second son of an Edinburgh burgess while Borthwick was the eldest son of a burgess of Haddington. Both were also listed amongst the nine general procurators practising before the college of justice in 1549.[122]

McCalzeane was the son of James McCalzeane, a burgess and notary, who died about 1536.[123] He was probably the nephew of another Edinburgh burgess, Robert McCalzeane, who was escheated for sending gold out of the country without royal licence during the governorship of Albany.[124] Thomas inherited his father's interests in two tenements in the High Street of Edinburgh over the head of his elder brother, a chaplain and notary also called James, which prompted James to raise a summons against him seeking to reduce their father's resignation of these lands in Thomas's favour.[125] The alleged ground of reduction, the law of death-bed, was rejected by the lords although no reason for the judgment was given. Thomas was acting as a procurator before the college of justice certainly before his father's death.[126]

Borthwick was the son of a Haddington burgess of the same name.[127] In July 1531 he himself became a burgess and, two months later, 'maister Dave' obtained possession of an acre of land within the burgh.[128] His education, part of which may have been abroad, no doubt lies behind his early promotion as one of the bailies of the burgh in October 1531.[129] But promotion had its dangers. In 1532 Borthwick was deforced by two men, one of whom, according to a witness, climbed a stairway and threatened to throw a large stone on his head.[130] Nonetheless, Borthwick had soon come to the attention of the king's secretary, Sir Thomas Erskine of Brechin, and this in turn brought him into contact with James Foulis, clerk register, and Nichol Crawford, justice-clerk.[131] Borthwick went to France with Erskine and the king in 1536 and by May of the following year his service had been rewarded

---

[122] *ADCP*, 584.

[123] For James's as a notary, see *Prot. Bk. Foular*, ii, no. 734: 31 Aug. 1526.

[124] CS 5/29 fos. 1v, 35v: 14 and 21 Feb. 1517. Robert McCalzeane witnessed a charter of sasine to Gilbert Lauder and Margaret McCalzeane in 1510, and through Margaret (his aunt?) Thomas was linked to Henry Lauder: *Prot. Bk. Foular*, i, no. 645: 2 May 1510.

[125] CS 6/10 fo. 88r: 1 June 1538; James was a notary by 1544: NAS, Swinton Charters, GD 12/119: 5 Apr. 1544.

[126] The first reference to him in the *acta* may be CS 6/6 fo. 30r: 1 Feb. 1535.

[127] David senior was dead by 1540: *RSS*, ii, no. 3383: 19 Feb. 1540.

[128] NAS, Transcript of Haddington Burgh Court Book, GD 1/413/1: 4 July 1531; NAS, *Prot. Bk. Alexander Symsoun*, B.30/1/2 fo. 25r: 11 Sep. 1531. Borthwick subsequently purchased a charter of this land: B.30/1/2 fo. 59r: 16 Jan. 1534.

[129] Ibid., 10 Oct. 1531. The other bailies elected were the master of Hailes and Patrick Lawson.

[130] Ibid., 26 Mar. 1532.

[131] Both of whom, along with Borthwick, witnessed one of of Erkine's charters: *RMS*, iii, no. 1308: 12 Sep. 1533. See also, *RMS*, iii, no. 1460: 27 Mar. 1535, which indicates Borthwick was a notary.

with the position of captain of Tantallon.[132] The fact that he had to borrow materials from his own burgh demonstrates that the castle had not yet recovered from the siege of 1528.[133] By August, 1537, the castle was in a fit enough state to play host to the king and his secretary.[134] This was not the last service which Borthwick performed for the king, nor did his career in government service end with the king's death.[135] For example, in 1553, having received a gift of the lands of Fenton Barns in East Lothian, the escheat of the late Gavin Borthwick (who had died illegitimate), he was named as one of the commissioners to meet an English delegation in the Borders.[136] Borthwick's association with the earl of Arran during this period clearly advanced him and brought some of the rewards which those who held the office of king's advocate in their own right were becoming used to.

Borthwick's early career indicates that James Wishart was not alone in having a background in royal service prior to his appointment as advocate for the king. Even so, it was many years before Borthwick was appointed principal advocate and a great deal had happened in between. The pattern first established with Henryson, a burgess with a university background, is found replicated not only in McCalzeane and Borthwick, but also in Otterburn and Lauder. But it also applied to many men of law who did not rise to the rank of king's advocate. There would appear to be nothing unusual in the backgrounds of these particular men that suited them to such service. Of the group as a whole Wishart was the odd man out, but his appointment was unique and, after his death, it was never again seen to be desirable to combine in one man the offices of king's advocate and justice-clerk. Nor does Wishart seem to have gained experience as a substitute for the king's advocate prior to his appointment, unlike Otterburn, Lauder and Borthwick. Personal factors not evident from the record must explain not only why Wishart was chosen in 1513 rather than the more experienced Otterburn, but also why Lauder in due course replaced Otterburn and, indeed, why James Henryson was originally chosen in the first place. It is however tempting to see in the practice of appointing substitutes to act when the advocate was occupied elsewhere, the beginnings of a system of evaluating the performance of potential replacements. If Henryson was grooming Otterburn as his replacement, the

---

[132] Borthwick at this stage was yet to establish himself as a lawyer. Nonetheless, lawyers were not unheard of as the captains of important strongholds; in 1497 Master William Scott of Balwearie, councillor and man of law, was captain of Falkland: NAS, GD 266 (Crawford Priory Collection): 15 May 1497.

[133] NAS, Transcript of Haddington Burgh Court Book, GD 1/413/1: 20 May 1537.

[134] *RMS*, iii, no. 1704: 18 Aug. 1537.

[135] In 1540 Borthwick appeared in Haddington with a letter from the king to the council which related that Archibald Borthwick (probably a relative), prebendar of the local kirk, was now in the king's service and was to be replaced by a substitute to prevent him losing his prebendary through absence: NAS, Transcript of Haddington Burgh Court Book, GD 1/413/1: 8 Oct. 1540.

[136] *RSS*, iv, no. 1945: 17 Apr. 1553; *R.P.C.*, i, 150: 18 Sep. 1553.

plan miscarried; and Otterburn himself was in no position to suggest his own successor twenty-five years later.

This chapter should not be concluded without some mention of the downside of acting as advocate for the crown. It has already been seen in the murder of Robert Galbraith that a dissatisfied litigant might resort to drastic measures if he felt cheated of justice.[137] It was not until George Lockhart of Carnwath's murder in 1690 that a king's advocate met the same fate, although there is evidence that things could occasionally become difficult. In 1544, Henry Lauder fell foul of an Edinburgh baker, George Seton, who appears to have laid claim to Lauder's lands of St Germains in East Lothian. Evidently the dispute ended in violence and Seton, under the nose of his chief and Henry Lauder's neighbour, Lord Seton, was obliged to confess to making 'greit iniure and wrang to Maister Henry Lauder and Agnes Stewart his spouse in the hurting of hir at hir awin place of Sanct Germanis'.[138] As well as making a profuse apology, Seton renounced any rights he may have had to the lands in question. Some twenty years later, Lauder's successor, John Spens of Condie, was subjected to an even more direct attack. One evening in May, 1564, Spens was on his way home to Gilmerton when he and his servants were attacked by a group of nine men. The assault had no serious consequences, perhaps because only one of the assailants was armed, but the reason behind it is obscure. John Ramsay, one of the attackers, made a formal and grovelling apology before the lords of session for having taken part, alleging that the attack occurred 'apoun suddantye without ony just occasioun'.[139]

It is a sobering thought that knowledge of these attacks survives only because culprits were caught and forced to apologise on the record. These attacks cannot be linked directly to ongoing activity before the courts but one example of intimidation that can be linked in this way occurred in 1544 and affected Thomas McCalzeane, although he was acting for a private client at the time. In 1546 Robert Douglas of Lochleven deponed before the lords that he had overheard the captain of Edinburgh Castle, James Hamilton, threaten McCalzeane, who was about to appear against him in an action brought by Alexander Sandilands. Hamilton is alleged to have said of McCalzeane, amongst other 'iniurious wordis', that 'he suld have his skin' if he acted against him.[140] There is no evidence that this threat was made good. Nonetheless, advocacy in general, and for the crown in particular, was liable to make enemies even though, or perhaps because, the rewards were good.

Conclusion

[137] See chapter six.
[138] NAS, Eglinton Muniments, GD 3/2/4/3: 1 Apr. 1544.
[139] CS 7/31 fo. 53r.
[140] CS 6/28 fo. 54r: 3 July 1546.

Despite the occasional threat of violence, there is no evidence that any of the early advocates felt the same way as the seventeenth-century lawyer Sir John Nisbet, who complained that he had been

> thrown against my will into the place of Advocate and Lord of the Sessione, my private statione as ane Advocate of the greatest practice being more profitable and more secure...[141]

although the sentiment may not have been unfamiliar at least to some of them. Rather, the evidence indicates that the rewards of the office could be substantial. Not until Otterburn and Lauder were advocates with a large private practice were they appointed to serve the crown. With so little known of the material rewards of private practice, it is impossible to say whether the balance had shifted by Nisbet's time. In terms of security of tenure, the early king's advocates had mixed fortunes. Henryson met his death at Flodden along with his king and, as pointed out in the last chapter, might well have been fortunate to escape retribution during the minority of James V had he survived. Wishart also held office until his death. Henry Lauder managed to steer clear of controversy and, unlike Otterburn, retained office until he died in 1561.

What seems certain is that, with the possible exception of James Wishart, the early king's advocates should be considered part of the mainstream of the legal profession in the sense that they continued to represent private clients during the time they held office. As time went on this becomes less obviously true as administrative and other demands placed upon their time increased. It may be paradoxical, but Henryson, appointed at a time when his appearance before the courts was still something of a novelty, spent a great deal more of his time while he was king's advocate dealing with private clients than did either Otterburn or Lauder, even though at the date of their respective appointments the latter had amassed many more years of legal experience.

[141]   NAS, Biel Muniments, GD 6/1005: n.d.

Conclusion

On 24 July 1535 John Cranston of that ilk personally pursued a summons against John, abbot of Lindores, Sir John Jardine, *oeconomus* of the abbot of Kelso, and the king's advocate and erstwhile Border commissioner, Adam Otterburn.[1] The action followed an English raid over the Border almost two years earlier which had resulted, on a day of truce in September 1534, in the Englishmen Hugh Ridley and John Heron being delivered up as hostages to be held until compensation was paid for the damage done during the raid. Ridley was delivered to the custody of the abbot of Kelso, while Cranston received Heron as a hostage. At another day of truce early in July 1535, the English had offered to pay Cranston for the goods which Heron had taken from him during the raid. Royal officials, including Otterburn, James Foulis, clerk tegister, and Thomas Scott, justice-clerk, prevented Cranston from accepting this offer. They wanted him to keep Heron in his custody as a guarantee that Jardine and the tenants of the abbey of Kelso would be compensated for the injury done to them. This prompted Cranston to appear before the lords of council complaining that Heron had been delivered to him because of the 'scaith' or injury which Heron had done to him, not for injury done to the inhabitants of Kelso.

To the lords sitting in Edinburgh this case was merely one among many resulting from Border raids and they did not hesitate to refer the matter to the warden of the Middle March so that he might deal with it in accordance with the appropriate law and practice. This is in spite of the fact that at this period, and until there were improved diplomatic relations with England from 1536, administration of the frontier was inadequate and characterised by ineffective or disorderly days of truce and considerable local feuding.[2]

In the web of jurisdictions in sixteenth-century Scotland, the lords often referred cases to other forums, such as that of the court of the admiral or of the bishop's official. The surviving record of the admiral's court, although relatively late, contains the names of many legal practitioners whose faces were not unfamiliar to the lords of session.[3] The practitioners before the official of Lothian in the 1540s have also been identified and, although they appear a more coherent and specialised group, some of them certainly had experience

---

[1]   CS 6/6 fol. 197r. Otterburn was part of a commission to the Borders in 1534: Rae, *Administration of the Frontier*, 258.
[2]   Rae, ibid., 171-2.
[3]   *Acta Curiae Admirallatus Scotiae*, ed. T.C. Wade (Stair Society, 1937).

in dealing with civil matters before the lords of session.[4] The essential point is that prior to 1550 only a fraction of any legal practitioner's career can be reconstructed. Even if in very rare cases there is evidence that the same man of law followed a case from its hearing before a sheriff up to its hearing in the tolbooth before the lords, there is no way of knowing how common a practice this was.

Indeed, where the record does survive, as it does for example in relation the sheriff court of Fife, the indication is that advocates with links to a particular sheriffdom who might be expected to act there regularly, such as Robert Leslie, did not do so. To conclude from this that these advocates were therefore specialists who concerned themselves exclusively with business before the lords of session would however be going beyond the evidence. Although the *acta* of the lords of session provide the best evidence for advocates' legal activity, as a source they also have limitations. Appearances by any particular man of law were recorded only on a minority of the days upon which there was a diet of the session, and the lords are recorded as sitting only on a minority of the days of any year. Even in the unlikely event that men of law were present on every day when the lords were recorded as sitting, that would still reveal what they were doing with merely a modest amount of their time. This *caveat* must necessarily be applied to any discussion of these men of law either as individuals or as a group.

More positively, what does emerge is that in the half century or so covered by this study the central administration of civil justice in Scotland underwent significant change. By 1550 a generation had grown up used to professional judges administering the law within the college of justice in Edinburgh. Professionalism such as this was viewed by contemporaries as a signpost to the future. This is demonstrated by the increasing numbers of new professional advocates eager to be admitted to practice before the court during and after the 1550s. These men, like their counterparts on the bench, were following directly in the footsteps of the men appointed in 1532. But, unlike the judges, the general procurators appointed at the foundation of the college of justice followed a longer tradition of professional legal practitioners whose activities, for the most part, remain hidden from view. It is true that a small proportion of royal councillors and lords of session during the reign of James IV and earlier carried out their responsibilities with a professional zeal. Figures both secular and spiritual, such as the Edinburgh burgess and St Andrews graduate Richard Lawson, and William Elphinstone, bishop of Aberdeen and student of Glasgow, Paris and Orléans, demonstrated how assiduous judges at the turn of

---

[4]   Ollivant, *Court of the Official*, 175-6.

the fifteenth century might be.[5] But in the strictest sense such men were not professional judges. Indeed they themselves followed in the footsteps of men such as the Cologne graduate David Guthrie of Kincaldrum whose royal service as treasurer, comptroller and justiciar during James III's reign was extensive.[6]

Before entering royal service Guthrie himself was a man of law and in this regard his success made him no less of a role model to those men who, at the turn of the fifteenth century, were regularly pleading before the lords. Of these, perhaps John Williamson, James Henryson, Thomas Allan, David Balfour and Matthew Kerr were the busiest.[7] They were all graduates and it is perhaps the case that by the time eight graduates were appointed in 1532 the die had long been cast in this regard. But the story is not quite so simple. Along with the graduates appearing regularly as procurators during James IV's reign were a considerable number of men who had not gone to university but who clearly knew the rudiments of legal procedure sufficiently well to represent the interests of others on an occasional basis. The most prominent of these was David Balfour of Caraldston. By 1532 such figures had not disappeared but they were much less significant. The graduates, and in particular the professional men of law, had taken over to the point where a fairly compact group of them held a dominant position. The appointment of professional judges in 1532 may even have taken its inspiration from the professionalisation of lawyers which was increasingly apparent during the 1520s.

The general procurators of 1532 who form the core of this study were men of differing backgrounds although all were well educated. They also appear to have been competent and honest practitioners. There are very few allegations of sharp practice. True Robert Leslie was posthumously accused of treason (on unconvincing grounds) while William Johnstone condemned himself as a heretic by fleeing the country. But no allegations of using false evidence, or suborning perjury, were made in regard to them or most of their contemporaries. Nor was it suggested that they were incompetent or greedy men. In practice the professional pleaders appointed in 1532 seem to have been skilled and experienced men with high ethical standards. Allegations of malpractice are very few and far between in the court record.

---

5   Chalmers, 'King's Council', *passim*. Although Chalmers has much to say about Lawson, he dates his death wrongly to 1508 (at 245). Lawson died probably during the summer of 1507: *Prot. Bk. Foular,* ii, no. 340: 25 Aug. 1507. As for Elphinstone, see Macfarlane, *Elphinstone, passim.*

6   On Guthrie see G. Crawfurd, *The Lives and Characters of the Officers of the Crown and of the State in Scotland* (Edinburgh, 1726), i, 360-1; A.R. Borthwick and H.L. MacQueen 'Three Fifteenth Century Cases' (1986) *JR* 149; ibid., "'Rare creatures for their age': Alexander and David Guthrie, graduate lairds and royal servants", *Church, Chronicle and Learning in Medieval and Early Renaissance Scotland,* ed. B.E. Crawford (Edinburgh, 1999) 227-239; MacQueen, *Common Law,* 82; A.R. Borthwick, 'The King, Council, and Councillors', 293-5.

7   See Finlay, 'Professional Men of Law', Appendix 4.

It is impossible from this distance and with the evidence available to assess adequately the importance of these men on the subsequent development of the legal profession. If such a skilled cadre had not existed in 1532 it is, to say the least, unlikely that the profession would have developed as it did during and after the 1550s. Much remains to be learned of the role which advocates played in the Reformation crisis and during the early years of James VI's reign. In some cases a significant amount is known, on the surface, about their contribution. But men such as James McGill, David Borthwick and Thomas McCalzeane had long careers and were engaged as the advocates of many distinguished clients. McGill in particular, as clerk register, was in the circle of the earl of Moray and took an active and very public part at his side in the first trial of Queen Mary which commenced in England in 1568.[8] As a leading Protestant McGill was in October 1574 one of the twelve elders elected to the first Edinburgh kirk session of which record survives.[9] Two other lawyers were also elected as elders in that year followed the next year by another four.[10]

An interesting anecdote involving Thomas McCalzeane is instructive. A former kirk elder, McCalzeane found himself embroiled with the kirk session in 1575 when, having slandered one of Edinburgh's ministers, he refused to perform public repentance.[11] Haughtily refusing to wear sackcloth, declining to sit on the stool of repentance and preferring instead to bring his own chair, McCalzeane is perhaps the liveliest example of the fact that, in social terms, by the third quarter of the sixteenth century the advocates had well and truly arrived.

[8]   G. Donaldson, *The First Trial of Mary, Queen of Scots* (London, 1969), 115, 119, 120.
[9]   Lynch, *Edinburgh and the Reformation*, 269.
[10] Ibid., 271.
[11] Michael F. Graham, *The Uses of Reform: 'Godly Discipline' and Popular Behaviour in Scotland and Beyond, 1560–1610* (Leiden, 1996), 269.

APPENDIX 1

General Procurators of the College of Justice, 1532–1549

27 May 1532[1]

1.	Mr. <u>Robert Galbraith</u>	5.	Mr. Robert Leslie
2.	Mr. *William Johnstone* [(St.A)]	6.	**Mr. *John Lethame* [(Gla)]**
3.	**Mr. Thomas Kincraigie**	7.	**Mr. *Thomas Marjoribankis* [(Gla)]**
4.	**Mr. <u>Henry Lauder</u>**	8.	Mr. *Henry Spittall* [(St.A)]

16 November 1537[2]

9.	Mr. <u>Henry Balnavis</u>	13.	**Mr. *Thomas Marjoribankis***
10.	Mr. James Carmuir	14.	**Mr. Thomas McCalzeane**
11.	**Mr. <u>Henry Lauder</u>**	15.	Mr. Hugh Rigg
12.	**Mr. *John Lethame***	16.	**Mr. George Strang**

1 March 1549[3]

17.	Mr. John Abercrombie	22.	Mr. <u>James McGill</u>
18.	Mr. <u>David Borthwick</u>	23.	Mr. <u>John Spens</u>
19.	Mr. Robert Heriot	24.	**Mr. George Strang**
20.	**Mr. Thomas Kincraigie**	25.	Mr. William Wychtman
21.	**Mr. Thomas McCalzeane**		

Key

Names in Italics: former procurators of the Scots Nation at the University of Orléans.

Names in Bold: these names are duplicated.

Abbreviations in superscript: these are the native dioceses, as recorded in the Book of the Scottish Nation (*liber nationis Scotie*) at Orléans, of those whose presence is recorded there i.e. Brechin, Glasgow, St. Andrews.

<u>Names Underlined</u>: these were elevated to the bench, acting as lords of session, although some of them did so *ex officio,* e.g. Marjoribanks (lord clerk register), James McGill (lord clerk register).[4]

---

[1] *Acts of Sederunt*, ed. I. Campbell (Edinburgh, 1811), 5. Names in italics are those of procurators of the Scots Nation, University of Orléans: Kirkpatrick, *Miscellany of the Scottish History Society, vol. II,* (Edinburgh, 1904), 70.

[2] EUL, La. III. 399, Lord Fountainhall's Collection, 'Statutes of Session', fo. 2.

[3] Campbell, *Acts of Sederunt,* 48.

[4] See A.L. Murray, 'The lord clerk register' (1974) *SHR* 134 where it is asserted that from 1532 the clerk register took a place on the bench almost as of right.

APPENDIX 2

Crown Advocates, 1493–1582

James Henryson of Fordell	October 1493/September 1513
James Wishart of Pittarow	31 September 1513/late 1524/early 1525
Adam Otterburn of Auldhame	late 1524/early 1525[5]/October 1538
Henry Lauder of St Germains	November 1538/18 July 1561
John Spens of Condie	21 October 1555/October 1573
David Borthwick of Lochhill	20 October 1573/January 1582
Robert Crichton of Eliok	1 February 1581/25 June 1582
David McGill of Nisbet	app. 26 June 1582

[5] Inglis, *Otterburn,* 25, citing CS 5/35 fo. 177v, places Otterburn's first appearance as king's advocate on 4 Dec. 1524. Unfortunately the record he refers to dates from 4 Dec. 1525. There is a gap in the record when Otterburn takes over as advocate and so the precise date of his assumption of office is impossible to pinpoint.

Bibliography

A. PRIMARY SOURCES

1. *Manuscripts*

Edinburgh City Archive:
Protocol Book of Vincent Strathauchin, Transcript.
Protocol Book of Alexander King, Transcript.

Edinburgh University Library, Special Collections:
La. III. 399, Lord Fountainhall's Collection, 'Notices and Observations out of the buikis of sederunt of the Lordis of Sessioun: Statutes of Session' [n.d., early 17th century].
La. III. 388a, Sinclair's Practicks.
MS Dc. 7.63, (Law, *De Cronicis Scotorum Brevia*).

National Archives of Scotland, Edinburgh [NAS]:
Crown Writs, AD.
Commissary Court of Edinburgh, Manuscript Register of Testaments, CC 8.
Manuscript Books of Sederunt, CS 1.
Manuscript Acts of the Lords of Council, CS 5.
Manuscript Acts of the Lords of Council and Session, CS 6.
Manuscript Register of Acts and Decreets, CS 7.
Manuscript Extracted and Unextracted Session Processes, CS 15.

Abercairny Muniments, GD 24.
Ailsa Muniments, GD 25.
Biel Muniments, GD 6.
Boyd Papers, GD 8.
Broughton and Cally Muniments, GD 10
Crawford Priory Collection, GD 20.
Eglinton Muniments, GD 3
Glencairn Muniments, GD 39.
Hay of Haystoun Papers, GD 34.
Haddington Burgh Court Book, Transcript, GD 1/413/1.
Henderson of Fordell, GD 172.
Hume of Wedderburn MSS, GD 267.
Inventory of Bruce of Kennet, GD 11.
Inventory of Leven and Melville Muniments, GD 26.
Lothian Muniments, GD 40.
Mar and Kellie Muniments, GD 124.
Morton Papers, GD 150.

Professor Hannay's Papers, GD 214.
Shairp of Houston Muniments, GD 30.
Swinton of Swinton, GD 12.
Viscounts and Barons of Elibank, GD 32.

Justiciary Court Books, JC 1/3, JC 1/4

Protocol Book of James Androsoun, NP 1/5A.
Protocol Book of Andrew Brounhill, B22/1/11.
Protocol Book of James Darow, B66/1/1.
Protocol Book of John Feyrn, NP 1/168.
Protocol Book of Thomas Keane, NP 1/2A.
Protocol Book of Alexander Makneil, B22/22/18.
Protocol Book of James Meldrum, B30/1/1.
Protocol Book of Alexander Symsoun, B30/1/2.

Register House Charters, RH6.
Register of Deeds, RD.

National Library of Scotland [NLS]:
Additional MS 1746 (Adam Abell).
Adv. MS. 25.5.6.
Adv. MS. 25.5.7.
Adv. MS. 25.5.9.

St Andrews University Library:
Cartulary 'Λ' b.
SL 110 PW 123.

2. *Published Primary Sources*

A History of the House of Hamilton, ed. G. Hamilton, (Edinburgh, 1933).
Acta Dominorum Concilii 1501–1503, ed. J.A. Clyde, (Stair Society, 1943).
Acta Facultatis Artium Universitatis Sancti Andree 1413–1588, ed. A.I. Dunlop, vol. II., (Scottish History Society, 1964).
Acts of the Lords auditor of Causes and Complaints, 1466–1496, ed. T. Thomson (Record Commission, 1839).
Acts of the Lords of Council in Civil Causes (Acta Dominorum Concilii), 1496–1501, edd. G. Neilson & H. Paton, (Edinburgh, 1918).
Acts of the Lords of Council in Civil Causes, 1478–1495 ed. T. Thomson, (Record Commission, Edinburgh, 1839).
Acts of the Lords of Council in Public Affairs, 1501–1554, ed. R.K. Hannay (Edinburgh, 1932).
Acts of the Lords of Council, 1501–1503, ed. A.B. Calderwood, (Edinburgh, 1993).
Acts of the Parliaments of Scotland, eds. T. Thomson & C. Innes, (Record Commission, 1844–75).

Auctarium Chartularii Universitatis Parisiensis Tomus III: Liber Procuratorum Nationis Alemanniae in Universitate Parisiensis, eds. C. Samaran, & Ae. van Moe, (Paris, 1935).

Auctarium Chartularii Universitatis Parisiensis, vol. 3, eds. H. Denifle, & E. Chatelain, (Paris, 1935).

The Binns Papers 1320–1864, eds. J Dalyell of the Binns & J. Beveridge (Scottish Record Society, 1938).

Bisset, Habakkuk, *Rolment of Courtis*, ed. P. J. Hamilton-Grierson, (Scottish Text Society, 1920–6).

Calendar of the Laing Charters, ed. J. Anderson, (Edinburgh, 1899).

Calendar of Writs preserved at Yester House, 1166–1625, eds. C.C.H. Harvey & J. Macleod, (Scottish Record Society, 1930).

Campbell, I., *Acts of Sederunt*, (Edinburgh, 1811).

Charters of the Abbey of Coupar Angus, 2 vols. ed. D. E. Easson, (Scottish History Society, 1947).

Charters of the Hospital of Soltre, of Trinity College, Edinburgh, and other Collegiate Churches in Midlothian, (Bannatyne Club, 1861).

The Commissariot Record of Edinburgh: Register of Testaments, (Scottish Record Society, 1897-9).

Concilia Magnae Britannicae et Hiberniae, A.D. 446–1718, ed. D. Wilkins, (vol. ii, London, 1737).

Correspondence of Sir Patrick Waus of Barnbarroch, knight, ed. R.V. Agnew, (Edinburgh, 1887).

The Court Book of the Barony of Carnwath, 1523–1542, ed. W.C. Dickinson, (Scottish History Society, 1937).

Davidis Humii de Familia Humia Wedderburnensi Liber, (Abbotsford Club, 1839).

Early Records of the University of St Andrews, ed. J. M. Anderson, (Scottish History Society, 1926).

Edinburgh Records: The Burgh Accounts, ed. R. Adam, (Edinburgh, 1899).

Extracts from the Council Register of the Burgh of Aberdeen, 1398–1570, (Spalding Club, 1844).

Extracts from the Records of the Burgh of Edinburgh, 1403–1528, ed. J. Marwick, (Scottish Burgh Records Society, 1869).

Fasti Aberdonenses: Selections from the Records of the University and King's College of Aberdeen, (Spalding Club, 1854).

Foedera, Conventiones, Litterae et cuiuscunque generis Acta Publica, ed. T. Rymer, xi, (London, 1710).

Fraser, W., *Memoirs of the Maxwells of Pollock*, (Edinburgh, 1863)

Fraser, W., *Memorials of the Family of Wemyss of Wemyss*, (Edinburgh, 1888).

Fraser, W., *Memorials of the Montgomeries Earls of Eglinton*, (Edinburgh, 1859).

Fraser, W., *The Book of Caerlaverock*, (Edinburgh, 1873).

Fraser, W., *The Douglas Book*, (Edinburgh, 1885).

Fraser, W., *The Lennox*, (Edinburgh, 1874).

Fraser, W., *The Melvilles Earls of Melville and the Leslies Earls of Leven*, (Edinburgh, 1890).

Fraser, W., *The Red Book of Grandtully*, (Edinburgh, 1868).

Fraser, W., *The Red Book of Menteith*, (Edinburgh, 1880).

Fraser, W., *The Stirlings of Keir*, (Edinburgh, 1858).

Fraser, W., *The Sutherland Book*, (Edinburgh, 1892).

The Hamilton Papers, ed. J. Bain, (Edinburgh, 1890-2).

Hectoris Boetii Murthlacensium et Aberdonensium Espicopurm Vitae, (New Spalding Club, 1894).

Historic Manuscripts Commission:

4th Report, (London, 1874)

5th Report, (London, 1876)

8th Report, (London, 1881)

10th Report, (London, 1885)

14th Report, (London, 1894)

Mar & Kellie, (London, 1904)

The House of Forbes, eds. A.N. Tayler, & H.A.H. Tayler (Spalding Club, 1937).

The Knights of St John of Jerusalem in Scotland, eds. I.B. Cowan *et al.*, (Scottish History Society, 1983).

The Lag Charters 1400–1720, ed. A.L. Murray, (Scottish Record Society, 1958).

Laing, D. ed., Knox, *History of the Reformation in Scotland*, (Wodrow Society, 1855–6).

Laing, D. ed., *The Poems and Fables of Robert Henryson, now first collected*, (Edinburgh, 1865).

The Ledger of Andrew Halyburton 1492–1503, ed. Innes, C., (Edinburgh, 1867).

Letters and Papers, Foreign and Domestic, of the Reign of Henry VIII, eds. J.S. Brewer *et al.*, (1862–1932).

The Letters of James V, eds. R.K. Hannay and D Hay, (Edinburgh, 1954).

Liber Officialis Sancti Andree, (Abbotsford Club, 1845).

Liber S. Marie de Dryburgh, (Bannatyne Club, 1847).

Liber S. Marie de Melros, (Bannatyne Club, 1837).

Liber S. Thome de Aberbrothoc, (Bannatyne Club, 1848–56).

Lindsay, R., of Pitscottie, *The Historie and Cronicles of Scotland*, ed. J. G. Mackay, (Scottish Text Society, 1899–1911).

Perth Guildry Book 1542–1601, ed. M.L. Stewart, (Scottish Record Society, 1993).

National Register of Archives (Scotland):

Surveys no. 0852 Hunters of Hunterston

0897 Skene of Halyards

0925 Inventory of Erroll Charters

1100 Roxburghe Muniments (including Bellenden Papers)

Pitcairn, R., ed., *Criminal Trials in Scotland from 1488 to 1624*, (Bannatyne Club, 1833).

The Practicks of Sir James Balfour of Pittendreich, ed. P.G.B. McNeill, (Stair Society, 1962–3).

Protocol Book of Cuthbert Simon, 1499–1513, (Grampian Club, 1875).

Protocol Book of Gavin Grote, ed. W. Angus, (Scottish Record Society, 1914).

Protocol Book of Gavin Ros 1512–32, (Scottish Record Society, 1931).

Protocol Book of James Young, 1485–1515, ed. G. Donaldson, (Scottish Record Society, 1952).

Protocol Book of John Foular, 1501–28, eds. W. MacLeod & M. Wood, (Scottish Record Society, 1930–53).

Protocol Book of John Foular, 1528–32, ed. J. Durkan, (Scottish Record Society, 1985).

Protocol Book of of Dominus Thomas Johnsoun 1528–78, (Scottish Record Society, 1920).

Protocol Book of Sir Alexander Gaw, 1540–58, (Scottish Record Society, 1510).

Protocol Book of Sir John Cristison 1518–51, ed. R.H. Lindsay, (Scottish Record Society, 1930).

Protocol Book of Sir Robert Rollok, 1534–1552, ed. W. Angus, (Scottish Record Society, 1931).

Quoniam Attachiamenta, ed. T. D. Fergus, (Stair Society, 1996).

Records of Aboyne, ed., Charles, ninth Marquis of Huntly, (Spalding Club, 1894).

'Records of the Scottish Nation at Orléans', ed. J. Kirkpatrick, in *Miscellany II,* (Scottish History Society, 1903).

Regality of Dunfermline Court Book, 1531–1538, eds. J. M Webster & A.A.M. Duncan, (Dunfermline, 1953).

Regiam Majestatem and Quoniam Attachiamenta, ed. T.M. Cooper, (Stair Society, 1847).

Register of the Great Seal of Scotland, (*Registrum magni sigilli regum Scotorum*), eds. J.M. Thomson *et al.*, (facsimile edition, Edinburgh, 1984).

Register of the Privy Council of Scotland, 1st series, vols. i-iii, (Edinburgh, 1877-1898).

Register of the Privy Seal of Scotland, (*Registrum secreti sigilli regum Scotorum*) eds. M Livingstone *et al.,* 7 vols. (Edinburgh, 1908–1966).

Registrum de Dunfermelyn, (Bannatyne Club, 1842),

Registrum de Ecclesie Sancti Egidii de Edinburgh, (Bannatyne Club, 1859).

Registrum Episcopatus Aberdonensis, (Spalding Club, 1845).

Registrum Episcopatus Brechinensis, (Bannatyne Club, 1856).

Registrum Episcopatus Glasguensis, (Bannatyne Club, 1843).

Registrum Honoris de Morton, (Bannatyne Club, 1853).

Registrum Monasterii de Passelet 1173–1529, (Maitland Club, 1832).

Registrum S. Marie de Neubotle, (Bannatyne Club, 1849).

Rentale Book of the Cistercian Abbey of Coupar Angus, (Grampian Club, 1879–80).

Rentale Dunkeldense, ed. R.K. Hannay, (Scottish History Society, 1915).

Rentale Sancti Andree, 1538–46, ed. R.K. Hannay, (Scottish History Society, 1913).

Roll of Edinburgh Burgesses and Guild Brothers, 1406–1700, ed. C.B.B. Watson, (Scottish Record Society, 1929).

Rotuli Scotiae, ed. D. Macpherson *et al.,* (Edinburgh, 1814–1819).

The Scottish Correspondence of Mary of Lorraine, 1543–60, ed. A. Cameron, (Scottish History Society, 1927).

Select Cases from the Ecclesiastical Courts of the Province of Canterbury, c. 1200–1301, eds. N.Adams & C. Donoghue, (Selden Society, 1981).

Selected Cases from Acta Dominorum Concilii et Sessionis 1532–33, ed. I.H. Shearer, (Stair Society, 1951).

Selections from the Family Papers preserved at Caldwell, (Maitland Club, 1854).

Selkirk Protocol Books 1511–1547, eds. T. Maley, & W. Elliot, (Stair Society, 1993).

The Sheriff Court Book of Fife, ed. W.C. Dickinson, (Scottish History Society, 1928).

Sir John Scot of Scotstarvet, *The Staggering State of Scottish Statesmen from 1550 to 1650* ed. J. Rogers, (Grampian Club, 1872)

Sir John Skene, *De Verborum Significatione* (Edinburgh, 1597).

Sir Richard Maitland of Lethington, *History of the House of Seytoun*, ed. J. Fullarton, (Maitland Club, 1829).

Wigtownshire Charters, ed. R.C. Reid, (Scottish History Society, 1960).
Works of Sir David Lindsay of the Mount 1490–1555, ed. D. Hamer, (Scottish Text Society, 1930–6).

B. SECONDARY SOURCES
1.　*Works of Reference*

Atlas of Scottish History to 1707, eds. P.G.B. McNeill & H.L. MacQueen, (Edinburgh, 1996).
Black, G.F., *The Surnames of Scotland*, (New York, 1946).
The Concise Scots Dictionary, ed. M. Robinson (Aberdeen, 1985).
Cowan, I.B. & Easson, D.E., *Medieval Religious Houses: Scotland*, 2nd edn., (London, 1976).
Crawfurd, G., *The Lives and Characters of the Officers of the Crown and of the State in Scotland*, (Edinburgh, 1726).
Dictionary of National Biography, eds. L. Stephen & S. Lee, 22 vols., (Oxford, 1917).
Douglas, R., *The Baronage of Scotland*, (Edinburgh, 1798).
Dowden, J., *The Bishops of Scotland*, (Glagow, 1912).
Fryde, E.B. and others, *Handbook of British Chronology*, 3rd edn., (London, 1986).
Guide to the National Archives of Scotland, (Edinburgh, 1996).
The Scots Peerage, ed. Sir J. Balfour Paul, (Edinburgh, 1904–14).
Tolbooths and Town-Houses: Civic Architecture in Scotland to 1833, (Royal Commission on the Ancient and Historical Monuments of Scotland, 1996).
Watt, D.E.R. ed., *Fasti Ecclesiae Scoticanae Medii Aevi ad annum 1638*, Second draft, (Edinburgh, 1969).

2.　*Monographs*

Anderson, P.D., *Robert Stewart, Earl of Orkney, Lord of Shetland, 1533–1593,* (Edinburgh, 1982).
Baker, J.H., *An Introduction to English Legal History*, 3rd edn., (London, 1990).
Baker, J.H., *The Reports of Sir John Spelman* (Selden Society, 1978).
Bawcutt, P., *Gavin Douglas,* (Edinburgh, 1976).
Brand, P., *The Origins of the English Legal Profession*, (Oxford, 1992).
Broadie, A., *The Circle of John Mair: Logic and Logicians in Pre-Reformation Scotland*, (Oxford, 1985).
Brooks, C.W., *Pettyfoggers and Vipers of the Commonwealth: The 'Lower Branch' of the Legal Profession in Early Modern England*, (Cambridge, 1986).
Brown, M., *James I*, (Edinburgh, 1994).
Brundage, J.A., *The Medieval Canon Law,* (Longman, 1995).
Brunton, G. and Haig, D., *An Historical Account of the Senators of the College of Justice from its Institution in MDXXXII*, (Edinburgh, 1832).
Buchan, J.W., and Paton, H., *History of Peeblesshire* (Glasgow, 1927).
Burns, J.H., *The True Law of Kingship*, (Oxford, 1996).
Cameron, J., *James V,* (East Lothian, 1998).
Chrimes, S.B., *Henry VII*, (London, 1977).
Clanchy, M.T., *From Memory to Written Record: England 1066–1307*, (Oxford, 1993).

Cooper, T.M., *Select Scottish Cases of the Thirteenth Century*, (Edinburgh, 1944).

Dawson, J.P., *A History of Lay Judges*, (Harvard, 1960).

Dawson, J.P., *The Oracles of the Law*, (Ann Arbor, 1968).

Delachenal, R., *Histoire des Avocats au Parlement de Paris, 1300–1600*, (Paris, 1885).

Dilworth, M., *Scottish Monasteries in the Late Middle Ages*, (Edinburgh, 1995).

Dingwall, H., *Late Seventeenth-Century Edinburgh: A Demographic Study*, (Aldershot, 1994).

Dingwall, H., *Physicians, Surgeons and Apothecaries: Medical Practice in Seventeenth-Century Edinburgh*, (East Linton, 1995).

Donaldson, G., *The First Trial of Mary, Queen of Scots* (London, 1969).

Donaldson, G., *Scotland: James V to James VII*, (Edinburgh, 1971).

Edington, C., *Court and Culture in Renaissance Scotland, Sir David Lindsay of the Mount*, (East Lothian, 1994).

Ewan, E., *Townlife in Fourteenth Century Scotland*, (Edinburgh, 1990).

Fawcett, R., *Architectural History of Scotland: Scottish Architecture from the Accession of the Stewarts to the Reformation 1371–1560*, (Edinburgh, 1994).

Ferguson, W., *Scotland's Relations with England: A Survey to 1707*, (Edinburgh, 1977).

Finlayson, C.P., *Clement Litill and His Library*, (Edinburgh, 1980).

Gray, D., *Robert Henryson*, (Leiden, 1979).

Graham, M.F., *The Uses of Reform: 'Godly Discipline' and Popular Behaviour in Scotland and Beyond, 1560–1610*, (Leiden, 1996).

Harding, A., *A Social History of English Law*, (Harmondsworth, 1966).

Helmholz, R.H., *Roman Canon Law in Reformation England*, (Cambridge, 1990).

Helmholz, R.H., *The Spirit of Classical Canon Law*, (Georgia, 1996).

Holdsworth, W., *History of English Law*, vol. vi, (London, 1937).

Howard, D., *Scottish Architecture from the Reformation to the Restoration, 1560–1660*, (Edinburgh, 1995).

Inglis, J.A., *Sir Adam Otterburn of Reidhall*, (Glasgow, 1935).

Irons, J.C., *Leith and Its Antiquities*, (Edinburgh, 1897).

Ives, E.W., *The Common Lawyers of Pre-Reformation England*, (Cambridge, 1983).

Kagan, R.L., *Lawsuits and Litigants in Castle, 1500–1700*, (North Carolina, 1981).

Kirk, J., *Patterns of Reform: Continuity and Change in the Reformation Kirk*, (Edinburgh, 1989).

Knecht, R.J., *The Rise and Fall of Renaissance France*, (London, 1996).

Lynch, M., *Edinburgh and the Reformation*, (Edinburgh, 1981).

Macdougall, N., *James III: A Political Study*, (Edinburgh, 1982).

Macdougall, N., *James IV*, (Edinburgh, 1989).

Macfarlane, L.J., *William Elphinstone and The Kingdom of Scotland 1531–1514*, (Aberdeen, 1985).

MacQueen, H.L., *Common Law and Feudal Society in Medieval Scotland*, (Edinburgh,

Mann, J., *Chaucer and Medieval Estates Satire*, (Cambridge, 1973).

Martines, L, *Lawyers and Statecraft in Renaissance Florence*, (Princeton, 1968).

Marshall, R.K., *Virgins and Viragos: A History of Women in Scotland from 1080 to 1980*, (London, 1983).

Mattingly, G., *Renaissance Diplomacy*, (London, 1955).

McGladdery, C., *James II*, (Edinburgh, 1990).

McKechnie, H., *Judicial process upon Brieves, 1219–1532*, (Glasgow, 1956).

Nicholson, R., *Scotland: The Later Middle Ages,* (Edinburgh, 1974).

Ollivant, S., *The Court of the Official in Pre-Reformation Scotland*, (Stair Society, 1982).

Omond, G.T., *The Lord Advocates of Scotland*, (Edinburgh, 1883).

Owen, D.M., *The Medieval Canon Law: Teaching, Literature and Transmission,* (Cambridge, 1990).

Owst, G.R., *Literature and Pulpit in Medieval England,* (Cambridge, 1933).

Palmer, R.C., *The County Courts of Medieval England, 1150–1350*, (Princeton, 1982).

Prest, W., ed., *The Professions in Early Modern England*, (New York, 1987).

Prest, W., *The Rise of the Barristers*, (Oxford, 1986).

Queller, D.E., *The Office of Ambassador in the Middle Ages*, (Princeton, 1967).

Rae, T.I., *The Administration of the Scottish Frontier 1513–1603*, (Edinburgh, 1966).

Reid, W. Stanford, *Skipper from Leith: The History of Robert Barton of Over Barnton,* (Philadelphia, 1962).

Sanderson, M.H.B., *Scottish Rural Society in the Sixteenth Century*, (Edinburgh, 1982).

Sanderson, M.H.B., *Cardinal of Scotland,* (Edinburgh, 1986).

Sanderson, M.H.B., *Mary Stewart's People*, (Edinburgh, 1987).

Sanderson, M.H.B., *Ayrshire and the Reformation*, (East Linton, 1997).

Sayers, J.E., *Papal Judges Delegate in the Province of Canterbury 1198–1254*, (Oxford, 1971).

Scarisbrick, J.J., *Henry VIII*, (London, 1981).

Shaw, D., *The General Assemblies of the Church of Scotland 1560–1600, Their Origins and Development*, (Edinburgh, 1964).

Shennan, J.H., *The Parlement of Paris*, (London, 1968).

Simpson, G.G., *Handwriting in Scotland 1150–1650*, (Aberdeen, 1973)

Stephen, W., *A History of Inverkeithing and Rosyth,* (Aberdeen, 1921).

Tweedie, M.F., *The History of the Tweedie or Tweedy Family,* (1902).

Willock, I.D., *The Origins and Development of the Jury in Scotland*, Stair Society vol. xxiii, (Edinburgh, 1966).

Wormald, J., *Court, Kirk and Community: Scotland, 1470–1625*, (London, 1981).

Wormald, J., *Lords and Men in Scotland: Bonds of Manrent, 1442–1603*, (Edinburgh, 1985).

3. *Articles (including volumes of essays)*

Auzary-Schmaltz, B. & Dauchy, S., 'L'assistance dans la résolution des conflits au civil devant le Parlement de Paris au Moyen Age', *L'assistance dans la resolution des conflits,* (Brussels, 1997).

Baker, J.H., *The Legal Profession and The Common Law*, (London, 1986).

Bennet, M., 'Careerism in late medieval England', *People, Politics and Community in the Later Middle Ages,* eds. J. Rosenthal & C. Richmond (Gloucester, 1987).

Borthwick, A. & MacQueen, H.L., 'Three Fifteenth-century Cases', (1986) *JR*, 123.

Bouwsma, W.J., 'Lawyers and Early Modern Culture', 78, (1973) *American Historical Review*, 303.

Brand, P., *The Making of the Common Law*, (London, 1992).

Brodie, D.M., 'Edmund Dudley: Minister of Henry VII' (1932) *Transactions of the Royal Historical Society* (4th ser.), 133.

Brown, A.L., 'The Scottish establishment in the later 15th Century' (1976) *JR* 89.

Brown, J., ed., *Scottish Society in the Fifteenth Century*, London, 1977.

Brundage, J.A., 'Legal aid for the poor and the professionalization of law in the Middle Ages', (1988) *Journal of Legal History*, ix, 169.

Brundage, J.A., 'The medieval advocates' profession', (1988) *Law and History Review*, vi, 439.

Brundage, J.A., 'The profits of the law: legal fees of university-trained advocates', (1988) *American Journal of Legal History*, xxxii, 1.

Cairns, J.W., 'Importing our lawyers from Holland: Netherlands influences on Scots law and lawyers in the eighteenth century', *Scotland and the Low Countries*, ed. G. G. Simpson (East Linton, 1996), 136.

Cairns, J.W., 'The formation of the Scottish legal mind in the eighteenth century: themes of Humanism and Enlightenment in the admission of advocates', *The Legal Mind*, eds. N. MacCormick & P. Birks (Oxford, 1986), 253.

Cairns, J.W., 'The law, the advocates and the universities in late sixteenth-century Scotland', *SHR* lxxiii, (1994), 171.

Carswell, R.D., 'Origins of the legal profession in Scotland', (1967), *American Journal of Legal History*, 41.

Cooper. T.M., *Selected Papers*, (Edinburgh, 1957).

Cowan, I.B., 'Patronage, provision and reservation: pre-Reformation appointments to Scottish benefices, *The Renaissance and the Reformation in Scotland: Essays in honour of Gordon Donaldson*, eds. I.B. Cowan & D. Shaw, (Edinburgh, 1983), 75.

Cowan, I.B., & Yellowlees, M.J., 'The cathedral clergy of Dunkeld', *The Renaissance in Scotland*, eds. M. Lynch *et al.*, (Leiden, 1994).

Donaldson, G., 'The legal profession in Scottish society in the sixteenth and seventeenth centuries', (1976) *JR*, 1.

Donaldson, G., *Scottish Church History*, (Edinburgh, 1985).

Durkan, J., 'Some local heretics', *Transactions of the Dumfries and Galloway Natural History and Antiquarian Society*, 3rd series, xxi, (1957–8), 67.

Durkan, J., 'The beginnings of humanism in Scotland', iv, (1953) *Innes Review*, 5.

Durkan, J., 'The cultural background in sixteenth-century Scotland', *Essays on the Scottish Reformation*, ed. D. MacRoberts (Glasgow, 1962).

Durkan, J., 'The early Scottish notary', *The Renaissance and the Reformation in Scotland*, eds. I.B. Cowan & D. Shaw, (Edinburgh, 1983), 22.

Durkan, J., 'The royal lectureships under Mary of Lorraine', (1983), *SHR* 73.

Durkan, J., 'Scottish "Evangelicals" in the patronage of Thomas Cromwell', (1982), *Records of the Scottish Church History Society*, 127.

Durkan, J., & Ross, A., 'Early Scottish libraries' (1958), *Innes Review*, 5.

Engelmann, A., 'System of the Romano-canonical procedure', *Continental Legal History Series*, vol. VII, (London, 1928).

Farr, J.R., 'Dijon's social structure 1450–1750', *Cities and Social Change in Early Modern France*, ed. P. Benedict, (London, 1992).

Finlay, J., 'James Henryson and the origins of the office of king's advocate' (2000) *SHR* 17-38.

Finlay, J., 'Robert Galbraith and the role of the queen's advocate' (1999) *JR* 277.

Finlay, J., 'Women and Legal Representation in Early Sixteenth-Century Scotland', *Women in Scotland, c.1100–c.1750*, eds. E.Ewan & M.Meikle, (East Linton, 1999).

Gane, G., 'The effect of a pardon in Scots law', (1980) *JR* 19.

Harding, A., 'The medieval brieves of protection and the development of the common law', (1966) *JR* 115.

Helmholz, R.H., *Canon Law and the Law of England*, (London, 1987).

Hillyard, B., '"Durkan and Ross" and beyond' *The Renaissance in Scotland*, eds. Lynch *et al.*,(Leiden, 1994).

Houston, R., 'Mortality in early modern Scotland: the life expectancy of advocates', (1992), *Continuity and Change*, 7 (1), 47.

Ives, E.W., 'The common lawyers in pre-Reformation England' (1968)*Transactions of the Royal Historical Society*, 145.

Ijsweijn, J. & Thomson, D.F.S., 'The Latin poems of Jacobus Follisius or James Foullis of Edinburgh', *Humanistica Lovaniensia*, 24, (1975), 102-52.

Jack, R.D.S. ed., *The History of Scottish Literature vol. 1: Origins to 1660*, (Aberdeen, 1988).

Lyall, R.J., 'Politics and poetry in fifteenth and sixteenth-century Scotland', (1976), *Scottish Literary Journal*, iii, 5.

Lyall, R.J., 'Scottish students and masters at the universities of Cologne and Louvain in the fifteenth century', (1985), *Innes Review*, xxxvi, 55.

Lynch, M., Spearman M., & Stell, G., eds., *The Scottish Medieval Town*, (Edinburgh, 1988).

MacDonald, A.A., Lynch, M., & Cowan, I.B., eds. *The Renaissance in Scotland Studies in Literature, Religion, History and Culture offered to John Durkan*, (Leiden, 1994).

Macdougall, N., ed., *Church, Politics and Society: Scotland 1408–1929*, (Edinburgh, 1983).

Macfarlane, L.J., 'The primacy of the Scottish church 1472–1521', (1969), *Innes Review*, 111.

MacQueen, J., ed., *Humanism in Renaissance Scotland*, (Edinburgh, 1990).

MacRoberts, D., ed., *Essays on the Scottish Reformation*, (Glasgow, 1962).

Madden, C., 'Royal Treatment of Feudal Casualties in Late Medieval Scotland, (1976), *SHR* lv, 172.

McKay, D. 'Parish Life in Scotland 1500–1560,' *Essays on the Scottish Reformation*, ed. D. MacRoberts, (Glasgow, 1962).

Murray, A.L., 'Exchequer and Council in the reign of James V, (1987), *SHR* lxvi, 125.

Murray, A.L., 'Sinclair's Practicks', *Law Making and Law-makers in British History*, ed. A. Harding, (London, 1980).

Murray, A.L., 'The comptroller, 1425–1488', (1973), *SHR* lii, 1.

Murray, A.L., 'The lord clerk register', (1974), *SHR* liii, 124.

Nicholson, R., 'Feudal developments in late medieval Scotland', (1973) *JR* 1.

Owen, D.M., 'Ecclesiastical jurisdiction in England 1300–1550', *Studies In Church History,* vol. 11, ed. D. Baker (Oxford, 1975).

Palmer, R.C., 'County Year Book Reports: the professional lawyer in the medieval County Court', (1971), *English Historical Review*, xci, 776.

Palmer, R.C., 'The origins of the legal profession in England', (1976), *Irish Jurist*, 126.

Perez, J. B., 'The science of Law in the Spain of the Catholic Kings', *Spain in the Fifteenth Century 1369–1516*, ed. R. Highfield (London, 1972), 279.

Philipson, N.T., 'Lawyers, landowners and the civic leadership of post-Union Scotland', (1976) *JR* 97.

Post, G., Giocarinis, K., & Kay, R., "The medieval heritage of a humanistic ideal: '*scientia donum dei est, unde vendi non potest*'", 11 (1955) *Traditio,* 195.

Powell, E., 'Arbitration and the law in England in the late Middle Ages', (1983), *Transactions of the Royal Historical Society,* 5th series, xxxiii, 49.

Powell, E., 'Settlement of disputes by arbitration in fifteenth-century England, (1984) *Law and History Review,* ii, 21.

Prest. W., ed., *Lawyers in Early Modern Europe and America,* (New York, 1981).

Rae, T.I., 'The Origins of the Advocates' Library', *For the Encouragement of Learning: Scotland's National Library, 1689–1989,* eds. P. Cadell *et al.,* (Edinburgh, 1989), 1.

Ramsay, N., 'Retained legal counsel, *c.*1275–*c.*1475' (1985) *Transactions of the Royal Historical Society,* 95.

Ranieri, F., 'From status to pofession: the pofessionalisation of lawyers as a research field in modern European legal history', (1989), *Journal of Legal History,* x, 180.

Rawcliffe, C., 'Baronial Councils in the Later Middle Ages', *Patronage, Pedigree and Power in Later Medieval England,* ed. C.D. Ross (Gloucester, 1979).

Reid, W. Stanford, 'Robert Barton of Ovir Barnton', (1948), *Medievalia et Humanistica,* v, 46.

Robertson, J.J., 'The development of the law', *Scottish Society in the Fifteenth Century,* ed. J. Brown, (London, 1977), 136.

Rousseaux, X., 'De l'assistance mutuelle à l'assitance professionelle le Brabant (XIVe– XVIIIe)', *L'assistance dans la resolution des conflits* (Brussels, 1997).

Rowlands, M.E., 'Robert Henryson and the Scottish courts of law', (1961-2), *Aberdeen University Review,* xxxix, 219.

Sanderson, M.H.B., "'Kin, Freindis and Servandis': The men who worked with archbishop David Beaton", (1974), *Innes Review,* xxv, 31.

Scott, P.H., ed., *Scotland: A Concise Cultural History,* (Edinburgh, 1993).

Sellar, W.D.H., ed., *Miscellany Two,* (Stair Society, 1984).

Sellar, W.D.H., 'The Common Law of Scotland and the Common Law of England', *The British Isles, 1100–1500: Comparisons, Contrasts and Connections,* ed. R.R. Davies, (Edinburgh, 1988), 82.

Shead, N.F., 'Glasgow: an ecclesiastical burgh', *The Scottish Medieval Town,* eds. M. Lynch *et al.,* (Edinburgh, 1988).

Simpson, G.G., *Scotland and the Low Countries,* (East Linton, 1996).

Simpson, J.M., 'The advocates as Scottish trade union pioneers', *The Scottish Tradition,* ed. G.W.S. Barrow, (Edinburgh, 1974), 164.

Stein, P., *The Character and Influence of the Roman Civil Law,* (London, 1988).

Van Caenegem, R.C., 'The developed procedure of the second Middle Ages XI-XV Century', *International Encyclopaedia of Comparative Law,* (Tübingen, 1971-), xvi, III.

Van Heijnsebergen, T., 'The interaction between literature and history in Queen Mary's Edinburgh: The Bannatyne manuscript and its prosopographical context', *The Renaissance in Scotland,* eds. A.A. MacDonald *et al.,* (Leiden, 1994).

Watt, H., 'Henry Balnavis and the Scottish Reformation', *Scottish Church History Society,* 5, (Edinburgh, 1935), 23.

Wijffels, A., 'L'assistance judiciare dans le Pays-Bas méridionaux 1. Avocats et procureurs au Grand Conseil de Malines', *L'assistance dans la résolution des conflits* (Brussels, 1997).

Williams, J.H., *Stewart Style, 1513–1542, Essays on the Court of James V*, (East Lothian, 1996).

Wilson, N., 'The Scottish bar: the evolution of the Faculty of Advocates in its historical setting', (1968), *Louisiana Law Review*, xxviii, 235.

Wormald, J., 'Bloodfeud, kindred and government in early modern Scotland', *Past and Present*, no. 87 (May 1980) 54.

4. *Theses/Dissertations*

Borthwick, A.R., 'The King, Council and Councillors in Scotland, c.1430–1460' (Ph.D. Thesis, University of Edinburgh, 1986).

Cameron, J., 'Crown-Magnate Relations in the Personal Reign of James V', (Ph. D. Thesis, University of St Andrews, 1994).

Chalmers, T.M., 'The King's Council, Patronage and the Governance of Scotland, 1460–1513', (Ph.D. Thesis, Aberdeen University, 1982).

Clark, G.B., 'The Remedy of Lawburrows in Scots Law', (LL.M. Dissertation, University of Edinburgh, 1985).

Emond, W.K., 'The Minority of James V', (Ph.D. Thesis, University of St Andrews, 1988).

Fulton, R.W.M., 'Social Criticism in Scottish Literature 1480–1560', (Ph.D. Thesis, University of Edinburgh, 1972).

Goodare, J.M., 'Parliament and Society in Soctland 1560–1603', (Ph.D. Thesis, University of Edinburgh, 1989).

Jamieson, I.W.A, 'The Poetry of Robert Henryson: A Study of the Use of Source Material', (Ph.D. Thesis, University of Edinburgh, 1965).

Kelham, C.A., 'Bases of Magnatial Power in Later Fifteenth Century Scotland', (Ph.D. Thesis, University of Edinburgh, 1986).

Kelley, M.G., 'The Douglas Earls of Angus: A Study in the Social and Political Bases of Power of a Scottish Family from 1389 to 1557' (Ph.D. Thesis, University of Edinburgh, 1973).

Meikle, M.M., 'Lairds and Gentlemen: A Study of the Landed Families of the Eastern Anglo-Scottish Borders c. 1540–1603', (Ph.D. Thesis, University of Edinburgh, 1989).

Murray, A.L., 'The Exchequer and Crown Revenue of Scotland 1437–1542' (Ph.D. Thesis, University of Edinburgh, 1962).

van Rhee, C.H., 'Litigation and Leglislation Civil Procedure at First-Instance in the Great Council for the Netherlands in Malines (1522–1559)', (Ph.D Thesis, University of Leiden, 1997).

Wasser, M.B., 'Violence and the Central Criminal Courts in Scotland 1603–1638', (Ph.D Thesis, Columbia University, 1995).

INDEX

Abell, Adam, chronicler, 64
Abercrombie, John, advocate, 57
Aberdeen, bishop, *see* Elphinstone, William
Aberdeen, burgh council, 96
acta of the lords of session, 1, 8, 21, 24, 25, 36, 48, 70, 102, 105, 172, 179, 226
action of error, 89, 111, 120, 177, 179, 183, 192, 193, 195, 197
advocate for the poor, 53, 63, 81, 82, 83, 84, 85, 86, 211; legislation of 1424, 82; remuneration, 84, 85. *See also* Blackstock, Andrew; Gledstanes, John; Henryson, Edward; Kincraigie, Thomas; Logie, John; Marjoribankis, Thomas; Williamson, John
advocates, 6, 7, 8, 12, 18, 19, 28, 30, 32, 38, 40, 43, 44, 60, 63, 65, 68, 71, 72, 75, 76, 82, 88, 90, 95, 103, 104, 105, 109, 119, 148, 170, 171, 172, 173, 174, 175, 176, 178, 179, 180, 181, 182, 183, 185, 186, 190, 192, 193, 194, 198, 200, 202, 217, 230; admission, 5, 7, 14, 53; admission oaths, 4, 70; advancement to the bench, 7; and notaries, 56; appearances in local courts, 132; appearing in secular and church courts, 87; appointed as sheriffs *in hac parte*, 63; appointed as sheriffs-depute, 63; arragements with clients, 46; as a group, 17, 55; as arbiters, 166; as assessors, 19, 20, 117; as custodians of evidence, 118; assassination of advocates made treasonable, 151; attendance, 164; booths, 94, 95, 96; circulation of legal texts amongst, 87, 88; comparison with foreign lawyers, 54; comparison with foreign lawyers, 54; compulsion, 73, 77, 78, 80; concentration in Edinburgh, 95; consultations, 96; co-operation amongst, 98; correspondence with clients, 21; *cum ceteris procuratoribus curie*, 68; delaying tactics, 122; designation, 15, 16, 18; distinguished from writers, 11, 14; distribution of clients, 62; drafting advice, 52; drafting defences, 109; dress, 93; duration of client relationships, 134; duty to act, 79; early dynasties, 64, 212; early organisation, 4; education, 57; entering court, 102; ethics, 160; giving counsel, 39; group of, 58, 68, 78; indication of presence in the *acta*, 67; judge's duty to provide an advocate, 74; litigation strategies, 108; not to see summons without taking case, 76;

number, 182, 183; number per litigant, 81; number permitted, 69, 70, 72; numbers admitted, 5; numbers permitted, 81; obligations, 73; power vis-a-vis judges, 81; probation, 14; probationers, 5; professional continuity, 67; professionalisation, 227; qualification, 53, 54, 55, 58; Reformation-crisis, 228; religion, 64; remuneration, 38, 39, 40, 41, 42, 44, 45, 46, 73, 160; retention of services, 39, 40; right of audience, 15, 73, 77, 93, 105; sanctions against, 77; servants, 12, 13; social status, 6, 7, 13; terminology, 9, 10, 17, 19, 170; trading activity, 41; wealth of, 42
Advocates, Faculty of, 2, 3, 4, 6, 8, 15, 38, 123
Advocates' Library, 6
Aiton, Robert, litigant, 61
Albany, Duke of, *see* Stewart
Allan, Thomas, advocate, 66, 227
Altavite, Bardo, litigant, 34
Anderson, Robert, witness, 114
Anderson, William, 17
Andreae, Johannes, 89
Andrew, Marion, 104
Angus, Earls of, *see* Douglas
Angus, Thomas, litigant, 114
arbitration, 11, 33, 44, 49, 99, 122, 151, 154, 158, 166, 167, 173, 177, 214
Arbroath abbey, 45, 46, 211
Arbuthnot, James, of that ilk, 216
Armstrong, John, 30, 145
Arnot, Robert, litigant, 120
Arran, Earls of, *see* Hamilton
Atholl, Earls of, *see* Stewart
avant parlier, 11
avocats, 11, 12, 55, 83
Ayton, John, king's master mason, 185
Azo, 10

Baker, J.H., historian, 3, 189
Balfour, David, of Burleigh, 199
Balfour, David, of Caraldston (Careston), advocate, 9, 45, 66, 91, 170, 175, 227
Balfour, Janet, of Caraldston (Careston), litigant, 111
Balfour, Sir James of Pittendreich, advocate and lord clerk register, 28, 31, 43, 48, 66, 75, 76, 152, 187, 194
Ballantyne, John, secretary to the 5th earl of Angus, 74

Ballon, Andrew, canon of St Andrews, 79
Balnavis, Henry, of Halhill,advocate and lord
    of session, 65, 66, 175, 184, 229; as
    treasurer clerk, 184
Baron, Andrew, litigant, 75
Baron, Patrick of Spittalfield, justice-depute,
    167
Baron, Patrick, of Spittalfield, justice-depute,
    168
Barr, Margaret, 156
barratry, 74, 79, 80, 173, 189, 190, 191
Bartolus of Sassoferrato, 62
Barton, Alexander, 17
Barton, Robert, of Over Barnton, 17, 35, 74,
    75, 125, 167, 184, 185, 186
Bas, John, witness, 114
Baty, Helen, 208, 217
Baty, John, Edinburgh burgess, 208
Beaton, David, abbot of Arbroath, archbishop
    of St Andrews and cardinal, 39, 65, 107,
    120, 129, 133, 135, 141, 186, 190
Beaton, James, archbishop of Glasgow and
    chancellor, 16, 107, 112, 129, 145
Beaton, John, of Creich, royal chamberlain, 185
Bellenden, Katherine, 61
Bellenden, Sir John, of Auchnoule, 203
Bellenden, Thomas, director of chancery, 19,
    46, 61, 65, 115, 146
Bennet, William, witness, 114
Blackadder, Beatrice, heiress, 155
Blackadder, Margaret, heiress, 155
Blackstock, Andrew, advocate for the poor, 44
Blackstock, Andrew, advocate for the poor, 85
Blackstock, William, advocate, 56, 68, 83
Boece, Arthur, canonist, 55
Boece, Hector, 56
bonds of manrent, 45, 46, 134, 145, 146, 160,
    161
books of sederunt, 4, 14, 53
Border raids, 225
Borthwick, David, of Lochhill, king's advocate
    and lord of session, 43, 110; family and
    background, 221
Borthwick, Gavin, 222
Borthwick, William, Lord Borthwick, 134, 141
Boswell, Sir Thomas, 19
Bothwell, Earls, *see* Hepburn
Bothwell, Francis, provost of Edinburgh, lord of
    session, 61, 63, 91, 95
Bothwell, Lady, *see* Stewart, Agnes
Bothwell, Margaret, wife of Henry Spittall, 56
Boyd, Margaret, countess of Cassillis, 108, 132,
    134
Brabant, council of, 11, 12, 14, 54, 69; number
    of *avocats* permitted, 69
Brady, John, litigant, 48
Brand, Paul, historian, 1, 2, 3, 4, 7, 38, 44, 69
brieve of inquest, 29, 63, 192, 197

Broun, Adam, witness, 114
Brown, James, litigant, 61
Brown, Laurence, 210
Brown, Marion, 217
Brown, Sir William, litigant, 75
Bruce, Hector, of Colpmalyndy, litigant, 44,
    115, 124, 135
Bruce, Robert, Edinburgh burgess, 44
Buchan, Earls of, *see* Stewart
Bunche, Walter, litigant, 132
burgh laws, 132

Calder, Alexander, 200
Cameron, Jamie, historian, 130
Campbell, Archibald, 4th earl of Argyll, 91, 219
Campbell, Colin, 3rd earl of Argyll, 167
Campbell, Helen, litigant, 47
Campbell, John, of Lundie, royal treasurer, 167
Campbell, John, of Skeldon, litigant, 137
Campbell, Marion, 177
Campbell, Sir Hugh, of Loudoun, sheriff of
    Ayr, 106, 136, 156, 177, 197
Campbell, Sir Hugh, of Loudoun, sheriff of
    Ayr, 154, 177
Campbell, Sir John, of Lundie, royal treasurer,
    126, 144, 166, 184; as justice-depute, 26,
    91, 107
Campbell, Sir John, of Lundie, royal treasurer,
    195
canon law, definition of poverty, 84
Carkettle, John, of Finglen, 151
Carmichael, John, 105
Carmichael, John of Meadowflat, litigant, 134,
    144, 145
Carmichael, John, litigant, 37
Carmichael, Peter, 97, 173
Carmuir, James, advocate, 28, 61, 64, 69, 76,
    229
Carnegie, Robert of Kinnaird, advocate and
    lord of session, 41, 58, 144
Castile, 54; *abogado de pobres*, 83; number of
    advocates, 69
Castle Campbell, 114
Charters, Patrick, 117
Chene, Alexander, king's advocate-depute, 181
Chernside, Ninian of East Nesbit, 155
church courts, 4, 18, 24, 26, 38, 40, 59, 63, 69,
    86, 99, 103, 190
clerks of council, 9, 10, 18, 21, 24, 31, 36, 51,
    64, 67, 68, 103, 105, 123, 164, 170, 183,
    188
clients, expectations, 46
Cockburn, Edward, parson of Ellon, 37
college of justice, 1, 2, 4, 6, 12, 14, 19, 42, 43,
    44, 53, 54, 55, 62, 63, 65, 66, 67, 69, 70,
    72, 76, 77, 84, 87, 143, 151, 182, 190, 219,
    220, 221, 226; asking instruments, 105;
    normally based in Edinburgh, 164; practick,

89, 90, 121; procedural delay, 120, 121; procedure, 87, 96, 99, 102, 107; registration of deeds, 105; sessions, 164

college of Justice: influence of Romano-canonical procedure, 122

Colquhoun, Patrick, 199

Colville, James, of East Wemyss, comptroller, 80, 126, 176, 203

comptroller, 35, 63, 80, 125, 126, 170, 178, 181, 183, 184, 185, 186, 187, 188, 196, 227

constitutions, 21, 23, 24, 25, 29, 31, 32, 35, 36, 46, 48, 66, 67, 68, 73, 161, 177, 178, 215; recorded constitutions relationship to actual appearances, 24; special, 177; special and general, 23

constitutionz: general, 22

Cooper, T.M., judge and historian, 66

Corry, Thomas, 185

council of Chalcedon, 82

Coupar Angus abbey, 39

Craig, Thomas, of Riccarton, advocate, 6

Craik, John, 149

Cranston , John, of that ilk, 225

Crawford, David, litigant, 37

Crawford, Earl of, *see* Lindsay

Crawford, James of Auchinhame, litigant, 135

Crawford, John of Drongane, 23

Crawford, Nicol, advocate and justice-clerk, 37, 61, 172, 175, 193

Crichton, Abraham, advocate and official of Lothian, 16, 27, 49, 87, 88, 150

Crichton, Adam of Ruthvenis, 150

Crichton, George, advocate, 43, 88, 183

Crichton, George, bishop of Dunkeld, 46, 126, 160

Crichton, John, 47, 150

Crichton, John of Strathord, 138

Crichton, Margaret, lady Sempill, 159

Crichton, Ninian, of Bellibocht, 58, 153, 156, 160

Crichton, Ninian, of Bellibocht, sheriff of Dumfries, 133

Crichton, Robert, 4th lord Sanquhar, 133, 155, 156, 160

Crichton, Robert, of Eliock, king's advocate, 40, 156, 173, 180, 181, 230; death, 181

Crichton, Sir James, of Frendraught, 132, 141

Crichton, Sir Peter, of Naughton, 133

Crichton, William, 47

Crichton, William, of Drylaw, 159

Culross abbey, 97

Cummyng, John, litigant, 43

Cunningham, Alexander, dean, litigant, 74

Cunningham, Cuthbert, earl of Glencairn, 220

Cunningham, John, 23

Cunningham, Sir William, feuar of Glencairn, 167

Cunningham, William, master of Glencairn, 106, 107, 111, 115, 214

Cupar, burgh, 26

Currour, James, treasurer's clerk, 184

Dacre, William, 4th lord, English warden, 26, 147

Danzig, town council,, 41

Darnick, skirmish at (1526), 202

Darow, James, notary, 16, 170, 207

David Beaton, abbot of Arbroath, archbishop of St Andrews and cardinal, 55

David Borthwick of Lochhill, king's advocate and lord of session, 18, 40, 41, 55, 57, 64, 90, 180, 199, 220, 228, 229, 230

David Borthwick of Lochhill, king's advocate and lord of session, 176

Davidson, Thomas, 185

de Beaumanoir, Vincent, 11

de Ferrarriis, John, 89

de la Bastie, Seigneur, 148

de Tudeschis, Nicolas, 89

Deer abbey, 154

Delachenal, Roland,. historian, 5, 11

Dijon, lawyers in,, 69

dilatory exceptions, 106

Dingwall, Helen, historian, 7

Dingwall, Sir John, provost of Trinity collegiate church, 128

Dishington, William of Ardross, litigant, 133, 134

Doles, Alexander, 30

Donaldson, Thomas, witness, 114

Douglas, Archibald, 5th earl of Angus, 15, 16, 39, 80, 112, 114, 129, 130, 143, 144, 145, 148, 151, 155, 157, 177, 201, 202, 203, 204, 211

Douglas, Archibald, 6th earl of Angus, 74, 76, 77, 129, 143, 147, 152, 153, 155, 156, 157, 158, 164, 167, 201, 202, 203, 204, 211, 214, 218

Douglas, Archibald, of Kilspindie, 104, 129, 186, 202, 203, 218

Douglas, Gavin, bishop of Dunkeld, 160

Douglas, George, 167

Douglas, James of Cavers, sheriff of Roxburgh, 153

Douglas, James of Parkhead, 129

Douglas, James, of Drumlanrig, 145, 155, 158, 160, 161

Douglas, Janet, Lady Glamis, 203

Douglas, John, of Balvenie, 199, 209

Douglas, Robert, of Lochleven, 223

Douglas, Robert, of Lochleven, 116

Douglas, Sir Ninian, 128

Drummond, John, Lord, 35, 153

Drummond, John, Lord, litigant, 152, 153

Dryburgh abbey, 39, 106

Dubh, Donald, of the Isles, 201
Dudley, Edmund, 204
Dunbar, Alexander, of Cumnock, 122, 187
Dunbar, Archibald, baillie of regality of
    Glasgow, 154
Dunbar, James, 97, 132
Dunbar, Sir Alexander, vicar of Crail, 97
Dunbar, William, poet, 19
Dundas, Adam, 167
Dunkeld, bishop of, *see* Douglas, Gavin
Durand, Guillaume, 87
Durham, Alexander, of Grange, 140
Durkan, John, historian, 55
Dysart, burgh, 33, 132, 134, 211

Eccles priory, 154
Edinburgh tax roll (1565), 12, 13, 14, 43, 183
Eggart, James, Hanseatic merchant, 35, 37
Eglinton, Earl of, *see* Montgomerie, Hugh
Elcho priory, 125, 127, 158
Elcho, Prioresses of, *see* Leslie, Eufame;
    Swinton, Elizabeth
Elemour, John, of Clifton, 213
Elphinstone, Alexander, canon of Aberdeen,
    157
Elphinstone, Alexander, Lord Elphinstone, 17,
    115, 118, 166
Elphinstone, Andrew of Selmes, 157
Elphinstone, Robert, parson of Kincardine, 56,
    118
Elphinstone, William, bishop of Aberdeen, 55,
    56, 60, 87, 88, 226
Emond, W.K., historian, 76, 91, 130, 147, 155,
    157, 161, 201, 202, 203
Empson, Sir Richard, 204
Erskine, John, Lord Erskine, 63, 154
Erskine, John, of Dun, 65, 140
Erskine, Robert, Lord Erskine, 29, 35, 36, 46,
    217
Erskine, Sir Thomas, of Brechin, royal
    secretary, 57, 180, 221
Établissements de Saint Louis, 11
exceptions, 110
excommunication, 103

Farnely, Marion, litigant, 210
Fenton, James, of Ogill, 97
Ferguson, Robert, 51
Ferguson, Thomas, of Craigdarach, 155
feud: Campbell-Kennedy, 156; Douglas-
    Crichton, 155; Forbes-Leslie, 138;
    Montgomerie-Cunningham, 137; Tweedie-
    Fleming, 77
Fleming, John, Lord Fleming, 78
Fleming, Malcolm, Lord Fleming, 33, 78, 98,
    101
Fleming, Mariota widow of Alan Heriot, 33

Flodden, battle of (1513), 22, 128, 155, 159,
    171, 208, 209, 213, 215, 218, 224
Florence, lawyers in, 46, 54
Forbes, Elizabeth, wife of Henry Spittall, 134
Forbes, John, master of, 203
Forbes, William, litigant, 41
foreign litigants, 34, 108, 163; depositions from
    abroad, 117
forespeaker, 3, 9, 10, 11, 17, 18, 19, 27, 62, 67,
    89, 97, 99, 107, 108, 111, 116, 124, 130,
    146, 157, 159, 164, 170, 177, 208
Forrester, Alexander, burgess, 27
Forrester, Alexander, of Corstorphine, litigant,
    80
Forrester, Archibald, of Corstorphine, 212
Forrester, David, of Garden, 80
Fortune, Simon, nephew of Robert Galbraith,
    148, 151, 166
Fotheringham, Alexander, chaplain in Bruges,
    35, 163
Fotheringham, Charles, 35
Fotheringham, Thomas of Powrie, litigant, 144
Foular, John, notary, 60
Foulis, Henry, 60, 207, 208
Foulis, Isabel, 60
Foulis, James of Colinton, advocate and lord
    clerk register, 10, 17, 19, 24, 35, 39, 41, 49,
    55, 59, 60, 62, 63, 65, 66, 69, 89, 98, 100,
    106, 110, 146, 148, 157, 172, 175, 179,
    207, 208, 221, 225; entry of Mary of
    Guise(1538), 57; return from France and
    early connections, 60; studied under Robert
    Galbraith, 57
Foulis, James, of Colinton, advocate and lord
    clerk register, 49, 62, 179; appointed lord
    clerk register, 61; family and background,
    60; family and background, 206; lands, 60,
    61; return from France and early
    connections, 61
Foulis, James, skinner, 206
Foulis, Thomas, notary, 60
France, 5, 7, 11, 14, 26, 57, 58, 69, 85, 109,
    117, 148, 163, 180, 185, 203, 206, 220, 221
Franciscan friars, 118
Fraser, Katherine, 78
Fraser, Robert, 85
Freir, George, advocate, 55
Frog, Marion, litigant, 26, 27, 163

Galbraith, Adam, executor of Robert G., 151
Galbraith, David, of Kimmergame, 50, 146
Galbraith, Robert, monk of Glenluce, 151
Galbraith, Robert, of East Windshiel, advocate
    and lord of session, 10, 19, 27, 37, 47, 49,
    50, 53, 55, 57, 58, 59, 61, 63, 66, 67, 68,
    76, 89, 96, 97, 98, 100, 101, 103, 108, 110,
    113, 117, 119, 120, 123, 124, 128, 134,
    137, 139, 140, 145, 146, 147, 148, 149,

150, 151, 152, 153, 154, 155, 156, 157,
158, 159, 160, 161, 162, 163, 164, 165,
166, 167, 168, 169, 175, 177, 179, 195,
212, 222, 229; acts for the crown, 177;
appointed lord of session, 150; arbiter, 166;
attendance, 164; early life, 146; family and
background, 146; *Liber Galbraith*, 152;
murder of, 151; property in Edinburgh, 150;
Quadrupertitum, 146; queen's advocate, 148;
return to Scotland from Paris, 147; status as
a notary, 165
Galbraith, Simon, 158
Galloway, Sir John, notary, 198
Gardner, John, royal gardner at Falkland, 185
Geddes, James, servant of Douglas of Kilspindie,
203
Geddes, William, 203
Glamis, Lady, *see* Douglas, Janet
Glamis, Lord, *see* Lyon, John
Gledstanes, John, advocate and lord of session,
68; advocate for the poor, 84; receives sum
from privy seal fees, 85
Glencairn, Earls of, *see* Cunningham
Glenluce abbey, 103, 154
Gordon, Alexander, 3rd earl of Huntly, 120
Gordon, George, 4th earl of Huntly, 132, 205
Gordon, James, of Lochinver, 145, 156, 161
Gordon, James, of Westpark, 120
Gordon, John, of Lochinver, 156
Gordon, Robert, of the Glen, 156
Gourlaw, William, 108
Gourlay, Walter, litigant, 120
Graham, Gilbert of Knockdoliane, litigant, 136
Graham, William, 2nd earl of Montrose, 59
Grant, Francis, historian, 2, 70, 123
Gray, George, litigant, 119
Gray, Patrick, Lord Gray, 65, 141, 158, 167,
204
Grote, Gilbert, notary, 18
Guthrie, Andrew, of that ilk, 144
Guthrie, David, of Kincaldrum, 62, 227
Guthrie, Thomas, 33

Haddington, burgh, 41
Haddington, Earl of, *see* Hamilton, Thomas
Hailes, Master of, *see* Hepburn
Haliburton, James, litigant, 61
Halkerston, John, Edinburgh burgess, 61
Hamilton, James of Kingscavil, sheriff of
Linlithgow, 133
Hamilton, James, 1st earl of Arran, 60, 132
Hamilton, James, 2nd earl of Arran, duke of
Châtelherault, 64, 76, 132
Hamilton, James, of Kincavil, 64, 65
Hamilton, John, abbot of Paisley, treasurer, 184
Hamilton, Sir James, of Finnart, 77, 129, 130,
176, 196, 203, 218
Hamilton, Thomas of Priestfield, macer, 13, 97

Hamilton, Thomas, 1st earl of Haddington,
king's advocate ('Tam o' the Cowgate'), 13
Hamilton, Thomas, 1st earl of Haddington,
king's advocate ('Tam o' the Cowgate'), 128
Hamilton, Thomas, advocate, 61, 62, 97, 162
Hamilton, William, litigant, 111
handfasting, 47
Hannay, R.K., historian, 1, 3, 4, 7, 8, 12, 14,
19, 38, 63, 85, 93, 96, 98, 101, 104, 109,
172
Haswell, James, king's chaplain, 192
Hay, George, 7th earl of Errol, 51
Hay, John, 3rd lord Hay of Yester, 26, 33, 98,
104, 113, 153, 154, 158, 216
Hay, William, 3rd earl of Errol, 45
Hay, William, 6th earl of Errol, 51
Hay, William, of Tallo, litigant, 48
Henry VII, king of England, 204
Henryson, Edward, advocate and commissary of
Edinburgh: as advocate for the poor, 86
Henryson, George, 207
Henryson, George, of Fordell, 208
Henryson, James, of Fordell, king's advocate
and lord of session, 39
Henryson, James, of Fordell, king's advocate
and lord of session, 3, 15, 48, 49, 51, 63, 66,
83, 88, 128, 146, 170, 171, 174, 186, 187,
189, 201, 204, 206, 207, 208, 209, 210,
211, 213, 215, 222, 224, 227, 230; as
notary, 56; family and background, 207;
studies in Paris, 57
Henryson, James, younger, of Fordell, 208, 216
Henryson, John, 207, 210
Henryson, Katherine, 128
Henryson, Robert, 60
Henryson, Robert, father of James, 207, 210
Henryson, Robert, poet, 18
Hepburn, Elizabeth, prioress of Haddington,
154
Hepburn, John, prior of St Andrews, 79, 106,
154
Hepburn, John, sheriff-depute of Haddington,
210
Hepburn, Margaret, litigant, 48
Hepburn, Patrick, 2nd lord Hailes, 1st earl
Bothwell, 29
Hepburn, Patrick, 3rd earl Bothwell, 19, 35, 56,
139, 150, 153, 184, 220
Hepburn, Patrick, master of Hailes, 83
Heriot, David, of Trabroun, 147
Heriot, Robert, 33, 40, 229
Heriot, Walter, of Burnturk, 133
Heron, John, 225
Home, Alexander, 3rd lord Home, 147
Home, David, of Wedderburn, 37, 147, 148,
155, 156, 157, 158, 159
Home, family of, 147
Home, George, 4th lord Home, 51, 119

Home, George, of Wedderburn, 148
Home, Margaret, of Wedderburn, 158
Home, Patrick, 97
Home, Sir John, 38
Honorius III, pope, 82
Hopper, Adam, Edinburgh dean of guild, 125
Hopper, Elizabeth, wife of Gilbert Lauder, 219
Hopper, Isobel, 115
Hopper, Janet, wife of Hugh Rigg, 219
Hoppringle, Isobel, prioress of Coldstream, 166
Hunter, Adam, 97
Hunter, Thomas, 97
Huntly, Earls of, *see* Gordon
Hutton, Alexander, royal messenger, 150

Innermeath, Lords, *see* Stewart
inns of court, 3, 54
Irvine, Sir Alexander, of Drum, litigant, 139

James I, king of Scots, 19, 82, 84, 190
James III, king of Scots, 96, 170, 190
James IV, king of Scots, 2, 3, 15, 16, 18, 38, 66,
    145, 146, 170, 171, 183, 187, 200, 201,
    204, 209, 213, 214, 215, 217, 226, 227; act
    of revocation (1493), 171
James V, king of Scots, 1, 2, 4, 5, 16, 18, 26, 55,
    57, 58, 61, 66, 76, 80, 83, 86, 90, 91, 122,
    123, 126, 129, 130, 137, 143, 147, 148,
    150, 154, 155, 157, 158, 161, 162, 164,
    171, 175, 183, 184, 187, 188, 190, 191,
    196, 200, 201, 202, 203, 204, 214, 218,
    220, 221, 224
James VI, king of Scots, 181
Jardine, Alexander, of Lauder, litigant, 42
Jardine, Sir Alexander, of Appilgirth,
    comptroller, 145, 184
Jardine, Sir John, 225
Johnstone, James, justiciar *in hac parte*, 219
Johnstone, William, advocate, 50, 55, 58, 60,
    63, 64, 66, 68, 124, 219, 227, 229;
    ambassador to England, 64; exile, 64; family
    and background, 60
Julius II, pope, 79
justice ayres, 126, 168, 184, 204, 210, 211, 216

Keith, Gilbert of Troup, litigant, 139, 156
Keith, William, 3rd earl Marischall, 51, 156
Keith, William, of Inverugy, litigant, 49
Kelham, Charles, historian, 50, 143, 144
Kelley, Michael, historian, 202
Kelso abbey, 106, 154
Kennedy, Alexander, of Bargany, 132
Kennedy, family of, 156
Kennedy, Gilbert, 2nd earl of Cassillis, 45
Kennedy, Gilbert, 3rd earl of Cassillis, 42
Kennedy, James, of Blairquhan, litigant, 116,
    128, 132, 134, 156
Kennedy, Sir Gavin, of Blairquhan, 156

Kennedy, Thomas, litigant, 47
Kerr, Matthew, advocate and commissary of St
    Andrews, 148, 227
Kincraigie, Andrew, 63
Kincraigie, James, dean of Aberdeen, 56, 61
Kincraigie, Thomas, advocate and lord of
    session, 16, 40, 53, 55, 58, 59, 60, 61, 63,
    68, 70, 85, 86, 98, 162, 176, 178, 198, 229;
    advocate for the poor, 63; family and
    background, 56
King, Alexander, notary, 18, 25, 50, 92, 95,
    151, 152
king's advocate, 3, 57, 58, 83, 90, 95, 102, 106,
    117, 120, 128, 171, 172, 173, 175, 176,
    178, 179, 180, 181, 182, 183, 184, 186,
    187, 190, 195, 197, 198, 202, 204, 205,
    214, 215, 216, 218, 220, 222; acting for
    minor royal officials, 196; advocates-
    depute, 65, 175, 178, 179, 180, 220, 222;
    affronts to royal authority, 189; and alleged
    inordinate procedure, 193; and barratry,
    189, 190, 191; and criminal justice, 200;
    and deforcement of messengers, 189; and
    ethical standards, 198; and financial
    officials, 183, 185, 186, 188, 205; and the
    administration of justice, 192, 196; and the
    royal demesne, 199; and treason, 201, 202;
    business management, 174; dangers, 223;
    designation, 173; early development of
    office, 170; joint advocates, 179; joint-
    advocates, 182; occupational hazards, 222;
    on bench, 172, 174; private clients, 171,
    224; remuneration, 187; right of audience,
    172, 174; security of tenure. *See also*
    Borthwick, David; Crichton, Robert;
    Henryson, James; Lauder, Henry;Lockhart,
    Sir George; Mackenzie, Sir George;
    McGill, David; Nisbet, Sir John; Otterburn,
    Adam; Spens, John; Wishart, James; and
    Appendix 2; subject to law, 188
king's day, 84, 100, 101, 197
Kirkcaldy, James, of Grange, 65, 186
Knollis, William, Lord of St Johns, royal
    treasurer, 170

Laing, Walter, advocate, 17
Lauder, David, litigant, 30
Lauder, Gilbert, Edinburgh burgess, 30, 50, 58,
    95, 218, 219, 221
Lauder, Henry, of St Germains, king's advocate
    and lord of session, 32, 57, 58, 59, 62, 63,
    70, 91, 95, 105, 107, 158, 174, 175, 176,
    178, 179, 180, 181, 184, 198, 199, 204,
    214, 219, 220, 222, 223, 224; death, 224;
    entry of Mary of Guise (1538), 57; famil and
    background, 219
Lauder, Henry, of St Germains, king's advocate
    and lord of session, 176

Lauder, Henry, of St Germains, king's advocate and lord of session, 182

Lauder, Henry, of St Germains, king's advocate and lord of session, 104

Lauder, Henry, of St Germains, king's advocate and lord of session, 19, 28, 30, 33, 43, 50, 52, 53, 55, 58, 59, 62, 63, 66, 67, 68, 95, 111, 122, 123, 148, 174, 175, 176, 178, 179, 180, 196, 198, 199, 203, 204, 218, 219, 221, 223, 229, 230; challenged as a partial judge, 107; entry of Mary of Guise (1538), 57

Lauder, Katherine, wife of John Swinton, 158

law: royal lectureships in, 182

Lawson, James, 63

Lawson, Richard, of Hie Riggis, advocate and lord justice clerk, 42, 45, 51, 63, 94, 171, 204, 209, 211, 212, 226

Lawson, Thomas, 128

lawyers: quotas, 69

Learmonth, Andrew, 215

Learmonth, David, provost of St Andrews, 162, 215

legal libraries, 88

legal services, 50

Leith, seamen of, litigation concerning prizes, 74

Lennox, Countess of, *see* Stewart, Isobel

Lennox, earldom, 76

Lennox, Earls of, *see* Stewart

Leslie of Rothes, family of, 124

Leslie, Andrew, 127

Leslie, Elizabeth, 127

Leslie, Eufame, prioress of Elcho, 50, 124, 125, 127, 158

Leslie, George, 127

Leslie, George, 2nd earl of Rothes, 210

Leslie, George, 4th earl of Rothes, 23, 26, 60, 108, 117, 129, 130, 132, 133, 134, 137, 138, 143, 144, 165, 174, 196, 210

Leslie, Gilbert, 127

Leslie, Isobel, 143

Leslie, Janet, 127

Leslie, John, 127

Leslie, Margaret, 124

Leslie, Norman, 65

Leslie, Robert, of Inverpeffer, advocate, 10, 13, 24, 25, 30, 37, 39, 44, 48, 50, 53, 55, 58, 59, 61, 65, 66, 67, 68, 75, 76, 79, 80, 97, 98, 99, 100, 101, 104, 106, 108, 109, 111, 112, 115, 116, 120, 123, 124, 125, 126, 127, 128, 129, 130, 131, 132, 133, 134, 135, 136, 137, 138, 139, 140, 141, 143, 144, 145, 146, 148, 152, 153, 155, 156, 158, 159, 160, 161, 162, 163, 164, 165, 166, 167, 168, 169, 173, 177, 197, 203, 212, 226, 227, 229; acts in Leith litigation, 124; arbiter, 166; attendance, 164; children,

127; clients, 130; death and exhumation, 129; ecclesiastical clients, 135; Elcho dispute, 125; family and background, 123; gives caution for client, 48; in criminal courts, 167; lands, 129; long-standing clients, 134; long-standing relationships, 134; possible activity as a notary, 165; Rothes affinity, 143

Leslie, Walter, commissary of Dunkeld, father of Robert L., 123

Leslie, William, 3rd earl of Rothes, 210

Lethame, Janet, 104

Lethame, John, advocate, 55

Lethame, John, advocate and lord of session, 3, 27, 28, 33, 39, 50, 51, 53, 55, 58, 59, 61, 62, 63, 66, 67, 68, 70, 78, 79, 98, 108, 109, 111, 146, 148, 229; as notary, 56; remuneration, 45

letters of maintenance, 46

letters of procuratory, 21, 25, 26, 29, 36, 37, 61, 97, 125

libels, 99, 108, 122, 193, 202

Liddel, Agnes, 149

Lindsay, Alexander, 7th earl of Crawford, 144

Lindsay, David, 8th earl of Crawford, 120, 130, 144

Lindsay, David, 8th earl of Crawford,, 220

Lindsay, David, master of Crawford, 144

Lindsay, John of Covington, 144

Lindsay, John of Covington, litigant, 134, 145

Lindsay, John, 3rd lord Lindsay of Byres, sheriff of Fife, 75, 133, 137, 140, 154, 195

Lindsay, John, of Covington, 144, 145

Lindsay, Sir David, of the Mount, 57

Lindsay, William of Airdrie, litigant, 134

Lindsay, William of Pyeston, litigant, 134

Litill, Clement, advocate, commissary, 6, 14, 41, 57, 88

Lockhart, George of Carnwath (d. 1690), 223

Lockhart, John, of Barr, 156

Logie, John, advocate for the poor, 86

lord justice-clerk, 39, 45, 46, 50, 61, 63, 65, 91, 94, 112, 146, 171, 172, 175, 193, 204, 205, 208, 209, 210, 213, 215, 216, 217, 218, 221, 222, 225

Lord of St Johns, *see* Knollis

lords auditor of exchequer, 178, 183

lords auditor of parliament, 208, 212

lords of session, 1, 2, 3, 4, 5, 8, 9, 14, 16, 17, 20, 22, 25, 26, 29, 30, 31, 33, 34, 36, 37, 38, 43, 44, 46, 47, 48, 49, 53, 54, 55, 56, 58, 59, 63, 66, 67, 68, 69, 70, 71, 72, 73, 74, 75, 76, 77, 78, 79, 80, 81, 84, 85, 87, 88, 89, 91, 92, 93, 94, 95, 97, 98, 99, 100, 101, 102, 103, 104, 105, 106, 107, 108, 109, 110, 111, 112, 113, 114, 115, 116, 117, 118, 119, 120, 121, 122, 124, 125, 126, 127, 128, 129, 130, 132, 135, 136,

137, 138, 143, 144, 145, 147, 155, 157,
159, 160, 161, 164, 165, 166, 168, 172,
173, 174, 175, 176, 177, 178, 179, 181,
182, 183, 184, 185, 186, 187, 189, 190,
191, 192, 194, 195, 196, 197, 198, 199,
201, 202, 203, 207, 209, 210, 211, 213,
214, 215, 216, 217, 219, 220, 221, 223,
225, 226, 227, 229; acting for clients, 107;
objections to, 93, 105, 106; procedural
rules, 87; voting rights, 107
luckenbooths, 94
Lumsden, William, of Airdrie, litigant, 133
Lundie, James, 162
Lundie, Walter, litigant, 118
Lundie, William, litigant, 133
Lyon, John, 7th lord Glamis, 158, 186, 203

Maben, Gude and Wallace, 109
MacDowall ,Gilbert, of Spott, litigant, 130
macers, 5, 13, 60, 72, 76, 92, 93, 95, 97, 99,
102, 103, 117, 189
MacGill, David, 63
Mackenzie, Sir George, of Rosehaugh, king's
advocate, 6
MacLellan, Thomas, of Bombie, 161
MacLeod, Torquil, of Lewis, 201
magnatial affinities, 50, 143
Maitland, Richard, of Lethington, 98, 166
Major, John, 146
Malines, Grand Council of, 12, 27, 37, 38, 49,
54, 89; number of *avocats* permitted, 69;
procureur for the poor, 83
Manderstone, William, 197
Margaret Tudor, queen of James V, 17, 26, 147,
148, 149, 153, 157, 160, 161, 162, 188, 215
Marischal, Earl, *see* Keith
Marjoribankis, James, 61
Marjoribankis, Thomas, of Ratho, advocate and
lord clerk register, 16, 19, 41, 52, 53, 55, 58,
59, 61, 62, 64, 65, 66, 68, 73, 78, 80, 84,
91, 101, 103, 105, 111, 115, 119, 123, 176,
178, 184, 195, 229; advocate for the poor,
84; business conducted in his dwelling, 94;
entry of Mary of Guise (1538), 58; fined, 91;
mint, 58; trading activity, 58; treasurer's
clerk and custumar, 64
marriage alliance, 139
Martin, Elizabeth, lady Fastcastle, 97
Martins, Kerstan, litigant, 57
Mary of Guise, 40, 57, 180, 182; entry to
Edinburgh (1538), 57
Mary, queen of Scots, 18, 54, 57, 58, 66, 176,
183, 184, 219, 228
Mauchane, Alexander, advocate, 58, 63, 95,
219
Maule, Robert, of Panmure, litigant, 133
Maxwell, Henry of Bishopton, litigant, 135
Maxwell, Robert, 5th lord Maxwell, 145, 160

Maxwell, Robert, Lord Maxwell, 30, 65, 145
McBrek, Alexander, litigant, 196
McCalzeane, James, notary, brother of Thomas
M., 221
McCalzeane, James, notary, father of Thomas
M., 95, 221
McCalzeane, John, 13
McCalzeane, Margaret, wife of Gilbert Lauder,
218
McCalzeane, Robert, Edinburgh burgess, 221
McCalzeane, Thomas, lord Cliftonhall,
advocate and lord of session, 12, 13, 18, 26,
40, 41, 43, 55, 66, 70, 88, 95, 106, 110,
116, 176, 219, 220, 223, 228, 229;
threatened, 223
McCalzeane,, Henry, advocate, 13
McCartney, James, notary, 13
McClellane, Thomas, of Bombie, 188
McDowall, Christian, prioress of Eccles, 154
McDowall, Gilbert, of Spott, litigant, 118, 134,
136
McGill, David, of Nesbit, king's advocate, 181
McGill, David, of Nesbit, king's advocate, 39
McGill, David, s. of James M. of Nether
Rankeillour, 14
McGill, David, younger, advocate-depute, 182
McGill, James, of Nether Rankeillour, advocate
and lord clerk register, 13, 14, 43, 52, 55,
66, 70, 109, 110, 118, 176, 181, 203, 228,
229
McGill, John, son of James M. of Nether
Rankeillour, 14
Meldrum, William, 128
Meldrum, William, archdeacon of Dunkeld,
128
Melrose abbey, 154
Melville, John, of Carnbee, 215
Melville, John, of Raith, litigant, 65, 134
Menzies, Gilbert, provost of Aberdeen, 35, 116
Mercer, Robert, of Balleif, 138
Middleburg, 41
Milne, Alexander, abbot of Cambuskenneth,
lord president, 32, 44, 123, 135
Mochrun, Lady, *see* Stewart, Janet.
Moffat, John, Scots conservator in Flanders,
117, 163
Moncreiff, Hugh, 173
Moncreiff, John, 14
Moncreiff, Margaret, 138
Moneypenny, David, of Pitmillie, litigant, 29
Monorgund, Robert, 34
Montgomerie of Eglinton, family of, 145
Montgomerie, Adam, 201
Montgomerie, Adam, litigant, 136
Montgomerie, Hugh, 1st earl of Eglinton, 132,
133, 134, 136, 141, 145
Montgomerie, John, master of Montgomerie,
137

Montgomerie, Sir Neil, 136, 146
Montgomerie, William, of Greenfield, 136
Montrose, burgh, 25
Monypenny, Alexander, Lord Monypenny, 211
Monypenny, Isobel, 141
Monypenny, John, advocate, 5, 88
Monypenny, Patrick, 212
Moscrop (alias McCalzeane), Patrick, advocate, 13
Moscrop, Adam, notary, 14
Moscrop, John, advocate, 13, 14, 18, 41, 43, 55, 88, 89, 183
Moutrie, John, of Seafield, 45, 48, 50, 121, 133
Mowbray, Eufame, wife of Adam Otterburn, 217
Mowbray, William, alleged poor litigant, 83
Muir of Caldwell, family of, 145
Muir, Christine, litigant, 48
Muir, John, of Caldwell, 135, 145
Muir, Margaret, 136, 146
Muir, William, of Skeldon, 136
Murray, Andrew, 167
Murray, Andrew, of Blackbarony, 44
Murray, James, of Falahill, 188
Murray, James, of Fallahill: sheriff of Selkirk, 153
Murray, John, notary, 213
Murray, Sir William, of Tullibardine, 97

Namur, Grand Council of, 38, 69, 84; representation of the poor, 84
Nether Loudoun dispute, 177, 179
networking, 145
Newbattle abbey, 154
Newton, Janet, poor litigant, 84
Niddry, Thomas, abbot of Culross, 117
Nisbet, John, of Newton, litigant, 48
Nisbet, Sir John, king's advocate, 223
nonentry, 111, 112, 129, 150, 177, 181, 184, 185, 187, 194, 213, 215, 220
notaries: receiving depositions form witnesses, 117

oath *de calumnia*, 198
oath-swearing, 116
Ogilvie, Patrick, of Inchmartin, litigant, 48
Ogilvy, John, Lord Ogilvy, 107
Ogilvy, Patrick of Inchmartin, litigant, 134, 140
Ogilvy, Thomas, of Clova, 144
Oliphant, James, Haddington burgess, 41
Omond, G.T., historian, 178
Ordonnance de Thionville (1470), 38
Orrock, Robert, of that ilk, 100, 133, 134, 196; as depute to royal master of works, 196
Otterburn, John, official of Lothian, 217
Otterburn, Nicholas, lord clerk register, 217
Otterburn, Sir Adam, of Redhall and Auldhame, king's advocate and lord of

session, 3, 16, 17, 33, 42, 44, 45, 48, 51, 60, 61, 63, 66, 76, 90, 95, 97, 112, 118, 148, 165, 170, 172, 175, 176, 177, 178, 179, 186, 197, 204, 205, 209, 216, 217, 218, 220, 225, 230; as notary, 56; diplomatic activity, 218; Edinburgh town clerk, 209; entry of Mary of Guise (1538), 57; family and background, 216; lands, 214
Otterburn, Thomas, 217

Palmer, Robert, historian, 2
Pantoun, James, litigant, 73
Parlement of Paris, 5, 11, 54, 83, 89
Paterson, Janet, 149
physical court environment, 90, 92, 93, 94, 102, 103
physical evidence, 110, 112
Pitcairn, David, archdeacon of Brechin, 111
poor litigants, 81, 82, 83
prelocutor, 9, 10, 41, 92, 98, 110, 115, 122, 177, 197, 210
Prest, Wilfred, historian, 4
procurator, 3, 9, 10, 11, 15, 16, 17, 18, 19, 21, 24, 25, 27, 28, 29, 30, 31, 32, 33, 34, 35, 36, 37, 39, 40, 41, 42, 44, 45, 46, 47, 48, 49, 53, 54, 56, 60, 68, 69, 70, 72, 73, 77, 81, 96, 97, 98, 100, 102, 104, 105, 106, 107, 108, 109, 110, 111, 112, 117, 119, 120, 124, 128, 133, 137, 138, 139, 144, 146, 147, 153, 154, 156, 157, 160, 171, 176, 186, 195, 198, 207, 209, 211, 216, 217, 221; *de negotia*, 30, 51; judicial, 27, 28, 29, 31; powers, 31; role, 28
prolocutor, 9, 11, 27
prosopographical approach: limits of, 139

Quoniam Attachiamenta, 89

Raiton, Beatrice, widow of Sir William Sinclair of Herniston, 159
Ramsay, David, of Cullothie, litigant, 133
Ramsay, Eurphemia, 79, 176
Ramsay, John, 91, 223
Ramsay, John, of Dunure, litigant, 198
ratification, 22, 31, 34, 47, 98
recognition, action of, 187
Regiam Majestatem, 18, 21, 31, 36, 54, 62, 88, 152, 193
registration of deeds, 51
Reichskammergericht, 89
Reid, Adam, 185
Reid, Robert, bishop of Orkney, lord president, 88, 152
representation: rules in regard to, 73
Rhynd, Janet, wife of Adam Otterburn, 217
Ridley, Hugh, 225
Rigg, Hugh, advocate, 19, 50, 52, 68, 69, 70, 80, 104, 105, 108, 111, 176, 178, 202, 229;

entry of Mary of Guise (1538), 58; family, 219; translates Dutch, 57
Rigg, John, 50
Rigg, John, Dumfries burgess, 50
Rigg, Thomas, 50
Rigg, William, 50
Ross, John, 203
Ross, Ninian, Lord Ross, 135, 159, 162, 166
Ross, Sir John, of Montgrennan, 170, 201
Rothes, Earls of, _see_ Leslie
Russell, John, advocate, 44
Rutherford, Helen, 98
Rutherford, Janet, 98, 101
Ruthven, William, 1st lord Ruthven, 44, 135
Ruthven, William, master of Ruthven, 44, 154, 159, 160, 195, 196

Borthwick, David, of Lochhill, king': death, 180
Sanderson, Hans, litigant, 34
Sandilands, Alexander, 223
Sauchy, John, 191
Scone abbey, 154
Scott, Robert, 19, 32
Scott, Sir Alexander, clerk, 105, 112, 118
Scott, Sir Walter, of Buccleuch, 202
Scott, Sir William, of Balwearie, lord of session, 50, 63, 97, 133, 167, 173, 175, 221
Scott, Thomas of Abbotshall, 35
Scott, Thomas, of Pigorno, lord justice clerk, 177
Scott, Thomas, of Pigorno, lord justice clerk, lord justice clerk, 225
Scott, Thomas, procurator, 119
Scott, William, son of William S. of Balwearie, 173
sea laws, 164
Sempill, Gabriel, of Cathcart, 159
Sempill, John, Lord Sempill, 159
Sempill, Lady. _see_ Crichton, Margaret
Sempill, William, 159
sequestration of children, 219
Seton, 3rd George, Lord Seton, 211
Seton, Alexander, of Meldrum, 132, 138
Seton, Andrew, of Parbroath, 133
Seton, David, parson of Fettercairn, 38
Seton, George, 3rd lord Seton, 32, 211
Seton, George, 4th lord Seton, 141, 166, 220, 223
Seton, George, 5th lord Seton, 66
Seton, John of Lathrisk, litigant, 133
Seton, Ninian of Tullibody, litigant, 114, 128, 159
Shairp, John, of Houston, advocate, 4, 13, 41, 55, 81, 119, 181
Shaw, George, of Knockhill, 42
Shaw, Helen, lady Dirleton, 83, 119
Shaw, John, 23

Shaw, Robert, abbot of Paisley, litigant, 135
Simson, James, advocate and official of St Andrews, 16, 19, 27, 97
Sinclair, Edward, 37
Sinclair, Elizabeth, 156
Sinclair, Henry, lord of session, 86, 88
Sinclair, Henry, lord Sinclair, 33, 156
Sinclair, Patrick, of Spott, 156
Sinclair, Sir John, of Dryden, 156
Sinclair, Sir William, of Hermiston, 148, 150, 151, 159
Sinclair, Sir William, of Roslin, 48, 62
Sinclair's Practicks, 1, 89, 93, 109, 117
Skene, Sir John, of Curriehill, advocate and lord clerk register, 6, 13, 18, 21, 27, 28, 29, 88
Somerville, Hugh, Lord Somerville, 30, 157
Somerville, John, of Cambusnethan, 157
Sommerville, John, of Cambusnethan, 157
Spens, David of Wormistone, litigant, 134
Spens, Hugh, provost of St Salvator's college, 215
Spens, John, of Condie, king's advocate and lord of session, 180, 182; attacked, 223
Spens, John, of Condie, king's advocate and lord of session, 5, 13, 40, 43, 55, 121, 179, 193, 223, 229, 230
Spittall, Alexander, 59
Spittall, Henry, advocate, 17, 19, 27, 43, 44, 53, 55, 56, 58, 59, 63, 66, 68, 75, 76, 77, 78, 100, 108, 118, 134, 138, 153, 154, 195, 229; family and background, 56, 59
Spittall, James, of Blairlogy, father of Henry S., 59
Spittall, James, son of Henry S., 59
spuilzie, 19, 29, 48, 74, 96, 97, 101, 103, 104, 108, 114, 116, 117, 129, 137, 146, 163, 166, 201
St Andrews university, 212
Steelyard, 35
Stewart, Agnes, lady Bothwell, 23
Stewart, Agnes, wife of Henry Lauder, 223
Stewart, Alexander, 23
Stewart, Alexander, of Grandtully, 30
Stewart, Elizabeth, 23
Stewart, Isabel, countess of Lennox, 76, 77
Stewart, James, earl of Moray, 177, 228
Stewart, Janet, lady Mochrum, litigant, 136
Stewart, John, 1st earl of Atholl, 199, 209
Stewart, John, 2nd earl of Atholl, 126
Stewart, John, 2nd lord Innermeath, 140
Stewart, John, 3rd earl of Atholl, 126, 130
Stewart, John, 3rd earl of Buchan, 89, 139, 153
Stewart, John, 3rd earl of Lennox, 130
Stewart, John, duke of Albany, 59, 78, 146, 147, 148, 158, 160, 161, 162, 174, 216, 221
Stewart, Matthew, 4th earl of Lennox, 29
Stewart, Richard, 3rd lord Innermeath, 130, 134, 140, 144

Stirling, George, advocate, 89
Strachan (Strathauchin), Henry, notary, 60
Strachan, Adam, 60
Strachan, Thomas, Edinburgh burgess, 42
Strachan, Vincent, 60
Stralsund, 19
Strang, (Strange) Richard, advocate, 30, 40
Strang, George, advocate, 70, 198, 229
summonses, 109
Swinton, Elizabeth, prioress of Elcho, 125, 126, 154, 158
Swinton, Sir John, 158
Sym, Alexander, advocate, 12, 13, 18, 41, 55, 182, 183

table of summonses, 73, 83, 84, 93, 96, 98, 99, 100, 101, 102, 104, 106, 118, 174, 183; privilege, 43, 72, 73, 101, 174, 187
Thornton, John, 173
Thounis, Nicol, notary, 18
tolbooths, 90, 91, 92, 204
torture, 203, 204
Touris, Andrew, 149
treason, 74, 75, 80, 129, 147, 186, 196, 201, 202, 203, 204, 227
treasurer, 40, 58, 63, 64, 65, 85, 86, 102, 104, 120, 126, 148, 150, 164, 167, 170, 172, 183, 184, 185, 186, 187, 188, 194, 195, 196, 197, 201, 202, 215, 218, 227
Tudor, Margaret. *see* Margaret Tudor, queen of James V
Tulidaff, Andrew, of that Ilk, 132
Tweedie, James of Drummelzier, 78
Tweedie, John, of Drummelzier, 74
Tweedie-Fleming feud, 78

Ulpian, 82
University of Aberdeen, 55
University of Bourges, 86
University of Glasgow, 226
University of Louvain, 7, 57
University of Orléans, 55, 56, 64, 206, 226, 229
University of Paris, 7, 57, 61, 146, 206, 207, 226
University of Poitiers, 14
University of St Andrews, 14, 55, 57, 60, 64, 65, 123, 207, 214, 220; provost of St Leonard's college, 29
University of Wittenberg, 7

Veere, 117
Vicherling, William, procurator, 35

Wallace, James of Craigie, 156
Wardlaw, Christine (Edinburgh), 124
Wardlaw, Christine, wife of Robert Leslie of Inverpeffer, 124
Wardlaw, Gelis, 124
Wardlaw, John, laird of Torrie, 143
Wardlaw, Thomas, Edinburgh burgess, 124
Wardlaw, William, 124, 133, 143
Waus, Sir Patrick, 44
Wawane, William, official of St Andrews, 61, 87, 211
Wemyss, David, of that ilk, 133
Wemyss, Eufame, 97
Wemyss, Thomas, 133, 165
West, Nicholas, English ambassador, 214
Whitehead, Margaret, 149
Whitelaw, David, 88
Whithorn burgh, 33, 132, 135
Wielant, Philip, 27, 28, 30
Wightman, William, advocate, 70
Wigtown, burgh, 33, 131, 132, 152, 153, 163
Williamson, John, advocate for the poor, commissary of Lothian, 85
Williamson, John, notary, 3, 37, 66, 227
Wilson, Alan, thief, 201
Wilson, Nan, historian, 15
Wishart, George, 64
Wishart, George, reformer, 214
Wishart, James, of Pittarrow, king's advocate and lord justice clerk, 171, 177, 214, 215, 230; family and background, 214; lands, 215
Wishart, John, of Pittarrow, 214
Wishart, John, of Pittarrow, younger, 214
Wishart, William, of Pittarrow, 214
witness evidence, 112, 113, 114, 115; commissions, 117; objections to witnesses, 116; witness expenses, 116
Wood, Andrew, of Largo, 165
Wood, David, comptroller, 184
Woodhouse, William, litigant, 34
Wormald, Jenny, historian, 139
writers to the signet, 3, 12, 38, 109, 183

Young, Alexander, 128
Young, James, notary, 199